Pushkin and Romantic Fashion

PUSHKIN
and Romantic Fashion

Fragment, Elegy, Orient, Irony

Monika Greenleaf

STANFORD UNIVERSITY PRESS, STANFORD, CALIFORNIA

Stanford University Press
Stanford, California

Printed in the United States of America

CIP data appear at the end of the book

Stanford University Press publications are
distributed exclusively by Stanford University Press
within the United States, Canada, Mexico, and Central America;
they are distributed exclusively by Cambridge University Press
throughout the rest of the world.

Original printing 1994

Last figure below indicates year of this printing:

05 04 03 02 01 00 99 98 97 96

For Veronika

Acknowledgments

A book pretends to seamlessness, yet is in reality a palimpsest of drafts, each rooted in a particular set of circumstances, books, conversations, inspirations. This book goes back not only to my Yale dissertation, which I was fortunate to write under Victor Erlich's wise and cosmopolitan supervision, with the benefit of Edward Stankiewicz's and Alexander Schenker's linguistic and theoretical expertise, but all the way back to my senior thesis at Stanford. On hearing that I wanted to compare Pushkin to Mickiewicz, my supervisor, Edward J. Brown, shot back with characteristic spirit, "You can compare that tree to Hoover Tower, but what's that going to prove?" jumped on his red racing bike, and rode away. I suppose this book is yet another long-winded attempt to catch up with and answer him.

First as a student, later as an assistant professor, I was struck by the lack of segregation at Stanford, both up and down the generations and across the various humanities fields. Slavic and comparative literature really did share concepts, students, dissertations, colleagues. Without specifying how often I imposed on them with my manuscript, or how unexpectedly a word dropped in the corridor would set me thinking on a new, more fruitful track, I would like to thank Herbert Lindenberger, John Bender, Richard Schupbach, Gregory Freidin, Lazar Fleishman, David Wellbery, Boris Gasparov, Irina Paperno, Irina Reyfman, Harriet Murav, and Nancy Ruttenberg. Above all, I want to thank William Mills Todd III, but for whom not only my book, but large chunks of my biography would be very different.

The book's evolution owes most to my graduate students at Stanford and Yale, for they were the captive audience on whom I tried out its drafts and who rewarded me with brilliant ideas of their own. I would like to mention in particular Katya Hokanson, David Kropf, Anna Brodsky, Jennifer Hixon, Nancy Anderson, Marina Worontzoff-Dashkoff, John Sobolewski, Daria Kirjanov, Izabela Kalinowska-Blackwood, Rachel Wilson, and James Morgon. I was extremely fortunate in my editors at Stanford University Press: Helen Tartar, with her wide-ranging and well-oriented intellect, helped to steer my project toward an audience and my manuscript into the hands of Jan Spauschus Johnson, my marvelously subtle and meticulous editor. On several critical occasions Ashe Kumar and Peter Brodsky, my computer experts, rendered me indispensible assistance. I will also take this opportunity to thank the American Council of Learned Societies for funding two terms of sorely needed free time for research and writing in 1985.

A portion of the Introduction was published in Boris Gasparov, Robert P. Hughes, and Irina Paperno, eds., *Cultural Mythologies of Russian Modernism: From the Golden Age to the Silver Age* (Berkeley: University of California Press, 1992). Part of Chapter 3 appeared in the *Slavic Review* 50, no. 4 (1991).

Finally, there are the people who sustain you through the entire messy process, who keep tunnel vision from destroying thought, and who inspire by the quality of their own work: Cathy Frierson, Paul Josephson, Anna Brodsky, Kevin Crotty, Maxim Frenkel, Mark Woloshyn, Pamela Ison, Robert Klein, Mark Dansereau, Sophie Chanin; Boris and Elena Frenkel and Maria Voronina, who stepped in time and again when I needed them; and most fundamentally, my parents Theodore P. Dudli and Christina M. Dudli, my grandmother, Jadwiga Kuczynska, and my sister Anita Shelton. Thanks above all to my husband and invaluable research assistant, Peter Greenleaf, for always picking exactly the book off the top shelf at the Strand that opens up a new path for me, and for awaiting the results year after year with unmitigated, if a little ironic, enthusiasm; and finally to my daughter, Veronika Frenkel, who on being told what my book was about sanely declared, "That's not a book, it's a book report."

Contents

A Note to the Reader

Unless otherwise noted, all quotations from Pushkin's work are cited by volume and page number in his *Polnoe sobranie sochinenii* (Moscow: Izdatel'stvo Akademii nauk, 1937–58, 17 vols.). Certain volumes have two sub-volumes, or parts; thus, for example, "2.1, 96" refers to vol. 2, sub-vol. 1, p. 96.

In Chapter 3, quotations from Byron's works are cited in the text by canto, stanza, and line. I have followed the *Poetical Works*, ed. Frederick Page (Oxford: Oxford University Press, 1970). In Chapter 4, quotations from Shakespeare are cited in the text by act, scene, and line. These are drawn from *The Complete Works*, ed. Alfred Harbage (Baltimore, Md.: Penguin, 1969). In Chapter 5, quotations from *Eugene Onegin* are cited in the text by chapter, stanza, and line, following the version found in volume 6 of the collected works listed above.

I have used a modified Library of Congress system of transliterating Russian (omitting most diacriticals), except for names whose Anglicized spelling is widespread and more familiar to readers (e.g., Dostoevsky, Tolstoy).

In quotations, spaced ellipsis points (. . .) indicate my omissions of portions of the original text; closed suspension points (...) replicate ellipses in the original. Except where noted, italicized words or phrases show the original emphasis. Translations are mine unless otherwise noted.

Pushkin and Romantic Fashion

Pushkin and the Fragment: An Introduction

Aleksandr Pushkin stands so solidly at the head of the Russian classical tradition that we forget how protean his relationship with his audience was. Until 1828 he occupied the absolute center of literary life, his poetry read ubiquitously in good society and popularized by imitators until it finally trickled down to the literate provincial public.[1] All of this was no mean feat if we consider that from 1820 until 1828 Pushkin was in uninterrupted exile, shuttled from one peripheral or provincial point of the empire to another. Pushkin was so confident of his hold on his readers' attention that he shifted gears constantly: subversive political lyrics, Romantic elegies, classical fragments, Byronic imitations or parodies, the chapters of a novel-in-verse, a piece of Voltairean blasphemy, a national-historical tragedy, a Romantic epic followed in quick succession, published in fragments in a variety of journals and almanacs, published in expensive and cheap editions, sometimes not published at all but handed around in manuscript, endlessly quoted and misquoted. Pushkin may have been absent, sequestered in Kishinev, Odessa, or Mikhailovskoe, but his poetry was ubiquitous.

Moreover, in his generic shifts and his heterogeneous publishing modes Pushkin seems deliberately to have cultivated an image of youthful, gentlemanly, amateurish, improvisational unpredictability. Each text, each appearance before the public pushed off from the last, as it were, and deflected the reader's projection of a single, consistent authorial persona and system of values. Whatever overarching impression was generated was one of accelerated creative diversity and protean potential, full of promise for a Russian literature intent on catching up with centuries of European culture.

Not only was Pushkin's oeuvre so heterogeneous that it resisted paraphrase or summary, but very early on Pushkin's critics were disturbed by a comparable "fragmentariness" and lack of "plan" in the internal structure of Pushkin's compositions. At first identified with Byron's notorious practice of stitching together narrative poems out of lyrical outbursts, nature descriptions, and garishly lighted fragments of plot, with a self-conscious emphasis on the open-ended process of his improvisation, the rubric "fragmentary" stuck to Pushkin and came to stand for more than stylistic eccentricity. No one could pretend not to know what a Byronic poem meant, where its center of value lay. Pushkin's poems, however, were genuinely ambiguous: as critics remarked over and over, their parts did not cohere in a uniperspectival whole. The evocative verse of "Prisoner of the Caucasus" aroused interest first in the landscape, then in the native ethnography, then in the personalities of the prisoner and the maiden, only, finally, to short-circuit this interest. The girl disappeared into a pool, the prisoner departed without a backward glance, and the last words of the poem celebrated the power of Russian bayonets. When even the confirmed Romantic P. A. Viazemsky voiced his concern about the issue of intelligibility, Pushkin airily replied, "It's not necessary to say everything. That is the secret of entertainment."[2]

As the 1820's progressed, the epithet "fragmentary" followed Pushkin persistently, its connotation changing to reflect the changing temper and expectations of his audience. "Fragmentariness" and "inexplicitness" (*nedoskazannost'*) were accepted as key ingredients in a Romantic poetics that exercised the imaginative participation of the reader. "Fragmentariness" and improvisation formed the dazzling structural hub of *Eugene Onegin*'s virtuoso display, the game in which it engaged an alert audience. But the hostile and bewildered reviews of *Boris Godunov* and of the final chapters of *Eugene Onegin* reveal a new impatience with "fragmentariness," an unwillingness on the part of the reader to grapple with a discontinuous, polymorphous structure, to make the effort to connect one semantically or stylistically disparate scene with another. Somehow Pushkin had lost his audience.

Abandoning poetry with much fanfare in 1830, Pushkin turned a series of new faces toward his public: historian, chronicler, journalist, novelist, editor of other writers' works, and surreptitious recycler of his own. Not surprisingly, the theme of Pushkin's last story, "Egyptian Nights," is precisely the concealment/exposure of the writer's essence from the public, vividly symbolized by the doubling of the poet figure. The very structure of the story, with its concentric embedding of poem within narrative frame, is an emblem of entrapment, and the predicament of the improvisatore perhaps Pushkin's most telling diagnosis of the historical displacement of his own protean, improvisational art and modes of being.

How did Pushkin's protean freedom congeal into the ultimate entrapment of his improvisatore? Why did the freedom to improvise, with its necessary reliance on an audience perfectly attuned to the artist's play, lead finally to the illegible performances of 1835 to 1837?

Refashioning Pushkin

Looking at the ten volumes of Pushkin's poetry and fiction on the one hand and at the veritable industry that has arisen to explicate its "clarity" and "simplicity" on the other, any critic who has found himself sucked into the bottomless pit of *Pushkinizm* must ask, as Iury Tynianov did: Is there something intrinsic about Pushkin's artistic structures that elicits the "multiple and contradictory interpretation of his oeuvre by contemporary readers and later literary generations"?[3] Let me make a brief overview of the way in which subsequent generations of readers and writers have selected facets of Pushkin's discontinuous image and oeuvre to create the particular "first poet" and literary values they needed.

Although one of Vissarion Belinsky's aims in his series of Pushkin essays is to sift out a solid classical canon from the bewildering array of Pushkin's creations, in his fifth essay he tackles the overarching issue of Pushkin's multiplicity:

> We have already spoken about the variety of Pushkin's poetry, about his astonishing ability to transport himself easily and freely into the most contradictory spheres of life. In this respect . . . Pushkin recalls Shakespeare. . . . His first-class pieces in the anthological genre, imprinted with the spirit of the ancient Hellenic muse, his imitations of the Koran, fully transmitting the spirit of Islam and the beauties of Arabic poetry . . . belong to the greatest works of Pushkin's genius-Proteus. . . . The more Pushkin perfected himself as an artist, the more his own identity concealed itself and disappeared behind the wonderful, sumptuous world of his poetic visions.[4]

What Pushkin's readers were reacting to, suggests Lidia Iakovlevna Ginzburg in a seminal essay,[5] was the contrast between Pushkin's authorial heterogeneity and the Romantic adherence to a single "lyrical hero," an autobiographical voice or persona that overarches an author's entire oeuvre or cycle of works. A poem by Mikhail Lermontov, for example, sounds like an excerpt from an ongoing diary. Pushkin observed instead the traditional eighteenth-century system of fixed genres or styles, whereby the persona of the "I," its values and emotions, were dictated by the genre: thus Pushkin could, at one and the same time, write elegiac verse full of pathos and idealism, incendiary and "freethinking" civic verse, and cynical epigrams, but how and whether these "occasional" utterances cohered behind the scenes remained an open question.

The "protean" theory represented an attempt to account for Pushkin's fragmentariness within the framework of the Romantic cult of the artist. Pushkin was given the standard attributes of the "culture hero," a figure so many-sided and autochthonous that he contains as in germ the entire subsequent cultural tradition.[6] Like Shakespeare, or for that matter Goethe, Dante, Mickiewicz, or any of the other "first poets" venerated by Romanticism, Pushkin had to be shown to be seminal, the origin without origin, pregnant with all the forms of his culture. Indeed, in Dostoevsky's Christian/Russian variation on this model, not only is the artist's ability to transcend himself as a man reinterpreted as kenosis, but the specifically *Russian* artist's ability to impersonate and incorporate any European nationality testifies to the millennial role of Russian culture itself. Vast conclusions are repeatedly drawn from Pushkin's "divine" capacity for disappearing behind the heterogeneous array of his creations.

In practice, however, each generation of Pushkin readers tended to create its own Pushkin anthology, foregrounding different works and fashioning a more homogeneous image of Pushkin in accordance with its literary and ideological agenda. Gogol's divinely irresponsible aesthete of the 1830's gave way to P. V. Annenkov's "metaphysical" Pushkin of the 1850's, a writer with serious political and religious values and a covert program.[7] For Tolstoy, on the other hand, Pushkin was the epitome of the irresponsible aristocratic artist, with all the positive and negative connotations that these words contained.[8] From his vantage point within the age of prose, Tolstoy dismissed virtually all of Pushkin's Romantic poetry as "fiddle-faddle," but salvaged such little-known prose fragments as "The guests were arriving at the dacha" as models of compositional compactness and swiftness (although it seems paradoxical that Pushkin's lesson in *ex abrupto* beginnings and sudden truncations inspired Tolstoy's five-year labor on *Anna Karenina*!). When Tolstoy praises Pushkin's instinctive understanding of the "proper hierarchy of objects,"[9] the phrase exudes an appreciation for aristocratic good taste and the old order that marked Tolstoy's novels, in Dostoevsky's eyes, irremediably as "landowner literature."

Dostoevsky instead made Pushkin a prophet for contemporaneity. Retorting to a critical condemnation of the titillating sensuality of Pushkin's unfinished story "Egyptian Nights," Dostoevsky leapt to the defense simultaneously of women's rights and of the story's very fragmentariness.[10] In the apparently pagan tale of Cleopatra's sexual bargain he discovered a kind of negative proof for the necessity of Christianity, and, by implication, for Pushkin's hidden status as a Russian Christian artist. By the 1899 jubilee Pushkin had been coopted as a virtually imperial writer, a classic of the old regime, even while many of his works continued to be banned from the school curriculum for containing elements of both political subversion and sexual indecency.[11]

Thus while in the process of his successors' formation neglected parts of Pushkin's legacy were continually being selected, highlighted, and incorporated into contemporary polemical contexts, inconsistencies were simultaneously being suppressed, ambiguities too easily clarified. The image of Pushkin as a whole, marking the beginning of

Russia's participation in world culture, was in danger of being petrified on its pedestal, turned into a sacred—and closed—text. This explains to some extent the violence of reactions such as Dmitry Pisarev's, and later Vladimir Mayakovsky's, to what they regarded as the dead weight of Pushkin's classical legacy. The rhetoric of violent change would often define itself as insistently anti-Pushkinian.

Nevertheless, Pushkin's image presides most pervasively over the beginning of the twentieth century, precisely when presentiments over the end of culture were rife. One hundred years of Euro-Russian culture were symmetrically and symbolically bracketed by the dates 1837 and 1937: "V Peterburge my soidemsia snova / Slovno solntse my pokhoronili v nem"[12] (In Petersburg we will converge again. Truly the sun we buried there). By a mute or expressed common consensus, this generation or two of poets incorporated into its sense of obligation as witnesses of historical cataclysm the recording of its experience of reading Pushkin for the last time, as the last members of his culture. In the face of erupting Eurasian forces and the long-suppressed collective unconscious of the people, memory, both personal and cultural, became the hidden theme of most of these "poets' poet" studies.[13] In opposition to the crude institutionalization of Pushkin as a collective national monument of the tsarist regime, however, each poet of the turn of the century cultivated his own idiosyncratic dialogue with Pushkin, resulting in a proliferation of "*moi* Pushkins." This is reflected in the casual, memoir-like or even conversational, sometimes unfinished form of such essays as Vladimir Khodasevich's "The Shaky Tripod" ("Koleblimyi trenozhnik") and "Pushkin's Poetic Economy" ("Poeticheskoe khoziastvo Pushkina"), Valerii Briusov's and Marina Tsvetaeva's respective "My Pushkin" essays, Osip Mandel'shtam's "Pushkin and Scriabin," Nadezhda Mandel'shtam's *Mozart and Salieri*, and Anna Akhmatova's *Notes on Pushkin*.[14]

Many of these poet-Pushkinists stress the improvisational, personal character of their readings. Khodasevich notes regretfully that lack of access to books and libraries forces him to work from memory. Tsvetaeva unapologetically flaunts "her" Pushkin—pieced together from childhood memories, creative misunderstandings occasionally more revealing than scholarly accuracy, and metaphorical flights—

composed in much the same style as her memoirs about contemporaries. Nadezhda Mandel'shtam reconstructs Mandel'shtam and Akhmatova's conversations about the respective roles of Mozart ("inspiration") and Salieri ("craftsmanship") in the creative process, incorporating Pushkin into the current Acmeist and post-Acmeist discussions that culminated for Osip Mandel'shtam in "Conversations About Dante." Both Khodasevich and Akhmatova investigate the function of the recurrent motif and "self-citation" (Akhmatova) or "autoreminiscence" (Khodasevich) in Pushkin's poetics, intimating in the course of their discussions certain focal issues in their own poetic practice.

Each of these essays is both lyrical and metapoetic, projecting Pushkin against the background of modern poetics and modern poetics against the background of Pushkin, as the combination of possessive adjective and proper name suggests. They testify to the compulsive, perhaps apocalyptic urge of Pushkin's readers to "finish speaking for Pushkin" (*dogovarivat' za Pushkina*),[15] to fill the structural gaps, supplement the allusions and historical or literary context, and halt the semantic oscillation of his works. Perhaps the most eloquent example of this is Briusov's actual "completion" of Pushkin's poetic fragment "Kleopatra," the poem at the heart of his prose fragment "Egyptian Nights." This story in particular appears to have posed an irresistible temptation to all sorts of would-be supplementers, from Dostoevsky to M. Gofman to D. M. Thomas.[16]

Perhaps the most possessive and most self-reflective of the writer-Pushkinists is Vladimir Nabokov. His commentary to *Eugene Onegin*,[17] while claiming to be no more than a modest pony to the original text, outgrows its source severalfold, every bit of Pushkinian text serving as a pretext for a veritable orgy of cultural free association in four or five languages. It is a vivid confirmation of the notion that Pushkin's texts are essentially metonymic and refer to an array of mutually coexisting possibilities, among which the reader picks and chooses. The problem, as we see with the commentary of Nabokov alone, is that what is perceived as an open structure can breed an infinity of complements. The only principle of selection is the taste and discretion of the reader, a guarantee of which was haughtily asserted by most of the elitist poets mentioned. Of all readers, the poet-addressee regarded himself as best equipped to trace the oblique logic of those "strange affinities," which Iu. M. Lotman calls the "law of the syntagmatics of the artistic text."[18] What is most striking about all of these Pushkin "testimonies" is the degree to which mere history is pushed into the background as the poet, in Osip Mandel'shtam's phrase, addresses himself over the heads of his own generation to a future "conversationalist," a transtemporal *kruzhok* (circle).[19] Simultaneously, the idiosyncratic poet-addressee's readings of individual texts are elevated to a norm, displacing the ordinary (nonwriting) reader to a secondary, muted position.

Postrevolutionary professional Pushkinism produced two basic "unified theories" of Pushkin. To Viktor Shklovsky, Pushkin is the eternal subversive for whom every text represents a chance to encode radical Aesopian messages, whose every ellipsis is both politically and playfully motivated; or rather, whose play *is* political.[20] Post-Formalist Pushkin criticism, on the other hand, tones down the element of subversive play to fashion a soberer Pushkin, a normative theory that subsumes all contradictions: Pushkin's "poetry of reality" was as various as life itself; Pushkin was simply the progenitor of Realism. The gaudy artifice of *Eugene Onegin*, the weird ventriloquism of *The Belkin Tales*, the surreally hypertrophied attention to detail in "Journey to Arzrum," the folktale naïveté of *The Captain's Daughter*, the overt perversity of the "Kleopatra" tales—in short, the accelerated diversification of literary forms and voices that marks in particular the latter half of Pushkin's development—is subsumed under the heading, tediously ubiquitous in Soviet Pushkin studies, of the "shift from Romanticism to Realism."

Amid these various extreme interpretations of Pushkin's meaning for the twentieth century arose the new Pushkin scholarship of the Formalists. One of its manifest aims was to liberate Pushkin, and with him aesthetics, from the aegis of nineteenth-century Realism and philosophy, from the grandiose ethical orientation of the literary "graybeards" of the previous two generations. Another was to scrape from the "imaginary Pushkin" of Tynianov's scathing article[21] the accumulated prejudices and banalities of taste of generations of common readers, critics, and professors, to destroy the notions of Pushkin's classical "transparency" and "plasticity" and his democratic accessibility.

To induce a sense of *ostranenie* from Gogol was not nearly so challenging a task as to make Pushkin difficult, "strange," "aesthetically isolated."[22] One way to do so was to turn the period into a field of such specialized scholarly expertise that a great deal of prior knowledge was required before a reader dare approach, much less speak about, the increasingly forbidding citadel of Pushkin's "poetics." Another was to reorganize the canon, displacing the most popular "central" works by peripheral ones or invoking new criteria for evaluation: not character, realism, psychology, internal coherence, "simplicity," but artistic process, autocitations, parody, *kruzhkovaia semantika* (the semantics of the in-group), symbols, ellipsis, complexity. Imperceptibly, the old classical model of artistic simplicity and universal accessibility was dismembered and replaced by a darker, more tormented, more difficult Pushkin who better satisfied modern taste. Simultaneously, the Golden Age of which his art had long been emblematic was reinterpreted as an age of historical crisis, linguistic ferment, and shattered discourses, analogous to the modern postrevolutionary *promezhutok* (interval).[23] It is tempting to conclude about this, as about other instances of the Silver Age's preoccupation with the Golden Age of a century before, that in its reconstruction of the Pushkin period, it was constructing an image of itself.[24]

Modernism and the Fragment

Recent scholars, particularly though not exclusively of the Anglo-American tradition, have pointed to the centrality of the fragment for Modernism. Beginning in the 1920's, the apparently accidental shard of some creative process and the collage-like accumulation of diverse "fragments" that the reader synthesizes into his own "whole" could be elevated to the status of a work of art.[25] That a similar structural tendency can be found in the poetry and prose of the Russian Modernists has also been noted.[26] It may be taken as an unconscious confirmation of its prevalence that in 1924 Formalist critics published two books, very different in subject and method, that coincided at one point: the identification of a genre, technique, or cult of the fragment in the Pushkin period precisely one hundred years before.[27]

Otryvochnost' (fragmentariness) was identified as a "device" in *Byron and Pushkin*, B. M. Zhirmunsky's exhaustive and at the same time narrowly Formalistic attempt to resituate Pushkin in Romantic discourse, preeminently vis-à-vis Byron. Zhirmunsky has two main goals: to prove by technical analysis, not by vague historical and "spiritual" analogies, the fact of Pushkin's youthful Romantic "apprenticeship" to the fashionable English poet; and to prove that the Romantic influence had been conclusively overcome before Pushkin's major works were written. Among the many technical "brush strokes" collated by Zhirmunsky as evidence of Pushkin's brief but intensive apprenticeship to Byron, the compositional innovation of fragmentariness (*otryvochnost'*) or "peak composition" (*vershinnaia kompozitsia*) figures prominently. Pushkin not only borrowed Byron's various devices of *ex abrupto* openings, truncation, ellipsis at climactic moments (often formally foregrounded by conspicuous punctuation), and juxtaposition of stylistically heterogeneous pieces, he also mimicked Byron's self-deprecating manner of describing his works as unplanned, casual, generically unclassifiable collections of disconnected fragments.

Most importantly, Zhirmunsky proves that *fragment* and *fragmentariness* were part of the conscious literary terminology of the 1820's in Russia. They were singled out by Pushkin's hostile and sympathetic reviewers alike to symbolize either the fatal flaw or the inimitable "genius" of Romanticism. The very rapidity of the assimilation of *fragmentariness* into the critical vocabulary, from the outraged repudiations of conservative critics in 1823 to its clichéd equation with poetic inspiration in 1828 (by the very same critics), testifies to its status as a recognized contemporary term and loaded issue.[28] The responses to Pushkin's Southern Poems reproduced the well-rehearsed critical controversies that had surrounded Byron's Turkish Tales as they were published. The terms *fragment* and *fragmentariness* also figure in Pushkin's correspondence, his system of generic labeling, and the literary polemics ignited by his innovations.[29]

Thus Zhirmunsky's study exactly one hundred years later identifies a bit of the cultural code that had faded to invisibility. He casts it, however, too narrowly, as a brief, purely technical episode of "Russian Byronism," with no deeper connections either to European Romantic literature and nineteenth-century cultural change or to the rest of Pushkin's oeuvre. According to Zhirmunsky, Pushkin slavishly imitated Byron's gimmicks for three years, only to discard them forever in 1824.

In Tynianov's scholarship, on the other hand, the concept of fragmentariness continually widens its sphere of influence. First he shows that the crystallization of the fragment as a genre is a recurrent historical phenomenon.[30] It occurs in the interlude or *promezhutok* between generic systems: from the debris of one system's disintegration are synthesized the new genres of the next. Tynianov characterized his own literary period, and more surprisingly, Pushkin's Golden Age, as similar intervals of transition, or *promezhutok*.[31]

Whether Tynianov directs his analysis at eighteenth-, nineteenth-, or twentieth-century poets, whether it be on the level of genre (the unfinished fragment), compositional unity (the "soldering" of diverse fragments to create a multicentered whole), or the syntagmatics of the line and stanza, Tynianov finds meaning generated precisely at the point of apparent rupture, from the juxtaposition of heterogeneous elements—a technique that by 1924 belonged to the terminology of cinema, as *montage*.[32] My hypothesis is that the new art of cinema, with its clear emphasis on segmentation and montage, led Tynianov to perceive and foreground similar principles in verbal art, both in the period he studied as a scholar (the late eighteenth and early nineteenth centuries), and in the period he inhabited as a contemporary. An art of fragmentation and recombination was considered congruent with the fractured identity of modern man.

Like modern poetry, cinema displays its modernity precisely in its treatment of boundaries between segments: where "old" cinema attempted to disguise them, foster an illusion of continuum and "unified discourse" from tactfully soldered segments, "new" cinema foregrounds the rift and uses it to generate a modern, juxtapositional, or as Sergei Eisenstein would call it, "collisional," semantics. This theory of "perceptible" montage or textual discontinuity forces the viewer into an active interpretive role. As Eisenstein wrote, "Two segments, placed side by side, invariably unite in a new notion, which emerges from this juxtaposition as a new quality."[33] The difficulty of the semantic bridging movement performed by the viewer becomes a positive artistic criterion by analogy with an economics of energy:

> "Big form" in literature is not determined by the number of pages, nor is it determined in cinema by footage. The concept of "big form" relates to energy and should be understood in terms of the level of effort expended by the reader or viewer in construal of the work. Pushkin created big form in verse on the basis of digressions. "Prisoner of the Caucasus" is not any longer than some of Zhukovsky's epistles, but it is big form because the digressions, which are far from the material of the plot, expand the "space" of the poem to a considerable degree. The amount of expended effort required of the reader to go through a given number of verses of "Prisoner of the Caucasus" as compared to Zhukovsky's "Epistle to Voeikov" is entirely different. . . . This "moment" of retardation, based on far-off material, is characteristic of big form.[34]

Tynianov's aperçu fits perfectly with Pushkin's own devil's advocacy of the *poema*'s famous flaws, with its facetious shift of the burdens of "composition" to the reader: "It is not necessary to say everything. That is the secret of entertainment."[35] "This rests primarily in the fact that the desired image is *not fixed or ready-made*, but *arises—is born*. The image planned by author, director, and actor is concretized by them in separate representational elements, and is assembled—again and finally—in the spectator's perception."[36]

"The analogy between film and verse is not obligatory," Tynianov concludes in "On the Foundations of Cinema,"[37] yet it leads him to locate the explanation for Pushkin's infinite interpretability in the structure of the compositions themselves. Thus, in his article "Pushkin," Tynianov finally singles out "fragmentariness" as the key to the riddle of Pushkin's polysemy. Like all of the foregoing readers of Pushkin, he grounds his interpretation in contemporary aesthetic issues. He foregrounds in Pushkin precisely what interested him as a Modernist and cinematographer. In doing so, he proposes his own "unifying theory" of the "catastrophically rapid course of Pushkin's development."[38] Nevertheless, his obsession with fragmentariness corresponds to early-nineteenth-century critical nomenclature and its evident preoccupations.

The intriguing kinship between the fragmentary modes of the 1820's and the 1920's may be more than a coincidence. It is possible, as Philippe Lacoue-Labarthe and Jean-Luc Nancy do in *L'Absolu littéraire*,[39] to trace the use of the fragment and fragmentariness to an age's conscious perception of itself as postrevolutionary, irrevocably severed from antiquity and cultural wholeness, and qualitatively modern and ironic. The fragment was *prescribed* and cultivated as the quintessentially modern form by the Athenaeum group of Friedrich and August Schlegel from 1799 to 1802, with far-reaching consequences for Romanticism—much as it was prescribed by Tynianov for the poets of his generation. Tynianov never quite uncovered the hum of signification which the issue of the fragment had for the late eighteenth and nineteenth centuries, but this is one of the avenues his provocative work has left open. It offers the possibility of connecting Pushkin's career with more fundamental aspects of European Romanticism—Romantic irony, rhetoric, mass literary fashions—than have heretofore been treated.

Writing from the very heart of the twentieth-century avant-garde, the period that invented cubism, collage, accidental poems, Dada, serial music, and cinematic montage, the generation that defined itself as insistently postrevolutionary, "transitional," and modern, Tynianov was able to recognize something akin to the Modernist aesthetics of open forms, to detect the same Modernist self-definition and formal ferment in the seemingly classical and closed poetic legacy of one hundred years before. If it is quite clear that in their cult of art for art's sake, lyrical poetry, *kruzhkovaia semantika*, intertextuality, elitist subversiveness, and specific personal myths the Silver Age poets consciously modeled themselves and their epoch on Pushkin and his, the reverse possibility must also be taken into account: the Silver Age may have remodeled Pushkin and his period in its own Modernist image. The model of classical harmony, lucidity, transparency, the image of Pushkin that had crystallized in the nineteenth century, was displaced by, or perhaps existed side by side with, a new, darker, more personally tormented and ambiguous, more fragmentary and symbolic Pushkin whose every text, if read slowly and imaginatively enough, yielded riddles; the Pushkin of "Insomnia," *The Little Tragedies*, "Journey to Arzrum," and the "Kleopatra" tales. The privileging of the structurally and semantically most "open" of Pushkin's texts, as well as the recasting of his poetic persona, were in great part the achievements of his Modernist readers.

A Word on Organization

Did the fragment-colored glasses donned by Tynianov and other Modernists allow them to see Pushkin's age from another angle, or only their own reflection? I tend to the former opinion, partly because their aperçus anticipate so much in recent Romantic study. Lucien Dallenbach and Christiaan Nibbrig's *Fragment und Totalität*, Michael Fried's *Absorption and Theatricality*, Anne Janowitz's *Parts and Wholes*, Lacoue-Labarthe and Nancy's *The Literary Absolute*, Marjorie Levinson's *The Romantic Fragment Poem*, Thomas McFarland's *Romanticism and the Forms of Ruin*, Jack Undank and Herbert Josephs's *Diderot: Distraction and Dispersion*, among others, have encouraged me in my belief that Pushkin's idiosyncratic penchant for fragmentary structures can be located in a larger cultural context; indeed, in a European code or discourse of fragmentation that can be traced back at least to the mid-eighteenth century, that cuts across the traditional boundaries between the arts, particularly between sculptural or archaeological fragments and the literary text, and that seems to arise with the culture's perception of itself as modern. Pushkin's choices as an artist creating the first and most potent model of the modern Russian writer will, I think, be freshly illuminated by re-embedding them in the context of both European aesthetic theory and the European literary marketplace.

In Chapter 1, therefore, I expand my study of the so-called Romantic fragment well beyond the Byronic confines generally designated by Soviet scholars. The recognition of the fragment as a meaningful form was made possible by a radical change in the role of the reader. Originating in the face-to-face social and literary interactions of eighteenth-century salon life, aesthetic theory from Edmund Burke and Denis Diderot to the Schlegels, Samuel Taylor Coleridge, and the English Romantics increasingly incorporated the reader, the perceiving subject, and the audience's reaction into the text itself. What better stimulus for audience participation than the fragment? Although the terminology and concepts of Romantic fragmentariness have been traced to the German intellectual circle that formed around the Schlegel brothers in Jena in 1799 with the purpose of prescribing and producing an art for modernity, I see the Athenaeum's project as the logical culmination of earlier eighteenth-century experiments in narrative and skeptical investigations into the workings of language. These are the origins of the Romantic irony and narrative polyphony that mark such works as Byron's *Don Juan* and Pushkin's *Eugene Onegin* as distinctively modern. It was the Schlegels who connected their philosophical conception of Romantic irony with the crystallization of a new European sense of its historical position, and with the elevation of the "authentic" sculptural, archaeological, or poetic fragment as the quintessential form for modern lyrical self-expression. In terms of literary practice, we will observe the way in which the Greek Anthology (the collected fragments of Greek epitaph verse) generated a new model of the modern European lyric poet (Novalis, Coleridge, Shelley, Byron, Chénier, Sainte-Beuve, Batiushkov, Pushkin) and an unconsciously Romantic way for the reader to interpret his fragmentary oeuvre.[40]

When I depart from Pushkin for long stretches in Chapter 1, therefore, it is to elaborate a European genealogy of the Romantic fragment and Romantic irony that I hope will frame Pushkin's poetic practice in an illuminating way in the succeeding chapters. I believe that of all major European poets Pushkin actually came closest to realizing what Schlegel and the Athenaeum writers prescribed, or diagnosed, as the poetics of modernity. This can be accounted for not by any direct "philological" links, but because as latecomers on the European cultural scene Russian and German figures shared a fascination with European fashions and an ironic talent for conflating or stepping outside them.

As an indirect justification of this procedure, I invoke the famous opinion of Gogol: "More events take place in Russia in ten years than occur in other states in half a century."[41] Together with Gogol, Lotman and Boris Uspensky, William Mills Todd III, and other analysts of Russian culture, I believe that Russian cultural formations are distinguished by their syncretism, the tendency of Russian society and art forms to conflate and play off against each other *simultaneously* "multiple modeling systems" of social behavior, consensual norms, and artistic and literary tradition, both indigenous and imported, sometimes up-to-the-minute but more often chronologically out of sync with European fashion.[42] Repeated efforts to streamline Pushkin's development to the conventional triad "Classical-Romantic-Realist" have obscured that syncretism which his oeuvre, above all, exemplifies.

Thus each of the following chapters will explore one of the issues raised in Chapter 1. Taking V. K. Kiukhel'beker's "complaint" in 1824 about the elegy's usurpation of Russian poetry as a point of departure, in Chapter 2 I investigate why in fact the "languid elegy" should have served as such an effective entry for Russian poets into European culture and such an apt expression of Russia's new political power. Something unexpected emerged for me from what began as a "neo-Formalist" study of some of the most conventional aspects of Pushkin's poetry. This was the realization that the highly repetitive structures of "light poetry," in particular, erotic elegy, could serve as a window on the period's culture and psyche. Similarly, it is precisely the emphatically foreign costume of the Byronic Oriental tale that allows Pushkin, as I show in Chapter 3, to dramatize the various extremes of his own Russian/alien, powerful/marginalized, intellectual/sensual "identity."

Nor does Pushkin leave behind a "fashion" once it has been mastered and "overcome." On the contrary, it becomes part of his elegiac language. His movement "forward" is always characterized by an elegiac spiraling back, an impulse to render as a collision of styles his own experience of time, psychological change, or discontinuity. Thus the end of Chapter 3 will show Pushkin in his "Journey to Arzrum" revisiting, rereading, and rewriting the Oriental South, which he himself had brought into being in his earlier poetry, from the perspective of Russia's expanding military-imperial power, and his own tense, increasingly silenced position within it.

That improvisational ability to communicate by means of partial, fragmentary revelations and concealments reflected the phantasmagoric forms of power relations in the Alexandrian epoch, forms that would disappear with Alexander I himself. *Boris Godunov*, which, I will show in Chapter 4, reduces to an elliptical essence both the dramaturgical innovations of Shakespeare's chronicle plays and their Renaissance philosophy of history, fell on deaf ears. The "fragmentariness" of its structure, the perpetually impeded view of "the facts" that is so crucial a part of the play's ironic understanding of history was dismissed merely as a failure to assimilate the Romantic tragedy of Shakespeare. Meanwhile, its truly Shakespearean analysis of "the improvisation of power" from "empty" language also went unrecognized, both as the unifying subject of the historical drama and as a covert commentary on its own procedures.[43]

Eugene Onegin, on the other hand, has never lacked legibility in the eyes of its audience, particularly when read as a mimetic "story" interspersed with authorial "digressions." What I attempt to show, in my rather close reading of the language of *Eugene Onegin* in Chapter 5, is that it is precisely the mercurial shifts of subject matter and "tone of voice" that should be followed attentively. *Eugene Onegin* fights the reader's tendency to seek closure, whether of plot, meaning, or tone; to call a passage "a digression" is to refuse to follow the ironic train of thought that links, at a one-hundred-eighty-degree angle, one discrete utterance to another. The common ground *Eugene Onegin* seeks to create with its reader is not one of shared emotion or retrospective wisdom, but the spiritual mobility of Romantic irony.

The story of Pushkin's changing relations with his audience, from the deft improvisational play of *Eugene Onegin* to what was perceived as the increasing fragmentation and illegibility of texts such as *Boris Godunov* and "Journey to Arzrum," testifies to the congealment of that writer/reader interaction. "Egyptian Nights," then, can be seen as a meditation on the relationship of audience and inspiration that goes far beyond the sententious insistence on the artist's independence of "the crowd" made by Charsky and repeated by too many Pushkin lovers. In Chapter 6, I will show that in the sequence of unfinished "Kleopatra" tales so beloved of his Modernist readers, Pushkin was refashioning his own classical fragments into a series of exemplary readings, an epitaph for his entire career.

Although this book spans Pushkin's career in more or less chronological order, it does not pretend to exhaustiveness. I hope, however, that the last five chapters, on the classical fragment, elegiac repetition, the Oriental feminine, Romantic irony, and finally, in "Egyptian

Nights," a synthesis of all these modes, will integrate Pushkin's poetic self-fashioning with the cultural options and narrative formulas of his time.[44] Far from "overcoming Romanticism," in the stock phrase of Soviet criticism, Pushkin may have played out the last scenes of his life within its discursive field.

Chapter 1

The Romantic Fragment: A Genealogy

Byron was Pushkin's first contact with Romanticism. Pushkin encountered the English poet out of chronological order, as it were, in sudden contrast to everything Pushkin knew in literature, rather than as the culmination of a long cultural groundswell. That Pushkin the would-be trendsetter, aristocratic radical, lover, exile, and poet felt a personal and stylistic affinity with Byron is only natural;[1] that he should have wanted to emulate Byron's fiery and explicit political rhetoric in a country where it was banned is even more so; that he found the erotic "Turkish tale" a ready-made vehicle for dramatizing, glamorizing, and even analyzing his own experience in oriental / "southern" exile is inevitable. The most obvious Byronic features, particularly the melodramatic Byronic hero, were quickly sloughed off, as they were by Byron himself in the 1820's.

What Pushkin and Byron continued to share was a Romantic deep structure that rested on three "legs": the fragment as the fundamental poetic building block, the form of original inspiration; an oscillation between lyricism and irony that created the disorienting yet captivating emotional climate of the poetry; and the reader's implication in the *process of communication* (rather than the finished object) that the text had become. This kind of revolution in what writers and readers expect and get from each other does not happen overnight. When Byron "awoke one morning to find himself famous," as he said after the publication of *Childe Harold*, it was because he had tapped into and satisfied a taste that had already evolved. And when

Pushkin was berated, then praised, for the fragmentariness, planlessness, and suggestive musicality of his poetry, which, with its logical gaps, was interpretable only by the reader especially attuned to it, the critics were merely repeating comments rehearsed on Byron a decade earlier.[2] Where had this terminology for new literary pleasures come from?

Neither Byron nor Pushkin would have paid attention to the writings of the Athenaeum, a group of eight to ten German intellectuals who gathered in Jena between 1797 and 1802 to form what has been called "the first avant-garde in history"; yet their work constituted just such a manifesto of modern "fragmentariness."[3] Like most manifestos, the Athenaeum's "fragments," as its members called them, did not so much predict future developments as discern and codify the changes of the previous fifty years, new kinds of thinking and writing that affected anyone who read.

Pushkin is generally associated with the witty and rationalist French tradition exemplified by Voltaire, and with the neoclassical school of erotic *poésie fugitive*. But this very narrow view of eighteenth-century genres leaves out some of the century's most radical inventions, those that explore the successiveness and leaping illogical associativity of thought, including some of Pushkin's favorite works: Voltaire's absurdly improvisational contes, such as *Candide* and "The world as it goes" ("Le monde comme il va"), "a series of impromptu statements (sentences, then paragraphs), each playing with the verbal substance of the one preceding it . . . puzzlingly misaligned when taken as a whole, but wholly suggestive and provocative in its various parts and moments";[4] epistolary novels from Samuel Richardson's *Clarissa* to Choderlos de Laclos's *Liaisons dangereuses*; Laurence Sterne's improvisational narratives, *A Sentimental Journey* and *Tristram Shandy*, which emerged from the same skeptical philosophy of language as Diderot's *Jacques the Fatalist* and "This Is Not a Tale" ("Ceci n'est pas un conte") and the French *roman d'analyse*, such as Benjamin Constant's *Adolphe*, which builds an impression of psychological complexity not through the characters' confessional introspection and the author's analysis, but rather through the reticences, gaps, and contradictions in the characters' utterances to each other and to themselves.

I will discuss three main areas in which the Athenaeum's theoretical pronouncements reflect changes fundamental enough to have trickled down to Byron and Pushkin a generation later: the concept of audience as creative partner, imaginative communion as aesthetic goal; the discovery of the ancient fragment as the form that provokes authentic communion and hence provides a model for modern art; and Friedrich Schlegel's synthesizing theory of Romantic irony, which by positing the partiality or fragmentariness of any utterance or text also found a creative and communicative, not obstructive or distorting, role for language. My discussion will move backward into the eighteenth century and away from Russia at certain points, but only in order to approach Pushkin, who was so steeped in this period intellectually, with a different understanding of what it gave him.

Denying Authorship: The Athenaeum

With apocalyptic optimism, the Athenaeum regarded its historical period as the end of an era. The French Revolution had done away with the old political and social order, society was in a state of "chemical" dissolution,[5] and the new forms that social life and literary activity would take were still barely visible. The Athenaeum considered itself an ongoing experiment, a kind of incubator for these new forms of life and literature, which the participants awaited with curiosity: whatever they ended up producing would be the literature of the future. Ignoring old generic prescriptions, just as socially they ignored class, racial, gender, and conjugal borders, they envisioned forms that would do away with the old-fashioned idea of an author altogether, that would preserve the impromptu, witty, collective inspirations of the group as a whole: aphorisms and fragments whose authorship was attributed to the entire collective; philosophical dialogues that recorded the oral spontaneity and mutual fertilization of their thoughts; symposium-like novels through which the society's many voices would speak; fragments of lyrical poetry that would resemble Sappho's in their decontextualized, impersonal intimacy, like fossils involuntarily bearing the imprint of their historical time.[6]

None of these stances was original in isolation, only in combination. The Athenaeum circle owed a great deal both to the customs of the Parisian philosophical salons of the mid- to late eighteenth century and to the philosophes' favorite genre, the *entretiens* or dialogues, written representations of the salons' fertile oral culture. As early as 1730, the very title of Bernard le Bovier Fontenelle's *Dialogues on the Plurality of Worlds* suggested a revolt against system. Not an authoritative treatise but a conversation, it introduced a genre that was by definition "dialogical," whose works usually featured at least two equally matched and persuasive speakers who together arrived at conclusions neither could have dreamed up alone. It therefore substituted at least the possibility of a "plurality of worlds" for either the theological or the encyclopedic idea of a single, universally valid system of knowledge, and announced with exhilaration the fracturing of old orders into a new, fertile disorder. "Let's allow the world to speak, and let's abandon ourselves to its whirlpools," the Marquise exclaims, reversing the usual Enlightenment privileging of human speech and intellectual order over a passive, inarticulate world.[7]

In the various contes, *entretiens*, and antifictional fictions for which they are now famous, the philosophes were inclined to undo with the left hand the unified science of life the right hand had created. Perhaps the most irrepressible questioner of all utterances, especially his own, the personification of the reader, the theater audience, the peripatetic museum stroller, and the girl trapped inside the painting, the hyperactive "nephew" of a "great man," whose multiple voices constantly interrupted the serene monologic wisdom of "Moi," the philosophe, was Diderot.[8] Regarded in his own time as fatally flawed, Diderot has become the darling of the twentieth century for his Romantic irony: for having realized, in the very midst of Parisian positivism, that every articulated, self-evident truth is erected on the silencing of other versions, and for having been incapable either of completing his grand encyclopedic scheme or of repressing his fragmentary ejaculations. For the Athenaeum, and for the belated French Romantics who gathered under his banner shortly before the July Revolution, Diderot's ideas on poetic language were seminal.[9]

Of course, it was no accident that so often in the *entretiens* a feminine speaker announced "the eruption of all of those partially or fully repressed readers who can now speak for themselves at last."[10] It was in the salon that writer and potential reader came face-to-face as interlocutors, that an oral culture of wit, anecdote, and improvisational repartee arose to rival the system of written genres. Writing would have to address itself to the pleasure and attention of the reader, who as often as not was an educated woman.[11]

> A private vernacular, behavioral and linguistic, energized by the circumstances of salon life, with its sporadic, conversational shifts and disjunctions, its playful or associative interruptions and flights, had pushed through a more public and regularized speech. . . . It is not accidental that in the peregrinations of eighteenth-century fictions those forms are favored that introject the audience, as though the only way to match or seize its errant attention was openly to converse with it.[12]

The criteria for successful aristocratic intercourse—wit, lightness, *l'imprévu*, play with implicit codes of behavior, veiled aggression—were transferred to literature. Digressions, in their realistic mimicry of the waywardness and improvisational freedom of oral conversation, became both a sign of a written text's authenticity and a way of establishing and continually testing the narrator's rapport with his reader. In his digressions, the narrator discloses a mind in the delightful process of rapid thought, its associative leaps and figures of speech unique to itself, and projects a reader who can keep up. The work of art is no longer viewed as a finished object bestowed on a passive public but as the point of intersection of two complementary cognitive processes, those of creation and reception, which are increasingly seen as necessary halves of the whole aesthetic experience. In Diderot's pregnant words, "One must be almost in a state to create art in order to feel it strongly."[13] In the case of Laurence Sterne's *Tristram Shandy* or Diderot's *Jacques the Fatalist*, digressions serve as a cognitive test: At what point will the reader give up the attempt to construct meaning from random fragments? How many times can a text be interrupted before it becomes unreadable?

The idea that the reader or viewer was someone to be addressed, played with, involved, puzzled, and seduced was in the very fabric of social and literary pastimes such as the *tableau vivant* or the epistolary novel.[14] Both in the sequence of *tableaux* and in the sequence of letters that makes up the epistolary novel, we can discern several common underlying features of a new aesthetic. The roles of performer and audience, character and reader are incompletely differentiated and potentially reversible, as they are in the salon. For example, in the *tableau vivant* members of the salon watch other members freeze in poses taken from literary or artistic texts. The living participants become the illustrations to a verbal inscription; it speaks through their silence. The audience to the spectacle must have experienced a peculiar self-estrangement when confronted, for example, with a favorite subject like the "Herculaneum Dancers":[15] we (the live audience) watch the performers impersonate an animated social life suddenly transfixed by death, dancing bodies turned to stone, as someone else might watch the spectacle / text of our own salon lives. Historical irony was a frisson that never palled.

In the epistolary novel, the reader is both the "you" to whom each letter is addressed and an external eavesdropper on the entire correspondence. As in the *tableau vivant*, the expressive moment is excerpted from an explanatory narrative. Nobody provides a final integrated reading of the bundle of "found" letters and their writers' contradictory, often aggressive or deceptive attempts to narrate reality; so into the vacuum must step the reader, the reader turned author. Moreover, "each having his eyes,"[16] the multiple interpretive "wholes" these readers construct will be beyond the novelist's powers of control (as the scandal-ridden history of the reception of Laclos's *Liaisons dangereuses* proved).[17] Formal fragmentation in the eighteenth century points to the possibility of that vertiginous "multiplicity of worlds" hovering in the margins of every unified representation of life.

It is clear, I think, that the Athenaeum owed a tremendous debt to the culture of the Parisian salons: the establishment of such oral values as wit, unpredictability, associative logic, dialogicity, and immediate pleasure in the written literature, as well as a sense of collective intellectual or creative endeavor. The skepticism aroused by any authoritative, "monological" discourse was reflected in the new convention of the "found manuscript"; in the formal absence of the author, the uncensored voices of his culture spoke through him. The authentic written text was no longer a consciously *authored* enterprise, but the product of a fortuitous spurt of collective creativity (the *entretien* or *Decameron*-like storytelling session), or of some accidental set of circumstances that eliminated the possibility of a single authorial intention (the found manuscript, "bundle of letters," or frame tale).

The implication was that the surviving document had reached an audience it never addressed, thus neutralizing the author's rhetorical control. Each reader reconstructed his own version of events from a discontinuous series of documents. "Open genres" like the epistolary novel were essentially exercises in the philosophy of language; each reader demonstrated the truth of Gottfried Wilhelm Leibniz's view of the human mind as a creative artist that fabricates its own world: "The connective act of the soul by which it views one in many is perhaps one of the principal acts of its most excellent part. . . . Were it not for this, even the sensible world would appear as unconnected as the words of an index."[18] In his "Letter on the deaf and mute" and "Letter on the blind," as well as numerous hypotheses involving hunchbacks, cripples, and other bearers of "deformed" perception, Diderot repeatedly and vividly illustrated the skeptical thesis that there is no "true" space and no true perception of space. Each sense has its own world, and each human being arrives at a slightly different way of correlating these fragmentary worlds into a single working model.[19] The kinds of works of art that interested late-eighteenth-century thinkers were the ones that exercised the reader's cognitive faculties, that demonstrated his ability to dispense with orderly logical exposition and leap actively, deductively, imaginatively to his own meaning.

Expanding the intuitive role of the interlocutor got around the central problem: that each language imposed its own set of cognitive structures and thus inflicted damage or distortion on the original moment of thought and feeling. Diderot expressed this paradox most memorably:

> Our soul is a picture in motion, according to which we paint ceaselessly; we use a great deal of time to render it with fidelity: but it exists in its entirety, and all at once; the mind does not proceed step by step like (verbal) expression. The paintbrush executes only at length what the eye of the painter embraces all of a sudden. The formation of languages required decomposition; but *to see* an object, *to judge* it beautiful, *to experience* an agreeable sensation, *to desire* possession, this is the state of the soul in a single instant, and what Greek and Latin render in a single word. Ah, Monsieur! how our

understanding is modified by signs; and how the liveliest diction is still a cold copy of what takes place there![20]

Why should Latin and Greek possess this mysterious capacity to capture "in a single word" "the state of the soul at a single moment"? The poetic superiority of the ancient languages rested, in the eyes of eighteenth-century grammarians, on their "inflected," as opposed to "analytical," structure; that is, a single word could contain grammatical markers of person, tense, mood, voice, number, repetition, even particles indicating affection, diminutiveness, or insult, in addition to which its more or less free placement in the syntactic and verse sequence could create through sheer spatial arrangement a sense of intense phonetic and associative linkage among words. In other words, the structure of the ancient languages had retained the primitive, poetic ability to say "all at once" in a passionate "mixture of gesture and speech," figure and sound.[21] The dispersion of the original unified expressive impulse along a linear syntactic sequence in the interests of logic and communicability belonged to a later, decadent stage. Thus the "natural order" of speech, which the analytical syntax of French had been proudly thought to exemplify, was now seen to be merely a compromise between the instantaneous complexity of the speaker's impulse and the necessity (frustratingly familiar to any writer) to communicate it in some sequence. Expressive possibilities were restricted by the analytical language's more or less fixed word order and sequential development of grammatical and logical relationships.

The mission of *poetic* language, Diderot concludes, is to circumvent the automatic decomposition and successiveness of conventional discourse and to render the layered multiplicity and simultaneity of thought:

There passes then into the discourse of a poet a spirit which moves and enlivens all of its syllables. What is this spirit? I have felt its presence; but all I know is that it is that which causes things to be said and represented all at once; so that at the same time the understanding seizes them, the soul is moved by them, the imagination sees and the ear hears them; so that the discourse is no longer only a chain of energetic terms which represent thought with power and nobility, but is also a tissue of hieroglyphs layered one on the other which paint it. I could say that in this sense, all poetry is emblematic.[22]

Poetic language reverses the trajectory of eighteenth-century analytical discourse away from its "origins"; its mission is to recover the lost conceptual unity from which it has fallen or been separated.

It is not insignificant that Diderot borrows the terminology of baroque poetics for his supposedly secular discussion of poetic language. In his article on emblems in the *Encyclopedia* he had cited a similar definition of devices and emblems "which represent in a moment, and by a simple and distinct notion, what our [writers] can represent only successively, and by a long sequence of expressions and machines."[23] What attracts Diderot to the emblem is precisely its fragmentation of form and unity of effect. The emblem, with its combination of "mute figure" and word, simulates Rousseau's expressive mixture of gesture and passionate speech, that original condition of language which poetry was supposed to recover. What is expected of the work of art, and implicitly of the artist, is a sacred function. Inspiration reunites what classification has separated: the spirit, the object, desire, volition, vision, all the senses, the world.

But what form is this original impulse to take if it is not to be misshaped by the "machines of language"? Once the aesthetic locus has been shifted from the object to the artist's invisible, internal moment of inspiration and the complementary moment of ecstatic reception in the beholder or reader, which resurrects it, the most effective form is the fragment. The quick sketch is not designed for public communication; it merely captures the essential features of a conception in a private, instantaneous ideogram. Paradoxically, Diderot found, the excitement of the original moment was literally killed in the drawn-out act of "executing" or completing the work. "The sketch, that is a word which awakens in me a great thought. In the violent transports of passion, a man omits the links, begins a phrase without finishing it, lets a word escape him, utters a cry, and falls silent. Nevertheless, I have heard everything."[24]

The sketch, the ellipsis, the fragment acquire a special eloquence, both by virtue of their real or implied closeness to the inarticulate moment of conception and by their opening up of a space for the audience. This brings with it a taste not only for the *non finito*, as in the Renaissance fascination with the traces left by genius, but also, not quite illogically, for the fragment in a state of decay. Like the preliminary sketch, the "ruin" detached from its original context requires an interlocutor, as the complete work of art does not. It is precisely the fact that the ruin is detached from the context in which it once had practical significance—the military victory it was supposed to celebrate, the famous name it was supposed to immortalize—that liberates it from discursive automatism into the unknown of the reader's "illiteracy." Just as the peripatetic art critic of Diderot's *Salons* creates a certain narrative associatively linking the individual paintings on display, a narrative that depends entirely on the accidental order in which he has encountered the paintings,[25] the artistic fragment wanders in time, eliciting ever-different explanatory narratives from its readers.

Fragmentariness actually becomes a positive criterion by which Diderot judges paintings.[26] He prefers pictures in which the angle of the frame has cut out an essential piece of the story, or the painting's narrative has been halted right before the denouement, or the ambiguity of the human expression and pose beg for interpretation; in short, pictures he can call "morceaux." A properly composed painting is a fragment, cut off from its narrative context by the formal frame. A painting that exposes too much of its narrative and leaves too little unsaid leaves Diderot, the beholder, cold. The beholder must be allowed to be a reader of paintings. Pushkin explained the fragmentary composition of his own Romantic narrative poems in much the same way: "It is not necessary to say everything. That is the secret of entertainment."[27]

In all of this eighteenth-century play with authorial convention one senses a search for a new transcendental theory of creativity, a desire to elude the aegis of the conscious mind altogether, to be surprised by creativity from some unknown source—if not from divine possession, then from the nonself of the unpredictable collective. The authentic text must be the occasion for a meeting of minds, a process of communication completed differently by each reader; it generates an interest in the way mental and linguistic intuition (or inspiration) leaps to bridge gaps in a narrative, rather than in the complete story an author chooses to tell. The focus of attention may, indeed, become the story the author has not told. In short, it seems to me that the eighteenth century's cultivation of "open forms," while perfectly explainable in terms of secular skepticism, worked ultimately to restore a sense of mystery, of the incomplete congruity between language and conscious human intention. Someone or something else speaks through the author, inspiring him to say more than he knows. What one century might call "God" or "nature" or "the unconscious," the turn of the nineteenth century, imbued with the historical perspective that made Napoleon act before an audience of forty centuries, began to call "culture." The poet's writing was the Rosetta stone of the future, through which his culture would speak to future ages.

From Greek Fragments to Modern Sensibility

Although the Athenaeum writers looked forward in theory to unheard-of new forms of creativity, they harked back to Greece for concrete examples. As their name indicates, their own cultural role had been defined by Greece. This in itself was scarcely a new position. The rediscovery of the "origins" of western culture appears almost inevitably to accompany the crystallization of any imperial, national, or urban entity's identity as civilized, European, and politically integrated. Such a preoccupation with the classical legacy was de rigueur for a culture like Germany's at the turn of the century, aware of its "youth" and "barbarism" relative to other, less recently unified European nations. In Johann Gottfried Herder's words, "If we do not become Greeks, we will remain barbarians."[28]

Why precisely Greeks, rather than the more general Greco-Roman "ancients"? In the following pages I will discuss the displacement of Rome by Greece as the prestigious cultural model, and the displacement of neoclassical "imitation" and "universality" by the "originality" and historical specificity of Greek cultural forms. Just as Greek sculpture, architecture, philosophy, and literature had come, in the eighteenth century, to be seen as the involuntary, "organic" expression of the healthy culture that had produced them, so the Athenaeum members believed that modern cultures ought to express themselves in their own native forms.[29] Through his study of Greek lyric poetry, Friedrich Schlegel had discovered the archaic "savage face" of antiquity, Greek art's original function as ritual observance and "orgiastic liberation."[30] Finding itself only at the beginning of its own political and cultural differentiation as the "classical" century drew to a close, Germany defined itself perforce as "modern." Schlegel reinterpreted Herder's dictum thus: The Greeks were the Germans of their time in their youth and vitality. To become "classical," one must first be "modern."

What was needed at the end of the eighteenth century was a deliberate cultivation of disorder, a chaos that would allow the artist to generate rather than reproduce his forms, at the beginning rather than the end of history. If these forms didn't look like anything a neoclassicist would recognize, so much the better. Only in retrospect, Schlegel explained in "On Incomprehensibility," would modernity discover its own identity in the strange, "incomprehensible" new forms it had spawned.[31] Meanwhile, in the absence of historical perspective, the Athenaeum critics stood ready to interpret modernity's own artifacts to itself. One of Schlegel's enigmatic dicta postulates, however, a curious analogy between the works of the ancients and moderns: "Many works of the ancients have become fragments. Many works of the moderns are so at their genesis."[32] Why should fragmentariness be the point of intersection of the ancients and the moderns? What can a complete work damaged by the centuries—an architectural, sculptural, or manuscript fragment—have in common with a "fragment," a "sketch," a conception not brought to completion by its author? Where did this equation come from, and what would it have implied to its readers? In order to plumb its implications I will ask the reader to bear with me while I reconstruct a bit of cultural context. This will enable me to draw a genealogical dotted line between the discovery of the sculptural fragment at the beginning of the eighteenth century and the invention of the poetic fragment toward its end.

The older European courts (the Italian principalities, the Vatican, the newly centralized monarchy of Francis I, Peter I and Catherine I's Russian empires) had followed comparable patterns of ostentatious appropriation of Greco-Roman symbols for new beginnings, for Golden Age and Empire, but with significant differences. One difference was the emblematic role played by classical sculpture, perhaps because of its amenability to actual physical appropriation and transport. In *Taste and the Antique*, Francis Haskell and Nicholas Penny map the various cultural flowerings of European states by following the fortunes of the sculpture market throughout European history. An essential sign of modernity for any flourishing court was its acquisition, in the words of Louis XIV's minister Colbert, of "everything there is of beauty in Italy."[33]

One of the interesting conclusions the art historians draw about the tremendous expertise deployed in the acquisition and organization of rival collections is that what we would consider artistic criteria played a relatively small part. The value of the sculptures inhered in their iconography of power. Thus for Peter I's court at Peterhof it was more important to acquire reproductions of the most famous statues in Florence, Rome, and Naples than a partial or damaged group of authentic ancient statuary, which would not tell its mythical story so legibly nor represent the current monarch's claims to inheritance so richly.[34] Not only was there no snobbish differentiation of "copies" versus "originals," except on the basis of the preciousness of the material and the technical excellence of the reproduction, there was no interest in differentiating the ancient parts of a statue from its recently added modern appendages. What was important was that the statue be restored to representational wholeness and recognizability.[35] Greco-Roman classicism was predicated on the notion of the imitability and recyclability of the Golden Age. As late as 1807 Lord Elgin transported his Parthenon fragments to England in the full expectation that they would first be "restored" to architectural completeness before they were put on display. The outcry this aroused then, and would arouse today, testifies to a sea change in taste.

The change has to do with Europe's discovery of a Greek civilization unmediated by Rome. The sculptural and architectural relics found by English collectors were incomparably older and worse preserved than the classical statuary that ornamented European cities, and since these were located in infidel (Turkish) territory, anything portable could be legitimately carted off for display in a properly European context.[36] This practice had important consequences: the fashionable and later the museum-going public became increasingly accustomed to the display of sculptural and architectural fragments, physically incomplete and excerpted from their original surroundings.[37] This fostered a new tolerance for and indeed valorization of the physical imperfection of authentic historical relics, as well as the habit of juxtaposition, in sculpture galleries, travelers' commentaries, and the imaginations of art lovers, not only of different sculptures but of different cultures.[38] The narrative and iconographic interest of the sculptures began to give way to an awareness of historical and stylistic difference. That the Elgin marbles were left in their state of "authentic" fragmentariness after over a decade of controversy testifies to the penetration of certain radical new ideas, first formulated by the self-invented art historian Johann Joachim Winckelmann, about the irreplaceable value of cultural artifacts.

Ironically, the two books accredited with inventing modern art history, *Thoughts on the Imitation of the Painting and Sculpture of the Greeks* (1755) and *The History of the Art of Antiquity* (1763–64), were written by a man who never visited Greece and whose most influential theories of Greek art and culture were based on his study of Roman copies.[39] Nevertheless, Winckelmann was the first to demand respect for the "authentic fragment," the sculptural shard in whatever state it had survived time, as opposed to the restored, perfected, "whole" composite of ancient and modern sculptors' hands. In placing such an emphasis on authenticity, Winckelmann simultaneously shifted attention from an eclectic "classical" tradition to a specifically and historically Greek art, and from the generalized "norms" handed down by copyists to the irreplaceable work of a single artist, the specific genius and technique of a Praxiteles or a Michelangelo. Withdrawing attention from the iconographic aspects of classical sculpture, he refocused it on individual mastery, the historical development of style and technique within the work of a single artist and from artist to artist, culture to culture. Classical sculptures were not all equal, and modern neoclassical statuary was not equal at all.

Before Friedrich Schiller published his famous distinction between the "naive" culture of the ancients and modern "sentimental" culture, nostalgically mesmerized by the former yet fatally exiled from it by its own self-consciousness,[40] Winckelmann's close scrutiny of modern and antique nudes had led him to the same unflattering conclusions. He turns the artistic rendering of flesh into a text that can be read, and from which the most global extrapolations can be made:

In most figures executed by modern masters, those parts of the body which are subjected to pressure will display small but all-too-conspicuous folds of skin; but where the same folds occur on the same constricted parts in Greek statues, each rises from the other in gentle undulations, so that they all form a single unit and seem to be the combined product of a single noble pressure. These masterpieces show us a skin which is not tightly stretched, but gently drawn over a healthy flesh, which fills it out without distended protuberances and follows all the movements of the fleshy parts of the body in a single unified direction . . . in keeping with the more perfect and complete nature of the Greeks; [the movements] are merely hinted at, and are often apparent only to a trained sensibility.[41]

Every comparison inculcates the same lesson: if the "whole" of Greek culture can be divined from even the most mutilated fragment, modern man, with his dimpled, unappetizing flesh, sterile ratiocination, and sedentary, one-sided social life, represents a mere fraction of human potential. This was the burden of Goethe's eulogy to Winckelmann, and the stimulus for the ideal of *Bildung*, the careful nineteenth-century cultivation of a complete, classical self that comprised at least in theory a gentlemanly liberal education. It was founded on the a priori assumption of modern man's deficiency, fragmentariness, and inauthenticity in comparison with the ideal and powerfully eroticized Greek. Distance and inaccessibility are built into Winckelmann's influential redefinition of beauty.[42] Not only is the beautiful body a rare amalgam of male and female traits, but it is impervious to desire, hovering on the border of the inanimate, and above all, located exclusively in an unrecoverable place and time, ancient Greece.

Exaggerated though it may seem, Winckelmann's style was assimilated by the nineteenth century as the appropriate language for artistic commentary, for built into his descriptions of the aesthetic ideal is the ubiquitous figure of "the very careful observer," who is uniquely qualified to traverse and interpret the distance and inaccessibility Winckelmann incorporated into that ideal. Paradoxically, the frozen laconism Winckelmann attributes to the Greek statue necessitates his own translation of "its" latent passions into words. What is repressed or sublimated in the sculpture returns in Winckelmann's "rhapsodies."[43]

Logically, then, Winckelmann's interpretive impulse finds its supreme challenge in sculptural fragments. Here, for example, is his famous commentary on the Apollo Belvedere:

At the first glance you may perhaps see in this trunk no more than a shapeless piece of stone: but if you have the ability to penetrate into the secrets of art, and if you contemplate this work with a quiet eye, it will reveal itself as a miracle. . . . At the point where the poets finished, there the sculptor began. . . . In every part of the body there is made visible, as though in a painting, the whole hero in each one of his exploits separately, and there can be seen, just as one can see the correct dimensions in the judicious building of a palace, the particular exploit for which each one of the parts has served. I cannot contemplate the little that still remains of the shoulder without recalling that upon its powerful breadth was supported, as upon two mountains, the whole weight of the celestial spheres.[44]

The truncated, mutilated fragment can at any moment open out into a vision of the Greek world, an alternate pagan paradise; every part testifies to the many-sidedness and integration, physical and spiritual, rational and religious, of the Greek personality, itself a microcosm of Greek culture. Historical distance is eroticized much as geographical distance, the metaphorical precipitate of Renaissance exploration, was eroticized by the Renaissance poets.

Winckelmann's "reveries" and "rhapsodies," quoted and imitated from Goethe to Walter Pater and Marcel Proust,[45] provided, much as Jean-Jacques Rousseau's "promenades" did for the encounter of the solitary self with nature,[46] a model language for the interior monologue before the work of art, a model for the inner life of the "aesthete." Not only, as Mario Praz says, did the homosexual / narcissist impose the imprint of his idiosyncratic sensibility on the aesthetic reception of an entire age, the middle-class man usurped "noble" and preeminently secular sculpture, the art form par excellence of aristocratic power, prestige, and physicality, for the purposes of "bourgeois" emotional self-expression and even the propagation of Protestant values of repression, self-conquest, and spirituality. The northern bourgeois "thinker" appropriated the legacy of the aristocratic Mediterranean "hero," and the "historyless," "cultureless" German intellectual invented for himself a genealogy and a vocation.

With his emphasis on technique, the unique signature of the artist, and on interpretation, the complementary creativity of the beholder,

Winckelmann looks forward to an avant-garde model of artistic production and reception where the opaque artifacts of genius demand the mediation of an interpreter, whose verbal distillation pretends to a kind of poetry itself. Thus arises the characteristic symbiotic dialogue of the "silent," "simple," artistic fragment and the passionate aesthetic response it elicits from the viewer, a dialogue that would make the "classical fragment" one of the favorite genres for the implication of intimate interior worlds. Winckelmann might well have said that where sculpture ends, modern poetry begins.

When Diderot advises his readers to throw away their Virgins and crucifixes and meditate on the handy desk-size copies of Gladiators, Apollos, and Venuses now so easily reproduced,[47] he, like Winckelmann, is crossing two different aesthetic traditions, two different sensibilities. The very development of the technology of reduction, which made possible the production of cheap and easily accessible miniatures, facilitated not only the popularization of antique art, but a profound shift in the aesthetic uses to which it was put. Transferred from the city square or the nobleman's palace to the bourgeois drawing room or study, the antique object changed its function: from an object of outward display aimed at the public it became an object of inward contemplation, a pretext for the inner monologue of the private, cultured subject, a secularized form of the previously religious practice of meditation. The antique object, for all its associations with pagan sensuality, secular humanism, and the public or civic forum, became the focus of a new mysticism, a new spirituality generated by the symbolic incursion of the past into the present. Confronted by an antique object, the surviving fragment of a lost civilization, the modern sensibility felt the solidity of its here-and-now fracture. The religious "otherworldly" was replaced by the "sublime" apprehension of other, vanished cultural worlds, of hidden layers beneath the surface of everyday reality.[48] European exploration, with its geographical expansion and its faith in temporal progress, had led, paradoxically, to the excavation of its own archaeological—and psychological—layers and origins.[49]

What could modernity substitute for geological layers and historical damage, in order to create artifacts of similar "authenticity" and suggestiveness? The "sham ruin" that sprang up in the wake of the Greek Revival is exactly such a hybrid art form, poised between an aesthetic of public display and an aesthetic of internality. All over England and Europe, Greek sculptural and architectural fragments were turned into centerpieces for private gardens and public parks.[50] The dissonance was at least twofold, geographical and temporal. The eye was startled to discover a Mediterranean structure interpolated into a northern landscape, and the imagination was jolted by the insertion of an ancient fragment into modern time. The sham ruin was a form of conceptual art, nonfunctional and purely aesthetic, relying for its sublime or ironic effect entirely on the viewer's response to the fabricated anachronism.

If the muteness of sculptural and architectural fragments invited a complementary interior monologue from the viewer, fragments of ancient texts stimulated readers to picture the context from which they had been torn, for which they served as an inscription. The literary equivalent of the sculptural fragment was the newly rediscovered Greek Anthology.[51] An ancient compilation that consisted basically of epitaph verses and statuary inscriptions, it had been shaped simultaneously "from the inside" by the organic laws of its culture and "from the outside" by the rough hand of history. The epitaphs testified eloquently to both the durability and the fragility, the skillfulness and the sheer fortuitousness of poetic artifacts.

It was difficult for the modern lyric poet not to conceive of his verses even as they were being written as analogous "epitaphs" for his culture. From here to the fabrication of objects that would induce that state of rapt reverie was but a step. But how, in practice, was Schlegel's dictum, "The poems of the moderns are often fragments at their genesis," to be realized? One obvious and popular solution was impersonation. Not surprisingly, just as the display of authentic Greek fragments led almost immediately to the fashion for sham ruins, ruins, as it were, in ironic quotation marks and aware of their own fashionable status, the cult of the Greek Anthology soon spawned its own progeny of sham literary ruins.[52] The cultic popularity of James Macpherson's literary hoax, his supposed "translation from the original Gaelic" of the fragments of an archaic Scottish epic poem by the bard "Ossian, son of Fingal," testifies to the privileged status of the fragment in the public imagination, as well as to its desire for a primitively expressive language. Ossian's was precisely the sort of primitive poetry the eighteenth-century debate on the origins of language had envisioned. A past was invented to satisfy new aesthetic needs.[53]

In Chapter 2 I will explore more fully the way the Russian elite, and in its context Pushkin, plunged into the European "romance with the classical." At this point I would like just to point out certain idiosyncrasies of the Russian situation. The Russian court since Peter I had whole-heartedly identified itself with Roman iconography, as a sign both of its imperial ambitions and of its new European orientation. The individual courts of the wealthy nobility had for the most part followed suit, although this often produced an extraordinary hybrid theater of European imports and old Russian-autocratic customs.[54] By the beginning of the nineteenth century, the Russian elite appeared to be polarized between two purifying drives: one that wanted to complete the process of refinement and was moving in the direction of an aesthetics of the interior life, infused by meditation on Greek or Italian culture (Batiushkov) or German mystical nature (Zhukovsky);[55] another that wanted to purge Russian culture of imported mannerism and subtlety and return to an unabashed culture of powerful display (the Beseda group, or archaists).[56]

Curiously, each of these groups could invoke Greece as a cultural model: the first group in the manner of Winckelmann, turning the Greek art object into an object of meditation, an object for the inculcation of internal, spiritual values; the second group in the manner of Schlegel, claiming that only in its primitive vitality would a Slavic culture truly be "in the spirit of the ancients." The latter "archaist" group of nobility identified itself with the interests of the monarchy, accepting its own subordinate role in the collective celebration of power; the former group attempted to stake out a higher ground of cultural refinement and greater autonomy.[57]

There was a certain incongruity in the latter position, however. The claim to superior internal values made by the non-courtly nobility was already a move dictated by its disempowerment. The values of a highly developed interior life, of self-mastery and self-government, had been instruments of cultural power for a rising middle class in seventeenth-century England or eighteenth-century

Germany: an enhancement of its prestige and a means of harnessing and sublimating the energy of a large population for societal institutions.[58] The Russian aristocracy's attraction to the culture of the interior, which had been developed in Europe for the most part by other classes, is one of the most fruitful cultural hybrids of Russian intellectual history. I believe that Pushkin, like Tolstoy, was intermittently conscious of the incongruousness of this adaptation, and temperamentally and culturally divided between the two orientations. (This might explain his liberal friends' recurrent perplexity over Pushkin's incurable "barbarism" when it came to questions of Russia's military might or realpolitik, including his attitude toward the Greek, Caucasian, and Polish independence movements.)

In Chapter 2, therefore, I will look at the way Pushkin adopts the refined and impersonal anthological fragment bequeathed to him by André Chénier and Batiushkov, only to reinfuse it with the direct experience and "virile" egoism of the aristocrat; and then at the way "disempowerment" leaves, after all, an unmistakable imprint on the obsessive forms of his erotic imagination.[59] My overall aim is to show that Pushkin's supposedly inherent "classicism"[60] was inspired by the ubiquitous *Romantic* fashion for "creation in the spirit of the ancients"; and that this romance with the classical provided him with a fund of images to which he returned again and again in order to represent the mystifying movements of his interior life.

The Imaginary Subject: From Schlegel to Pushkin

When we think of Romantic subjectivity we tend to think of the Rousseauist or Wordsworthian "authentic self in nature," secondarily vitiated by its dealings with other men in society and the necessity of mediation through an inherently corrupt language.[61] The fragment then becomes the solution to the problem of linguistic skepticism: a product of the natural self in a moment of incandescent thought, it has exploded accidentally into words without submitting to the deadening structures and habits of language. However, there existed within Romanticism an alternate branch: the far more radical theory of the self and language developed by Immanuel Kant and Friedrich Schlegel. In his interpretation of the fragment, Schlegel went beyond his predecessors. He incorporated the sentimental cult of ruins and nostalgia for origins, the radical eighteenth-century skepticism about language, the inclusion of the audience and its interpretive role in late-eighteenth-century aesthetic theory and literary "open works," and finally Kant's philosophical redefinition of "the subject" and his world into a new conception of human communication: Romantic irony. I believe that Schlegel's ideas about the ironic subject and his language can be used to illuminate Pushkin.

Perhaps the simplest way of putting it is that the "self" in Kant does not precede (as a "soul," "psyche," or any other metaphysical entity) its communicative representations. It comes into phenomenological existence only through its interactions with the world. Or, as Lacoue-Labarthe and Nancy put it in their thought-provoking book *The Literary Absolute*, "All that remains of the subject is the 'I' as an 'empty form' (a pure logical necessity, said Kant; a grammatical exigency, Nietzsche will say) that 'accompanies my representations.' "[62] If, as Kant says, "I" is an empty grammatical form until it speaks, then, Schlegel continues, the "provisional and fragmentary individual subject" finds out who she or he is by entering into dialogue. The subject does not precede his life, but comes into being, or "builds himself," through interaction with other subjects, nature, and the world, and they with him; his life is the representation of his "inner self."

Similarly, meaning does not precede the communicative interaction but comes into being through it. Meaning is not a brilliant insight conceived independently in one man's mind, then conveyed intentionally to a passive object-listener and in the process "damaged" by the corrupt medium of language that unavoidably inserts itself between them. Instead of setting up a quasi-theological contrast between authentic self-expression and debased social language, Schlegel sees *all* language use as approximate, negotiable, and interactive. Meaning is not the origin but the end product of a creative process of communication. The "self" is not primarily the thinker and secondarily the speaker of its originally perfect thoughts; the "self" is actually the by-product of its communication with others and is therefore in a continuous process of development or self-fashioning, which halts at a stable and finished "identity" only in death. This means that at any given moment the "self" is fragmentary in relation to the accumulation of its past and future representations, and any utterance it makes is partial in relation to the "whole" process of its communication with the world.

Human understanding structures its world through the recurrent images and categories to which it has recourse and then finds itself essentially sealed off from the world by that limited language. Gary Handwerk calls Schlegel's irony "the systematic undoing of understanding,"[63] where by understanding he means the smooth appearance of understanding, what Diderot called "the automatic enchainment of notions." By drawing the conversationalists' attention to the possible other meanings of the linguistic formulas they use, irony generates a shared sense of relativity and freedom from linguistic "literality"; it mocks accepted meanings in order to regenerate a *reflective*, rather than reflexive, community. The kinds of irony that Handwerk links to Schlegel are united by

> their intersubjective character, that is, by the ironist's awareness of how dependent the signifying process is on its constant relocation of meaning within verbal interactions. All discourse is typified by what Schlegel calls the "hovering" (*schwebende*) quality of signification; an ironic discourse differs essentially in the greater or more constant awareness on the part of the interlocutors of how inextricable their identities are from that discourse. (viii)

Irony has a number of means of breaking out of the conceptual prison of accepted meaning. One is *Witz*, "a flash from the unconscious world" (24); erupting from some intuitive sense of the interconnectedness of phenomena, it overrides language's effort to maintain order. True wit always surprises the speaker as much as his listeners, because it transcends the well-worn logical and lexical paths he himself uses in everyday life. A second, more extended liberation of the ironic self is represented by the ecstatic, Sapphic lyric, which articulates a desire so intense that it transcends personal and social circumstance and attains universality. Third, allegory (whether in the form of dialogue, drama, or novel) allows the ironic awareness of a universe of relations to be represented in time and in tangible form.

In Handwerk's words, "the artwork's presence for analysis and its fixing of patterns long enough to permit the dialectic of ironic self-recognition to occur do privilege it in the Athenaeum period"

(34). But the key, according to Schlegel, is nevertheless the ironic self-recognition allegory provokes in its audience, not the art object sufficient unto itself: "Should, through representation, that occur in the other person which took place in us, then it has attained the aim of communication. In communication should be contained, not always a representation of the results, but rather of the manner and way in which it came to be" (21). In short, "Irony is a linguistic act used to define the place and movement of the subject" (3).

Every reader of Pushkin is aware of his habitual irony; it is generally regarded as a legacy of his favorite eighteenth-century writers, his social milieu, the aristocratic salon, and the life of the literary circles he frequented. It is as recognizable in his poetry as it is in his fiction and letters. But is it always the same irony? I have found that the distinctions Gary Handwerk makes between various types of irony ("normative," "aesthetic," and "ethical") can be used to identify changes in Pushkin's writing and in the varying degrees first of misunderstanding and later of semantic multiplicity it engendered.

In Pushkin's Lycée, Arzamas, and "southern" periods, what Soviet scholars often characterize as *kruzhkovaia semantika* (the semantic code of the in-group) conforms to Wayne Booth's definition of "normative irony": "saying one thing to mean another" with the purpose of creating ingenious, intellectually and ideologically compatible, "amiable communities of interpretation."[64] "Contextual loading" of certain words creates "competing significations," which a combination of prior knowledge and social intuition allow the interlocutor to decide between.[65] Needless to say, the amiability is strictly limited to the members of the community.

For example, in a letter to his brother—and by extension, to their entire *kruzhok* (circle)[66]—in St. Petersburg, shortly after the flood that would, ten years later, inspire his greatest and most tragic narrative poem, Pushkin wrote in the following vein:

Что это у вас? потоп! ничто проклятому Петербургу! Voilà une belle occasion à vos dames de faire bidet. Жаль мне «Цветов» Дельвига; да надолго ли это его задержало в тине петербургской? Что погреба? признаюсь, и по них сердце болит. Не найдется ли между вами Ноя, для насаждения винограда? На святой Руси не штука ходить нагишом, а хамы смеются. . . . Верно есть бочки *per fas et nefas*, продающиеся в Петербурге—купи, что можно будет, подешевле и получше. Этот потоп—оказия. (13, 122–23)

What are you having? a flood? It serves accursed Petersburg right! Voilà une belle occasion à vos dames de faire bidet. I am sorry about Del'vig's *Flowers*; and will he be delayed long in the Petersburg mire? What about the wine cellars? I confess that my heart aches for them, too. Will no Noah be found among you, to plant a vineyard? It is no joke to go about stark naked in Holy Russia; the Hams would laugh. . . . Barrels no doubt *per fas et nefas* are being sold in Petersburg—buy what you can, the cheapest and the best. This flood is an occasion.[67]

Pushkin later made a contribution to the victims of the flood, but his epistolary impulse is to use the *potop* as a theme for associative variations, the more outrageous the better. Beginning his letter with a biblical malediction against St. Petersburg, from which, a baleful prophet, he has been exiled for several years, he reduces the flood of 1824 to an instrument of personal revenge against the sinning capital. An additional shade of irony is added by the fact that he echoes the *feminine* curse of Peter I's banished wife, Eudoxia: "Let this place be empty!" The elevated Church Slavic syntax of his blasphemous curse is immediately followed by a scatological French epigram. The two contrasting keys set the tone for the whole letter, playing a game of sacrilegious juxtapositions that create a vivid patchwork portrait of their absent author: irreligious, inhumane, frivolously literary, hedonistic, and fragmentary. The one thing that is missing is any mention of death or tragedy. Instead Pushkin's thoughts dance tangentially around the gap, motivated by shock value and, on closer inspection, a punning, paronomastically driven train of thought: *pogreba* (cellars) leads to Noah's planting of vines, which leads to a macaronic pun on Ham (the son who ridiculed Noah's nakedness) and *kham* (the Russian word for boor), then, offhandedly, back to the news of the *pogrebenie* (burial) of his aunt. Death has, indeed, been turned into a linguistic predicament, or rather an occasion for verbal vitality. The last words summarize the latent content of the whole letter: "This flood is an occasion!"—an occasion for acquiring cheap wine, venting his spleen against the government, flaunting his incorrigibility, and finally for confirming, across the geographical distance of his exile, his insider's status as a Petersburger (after all, only the victims of a tragedy have the right to laugh at it).

Denser and more indirect than ordinary communication, irony automatically eliminates the literal-minded, who do not recognize the invisible quotation marks that surround language aware of its own history of usage. As I will show in Chapters 2 and 3, both "Greek authenticity" and Byronic-Oriental dandyism can be seen first of all as consciously adopted and ironic fashions whose aim was to establish "amiable communities of interpretation" among like-minded (and often geographically isolated) writers and readers. But, Handwerk points out, this is irony at its least ambiguous:

> Irony's complexities are, after all, shared; the whole thing cannot work at all unless both parties to the exchange have confidence that they are moving together in identical patterns. Yet when hermeneutic patterns become identical, irony necessarily ceases to be, as it was for Schlegel, a heuristic device. . . . Booth's analysis prematurely resolves incompatibilities at the level of coherence of the individual subject in the form of a conscious intentionality. His irony enacts and relies upon accepted human values within a clearly defined context; it is essentially normative. (6–7)

The point of *kruzhkovaia semantika*, whether overtly political or not, was to reaffirm its members' rapport against the background of authoritarian or rival social discourses,[68] not to test the true limits of communication.

The second kind of irony with which Pushkin can readily be identified is aesthetic irony. The Romantic achievement has been seen as the shifting of irony from a rhetorical device in the text to a characterization of its process of creation, hence of the artist's mind itself. Romantic aesthetic irony is usually equated with the gesture of parabasis, in which the author breaks the illusion of his work by addressing his audience directly, thereby shifting the act of creation into the foreground and the narrative he happens to be telling into the background, and shares the ironic moment with his audience.[69] The extent of the artist's irony is to show how relative various limited human viewpoints are compared to his own all-inclusive and mobile vision. He can project himself *at will* now into this figure, now into that one, as Pushkin enthused about Shakespeare and Gogol enthused about Pushkin, but these are "descents" into human nature, not ambivalent explorations of his own.

Pushkin study tends to fuse normative and aesthetic irony into a single amalgam, a kind of prolonged wink of complicity shared between Pushkin and the aesthetically select few. Too often Pushkin commentary devotes itself to hunting down the subtexts that motivate Pushkin's intertextual "play," without which no sophisticated understanding can be contemplated. The literal level of the text is relegated to popular culture, while initiated readers listen for echoes of a poetic tradition whose richness is also a test of their own cultivation. Any irony is directed only at the philistine world.

Since my own readings of individual poems and scenes often rely on intertextual dialogue, I should explain where I think the difference lies. It seems to me that Pushkin becomes interested in any poetic ancestor who provides him with a new way of analyzing and representing his own situation. In exile, for example, he discovers an affinity with other banished poets—Ovid, Dante, Byron—although he often disengages himself from their background with his flippant trademark phrase "A ia" ("While I, ever-idle scapegrace" [2.1, 96]). He defines himself by trying on a hypothetical linguistic identity, whether it be the "naked simplicity" of the Greek lyricist's relationship to nature, the elegiac poet's inability to enter into a relationship with any experience except through repetition of a previous one, the Shakespearean character's conscious manipulation of the power structures of language. What attracts Pushkin to a certain poem by Chénier or a certain scene from *Romeo and Juliet* is the possibility it offers him of translating himself anew.

As we shall see, many of the scenes Pushkin selects from world literature turn out to be re-presentations of a remarkably repetitive structural core. By entering into dialogue with different models, Pushkin discovers the ramifications, the many possible facets of what would otherwise be a fixed psychic drama. In the mid-1820's he begins to liberate himself from the narrowly repetitive subject matter and phraseology of elegy, only to preserve the principle of elegiac repetition secretly, where we would least expect to find it: in his ostensibly non-lyrical (because historical, dramatic, social-realistic, or self-ironizing) works. Yet I hope to demonstrate that each new departure can also be seen as an ironic re-presentation "of the place and movements of the subject."

What Pushkin learned from Byron, I believe, was the possibility of juxtaposing in a single work utterly different, simultaneous points of view on the same subject matter. The jumps from style to style marked the *movements* of a mercurial subjectivity. This was Schlegel's idea of Romantic irony in the flesh. One of Byron's verse passages might address a girl in heartfelt tones, while another hobnobbed with his publisher; a third voice wove a melodramatic story full of factual holes, with interpolated hints about the author's own tragic secrets, while yet another commented sociably on details of local color the author had used to flesh out his narrative. Pushkin pushed the Byronic twists and turns even further. The preface to "Prisoner of the Caucasus" depicted with visceral sympathy the struggle of native tribes for survival, while the epilogue announced their defeat with the triumphant voice of a military ode—a radical departure from what we might call the "political correctness" of Byron's cluster of styles.

It was the suturing of stylistically and perspectivally clashing fragments that made Pushkin's Byronic poems so mystifying, not just to the uninitiated public but to his *kruzhok* (Viazemsky, Turgenev, Zhukovsky, Nikolai Karamzin). This was no longer "normative" or even "aesthetic" irony, but irony that brought together utterly different discoursive perspectives within the same ostensible narrative framework and did not even begin to articulate a decision. The reader was left uncomfortably "holding the bag," which contained, in unresolvable admixture, a lively sympathy for a Cherkess girl and a peculiar indifference to her fate, a vivid love of nature and an admission of spiritual deadness, rebellious language and patriotic language, feminist sentiments and misogynist sentiments, and, quite probably, many different readers' coexisting views.

Later writers would mythologize this all-inclusiveness as the stamp of an extraordinary identity: the self-destructive, modern perversity of Lermontov's Pechorin, or the uniquely Russian breadth of nature, to which no human experience is foreign, of a Dmitri Karamazov. Tolstoy would treat acting "in or out of character" as a moral issue: only the man in harmony with nature can have a peacefully consistent identity; it is society's artificial and multiple roles that push him into self-betrayal and sin. Goethe in later life adopted an Olympian persona to integrate bursts of what he called second and third "adolescences" that would have destroyed the "wise and harmonious" reputation of any other celebrity. Stendhal simply adopted the pseudonym, the explicit refusal of identity, as his identity. Byron and Pushkin, it seems to me, never give up their right not to coincide with themselves, to create a sincere new identity with every utterance—a series of "stills" of a subjectivity in constant motion.

According to Friedrich Schlegel, truly ironic creativity is *unverständlich* or "incomprehensible" not just to its audience, but to its author. Why should this be? That Schlegel's theory of the "fragmentary and provisional subject" has been likened to Jacques Lacan's "decentered subject" should not seem too anachronistic; the eighteenth-century skeptics, no less than Lacan, were groping for a theory of an "unconscious" grounded in language. It could be said that after the nineteenth century's detour into explanatory myths, Lacan goes back to Kant's dissolution of the traditional discrete subject and completes the job. It is as if the nineteenth century's myths of a previous or future unity—Greece, childhood, Oriental sexuality, nature, world-historicism, and finally the ultimate myth of the Freudian family romance, the story of the subject's banishment from emotional unity into alienation—allowed it to avoid the more radical eighteenth-century perception of human fragmentation. "The Freudian unconscious provides the subject with a preexistent and simultaneous fullness that counteracts its experience of partialness"[70]—in fact, that labels the latter as an abnormal symptom.

Instead of attributing "the experience of partialness" to individual sexual development, Lacan grounds it in universal human language development. As Lacan has shown in his analysis of the stages of infancy, psychological individuation accompanies the stages of language development. The conceptual apparatus of language makes possible, indeed inevitable, the human being's perception of himself as separated. He becomes "himself" precisely when he internalizes what is external to himself, that is, the symbolic function of language. He is "present" when he speaks: that is, when he substitutes a linguistic form for his relationship to another subject or thing. As Lacan would say, the simultaneous presence/absence of language is inscribed into subjectivity itself.

Lacan uses Ferdinand de Saussure's terminology of *langue* and *parole* to characterize the speaker's relationship to his own surprising utterance or *parole*, a sudden concrete "signifier" from his own internal fund of *langue*, an utterance from which he is fading even as he completes it. The only thing that saves his speech from utter reification, as Handwerk elucidates, is the reply it provokes.

> Ironic utterances are . . . partial utterances requiring completion, which make evident the partialness of the utterer as subject. Unable to play all the parts at once, the ironic subject is forced to proceed to an enactment that must be an interaction as well. . . . The uniqueness of human language lies in the fact that 1) the message is addressed not only to another person, but from the subject to itself; and 2) the message is recoverable by the subject only in [the] inverted form [of the other's response]. (132)

The subject's speech always consists of what he has verbalized plus the large number of simultaneous impulses, thoughts, and emotions that have been eliminated from the utterance (though they may leave a legible trace in fleeting expressions, "body language," and what we call "Freudian slips"). In other words, any utterance is a fragment, from which only another human being can reconstruct the unspoken part.

It is precisely language, the foreign element people have internalized, that is the human common denominator. When a human subject addresses another human subject, he is addressing the only entity that shares the common, linguistically determined predicament of "selfhood." Each is aware that the pieces of language he produces are not himself, and yet external confirmation of his existence can be gained only through language. Language is authentic not as "self-expression" per se, but only to the extent that it is understood. Or, to quote again Handwerk,

> The subject is a radical in a chemical sense—a compound not found unattached in nature. Insofar as it has any content, it is the sum of its interrupted encounters with all its significant others. . . . The integrity of the subject is

therefore not so much denied as displaced into the symbolic structure where its identity is realized. (127)

Subjectivity is not to be equated with the human individual; it is brought into being during the encounter. Its material form is the unfolding linguistic drama of that encounter.

Such a description of human interaction not only saves it from the Rousseauist-Romantic prejudice against social language as inherently debased, automatic, and uncreative, but also opens the way to understanding human linguistic interaction and artistic-receptive interaction as essentially kindred, not opposite, phenomena. In other words, the artist, like any human being, creates his *parole* from a fund of language that is in him and in his audience and that exceeds the conscious intentions of both. If "the fragmentation characteristic of the subject is its most effective tie to others" (135), it is also the most effective tie to an audience. The writer who has something to say to each new audience may be the one who explores his own irresolution aloud, who gives his reader not just an opportunity for emotional response, but the project of comprehending the whole of what he has said and left unsaid.

The common response, as we have seen, to the awareness of fragmentariness was melancholy nostalgia for a previous state of integration. Schlegel's solution was an exhilarating embrace of irony's double or mobile awareness, both of the limitations of one's own viewpoint at any given moment and the multiplicity of other, equally self-centered and logical viewpoints in simultaneous coexistence. The flash of wit and the lyrical fragment are analogous artifacts of this inexplicable altered state that is identified with ironic creativity. The lyric thus becomes not a genre of personal, empirical intimacy, but the genre that instantly captures those invasions of the narrow empirical self by its demonic other, or "true" self. Such intermittent lyrical intensity can only be apprehended by the empirical mind as "that which has been lost. . . . The Absolute remains accessible to self-consciousness only in its absence" (29). In other words, the stage is set for elegy. For although elegy may mourn a variety of concrete objects, its most essential concern is to dramatize the psychological process of creation, the empirical subject's alternation between mourning and lyrical release. "Poetry makes the Absolute, as dialectic of presence and absence, tangible in an indirect way, through representation" (34).

This, I will argue in Chapter 2, is the most fundamental answer to Kiukhel'beker's percipient question, "Why is Russian literature in 1824 so obsessed with elegiac repetition?"[71] Each poet had his own trademark elegiac experience, Batiushkov the mystical repetition of classical elegiac motives, Zhukovsky the otherworldly visitation, Pushkin the repetition of erotic loss or frustration. Each poet, in other words, used a specific allegory to dramatize the experience of lyrical inspiration, then began to seek the *repetition* of that form as a means of regaining access to that other or truer self. The result was a self-perpetuating cycle: repetition only sharpened the subject's elegiac awareness of the absence of the original, and from this lack was generated a language of mourning, for what was essentially the poet's linguistic predicament. In the words of Paul de Man,

> The meaning constituted by the allegorical sign can then consist only in the *repetition* . . . of a previous sign with which it can never coincide, since it is of the essence of this previous sign to be pure anteriority. . . . Allegory can only blindly repeat its earlier model, without final understanding. . . . Language thus conceived divides the subject into an empirical self, immersed in the world, and a self that becomes like a sign in its attempt at differentiation and self-definition, . . . [leading to the idea of] selfhood as not a substance but a figure.[72]

The elegiac poet experiences selfhood amid the random array of his experiences only when the configuration which he has come to regard as his leitmotiv is repeated. Non-repeating experience is dead, meaningless—a theme we will encounter in Pushkin time and again.

Although the pattern that I call Pushkin's elegiac repetition compulsion will be explored in much greater detail in Chapter 2, let me cite here an elegy so saturated with both the theme and the devices of repetition that it constitutes a veritable meta-elegy on its own procedures.

K***

Я помню чудное мгновенье;
Передо мной явилась ты,

Как мимолетное виденье,
Как гений чистой красоты.

В томленьях грусти безнадежной,
В тревогах шумной суеты,
Звучал мне долго голос нежный
И снились милые черты.

Шли годы. Бурь порыв мятежный
Рассеял прежние мечты,
И я забыл твой голос нежный,
Твои небесные черты.

В глуши, во мраке заточенья
Тянулись тихо дни мои
Без божества, без вдохновенья,
Без слез, без жизни, без любви.

Душе настало пробужденье;
И вот опять явилась ты,
Как мимолетное виденье,
Как гений чистой красоты.

И сердце бьется в упоенье,
И для него воскресли вновь
И божество, и вдохновенье,
И жизнь, и слезы, и любовь.

(2.1, 406)

To *. I remember a miraculous moment; before me you appeared, like a transient apparition, like the genius of pure beauty. In the anguish of hopeless sadness, in the troubles of tumultuous vanity, your gentle voice long sounded and your sweet features appeared in dreams. Years passed. A stormy gust dispersed the previous dreams, and I forgot your gentle voice, your heavenly features. In the sticks, in dark captivity my days quietly dragged on without a divinity, without inspiration, without tears, without life, without love. The soul was roused; and again you appeared, like a transient apparition, like the genius of pure beauty. And the heart beats in ecstasy, and resurrected for it again are divinity, and inspiration, and life, and tears, and love.

As an expression of passionate love, the poem may strike one as excessively formal, symmetrical, and calculated. The addressee's name does not matter; she is a function of the structure in which she finds herself, and her role is very strictly defined: to be a sign. Her first appearance attracted his attention precisely because it reminded him of something absent: "*Kak* mimoletnoe viden'e / *Kak* genii chistoi krasoty"—she reminded him, to be precise, of the mysterious ideal visitor in some well-known elegiac lines of Zhukovsky's.[73] In the first stanza she has already set off the impulse of recognition that "reads" a phenomenon as the "repetition of an anterior sign," hence as a meaningful message.

We notice two things about the following stanzas. Their rhyme schemes are repetitive in an interesting way. The first stanza, in which the addressee makes her original appearance, is *abab*. In the following three stanzas, which tell of the increasing attenuation of her image in the poet's imagination, the rhyme scheme appears to try unsuccessfully to approximate the original stanza: *cbcb*, *cbcb*, *ab'ab'*. *Ty* (you) is hidden in each stanza's second and fourth end rhymes (sue*ty*, cher*ty*, mech*ty*, cher*ty*) until the fourth stanza, the low point of the poem, when the addressee's image, together with that phoneme, disappear. The fifth stanza talks about the soul's resurrection, but what is noteworthy is the utter lack of novelty of the stanza's language: the very same rhyme scheme and indeed practically the same lines are repeated, underlining their emblematic character. We know as little about the addressee this time as we did the first; the actual quality of the experience is immaterial. It is the pure *repetition* that releases the poet from the spiritual torpor of meaningless temporality. And in stanza six this is reflected not only thematically, by the restoration of the poet's deprived emotional life, but also formally, by the poet's splashing out at last into a new rhyme scheme: *adad*!

I am of course being facetious. Instead of a liberation into rhapsodic new poetry, there is a pedantically exact removal of the curse. Exactly what had been lost—"Bez bozhestva, bez vdokhnoven'ia, / Bez slez, bez zhizni, bez liubvi"—is symmetrically, incantationally restored: "I bozhestvo, i vdokhnoven'e / I zhizn', i slezy, i liubov'." In much the same way that young children object if any word of a bedtime story is altered or misplaced, the magic ritual must be repeated exactly. As a passionate love poem it may leave something to be desired, but as an ironic representation of the procedures of the elegiac imagination it is brilliant. This is, as I hope to show in Chapter 2, what makes Pushkin's elegiac lyrics so interesting: they not only represent, with countless variations, the genesis of elegiac language from erotic loss, but also, as in this poem, suggest a half- or unconscious, ironic awareness of the imagination's own compulsive patterns.

One of those patterns is repetition, particularly repetition of loss; another is attraction to representations of the subject's own pain, another's power (or the subject as the text on which is inscribed another's power). Although traditionally elegiac poetry is treated as the province of the personal, from which the young poet gradually weans himself to genres and subjects of public or historical import, I agree with Lidia Ginzburg that the lyric is a window on the values, conception of subjectivity, and conduct of relationships in a culture.[74] Above all, the erotic elegy reveals the *conceptual language* that governs sexual and indeed all power relations in a given culture; it is dramatized as the individual's erotic imagination.[75]

Not surprisingly, in view of Pushkin's own disempowerment in his society, his erotic elegies are very much concerned with power and humiliation; indeed, they seem to revel in it. The experiencing of humiliation at the hands of a sexual goddess becomes *the* obsessive leitmotiv of his poetry. Pushkin uses this erotic fragment again and again, interpolating it into ever-new contexts. Repetition of this psychological figure allows him to appropriate his own life as meaning and eventually to find that same figure embedded in "realistic" relationships in society and history. We can trace it from elegy to elegy (for example, from "Kak nashe serdtse svoenravno" to "Proserpine") and across a generic divide into historical elegy ("Kleopatra") and dramatic scene ("The Stone Guest" and the "Kleopatra" society tales). Less obviously, in Chapter 4 we will find Pushkin's historical lovers Dmitri and Marina bartering erotic for symbolic-linguistic power in one scene of *Boris Godunov*.

If in erotic elegy the language of power spoken by lovers is a microcosm of their culture, in historical drama the "lovers' quarrel" of Dmitri and Marina is a simulacrum of all of the power relationships in the play. The glimpses of human interactions that Pushkin first offered as the idiosyncratic vocabulary of his psyche in his anthological and erotic lyrics are projected, in different but recognizable guise, into the courtly power plays, monastic maneuvers, and lovers' skirmishes for dominance that make up the fragmentary tapestry of

Boris Godunov's culture. To a great extent the question of domination in *Boris Godunov* can be reduced to the question of who determines what language should be used, who forces others to accept his names for things. Pushkin uses specific scenes from Shakespeare to help him imagine the underlying dynamics of his chronicle characters and to liberate them from the interpretation of Karamzin, Pushkin's "spiritual father." But in the process of his ostentatious move from the "personal" lyric to a historical "tragedy without love," I think that Pushkin selects scenes from Shakespeare that allow him to continue to explore through new allegorical representations the drama of his subjectivity, including his relationship to various father figures and his relationship to the audience his texts had brought into being.

This may seem like an absurd elision of the boundary between lyricism and drama or Realism that has always seemed so important in tracking Pushkin's development. From a Lacanian point of view, however, Realism may be the most covertly imaginary of all modes. The characteristic error of the imaginary is narcissistic self-omission, Handwerk explains, "for it takes place only through a projection of [self] into discourse that is so complete that [it] need not appear there as an agent."[76] Or, in de Man's words, "The fundamental structure of allegory reappears here in the tendency of the language toward narrative, the spreading out along the axis of an imaginary time in order to give duration to what is, in fact, simultaneous within the subject."[77]

What I will try to show in my mildly deconstructive reading of *Eugene Onegin* is that its "realistic" plot, which can be so readily interpreted as the story of the poet's own maturation and renunciation of the youthful elegiac poet caricatured as Lensky, can be read as a perfect allegorical representation of "the place and movements of the subject" (3). Although the ability to tell the story of Eugene, Tatiana, and Lensky is treated as a kind of vocational stepping-stone from a poetry of "absence" (ironized as Lensky) to a more mature and realistic future of family novels (identified with Tatiana), segments of *Eugene Onegin* push and pull in different directions, refusing to go along with the moral. The language often does the exact opposite of what the characters' lives are supposed to exemplify; or, as Handwerk puts it, "the rhetorical and the declarative are absolutely polarized" (99). The assumption that *Eugene Onegin* records the outgrowing of the empirical self's shortsighted self-involvement in favor of the ironic, integrative wisdom of Tatiana cannot stand as Pushkin's final position: before we know it, he has begun to ironize ironic wisdom in its turn. Indeed, as de Man has suggested, the elegist and the ironist turn out to share a structural core. In the end, Pushkin can be located only in the hovering, the shifting among the tropes that create different points of view. The classic work of "undecidable" modern irony, which the Athenaeum critics could only dream about, was *Eugene Onegin*.

As Pushkin moved away from *kruzhkovaia semantika* (and the *kruzhok* itself disappeared or lost power) toward a truly vertiginous irony, there were fewer readers willing to follow, as the indifferent reception of *Eugene Onegin*'s last chapters testifies.[78] It is not that Pushkin objected to not being comprehended; it is that readers were no longer aware that his writing challenged their comprehension. It was being dismissed as all too comprehensible. This helps explain the stiffening of Pushkin's belated "misunderstood Romantic" posture in his last years. In such works as "What is in my name for you?" ("Chto v imeni tebe moem," 1830) and the several "Kleopatra" tales, Pushkin re-presents the writer-reader interaction in full Romantic ironic regalia to an audience that he clearly suspects has forgotten how to read. It was these intricately obscured frame tales, these "allegories of their own unreadability," to borrow de Man's phrase, that spoke so volubly to the aesthetes of the twentieth century, who stood ready to step into the hermeneutic role of posterity and understand their philistinely misunderstood poet. At the end of his elegiac career, Pushkin left these instructions, a virtual synopsis of the epitaphic, fragmentary, and intersubjective theories of language we have been exploring, for his past lover and future reader:[79]

> Что в имени тебе моем?
> Оно умрет как шум печальный
> Волны плеснувшей в берег дальный,
> Как звук ночной в лесу глухом.
>
> Оно на памятном листке
> Оставит мертвый след, подобный

Узору надписи надгробной
На непонятном языке.

Что в нем? Забытое давно
В волненьях новых и мятежных
Твоей душе не даст оно
Воспоминаний чистых нежных.

Но в день печали, в тишине
Произнеси его, тоскуя,
Скажи, есть память обо мне,
Есть в мире сердце, где живу я.
(3.1, 210)

What's in my name for you? It will die like the sad roar of a wave splashing on a distant shore, like a nocturnal sound in a dense/deaf forest. On the leaf of memory it will leave a dead trace, reminiscent of the design on a tombstone in an unintelligible language. What's in it? The long forgotten, in new and tumultuous excitement will not give your soul pure and tender memories. But on a sad day, in quietness, pronounce it grieving; say: there is a memory of me; there is a heart in which I live.

I will try to show in this book that far from aiming at denotative *tochnost' i kratkost'* (exactitude and brevity),[80] the language of Pushkin's texts always stops short of meaning, reserving for his readers the pleasure of speaking endlessly in his name.

Chapter 2

From Epitaph to Elegy: Russia's Entry into European Culture

Styles of Empire

The most durable tripartite division of Pushkin's career, first enunciated by the philosophical critic Ivan Kireevsky, shows Pushkin passing through a youthful "classicism," followed by a brief bout of Romanticism, quickly "overcome" to yield a dramatic and objective "realism."[1] Thus Pushkin's trajectory was thought to recapitulate the epochs of European culture and to accelerate Russia's momentum. Although the parameters of Pushkin's career coincide with the Romantic period, Pushkin criticism in Russia has almost invariably given it very short shrift in his development.[2] In the following chapters I will seek to demonstrate points of contact between contemporary European trends and, to borrow Stephen Greenblatt's phrase, Pushkin's modes of "self-fashioning"[3] as a fledgling writer in a profession that was itself only a few decades old, in a country eager to prove its cultural as well as military credentials on the European scene.

It is perhaps an inevitable corollary of Pushkin's retrospective monumentalization that he would be pressed into the mold of what Goethe was to Germany: the nation's first "classic." In his 1941 article "Antiquity in the Oeuvre of Pushkin," D. P. Iakubovich inveighed against a pursuit of classical allusions in Pushkin's texts that made no effort to contextualize the practice itself.[4] Pushkin was being wrested from the idiosyncratic readings of the Silver Age poets and Formalist critics and handed back to academic philologists for safekeeping and learned embalming. Titles such as "Pushkin and Tacitus," "Pushkin and Horace," "Pushkin and Antiquity" implied an unmediated legacy between the first poets and historians of the Roman Empire and Pushkin.[5] Meanwhile, Iakubovich objected, there was no attempt to interpret the function of Pushkin's classical allusions within the sign system of nineteenth-century Russian culture, or their changing role in Pushkin's own oeuvre.

Since Peter I the Russian court had made ever-increasing use of classical iconography to demonstrate its European affiliation, visibly in its architectural ensembles, the sculpture parks of Peterhof, Tsarskoe selo, and Pavlovskoe, as well as at the individual estates of prominent noblemen like N. B. Iusupov.[6] Iakubovich asks us to consider the effect of the Tsarskoe selo surroundings, saturated with "images of the ancient world, concrete incarnations of bookish mythology in plastic art. Tsarskoe selo in its very artifice" fostered that "domestic intimacy" with classical images we see reflected in the in-jokes of the Lycée and in Batiushkov's domestic idylls.[7] The Lycée, Pushkin never tired of repeating, was his spiritual home, implicitly opposed both to family life and to the reality of Russian society that lay beyond its conventional spaces.[8] In "At the beginning of my life I remember" ("V nachale zhizni pomniu ia," 1830), Pushkin would identify the frisson of vocational recognition with the transfixed sculptures scattered around the park, marking almost demonically the boundary between (Russian) nature and (European) culture that art had to cross:

И часто я украдкой убегал
В великолепный мрак чужого сада,
Под свод искусственный порфирных скал.

Там нежила меня теней прохлада;
Я предавал мечтам свой юный ум,
И праздномыслить было мне отрада.

Любил я светлых вод и листьев шум,
И белые в тени дерев кумиры,
И в ликах их печать недвижных дум.

Все—мраморные циркули и лиры,
Мечи и свитки в мраморных руках,
На главах лавры, на плечах порфиры—

Все наводило сладкий некий страх
Мне на сердце; и слезы вдохновенья,
При виде их, рождались на глазах.

Другие два чудесные творенья
Влекли меня волшебною красой:
То были двух бесов изображенья.

Один (Дельфийский идол) лик младой—
Был гневен, полон гордости ужасной,
И весь дышал он силой неземной.

Другой женообразный, сладострастный,
Сомнительный и лживый идеал—
Волшебный демон—лживый, но прекрасный.

Пред ними сам себя я забывал;
В груди младое сердце билось—холод
Бежал по мне и кудри подымал.

Безвестных наслаждений темный голод
Меня терзал. Уныние и лень
Меня сковали—тщетно был я молод.

Средь отроков я молча целый день
Бродил угрюмый—все кумиры сада
На душу мне свою бросали тень.

(3.1, 254–55)

And often I secretly escaped into the grand gloom of an alien garden, beneath the artificial vault of porphyry cliffs. There the coolness of shadows caressed me; I turned my young mind over to dreams, and idle thought was my delight. I loved the rush of bright waters and leaves, and amid the trees' shade the white idols, and in their visages the imprint of motionless thoughts. Everything—the marble compasses and lyres, swords and scrolls in marble hands, on heads laurels, on shoulders the purple [of mantles]—everything cast a certain sweet terror over my heart; and tears of inspiration, at their sight, were born in my eyes. Two other miraculous creations drew me with their bewitching beauty: they were representations of two demons. One young visage (the Delphic idol) was wrathful, full of terrible pride, and breathed an altogether unearthly power. The other womanlike, passionate, a doubtful and deceitful ideal—bewitching demon—deceitful, but beautiful. Before them I myself forgot; in my breast the young heart beat—a chill ran over me and stood my hair on end. A dark hunger for unknown delights preyed on me. Dejection and indolence paralyzed me—in vain was I young. Among the youths the whole day I mutely wandered gloomy—and still the idols of the garden cast their shadow over my soul.

While fragments of classical architecture or statuary interpolated into a northern setting cast an aura of unreality on contemporaneity, introducing the possibility of evanescence into the lived moment, living people interpolated into the classical stage set of Tsarskoe selo began to conceive of themselves in its terms. Thus the sculptural icons absorb into themselves Pushkin's youthful energy, leaving him listless and paralyzed, alienated from his own life. They interpose a seductive set of ideal, alien images between the subject and his own experience.

This ubiquitous modeling system bore a strong connection with Russian imperial iconography and ambitions. Under Catherine II in particular, Russian poets had struggled to give birth to a poetic Golden Age concomitant with her pretensions. Pushkin derided his friends' efforts to construct a pantheon of Russian "classics" out of the valiant but outdated efforts of late-eighteenth-century writers such as M. V. Lomonosov, A. P. Sumarokov, and I. I. Dmitriev; even G. R. Derzhavin's "barbaric" muse was only "¼ gold, ¾ lead," he reminded the enthusiastic A. A. Del'vig and A. A. Bestuzhev.[9] In 1824, at the height of the classics versus Romantics controversy, he voiced his skepticism to Viazemsky: "Does the old classical whore you attack fully exist in Russia [*u nas*]? That's still the question."[10]

Under Alexander I the Augustan analogy was explicitly encouraged. The ideal of a classically cultivated cultural elite was enunciated in the Lycée's founding charter, and a full-time teacher of both Greek and Latin hired to implement it. N. F. Koshansky's course, based on his own textbook, consisted primarily of the inculcation of stirring heroic exempla from Roman history and a thorough acquaintance with classical mythology and the Roman elegiac poets—essentially the same course used throughout nineteenth-century Europe as the obligatory finish to a gentleman's education. Indeed, an indifferent scholar of Latin like Pushkin resorted to Russian and particularly French translations of the Latin poets; numerous studies have demonstrated the mediation of J. B. Gresset, Evariste Parny, André Chénier,

Derzhavin, and Batiushkov.[11] The saturation of Pushkin's Lycée lyrics with classical nomenclature and epigrammatic allusions to ancient poets, often demonstrably lifted from Koshansky's handbook, merely testify, Iakubovich concludes, that Pushkin, like Eugene Onegin with his epistolary Latin, was

> a man of his epoch, nothing more. Apart from the role of French classicism, which served as a surrogate for authentic antiquity and popularized in its stead its external apparel, one must take into consideration that the images, mythological situations and personages, Latin epigraphs and expressions were in Pushkin's time the natural external ornament of a schoolboy and courtly salon education, in no way testifying to a profound penetration into the philosophical or mythological depths of the texts of ancient authors.[12]

Indeed, the semiotic significance of classicizing gestures seems to have been much more apparent to Pushkin's contemporaries than it has been to learned scholarship. For example, in his maiden speech before the conservative Society of Amateurs of the Russian Language (Beseda liubitelei russkogo iazyka) in 1816, Batiushkov stressed the paradoxical connection between "light poetry" and nation building. In a consummate rhetorical performance designed to mollify the specifically archaist-Slavicizing preferences of his audience, Batiushkov took pains to dress his argument for literary enrichment in patriotic exhortation [to promote] "the future wealth of the language, so closely linked to civic education, with enlightenment, and consequently—with the welfare of the most glorious and expansive nation on earth." Batiushkov never defends the content of intimate poetry. Instead, he argues that every Golden Age of human culture has produced not only great forms, but a symbiotic correlative of light poetry; indeed, that the proliferation of intimate poetry can be regarded as a product and sign of political power and cultural dominance: "Complete the splendid, great, sacred work: enrich and refine the language of this most glorious people, who inhabit one half of the world; let the glory of its language equal its military glory, the successes of its mind with the successes of its arms." Playing expertly on the recent upsurge of patriotic feeling, the Napoleonic campaigner locates the whole endeavor not in St. Petersburg, after 1812 the foreign capital, but in Moscow—like Rome, "so eloquent in its ruins, near fields identified with unprecedented victories, in the ancient fatherland of glory and the new greatness of our people!"[13]

But the codes of classicism could easily be kidnapped for other uses. By the 1820's the mythology of the Roman Republic had been thoroughly assimilated into French revolutionary-republican, then Byronic-libertarian rhetoric. If, as G. A. Gukovsky notes, "antiquity, initially adopted by Pushkin as a system of mythological symbolism, as a certain class code of the western aristocracy, later became a feature of the civic lyric poetry" of Pushkin and the Decembrists,[14] they were following the well-established subversive track of Byron, Shelley, and other political radicals.

We find ample testimony to the classical code's appropriation in the "Aesopian language" of Pushkin's correspondence. The very writers who were supposed to furnish Alexander's Augustan Golden Age played havoc with the metaphor's automatic imperial associations:

Я карабкаюсь, и может быть, явлюсь у вас. Но не прежде будущего года [...] Жуковскому я писал, он мне не отвечает, министру я писал —он и в ус не дует/ О други, Августу мольбы мои несите! Но Август смотрит сентябрем... Кстати: получено ли мое послание к Овидию?

I am floundering about, and perhaps shall manage to visit you. But no earlier than next year [...] I have written Zhukovsky, but he does not answer me; I have written to the minister—he doesn't give a rap—'O friends, take my entreaties to August(us). But August looks like September... By the way, has my epistle "To Ovid" been received?[15]

The central punning metaphor is borrowed from N. M. Iazykov's "Pesnia," "We like noisy feasts" ("My liubim shumnye piry," 1823):

Наш Август смотрит сентябрем—
Нам до него какое дело!
Мы пьем, пируем и поем
Беспечно, радостно, и смело.
Наш Август смотрит сентябрем—
Нам до него какое дело![16]

Our August looks like September—what do we care about him! We drink, feast, and sing carelessly, joyously, and daringly. Our August looks like September—what do we care about him!

Pushkin augments the pun with phonological echoes that humorously link incongruous segments: "v us ne duet" and the pathetic apostrophe "O drugi, Avgustu." These refer in turn to Pushkin's epistle "To Ovid," in which the standard Augustus-Alexander parallel had yielded the corresponding self-glorifying analogy Ovid-Pushkin, as poets of love and victims of unjust exile. This then culminated in Pushkin's provocative assertion of greater independence vis-à-vis *his* emperor, in lines that were removed before publication but of course circulated by word of mouth. Thus Pushkin's letter alludes to a whole underground network of texts that held up a mocking mirror to Alexander's allegorical pretensions and put them to their own uses.

There were many ways in which the imperial code of neoclassicism could be appropriated for politically subversive or at least irreverent ends: an emphasis on the historical exempla of Republican Rome or democratic Greece; a focus on the dissidents or persecuted writers of imperial Rome, Ovid and later Petronius; and the correlation between political liberty and hedonistic pleasure—classical or Oriental leisure, indolence, poetry, and the private erotic adventures of the famous classical lovers Tibullus, Catullus, and Propertius. In this context, classical impersonations like Pushkin's "godson of Tibullus" and Eugene Onegin's Ovidian *Art of Love* can be read as signs of a subtly subversive, libertarian dandyism.

The most subtle subversion of the imperial code of neoclassicism was offered by the alternative and more "authentic" antiquity of Greece. Greece offered a new model for Russian self-presentation. If to be an educated Russian once meant to be a "European," a self-made, self-conscious foreigner in one's own country, to be "Greek" in spirit a Russian now needed to reject the theater of neoclassicism and return to his own authentic cultural origins. As early as 1790 N. L'vov had suggested a direct link between Greek culture and Slavic folklore.[17] Curiously, then, Batiushkov's Grecophilia and A. S. Shishkov's Slavonicism can be seen as two aspects of the same trend. Shishkov's efforts to trace the origins of the Russian language to Slavonic, and via Slavonic back to Greek, turned out to be a "sham ruin," but they were motivated by the same impulse to locate the present in relation to (sacred) origins, to reinvent a national genealogy that was both authentic (autochthonous, nonimitative, and antiforeign) and "essentially Greek." Even Pushkin cited Lomonosov's "discovery" of the Greek heritage of Russian linguistic structures as proof of the poetic superiority of the Russian language.[18] Ever since the mid-eighteenth century the excessively analytical, linear syntax of modern European languages, especially French, had been denigrated in comparison with the synthetic forms, capable of saying "everything simultaneously," of ancient Greek. Thus Russia was imaginatively remodeled into a country still miraculously in touch with the archaic sources of poetry, still uncontaminated by derivative and eclectic modernity.

S. S. Uvarov's "Preface" to the project undertaken by him and Batiushkov jointly, their publication of twenty exemplary translations from the Greek Anthology into French and Russian verse respectively, provides a revealing simulacrum of Russian Grecophilia at the time. Uvarov emphasizes the relatively recent rise of European interest in the Anthology—even in Germany, "the cradle of philology," no one before Herder had singled it out. French scholarship had in the main proved unequal to the philological deciphering of the Anthology's various dialects, while its poets lacked a rhythmic prosody to do it justice. German poets had provided accurate but graceless translations. Uvarov and Batiushkov's joint project is, in both scholarly and poetic terms, on a par for once with the best contemporary achievements in Europe. At the end of the essay, Uvarov demonstrates his own detailed acquaintance with the textual history of the Anthology and inserts each fragment into a philological commentary.

Uvarov's commentary gives a clear indication of the differences between the poetics of the Greek Anthology and the familiar poetics of neoclassicism. He begins by drawing a remarkably clear distinction between the modern and the ancient Greek epigram:

> By epigram we mean short verses with a satirical content, terminating on a witticism, a reproach, or a joke. The ancients gave this word a different meaning. For them any small piece written in elegiac meter (that is, a hexameter followed by a pentameter) was called an epigram. Anything can serve as its subject: now it instructs, now it jests, and almost always it exudes love. Often it is nothing but an instantaneous thought or a fleeting feeling, inspired by the beauties of nature or the monuments of art. Sometimes the

Greek epigram is complete and perfect, sometimes careless and unfinished . . . like a sound fading in the distance. It almost never concludes with a sharp, striking idea, and the more ancient it is, the simpler. This genre of poetry embellished both feasts and graves. Reminding them of the insignificance of life passing by, the epigram said, "Mortal, catch the fleeting moment!" . . . A true Proteus, it adopts all forms.[19]

Upon the initial opposition of "moderns" and "ancients" is quickly superimposed the opposition of north and south. A northerner attains by the effort of intellect what for the southerner is a spontaneous, undivided response to nature. A southerner turns his attention outward, is satisfied by external impressions, while the northerner is forced by an inhospitable nature to turn his attention inward. For the ancients, therefore, life was all; for us moderns, it is only a transitional stage. The anthological fragment perfectly symbolizes the antique attitude to life: fully engaged, sensuous, short.

And masculine. Uvarov finds in the anthological fragment, as Winckelmann had in the sculptural fragment, a respite from the coyness of a neoclassical literature imprinted, as he thought, with the feminine values of the salon.

Let us note one peculiarity: the Greeks did not write for women, but were more modest in their thoughts and expressions than most modern writers, whose creations are read by both sexes. I do not wish to deny that some of the epigrams of the Anthology and most of Aristophanes' comedies are distinguished by their unbridled freedom; but nakedness in the Anthology, and especially in Aristophanes, resembles the nakedness of Greek statues: it does not arouse the senses. The habit of calling all things, all objects by their real and natural names subdues the imagination. This crudity can even be united with a certain simple-heartedness, completely opposite to our art of expressing everything in half-words and perverting the heart without offending the ear and taste. . . . One can only wonder that the shameful vice to which [the Greeks] gave their name not only did not inspire in them crude words, but even inspired the most tender and beautiful expressions. In short, the sensuous poetry of the Greeks resembles ours, as much as the passionate pleasures of an athlete resemble the whims of an exhausted sybarite.[20]

As in Winckelmann, the characteristic underlying contrast of antique wholeness versus modern insufficiency or superfluity manifests itself. Language is used in modern society not to display vividly but to conceal. Uvarov is less inclined to philosophize about the intrinsic differences in sensibility between the ancients and the moderns and more inclined to purge the audience of its unworthy feminine members and tastes. The need for speaking in "half-words" and periphrasis for the benefit of a feminine or effeminate public is harmful because it deflects the writer from the "naked truth," from a direct, masculine relationship with life, indeed from a direct, passionate relationship with other men.[21] The tastes of feminine or salon-bound readers should not determine how life will be represented in modern times. "Fragments" of poetry bear the most authentic witness to a great people's history and way of life. The Greek Anthology, with its "protean" heterogeneity of subjects and attitudes to life, should be taken as a model for the "protean" creativity and masculine freedom that ought to distinguish the modern poet. It is by his artifacts that modern civilization will be judged.

Uvarov does not propose the Anthology merely as a model for modern literary language. His proposal, like Winckelmann's, is more radical:

> Through the Anthology we become contemporaries of the Greeks, we share their passions, we even discover traces of those rapid, instantaneous impressions, which, like the traces left in the sand at the ruins of Herculaneum, make us forget that two thousand years separate us from the ancients. Through the Anthology we participate in their celebrations, their games, we follow the citizens onto the square, into the theater, inside their homes: in a word, we breathe and live with them.[22]

Why should Russians share the Greeks' passions, live and breathe with them, displace their modern Russian desires to a geographically and historically distant, inaccessible realm? Herder had articulated this notion in 1793: "If we do not become Greeks, we will remain barbarians."[23] Barbarians in whose eyes?

I would like to suggest that the way Greek culture was being used by a modern culture in the self-conscious throes of being born into history was as a "*stade du miroir*—the vision of harmony by a being in discord" posited by Lacan as the key juncture in human psychological development and socialization.[24] To propose the Greeks as a model for "living, breathing, playing, experiencing passions," all presumably natural functions that do not need to be learned, is to construct a coherent image of the subject as other, rather analogous to "the child's fascination with the images of other human beings as harmonious totalities at a time when he himself is still unable to control his own functions or movements." Symptomatic of this stage is a fascination with "stature, status, and statues," which we have seen play a large role in the cult of Greece as well. By contrast, the incoherent subject tends to conceive of itself as a *corps morcelé*, " 'the body in bits and pieces,' or . . . put together like a mismatched jigsaw puzzle. . . . The paranoid twist of the *moi* in the Imaginary is directly related to the peculiar twists we give to our own body image."[25] Winckelmann's readings of antique-whole versus modern-fragmentary or distorted bodies was an influential enactment of this basic paradigm. It is only by "introjecting" the Greek ideal and alienating their own subjectivity that modern Europeans, Germans, Russians could be "born into language," culture, recognition.

The Greek Anthology thus offered a curious antidote to the neoclassical doctrine of the imitation of the ancients. For the neoclassical fixation on reproducing the canonical genres of ancient or Roman literature—epic, tragedy, comedy, satire, odes, elegies—the Greek Anthology substituted a culturally prestigious, yet flexible form capable of assimilating a poet's immediate, contradictory, contemporary responses to life. A collection of ancient epitaphs became the liberating form for the modern lyric, precisely because it corresponded to Romantic values.

The epigram's emphasis on what the eye can seize instantaneously and truly puts a premium on vision as a creative act. In the foreground of many classical anthological poems thus appears the voyeur, a framing figure who points to the act of seeing recorded in the poem. The voyeur is hidden, uninvolved in the action, as though the better to see, to disclose the essence of another. The voyeur poses the possibility of another relationship to the object of desire described besides the direct relationship of address, praise, seduction, castigation. It is a relationship of aesthetically mediated desire, the relationship of the artist. It presents the object to the reader in a new light, as though refreshed by the obliquity of the voyeur's gaze. This freshness and instantaneousness of perception is meant to characterize the poet's unique relation with the world.

For this reason, then, it was logical that the anthological fragment would be assimilated into Romantic values—in particular, as M. H. Abrams points out, "the extraordinary emphasis throughout this era on the eye and the object and the relation between them."[26] Or as Abrams quotes Coleridge, "To combine the child's sense of wonder and novelty with the appearances, which every day for perhaps forty years had rendered familiar . . . this is the character and privilege of genius."[27] The identity of poetry and a new way of seeing are central to both Romantic theory and practice: "Since to see the world anew is equivalent to making a new world, the Latin *vates* and the Greek *poeta* (maker) fall together. . . . As Ruskin . . . put it: 'The greatest thing a human soul ever does in this world is to *see* something, and tell what it *saw* in a plain way. . . . To see clearly is poetry, prophecy, and religion—all in one' " (375–76). A contrast is often set up between the ordinary physical sight the poet shares with other men when he is uninspired—"the slavery of the mind to merely material objects—and the liberated, creative, and resurrective mode of sight 'thro', and not with the eye' " (377). At such moments, Abrams summarizes, "the eye, altering, was said to yield, at least momentarily, a re-created world. . . . As a child sees now, so did all mankind see in the childhood of the human race" (379–80).

The Greek Anthology thus had a double value. As Batiushkov and Uvarov had said, the Greeks taught modern people to see; "we learn to play, to breathe with them," to rediscover the freshness of perception of people living at the beginning of civilized time, not in its decadence. At the same time, as Schiller argued in his famous essay on "The Naive and the Sentimental," modern men's *recovery* of the natural was qualitatively different from the Greeks' uncomplicated relationship:

> Nature in us has disappeared from humanity and we rediscover her in her truth only outside it, in the inanimate world. . . . It was quite otherwise with the ancient Greeks. With them civilisation did not manifest itself to such an extent that nature was abandoned in consequence. The whole structure of their social life was founded on perceptions, not on a contrivance of art. . . . At one with himself and happy in the sense of his humanity [the Greek] was obliged to remain with it as his maximum and assimilate all else to it; whereas *we*, not at one with ourselves and unhappy in our experience of mankind, possess no more urgent interest than to escape from it and cast from our view so unsuccessful a form.

> The feeling of which we here speak is therefore not that which the ancients possessed; it is rather identical with that which *we have for the ancients*. They felt naturally; we feel the natural. . . . Our feeling for nature is like the feeling of an invalid for health.
>
> Just as nature began gradually to disappear from human life as *experience* and as the (active and perceiving) *subject*, so we see her arise in the world of poetry as *idea* and *object*.[28]

When a modern poet manages to produce a moment of intense, unmediated vision reminiscent of that of the Greeks, it is a transcendental act of recovery, not just a natural act of observation. He is recovering for mankind what it has lost. The highly visual poetry produced "in the spirit of the ancients" during the Romantic period is thus surrounded by a miraculous aureole, implying a paradisial unity of spirit and matter once lost and now at least momentarily redeemed. The anthological fragment provided the ideal form for those instants of heightened consciousness when the temporal moment seemed to stand still, when an object visually perceived became charged with revelation—what Wordsworth called "spots of time" (77). First, its brief, often accidentally ruptured form calls attention both to the brevity of "this experience of eternity in a moment, which, Augustine suggests, anticipates the translation of all time into eternity at the apocalypse" (381) and to its fragility, haunted by the inevitability of relapse into the temporal continuum. Second, the more ordinary the object, the more its "transvaluation" testifies to the power of the poet's vision. As Abrams points out, for Wordsworth the Bible was the ultimate model for such an inversion of the relative values of physical object and spiritual vision:

> By exploiting the implications for secular literature of what, to readers trained in Neoclassic decorum, seemed the drastic impropriety of the literature of the Bible, [Wordsworth] accomplished an egalitarian revolution in poetry, deleting the traditional hierarchy and decorums of literary kinds, subjects, protagonists, and styles, with their built-in class structure and inherent scale of aristocratic values. (398)

The Greek Anthology, read through nineteenth-century eyes, could contain many of the same implications. It also introduced the possibility of mixture, for in it are juxtaposed a variety of lyrical subjects—erotic pleasure, seduction, complaints of romantic failure, enjoyment of nature, satirical observation of mores, elegiac mourning of loss and death, the specific and the abstract, the crude and the elevated, the "life of the body" and the "life of the mind"—in democratic adjacency. Any moment, vividly apprehended, was a fit subject for the lyrical epigram. Moreover, if the epigram can often be a wail or exclamation of intense emotion, that emotion is anonymous, not personalized; uprooted from biography, context, social hierarchy, historical epoch, it emerges as an emblematic human experience.

It is the epigram's fragmentary status, the fact that it is a vestige of an invisible context to which it continues to refer, that intensifies its lyrical suggestiveness and immediacy. Abrams summarizes:

> The Romantic Moment in which, as Frank Kermode puts it, *chronos* suddenly becomes *kairos*, has had an enduring and multiform literary life. The illuminated phenomenal object, if transparent to a significance beyond itself, reappears as the symbol of the Symbolists, but if opaque, as the image of the Imagists; in both cases, however, the Romantic object is usually cut off from its context in the ordinary world and in common experience and assigned an isolated existence in the self-limited and self-sufficing work of art. (418)[29]

The genre offers a way of discovering, to borrow the Schlegels' formulation, "the possibility of the classical" in the present. The modern young poet, by borrowing the form of the anthological fragment, also invests his own lyrical experiences with its historical irony and distance.

The Romance of the Classical: Pushkin's Anthological Fragments

Batiushkov's career embodies the transition from the neoclassical discourse of imitation and translation, which prescribes that the poet construct a "self" or a persona out of repetitive tropes inherited from the elegiac tradition, to the more individualistic poetic voices extrapolated from Greek epitaphic poetry.[30] Batiushkov fulfills Schiller's characterization of a modern "sentimental" poet with remarkable fidelity. It is precisely in his oeuvre that we find the classical fragment renewed as the exemplary form for the modern lyric, framed on the one hand by an acute sense of historical modernity and cultural loss, the crumbling of the old world, and on the other by the encroaching threat of insanity and silence. The epitaphic shards of the Greek Anthology provided the perfect vehicle or collective persona for Batiushkov's last utterances, while suggesting a startlingly fresh point of departure for Russian poetic language. Perhaps nowhere so much as in Batiushkov's last lyrics does the silence preceding and succeeding the text play such a constitutive role: the disembodied lyrical voice emerges from and returns to a silence that can variously be interpreted as the past, death, eternity, or the pre- or nonverbal depths of the mind. Each poem "cuts a figure," creates an acoustic arabesque, in the surrounding silence.

For Pushkin, the situation was different. If Batiushkov was sinking into silence, Pushkin was just breaking into print. If classical allusion and self-parodying periphrasis were the obligatory code for Russian poets at this time, how could a young poet participate and yet distinguish himself from the crowd? Pushkin's early lyrics have to be read in the context of what Savely Senderovich has called the "symposium spirit" of Russian poetry. Poets wrote poems for other poets, that is, for their friends and colleagues; every "friendly epistle" in verse was a fragment of that ongoing polylogue with other poets, projecting each poem against a cumulative, allusive semiotic code.[31] Above all, the symposium practice established "dialogicity" as the hidden spring of lyric poetry. Not only the sociable genres such as poetic epistle and "occasional" verse, but even the most intimate genres such as elegy and anthological epigram manifested their common origins in the "symposium"—by their allusiveness to a common fund of events, utterances, and written texts shared by the circle of writer/readers, their adherence to a shared (if often self-parodying) classical code, and their associative logic. Kiukhel'beker quite astutely excoriated both the comical epistle and the gloomy elegy for perpetuating "a little jargon of the coterie."[32] The members of the Athenaeum, on the other hand, might have recognized their own aesthetic principles in practice, producing a fecund modern poetry they could only theorize about.

The anthological fragment presented the young Pushkin with an opportunity for escape from the metaliterary allusiveness and coy wordiness of the symposium mode into an "authentic," unmediated recording of sensory experience—a literary genre liberated, as it were, from literature. Although Pushkin never made a statement comparable to Batiushkov's "On Light Poetry" or Uvarov's preface that clearly recommended the Greek Anthology as a model for stylistic purification, his increasingly negative attitude toward ornamental style in both prose and poetry was formulated in similar terms: "The charm of naked simplicity is still incomprehensible to us. . . . Poetry, free from conventional ornamentation of poetic composition, we still do not understand."[33] And in a letter to Viazemsky in December 1823 he wrote, "I do not like to see in our primitive language traces of European mannerism and French refinement. Coarseness and simplicity suit it better."[34] V. B. Sandomirskaia and Roberta Reeder have made convincing cases for tracing the genesis of these "archaistic" literary principles back to Pushkin's early, mediated acquaintance with the Greek Anthology. It is in Pushkin's anthological lyrics that we first find the economy of means, physical rendition of emotion, and precise selection and positioning of words within a constricted space that are the hallmarks of his mature style.[35] My analyses will certainly corroborate their conclusions, while enlarging the cultural context within which Pushkin made his choices.

As we have seen in Chapter 1, the nineteenth century revaluation of Greek antiquity was often synonymous with a relative upgrading of "original," "barbarian" virtues, such as simplicity, crude strength, and directness of expression, over the decadent polish of the dominant civilization. The Greek enthusiast often claimed for himself sources of inspiration different from those of the reigning elite—nature, primitive directness of experience, "untaught" expression, Dionysian fervor. I would like to suggest that Pushkin's removal from the literary center of St. Petersburg to the climate and archaic cultures of the south demanded a concomitant displacement of his language. What more appropriate form could be found for a poet in exile than "classical fragments"? This was the ideal marriage of ready-made form and lyrical occasion. Pushkin, however, went beyond simplicity and precision to explore the psychological possibilities of the anthological epigram's fragmentary form—a discovery that would become as essential to his poetic system as "tochnost' i kratkost'."

Unlike Batiushkov's, Pushkin's anthological pieces were neither primarily translations nor written as a deliberate cycle, and they were published in scattered fashion in different journals and with considerable delay.[36] If we read these pieces as somehow related it is because Pushkin, carefully preparing his first collection of poems for publication in Mikhailovskoe in 1826, gathered all those anthological poems written during his southern exile under a common rubric, "Imitations of the Ancients." Indeed, Pushkin's original heading, "Essays in Imitation of the Ancients" ("Opyty v podrazhaniakh drevnim") more clearly underscored his debt to Batiushkov and his collected poems, *Essays in Prose and in Verse* (*Opyty v proze i v stikhakh*).[37]

Examining their appearance as rough drafts in Pushkin's notebooks, however, Sandomirskaia has noted that many of the poems that appeared under the classical rubric in the 1826 collection were originally subtitled "Fragment." Although "fragment" is nowhere listed as a classical genre, there was certainly one neoclassical source where an up-to-date reader would have found "fragments" in profusion: in the posthumous edition of André Chénier.[38] There Pushkin would have found precisely that classical organization by genre (odes, idylls, epigrams, eclogues, imitations of specific Latin and Greek poets)—as opposed to the more modern chronological organization focusing on the individual poet's development—yet with the novel inclusion of "fragments."[39] Among the fragments included by editor Henri de Latouche were works in progress at the time of the poet's death, studded with suspension dots where words were missing, collages of incomplete stanzas and isolated poetic exercises, exquisite but broken off. It is in Chénier's volume that we find conflated the two principle implications of the rubric "fragment": on the one hand a short, vivid epitaph in the manner of the Greek Anthology, and on the other a rough draft, a verbal experiment, an isolated bit of the poet's ongoing creative process. In fact, Chénier's completed odes, elegies, and idylls are often sonorous but long-winded, and it is precisely the pieces broken off or not yet finished—momentary jottings in the heat of inspiration, still unintegrated into a composition—that seize our attention.

One of Chénier's many interrupted projects that must have attracted Pushkin was a collection of short pieces on erotic mythological subjects, "The Art of Love." Modeled on Ovid's in both title and manner, the manuscript is a collage of lyrics in different stages of completion—epigrammatic vignettes consisting of a few lines, occasionally beginning or ending abruptly on an unrhymed line, as well as longer pieces with internal lines or passages missing. The shape of the entire narrative is far from clear, but individual fragments stand out vividly:

Ou ton projet sera la toile fugitive
De cette Pénélope assiégée et captive
Qui, d'Ulysse en secret implorant le retour,
Va défaire la nuit son ouvrage du jour.

Souvent de tous les Dieux une Vénus chérie,
Par les décrets jaloux d'un bizarre destin,
A reçu dans son lit quelque absurde Vulcain.

L'obstâcle encourage l'amour.
J'épargne le chevreuil que nul bois, nul détour
Ne dérobe à mes traits dans la vaste campagne;
Je veux le suivre au haut de la sombre montagne,
Et, trempé de sueurs, affronter en courant
La ronce hérissée et l'orageux torrent.[40]

Or your project will be the fugitive cloth of this Penelope assaulted and captive who, imploring in secret the return of Ulysses, will undo during the night the day's handiwork.

Often a Venus cherished by all the gods has, by the jealous decrees of a bizarre destiny, received into her bed some absurd Vulcan.

The obstacle inspires love. I spare the roe which no wood, no curve steals from my shot in the vast countryside; I want to follow him to the height of the dark mountain, and, soaked in sweat, brave at a run the bristling bramble and the stormy torrent.

It is my hypothesis that many of Pushkin's short classical lyrics shared a similar dual status: they were poetic exercises in the new mode of the anthological fragment, a trying out of its expressive and technical possibilities, and at the same time excerpts from Pushkin's "southern" notebook, "fragments" of his creative life that he sent back to St. Petersburg, much in the manner of the exiled Byron. The subtitle *otryvok* (fragment) immediately conjured up the pathos of Romantic exile, as though the fragment had somehow survived distance and censorship to reach the reader in damaged form. Pushkin's oeuvre of the early 1820's is littered with fragments, real and simulated; complete works were often first previewed as fragments to arouse interest.[41] To supply a poem with the subtitle "A Fragment" clearly framed it for the reader in a particular way, encouraging him to bear in mind the creative process the fragment had been detached from: the poet's original conception, the reasons for its interruption, how the parts visible and invisible interacted, the poem's absent "origin."

Pushkin's anthological fragments played an even more complex role: even while they invoked the fashionable Romantic framework of exile and fragmentation, poems such as "Earth and Sea" ("Zemlia i more") and "The Nereid" ("Nereida") enviably projected Pushkin's new "incarceration" in the south onto a carefree classical idyll. Whatever anthological verses made their way back to St. Petersburg must have had a provocative ring: exiled from the center of Russian imperial culture to the empire's periphery, Pushkin found himself (tauntingly) in the land of true classicism. Every anthological fragment drove this point home. For what is finally remarkable about Pushkin's classical poems is the degree to which they project a vibrant, youthful self: if Batiushkov's anthological fragments are a poetry about endings and fragility, Pushkin's exude a sense of new beginnings; if Batiushkov's self tends to get lost in translation, in the traditional personae he evokes, Pushkin's defines itself precisely at the moment of disjuncture with tradition. And needless to say, the frank sensuality of the classical fragment became one of the enduring attributes of Pushkin's poetic persona.[42]

Whereas Pushkin's 1826 collection has often been viewed as proof of his essentially classical, still genre-oriented and learned approach to poetry,[43] I see it as one of Pushkin's many acts of retrospective literary self-fashioning. None too subtly in view of the recent Decembrist debacle, he attached as the book's epigraph one of those breathtakingly enjambed lines from the famous "Last Iambs" of Chénier, broken off literally at the moment he was conducted to the scaffold: "Ainsi, triste et captif, ma lyre toutefois / S'éveillait..."[44] (Thus, sad and captive, my lyre still awakened...). In other words, Pushkin is his own Henri de Latouche, molding an image of literary beginnings against historical odds. The deliberately old-fashioned format of the book creates a kind of historical perspective on the poetry of Pushkin's youth, a period he presents as closed, historically stylized. What emerges is a portrait of the artist as a young man, a portrait that retains both the marks of a "classical apprenticeship," complete with "imitations of the ancients," and of a sojourn in exile explicitly identified with André Chénier's political imprisonment. Some of those anthological fragments from 1819–20 now promoted Pushkin's historical self-characterization: unfinished rough drafts overlapping with academic exercises in "imitation" afforded vivid glimpses of the creative processes of a still youthful poet.

Many of Pushkin's poems of this period project the landscapes he was encountering for the first time in the south onto the pictorial conventions of classical poetry. "The Nereid" (1820), with its flamboyant opening rhyme "Tavridu/Nereidu," exploits the southern/classical palimpsest most effectively. The genre of the poem is highly conventional: a young girl (or boy) depicted as living sculpture.[45] Wittily, Pushkin's poem renders both the explicit and the implicit meanings of anthological "nakedness" as it had been defined by Batiushkov: unadorned economy and directness of language and a natural attitude toward the naked body. Sight is characteristically emphasized by stationing the poet/narrator explicitly in the position of a voyeur. Yet the poem's visual and verbal precision serve ultimately to remove "sight" from the temporal dimension and into the transcendental realm of "vision."

Среди зеленых волн, лобзающих Тавриду,
На утренней заре я видел Нереиду.
Сокрытый меж дерев, едва я смел дохнуть:
Над ясной влагою—полубогиня грудь
Младую, белую как лебедь, воздымала
И пену из власов струею выжимала.

(2.1, 156)

Amid the green waves that kiss Tavrida, at dawn I saw a Nereid. Concealed among the trees, I scarcely dared to breathe: above the clear moisture, the demigoddess puffed out her breast, young and white like a swan, and wrung foam from her hair in a stream.

"The Nereid" shows how well Pushkin understood the innovative possibilities of the classical fragment as genre. There is an implicit analogy between the accidentally glimpsed moment and the accidentally found or preserved text the anthological fragment pretends to be. It offers a means for "classicizing" the personal moment and begins to legitimate a private sphere of experience as the shared domain of author and reader. Yet its "simplicity" is illusory. The very exposure of the six lines of "The Nereid," the fact that there is nowhere to go but back to the beginning, puts a heavy premium, as Batiushkov had predicted in his article on light poetry, on formal perfection and maximal compression—every word is wedged into place, irreplaceable in the tight semantic, phonetic, and syntactic structure. Although the anthological fragment appears to focus on commonly experienced moments of human life, particularly physical and readily visualizable ones, its ultimate effect is metapoetic: to sharpen the reader's awareness of virtuosity, of difficulty overcome, of the contrast, so fundamental to the genre, between the fragile perfection and transience of the temporal moment and the permanence of the perfectly crafted artifact or image that has survived.

Perhaps most interesting is Pushkin's inventive exploitation of the very boundary of the *otryvok*, his many ways of framing and motivating ellipsis or broken-off speech. "To Dorida" is a particularly striking instance of a lyrical utterance by an "interested" narrator. It begins abruptly, with three exceedingly short predicate clauses, all fitted into the space of the first line: "Ia veriu: ia liubim: dlia serdtsa nuzhno verit'" (I believe: I am loved; for the heart one needs to believe). One pictures the line as a response to a preceding statement that has been cut off by the border of the poem. Moreover, the sequence of exaggeratedly short syntagms has the effect of reversing what the speaker thinks he is saying; we understand that this statement of belief in her love is an effort of will, undertaken for the sake of his peace of mind. But by the second line, the apparent address has revealed itself to be an argument with himself:

> Нет, милая моя не может лицемерить;
> Все непритворно в ней: желаний томный жар,
> Стыдливость робкая, Харит бесценный дар,
> Нарядов и речей приятная небрежность
> И ласковых имен младенческая нежность.
>
> (2.1, 137)

No, my love cannot dissemble; everything about her is spontaneous: the languid heat of her desires, the timid modesty, the priceless gift of the Charites, the pleasing carelessness of her dress and speech, and the babyish tenderness of her caressing nicknames.

With "net" the speaker contradicts a thought that has already formed in his mind (again, beyond the bounds of the poem). As the speaker enumerates the attributes that are supposed to contravene the unspoken suspicion of Dorida's faithlessness—spontaneity, flightiness, childlike and careless demeanor—the measured length of his syntagms, which apart from the first line fit neatly into the two distichs of the hexameter, begins to extend. Logical colon and period give way to semicolon, semicolon to commas, until the penultimate line does without punctuation altogether and flows uncontrollably into the last line, giving us the sense of a speaker carried away by the flow of his own images and language. Moreover, his final, emotionally most persuasive argument is *her* babbling, irrepressible language.

Here, however, is the rub. Not only has language, the basis of his professed belief in her veracity, exposed itself by the end of the poem as a medium of duplicity and self-persuasion and the speaker as someone profoundly enmeshed in, seduced by, his own language; the devastating *pointe* of the epigram comes at the moment the reader recognizes that final rhapsodic line, "I laskovykh imen mladencheskaia nezhnost'," to be a quotation, a very precise translation of a line from one of the most perverse fragments of André Chénier's "The Art of Love":

> Sache inventer pour lui mille tendres folies.
> Il faut en le grondant le serrer dans tes bras,
> Lui dire en le baisant que tu ne l'aimes pas;
> Et les reproches feints, la colère badine,
> Et des mots caressants la mollesse enfantine,
> Et de mille baisers l'implacable fureur.

Know how to invent for him a thousand tender follies. You must, while scolding him, enfold him in your arms, tell him, while kissing him, that you don't love him; and the feigned reproaches, the playful anger, and the childish softness of caressing words, and the implacable fury of a thousand kisses.

The girl's lack of pretence is confirmed, ironically, when her demeanor coincides fully with the disingenuous advice offered by a speaker experienced in "the art of love." Indeed, Pushkin's poem seems to reproduce the effect that, André Chénier's next stanza suggests, such behavior inspires in its hapless victim:

> Souvent d'un peu d'humeur, d'un moment de caprice
> (Toute belle a les siens), il ressent l'injustice;
> Il se désole, il crie, il est trompé, trahi;
> Tu ne mérites pas un amant tel que lui;
> Il a le coeur si bon! Sa sottise est extrême!
> Il te hait; te maudit; plus que jamais il t'aime.[46]

Often he feels the injustice of a bit of bad humor, a moment of capriciousness (every beauty has hers); he is desolate, he cries out, he is deceived, betrayed; you don't deserve such a lover as he; he has such a good heart! His stupidity is extreme! He hates you; curses you; more than ever he loves you.

We recognize in the construction of the last line the prototype for Pushkin's opening line: "Ia veriu: ia liubim: dlia serdtsa nuzhno verit'." Ultimately, perhaps, the whole scene with the beloved has been devised for the sake of this convergence with his poetic predecessor.

Pushkin's early anthological pieces do tend to cut off precisely at the moment of psychological revelation or reversal, often just when the reader realizes that there is an ironic gap between what the speaker thinks he is saying and what the reader has pieced together. Even in his classical fragments, language—both its words and its silences—is motivated by psychological analysis and dramatic irony; it is framed as theatrical utterance, language spoken for a purpose, as self-presentation, persuasion, self-deception, or involuntary self-exposure. An anthological fragment like "To Dorida" looks forward to the peculiarly Pushkinian elegy of dramatic self-deception, in which a speaker's language betrays a knowledge he refuses to face consciously.

In "The foul day is extinguished" ("Nenastnyi den' potukh") for example, Pushkin clearly uses fragmentation and ellipsis, and the reader's understanding of the silences in the text, to dramatize psychological denial. After establishing the theme of geographical and temporal distance between himself and his mistress, Pushkin graphically pictures her actions at the very moment he is thinking of her:

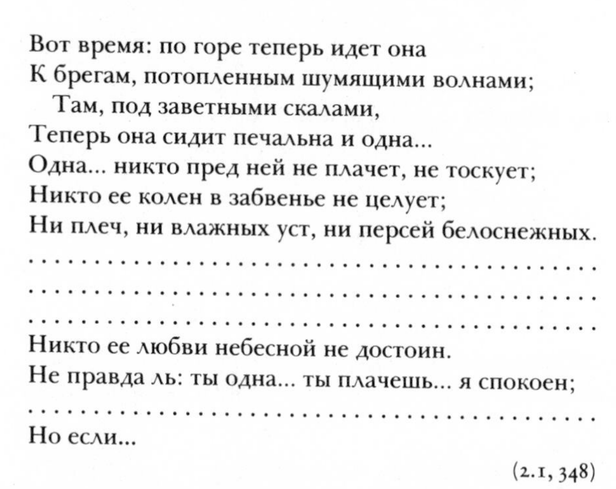

Вот время: по горе теперь идет она
К брегам, потопленным шумящими волнами;
  Там, под заветными скалами,
Теперь она сидит печальна и одна...
Одна... никто пред ней не плачет, не тоскует;
Никто ее колен в забвенье не целует;
Ни плеч, ни влажных уст, ни персей белоснежных.
. . . .
. . . .
. . . .
Никто ее любви небесной не достоин.
Не правда ль: ты одна... ты плачешь... я спокоен;
. . . .
Но если...

(2.1, 348)

Now's the time: along the mountain she's now walking to the shore, drowned by rushing waves; there, beneath the fateful cliffs, she now sits sad and alone... alone... no one weeps before her, nor grieves; no one kisses her knees in oblivion; nor her shoulders, nor her moist lips, nor her snow-white breasts... No one is worthy of her heavenly love. Isn't that true: you are alone... you are weeping... I am calm; but if...

The word *odna* (alone) followed by three dots appears repeatedly to draw him into reverie, while the three lines of suspension points tactfully omit some of the more intimate details of his reminiscences; after these he draws the apparently satisfactory conclusion "No one is worthy of her love." The next line reaffirms, as though rhetorically, "Isn't it true: you are alone... you are weeping... I am calm," and tries to fix her in this sacred image of solitude. But now another row of dots masks the mental transition from secure fantasy to self-deception and doubt, as *nikto* (no one), the grammatical subject, acquires a shadowy identity. The final switch to jealousy is telescoped into two words: "But if..." By this time the suspension dots have done their work, and the poet's train of thought has betrayed itself to the reader. Here we see Pushkin moving from the transparency and emphasis on visual observation of the classical poem to the "analytical elegy" or erotic poem developed by him and Baratynsky in the late 1820's, in which the specific and concrete becomes a surface from which must be deciphered a complex and paradoxical train of thought. Yet that psychological complexity was already infiltrating the gaps and laconisms of his classical poems.

Consider another minimalist tour de force, "The beauty before the looking glass" ("Krasavitsa pered zerkalom"):

> Взгляни на милую, когда свое чело
> Она пред зеркалом цветами окружает,
> Играет локоном—и верное стекло
> Улыбку, хитрый взор и гордость отражает.
> (2.1, 163)

Glance at your beloved, when her brow before the mirror she encircles with flowers, plays with a lock—and the true glass reflects her smile, cunning look, and pride.

The poem has ostensibly the same subject matter as "The Nereid"—a momentary glimpse of a woman when she thinks she is alone, absorbed in the classical gesture of twining flowers into her hair.[47] This time Pushkin gives us something quite different. Instead of a perfect moment suspended in time, the poem's four lines record the image's decomposition. With every word the initially innocuous or innocent image of *milaia* is irrevocably altered. What the lover's glance cannot discover directly will be revealed to him in the faithful mirror's "double": essentially a body that even in solitude is conscious of being looked at, that has internalized the *vzgliad* of the first line (and of the mirror) so thoroughly that there is nothing there but the reflection, an image of flower-like innocence prepared with deliberation and discipline. In four lines the image of the beloved has been replaced by the more interesting image of an artist whose material is her own body and others' emotions.

Close reading of Pushkin's anthological fragments persuades us of his inventiveness in exploiting the brevity and "nakedness" of the genre for his own purposes. He forces the reader to take into account what has been cut off by the borders of the utterance: what has preceded and succeeded the given segment, and what lies under the spoken words. His anthological epigrams invite analysis, not just pleasurable contemplation; in this they look forward to the sharp psychology of the works of his maturity. Moreover, as a genre of poet's poetry—poetic tours de force aimed at other poets—Pushkin's classical fragments play very much on the metapoetic dimension of "recognition,"[48] the fabrication of new images out of the old repertoire of poetic language.

I will end this section with "Dorida" ("V Doride nraviatsia i lokony zlatye"), Pushkin's variation on Batiushkov's then recent translation of an erotic epigram by Paulus Silentiarius. Batiushkov writes:

> В Лаисе нравится улыбка на устах,
> Не пленительны для сердца разговоры,
> Но мне милей ее потупленные взоры
> И слезы горести внезапной на очах.
> Я в сумерки вчера, одушевленный страстыо,
> У ног ее любви все клятвы повторял
> И с поцелуем к сладострастью
> На ложе роскоши тихонько увлекал...
> Я таял, и Лаиса млела...
> Но вдруг уныла, побледнела
> И слезы градом из очей!
> Смущенный, я прижал ее к груди моей:
> «Что сделалось, скажи, что сделалось с тобою?»
> —«Спокойся, ничего, бессмертными клянусь;
> Вы все обманчивы, и я... тебя страшусь.»[49]

What is pleasing about Laisa is the smile on her lips, her conversation, so capitivating for the heart, but even sweeter to me are her downcast looks and the tears of sudden grief in her eyes. Yesterday at dusk, carried away with passion, I repeated at her feet every oath of love, and with a kiss was quietly drawing her to voluptuousness on the luxurious couch... I was melting, and Laisa was swooning... When suddenly she drooped, paled, and tears cascaded from her eyes! Confused, I hugged her to my breast: "What happened, tell me, what happened to you?" "Don't worry, I swear by the immortals; I was agitated by one thought: You are all deceitful, and I... am terrified of you."

Batiushkov masterfully reproduces not only the plot but the ironic tension of Paulus Silentiarius's lyric, perhaps even intensifying its central paradox of a masculine pleasure sweetened by the beloved's fear and tears and by the telling of the episode. This last aspect is particularly clear in the Greek lyric, which begins with a genial address to the poet's male "friends" and ends symmetrically with the beloved's (under the circumstances, pathetically justified) fear that "all you men" are treacherous:

Sweet, my friend, is Laisa's smile, and sweet again the tears she sheds from her gently waving eyes. Yesterday, after long resting her head on my shoulder, she sighed without a cause. She wept as I kissed her, and the tears flowing as from a cool fountain fell on our united lips. When I questioned her, "Why are you crying?" She said, "I am afraid of your leaving me, for all you men are forsworn."[50]

Although Batiushkov does not reproduce the poem's distich, his free variation of long and short lines captures the poem's emotional duality. In particular, he introduces truncated lines and suspension dots, pauses in the poem's metrical inertia, at moments of heightened erotic and emotional tension, to render Laisa's alternations between passion and doubt: "Vy vse obmanchivy, i ia... tebia strashus'."

In Pushkin's poem, the undercurrent of ambivalent thoughts is his own.

В Дориде нравятся и локоны златые,
И бледное лицо, и очи голубые...
Вчера, друзей моих оставя пир ночной,
В ее объятиях я негу пил душой;
Восторги быстрые восторгами сменялись,
Желанья гасли вдруг и снова разгорались;
Я таял; но среди неверной темноты
Другие милые мне виделись черты,
И весь я полон был таинственной печали,
И имя чуждое уста мои шептали.

(2.1, 82)

Pleasing in Dorida are her golden curls, pale face, and blue eyes... Yesterday, leaving my friends' midnight feast, in her embrace I drank voluptuousness with my soul; rapture quickly succeeded rapture, desires were suddenly snuffed out, then flamed up anew; I was melting; but amid the uncertain darkness, other sweet features appeared to me, and I was full of mysterious sadness, and my lips whispered an alien name.

Pushkin begins as if with a cliché, a series of feminine attributes conventionally pleasing to men: "*i* lokony zlatye, / *I* blednoe litso, *i* ochi golubye," the repeated "i" suggesting just a trace of ironic detachment vis-à-vis his own list (we recognize here already a distant anticipation of Eugene and Pushkin's weary attitude to the clichéed attractions of Olga). The opening two lines break off, as though the poet had drifted into a reverie. Like Batiushkov, he starts over, this time with a tale of last night's feast with "friends," interrupted by his tryst with Dorida.

Formally, too, Pushkin retains and develops a number of Batiushkov's distinctive features: he introduces the high-Slavic forms "lokony zlatye," "ochi," and "ia negu pil dushoi" in a patently erotic context, together with the conventional flame/extinction metaphor so often used by Batiushkov. Less obviously, Pushkin reproduces the harsh s/z-r-g-v phonetic repetitions that are so noticeable an organizing principle of Batiushkov's vertical chains in this poem:

> serdtsa razgovory
> slezy goresti vnezapnoi
> sumerki vchera
> odushevlennyi strast'iu
> slezy gradom
> smushchennyi . . . grudi

In Pushkin:

> Vostorgi bystrye vostorgami smenialis',
> Zhelan'ia gasli vdrug i snova razgoralis'

Just at the moment Pushkin's text coincides fully with Batiushkov's, at the point where the resemblance that a contemporary reader would have recognized finally becomes identity, namely at the words "Ia taial," Pushkin detours away from the expected anthological text and into new territory. Instead of Batiushkov's continuation, "Ia taial, i Laisa mlela," Pushkin interrupts with "*no* sredi nevernoi temnoty," and the rest of the poem is quite different, and suddenly familiar to readers of Pushkin's future elegies.

The fear of betrayal openly expressed in her last words by Paulus's and Batiushkov's feminine protagonist is in Pushkin's poem displaced metonymically onto his *own* figurative language: "Vostorgi bystrye vostorgami *smenialis'*" and "sredi *nevernoi* temnoty." Whereas Paulus and Batiushkov begin with a visual evocation of the girl's lips and smile and end with her self-revelation in speech, Dorida's features, the ostensible stimulus for the poem, are canceled out by "Drugie milye mne . . . cherty," and her voice is eliminated from the poem altogether. It is not her sadness but *his* that is expressed—not "Vy vse obmanchivy" but "*ves'* ia *polon* byl tainstvennoi pechali."

His sadness is occasioned by the discrepancy between physical presence and the "other's" absence, by an *obman* (deception), which is nevertheless linked to plenitude: Pushkin ends with the birth of his own speech—the whispered revelation of "imia chuzhdoe," the unspoken alien name for which Dorida was only a surrogate and a stimulus.

Another poem by Paulus Silentiarius suggests an interesting contrast with Pushkin's treatment of the theme:

> Kissing Hippomenes, my heart was fixed on Leander; clinging to Leander's lips, I bear the image of Xanthus in my mind; and embracing Xanthus my heart goes back to Hippomenes. Thus ever I refuse him I have in my grasp, and receiving one after another in my ever shifting arms, I court wealth of Love. Let whoso blames me remain in single poverty.[51]

What for Paulus remains in the erotic realm, for Pushkin enters the metapoetic. Pushkin's tiny poem reveals the essence of the elegiac bargain: displacement as the essential creative act, the fecund source of language. In Pushkin's poem the "real girl" with whom he spends the night turns out to be as clichéed and dispensable as her name, Dorida; her purpose is merely to trigger that plenitude of sadness, of loss pregnant with language, that is the raison d'être of elegy. Not only the conventional Dorida, the girl with the golden locks, but erotic experience itself is dismissed as counterfeit, valuable only for its ability to generate mourning for the original—the whispered alien name kept outside the poem and inaudible to its reader—that is its source.

Read in the way I propose, a poem that began as an imitation of an "imitation of the ancients" reveals the Romantic core of the early-nineteenth-century cult of antiquity. While the erotic poetry of the Greek Anthology often bewails either the frustration of the lover's desire or the loss of the beloved, it never questions the value of sensual fulfillment, of the prize being striven for. Pushkin's poem reveals a permanent deficiency at the heart of being, the characteristically modern rift between the gnawing desire and concrete pleasures which are always *ne to*, that instead gesture toward some anterior, lost experience of completeness. Pushkin's poem deconstructs the modern nostalgia for the "whole" Greek body and being, expressed among others things precisely in its fascination with the anthological fragment. Laisa or Dorida has all the attributes of a classical beloved, the ability to inflame and quench the senses, but not to touch the infinity of the poet's underlying desire. As Paul de Man writes in "The Intentional Structure of the Romantic Image," such a poem "describes the passage from a certain kind of nature, earthly and material, to another nature which could be called mental and celestial."[52]

A classical epigram that claims to be about Dorida and the poet's graphic encounter with her turns out to be about the "epistemologically inaccessible event" that is kept outside it, unrepresented and unnamed—the dark source of its language.[53]

Mille e tré: Elegy and Repetition Compulsion

Read any one elegy by Zhukovsky, Pushkin, or Baratynsky, and you know them all. There have been no feelings among us for a long while now: the one feeling of melancholy has swallowed up the rest. We all vie with one another in yearning for our lost youth; we endlessly chew the cud of this yearning and race to parade our faintheartedness in periodical publications. If this sadness were not simply a rhetorical figure, one might, judging by our Childe Harolds barely out of their swaddling clothes, conclude that here in Russia poets are already born old men. The images are everywhere the same: *the moon*, which—needless to say—is *melancholy* and *pale*, cliffs and groves, where they could never be, a wood, behind which a hundred times they've pictured the setting sun, the evening glow; occasional long shadows and apparitions, something invisible, something ineffable, trite allegories, pale, unpalatable personifications of *Labor, Pleasure, Peace, Gaiety, Sadness*, the *Indolence* of the writer and the *Tedium* of the reader; and above all—fog: fog over the waters, fog over the forest, fog over the fields, fog in the author's head.[54]

In a footnote to his tirade, Kiukhel'beker adds that he would have nothing against one or two youthful laments about lost hopes and premature intimations of mortality, but "What can be said about a literature founded almost entirely on this one idea?" The passage trembles on the verge of the ridiculous as implicit political metaphors struggle to dramatize and ennoble a shift in poetic fashion: "the mighty tribe" of eighteenth-century poets has no descendants; the elegy has ousted the ode.

Kiukhel'beker's diatribe rests on two arguments. The first is that lyric poetry should be concerned with the sublime and the extraordinary, public and not private life. The elegy, in its preference for private, individual subject matter over public, historical, and heroic themes, can evoke only "sympathy" in the reader, not awe, much less the reverence and "enslavement of the hearing and soul of the people" Kiukhel'beker requires of poetry. The second is that the invasion of the Russian language by German and English elegiac fashion is tantamount to cultural colonialism: "We won't permit him [Zhukovsky], or anyone else . . . to impose on us the shackles of a German or English dominion." Russia, by virtue of her geographical position and her independence, is instead in a position to appropriate for herself all the intellectual treasures of Europe and Asia: "Ferdousi, Gafis, Saadi, Dzhami await Russian readers."[55] By 1824 the idea of Russia as cultural mediatrix between Europe and Asia was, as we shall see, gaining currency. It was a cultural role more in keeping with Russia's new power and prominence on the European political scene. Why, Kiukhel'beker's syncretic metaphors imply, should Russia submit to Jean François La Harpe when she had liberated Europe itself from the "monster" Napoleon, had repeatedly outshone the German generals on the battlefields of Europe, and was maneuvering against her former ally England for domination of Europe's Holy Alliance and the beckoning imperial territories of the near east? It was time to abandon the anachronistic posture of a European cultural colony and speak out in Russia's own vigorous idioms and genres.

Kiukhel'beker ends on a peroration, saturated with Slavonic formulas, that might easily have been excerpted from Dostoevsky's Pushkin speech half a century later:

> But it is not enough—I repeat—to appropriate foreign treasures: let there be created for the glory of Russia a poetry truly Russian; and let holy Russia not only in the civic, but also in the moral world be the first power in the universe! The faith of our forefathers, their patriarchal mores, chronicles, the people's songs and tales—are the best, purest, truest sources for our literature. Let us hope that at last our writers . . . will choose to be Russian.[56]

This last exhortation, directed by Kiukhel'beker at Pushkin, has been read as a de facto program for Pushkin's development. Didn't Pushkin's last Southern Poem, "The Gypsies," inscribe the demise of the modern hero and the bankruptcy of his individualistic values into the very plot of the poem, appending to it a crashing, "anachronistic," patently Derzhavinian ode to Russian arms that swept the elegiac-primitive-natural world of the poem into oblivion—or into Russian history? Didn't Pushkin kill off his moonstruck Germanic elegist Lensky—who may owe his very name to Kiukhel'beker's excoriation of the *len'*, or indolence, of Russia's elegiac poets—in the chapter written after Kiukhel'beker's article came out, and consign that creature of European fashion, Eugene Onegin, to historical supercession by the end of the novel? Did not Pushkin's "historical elegy" of 1825, "André Chénier," dramatize the duel between the private, elegiac impulse and the poet's public, odic responsibility? Most clearly of all, shortly after the publication of Kiukhel'beker's piece, Pushkin embarked on the first and most ambitious of his many historical projects, a national tragedy based on Karamzin's *History of the Russian State* and ancient chronicles, a tragedy, he proudly asserted, "without love," while his letters continually demanded "dry historical sources" for his work and advertised the demise of his interest in lyrical poetry altogether. Although virtually all his historical works, even his epic "Poltava," are built on the structural conflict of private and public, elegiac and historical concerns, his increasing interest in historical subjects seems to hew closely to Kiukhel'beker's prescribed path, as does his budding interest in Russian chronicles and folklore.

Because the trajectory outlined for Pushkin by critics has always moved him rapidly past the derivative formulas and narrow egotism of the elegy, a very minor place has been reserved for it in Pushkin's oeuvre. Quite typical is B. Tomashevsky's immunological interpretation of the elegiac episode in Pushkin's development:

> That illness of the age, which was reflected in Batiushkov's poems, turned out to be completely essential to Pushkin's schooling, and it was essential that he pass through this school, if only the sooner to overcome [*preodolet'*] it. The assimilation of elegiac literature was for Pushkin that stage of apprenticeship that abridged for him the "experiences of fast-flowing life." Before becoming himself [*samim soboi*], Pushkin had to pass through this literary school.[57]

The entire genre of the elegy is disposed of at this early juncture, leaving the 1820's for maturer achievements. In fact, however, the elegy remained, through the famous Boldino autumn of 1830, that watershed of Pushkin's career, one of his—and Russian literature's—most fruitful genres.

In this section I propose to take Kiukhel'beker at his word: to examine precisely the repetitive features of Pushkin's erotic elegies and try to determine their function. The key year appears to have been 1823, a year of multiple involvements with several prominent society women in Odessa. We will note not only the fixed features of each erotic "narrative," but also, more importantly, Pushkin's characteristic "delayed reaction" in working out his poetic response to each: it was only after his return to the north, over the course of five years (1825–30), that he produced clusters of elegies retrospectively addressed to specific women in his past, this despite his self-proclaimed abandonment of lyric poetry for the higher matter of history. Rather than insist on the young Pushkin's rejection or overcoming of the elegy, it would probably be more interesting to discover in what way Pushkin uses and alters its language of conventions to shape an image of his interior life. What kind of problems are being worked out, or avoided, in the poetic discourse of Batiushkov, Pushkin, Baratynsky? Does Pushkin outgrow the elegy, or do elegiac patterns continue to recognizably shape his poetic thought?

Savely Senderovich has already answered this question in the affirmative in his innovative book *Aleteiia. Elegiia Pushkina "Vospominanie" i problemy ego poetiki* (Aletheia: Pushkin's elegy "Reminiscence" and the problems of its poetics). For Senderovich, "Reminiscence" represents the essence of elegy in its *rejection* of elegiac conventions and allusiveness, its abandonment of the "symposium" of poets for the pure introspection of soliloquy.[58] I am interested rather in the repetition compulsion that Kiukhel'beker astutely recognized as the distinctive feature of elegiac poetry and that makes it, contrary to Kiukhel'beker's assessment, the logical genre for Russia's entry into European literature.

Although Kiukhel'beker stresses the thematic narrowness of the elegy, historically it is one of the most broadly defined genres. Identified originally by its distich meter (a heroic hexameter line followed by a more lyrical, relaxed pentameter), and only secondarily by its subject matter, the Greek elegy (from *elegeia*, lament) could treat subjects as diverse as mourning for the dead, the fortunes of war, political satire, and erotic failure. (The fixed features and tone of pastoral elegy, which is the particular form Kiukhel'beker has in mind, became popular in the eighteenth century, both in French *poésie fugitive* and in English "graveyard verse," but originated in what were technically Theocritus's idylls, not elegies at all.) For the famous Roman elegiac poets such as Catullus, Propertius, and Tibullus, who were André Chénier's models, the tone of complaint and the theme of love became the dominant mode of the elegy, which Ovid extended further in *Tristia* and *Ex Ponte* into a form of introspective meditation and autobiographical notation written *from a distance* and *in retrospect*.[59] However, eighteenth-century definitions of the elegy are unanimous in their emphasis not only on diversity of subject matter, but also on *mixture of emotions*.[60] What is perhaps most interesting, then, is that in the very midst of neoclassicism's systematic classification of genres, the elegy was singled out as the poetic genre of unclassifiable heterogeneity and private ambivalence.

It nevertheless makes sense that modern elegiac verse has tended to make its appearance as part of a nation's or city-state's Golden Age, as a correlative of national formation and empire building. Just as the Roman elegiac poets were criticized for trivial, personal pursuits out of keeping with Rome's civic and historical mission, modern elegy appears to rise on the back of political centralization, either as a product of the civilized leisure and education it enables or as a subversive response to the official discourses of public life. Batiushkov's career, divided between his public roles as frontline officer and post-Napoleonic Russian diplomat, and his private vocation of "light," preeminently elegiac poetry, illustrates this characteristic symbiotic relationship. Similar cases might be made for Karamzin and Zhukovsky, their identities split between official governmental appointments and a literary orientation toward the private lyric. The very submission of the personal life to the strict, repetitive codes of elegy make it the best place to study the shaping of the self by public discourse.

Elegies are concerned with the recoding of personal experience into the traditional language of elegy; or, as Senderovich says, with recoding personal memory as *the memory of the genre*.[61] By expressing his idiosyncratic pain in socially intelligible and binding language, the elegiac poet in fact reintegrates his radically and even destructively solitary experience into the community. This, as Peter Sacks has shown in his illuminating book *The English Elegy*, was the original function of the elegiac singer: to express the pain of loss in an inherited, profoundly repetitive language.[62] At the same time, the elegiac ritual involves the poet in another relationship: the relationship of rivalry. If originally the elegist competed by the excellence of his song for the right to inherit the property of the dead, the poet's mourning implicitly lays claim to his poetic inheritance: he establishes himself as the next living link in the elegiac tradition. This is one clear way that the elegy, precisely in its repetition compulsion, figures as the logical "entry into language" for young poets (1–37).

Many of the elegiac formulas in question in fact point metapoetically to the function of their repetition. The "begin again" convention, for example, suggests that the poet is merely resuming an old song, continuing an old tradition. Implying "an unbroken pattern such as one may oppose to the extreme discontinuity of death," it "is only one indication of this reenforced entry into a preexisting order of signs or conventions"(9). The elegy is thus almost by definition meta-elegiac, taking the history of the elegy into account. By a similar token, the "echo-convention" "might represent the elegist's particular sensitivity to the fact that the language he uses is and is not his own"; it figures the poet's submission to the "echoing language of dead poets" (25). Rhyme, particularly a markedly repetitive rhyme or refrain, might serve the same function. Anáklisis, the ritual repetition of the dying person's name, can be regarded as the first step in the sequence of substitutions by which the living and desired being is converted into a reified and separate object. By the same token, the necessity for the poet's cutting himself off from the beloved object is often symbolized within the poem by a cutoff or broken object: the branch cut from Daphne-as-tree by Apollo is fashioned into a laurel wreath that becomes the symbol of his divine creativity. The poet must sever himself from his love and reinvest his libido in the cutoff artifact, the symbolic product of his rerouted creative drive. The choral convention reinforces this impression of splitting or self-suppression by substituting for the poet's outgrown old self a new, collective identity (35).

The poet performs a certain feat in facing the abyss of death on behalf of society, hence the traditional motif of the descent and ascent of the poet-lover as a version of the dying and self-renewing vegetation god (whether Dionysus, Orpheus, or Christ). The poet descends into grief, crisis, and nonlanguage and ascends with a revelation: consolation for others, immortality for himself. The price for this transformation into substitutive language is the castration of his primary desire and attachment. In fact, this is the paradigmatic trade-off of elegy: the poet's erotic loss or sacrifice forces him again and again into language, and thus becomes the origin of the renewed poetic impulse (5–8). We shall see precisely this bargain enacted in Pushkin's "Proserpine." If one were to ask why Pushkin's erotic narratives so often focus on loss or separation at the very moment of consummation, the answer might lie in Pushkin's words: "But I, loving, was stupid and mute" (*Eugene Onegin*),[63] whereas *loss*, and above all *repetition* of loss, releases writing. One might hypothesize that Pushkin was addicted to the "elegiac work of mourning," to elegiac repetition itself.

Drawing on Freud and Lacan, Sacks shows that the elegiac "work of mourning" replays the original relationship between loss and language: namely the loss or absence of the mother, which the child first learned to name, represent, control, and finally substitute for with language. Thus the "fort / da" scene observed by Freud can be seen as the prototype for any subsequent work of mourning.[64] Identifying the spool with its mother, the child casts it away with the exclamation "Fort!" then draws it back with the incantatory repetition of the word "Da!" Through this substitutive use of language, the child gains for himself a new identity: he is no longer the object left behind but the author, the dramatist, of the action.

> The groundwork has clearly been laid for subsequent and more thorough suppressions of an inchoate self in favor of a formalized identity, one based not so much on the images of a private fantasy as on the intervening signs and positional codes of society. So, too, this phase foreshadows the elegist's consoling construction of a fictional identity not only for the dead, but for himself as well. (10)

The child's discovery of its ability to interpose language between itself and its loss, to turn a position of helplessness into a representation of power, anticipates the later, one might say more crudely concrete plot of the "Oedipal resolution," in which the child learns to assimilate himself to the father who has intruded on the mother-child relationship as a rival. According to Lacan, the first encounter with language, the preexisting symbolic order, is analogous to the later encounters with the father and with death, in that all three force the psyche out of a state of undifferentiation into a separate and mediated identity.

> It is the figure of the father, representing the symbolic order, that formally intervenes between the child and the child's first attachment. The child's imaginary, dyadic relationship with its prior "love-object" is thus interrupted and mediated by a signifying system, which acts as a third term, much as the laurel sign or the pipes come between the gods and the nymphs. In the elegy, the poet's preceding relationship with the deceased (often associated with the mother, or Nature, or a naively regarded Muse) is conventionally disrupted and forced into a triadic structure including the third term, death (frequently associated with the father, or Time, or the more harshly perceived necessity of linguistic mediation itself). The dead, like the forbidden object of a primary desire, must be separated from the poet, partly by a veil of words. (8–9)

From this perspective, the Oedipal resolution actually governs the child's "entry" into language, an entry that the work of mourning and the elegy replay.

Whether an elegy mourns the loss of a woman, the failure of erotic love, or death per se, it thus contains another implicit subject as well: a confrontation with the authority of a paternal figure or language. The woman may in fact figure as a pretext for a life-and-death struggle with a male authority figure in the guise of a father, husband, or rival lover. If we examine the three erotic attachments of Pushkin's Odessa period that left such long-lasting traces on his poetic production, certain similarities emerge. Within the course of two years Pushkin found himself courting three married women of foreign descent, each married or attached to a man of wealth and/or political influence. He first met Karolina Sobańska on February 2, 1821. She was the Polish mistress of the Third Section agent I. O. de Witt, who reported to St. Petersburg about all political activity in the south, including Pushkin's.[65] Amalia Riznich, the Italian wife of a wealthy businessman, lived in Odessa from the spring of 1823 to May

1824; and K. F. Vorontsova was the Polish wife of Count Vorontsov, the governor of Odessa, under whose jurisdiction Pushkin chafed from July 1823 through July 1824.

Pushkin could mock his wealthy host Riznich with impunity, counterpointing his torrid outpourings to Riznich's wife with mocking vignettes such as the one he later inserted in "Fragments of Onegin's Journey":

> А ложа, где, красой блистая,
> Негоциантка молодая,
> Самолюбива и томна,
> Толпой рабов окружена?
> Она и внемлет и не внемлет
> И каватине и мольбам,
> И шутке с лестью пополам...
> А муж—в углу за нею дремлет,
> Впросонках фора закричит,
> Зевнет и—снова захрапит.
>
> (6, 205)

And the loge, where, sparkling with beauty, the young wife of a merchant, self-absorbed and languid, is surrounded by a throng of slaves? She attends and does not attend to the cavatina and the prayers, to the joke half mixed with flattery... while her husband dozes in the corner, shouts out "Fuora!" in his sleep, yawns and goes back to snoring.

But Vorontsov and de Witt were more dangerous opponents. De Witt and Sobańska apparently included Pushkin in their reports throughout the time of Pushkin's sojourn in Odessa. Vorontsov repaid Pushkin for his amorous attentions and his epigrams by dispatching him on a locust-hunting expedition, then writing a denunciation that effectively resulted in Pushkin's transfer to northern exile in early August of 1824.

V. F. Viazemskaia, perhaps the most intimately initiated in Pushkin's affairs, was also the least inclined to romanticize them, reporting to her husband on July 15, 1823, that "Pushkin, I know, finds himself in very straitened circumstances. . . . [He] is much more melancholy than I: the three women with whom he has been in love have recently left. Luckily, one of them is about to return."[66] Pushkin's erotic lyrics tend to describe, however, a quite opposite situation with all the traditional elegiac features: the beloved is depicted in classical Roman style[67] as the glittering, passionate, but ambivalent object of desire of a mob of courtiers, among whom the poet struggles to retain a foothold.

> Простишь ли мне ревнивые мечты
> Моей любви безумное волнение?
> Ты мне верна: зачем же любишь ты
> Всегда пугать мое воображение?
> Окружена поклонников толпой,
> Зачем для всех казаться хочешь милой,
> И всех дарит надеждою пустой
> Твой чудный взор, то нежный, то унылый?
> Мной овладев, мне разум омрачив,
> Уверена в любви моей несчастной,
> Не видишь ты, когда в толпе их страстной
> Беседы чужд, один и молчалив
> . . . Но я любим
> . . . Но я любим...
>
> (2.1, 300)

Will you forgive my jealous fantasies, the mad agitation of my love? You are faithful to me; why then do you love to startle my imagination? Surrounded by a throng of admirers, why are you sweet to all of them, why does your marvelous gaze, now tender, now sulky, bestow empty hope on all of them? Having taken possession of me, having darkened my reason, certain of my unfortunate love, don't you see, when in the crowd, alienated from their passionate conversation, alone and taciturn. . . . But I am loved. . . . But I am loved...

As usual in the Pushkinian elegy of jealous self-deception, the reader is aware that the speaker's point of view has introduced an angle of distortion; but to what extent his attempt to correlate the outward signs of her behavior with the inner meaning he ascribes to them is wishful thinking is one of the questions left open in the text.

What is clear is that Pushkin's language is saturated with a rhetoric of domination and submission. His first words are not an accusation against her arbitrary behavior, but an anxious request for forgiveness of his jealous fantasies. "Surrounded by a throng of admirers," she queens it over her court with the arbitrary distribution of signs of her favor, her ambiguously speaking glances. Phrases akin to "tvoi chudnyi vzor" in fact echo throughout the lyrics of this period as an apocalyptic feature of men who overpower other men's minds. In "The Demon," for example:

> Его улыбка, чудный взгляд
> Его язвительные речи
> Вливали в душу хладный яд.
> (2.1, 299)

His smile, marvelous glance, his corrosive speech poured cold poison into my soul.

And Napoleon in "A guard dozed motionless on the Tsar's threshold" ("Nedvizhnyi strazh dremal," 1824):

> Нет, чудный взор его, живой, неуловимый,
> То вдаль затерянный, то вдруг неотразимый,
> Как боевой перун, как молния сверкал.
> (2.1, 310)

No, his marvelous gaze, lively, elusive, now lost in the distance, now suddenly irresistible, like a thunderbolt, like lightning gleamed.

The effect of her "marvelous gaze" is comparable: it has "conquered him," "darkened his reason," alienated him from language, left him "alone and mute." As always in Pushkin, the distribution of verbs says it all: *she* "forgives," "likes to frighten," "wants to seem gracious," "bestows," and "having conquered," "having darkened his mind," finally *does not see* him. Meanwhile, he fragments himself metonymically into a sequence of indirect objects, possessive pronouns, and nouns: "my jealous fantasies," "the mad agitation of my love," "my imagination," "my mind," "my unhappy love," and above all, into the grammatical object of *her* actions: "having conquered me" ("*mnoi* ovladev"), "but I am loved" ("no ia *liubim*"). Clearly, Pushkin has inscribed the relationship into a language of quasi-political domination and submission, with himself cast in a suppliant role.

Later critics, more romantic than Pushkin's contemporaries, have been eager to assign to Vorontsova the exclusive role of his "secret love":

Legends of that epoch mention a woman, surpassing all the others in the power with which she governed the thought and existence of the poet (Count-

> ess E. K. Vorontsova). Pushkin makes no mention of her anywhere, as though desiring to preserve for himself the mystery of this love. It reveals itself only in the multitude of profiles of a beautiful woman's head, of a calm, noble, grand type, that are scattered over almost all his papers from the Odessa period of his life.[68]

Viazemsky's son detected a more pointed connection between Pushkin's "empire-style" portraits of Vorontsova and the locust expedition inflicted on Pushkin by Count Vorontsov,

> making a fool of the Lovelace who was already anticipating his triumph. The decimation of Pushkin's amorous plans was long reflected in the sketches on his rough drafts of a refined Roman profile in an elegant classical headdress, with an imposing ruche around her neck.[69]

In other words, Viazemsky confirms the transfer to Vorontsova's iconic image of the attributes of imperial power her husband wielded over Pushkin. The abasement Pushkin suffered at Vorontsov's hands, which in fact he seemed to court, is thus eroticized in Pushkin's fetishistic portrayals of Vorontsov's spouse.

This is most clearly evident in "Proserpine," a poem dated quite specifically August 26, 1824—shortly after Pushkin's forced departure for Mikhailovskoe—although the first twelve lines had actually been written in April of 1821. The poem is a free translation of "Tableau XXVII" in Parny's *The Disguises of Venus: Pictures Imitated from the Greek*,[70] and thus belongs to a category we have come to recognize in Pushkin: the imitation of a (neoclassical) imitation of "the ancients." The first twelve lines of "Proserpine" focused more pointedly on the mutual seduction of "timid youth" and "indifferent and jealous goddess": "I boginiam l'stit izmena: / Prozerpine smertnyi mil" (Even goddesses are gratified by betrayal: the mortal appeals to Proserpine). (2.1, 319). Ending here, the fragment sounds like a courtly appeal to a society "goddess," who might be similarly tempted to condescend to a "timid mortal." Pushkin had met the grand-mannered consort of de Witt, Karolina Sobańska, two months before, and knew that she was inclined toward literary-erotic games.[71] By 1824 the concrete names had changed, but the underlying erotic structure was remarkably the same. The fact that "Proserpine" was completed and published without delay in Del'vig's *Northern Flowers* in 1824 suggests that a poem that may have begun in 1821 as a courtly tour de force had by then acquired a (or several) new raisons d'être.

First of all, Pushkin was entering the polemical fray against Kiukhel'beker's recently published essay "On the direction of our poetry." One line of Kiukhel'beker's argument had particularly attacked the Russian elegiac poets for their derivative relationship to the equally derivative "pygmies" of French literature, such as Parny: "Translators are translated by no one but our own humdrum translators. An imitator cannot know inspiration: he speaks not from the depths of his own soul, but rather forces himself to relate the conceptions and sensations of another."[72] "Proserpine," like other Pushkin "imitations," demonstrates the reverse: that his poetic "self" peeps out most readily from behind a mask, expressing itself precisely in its irreverent alteration of the inherited form. Indeed, the form of "imitation" or "elegiac repetition" dismissed by Kiukhel'beker is wittily congruent with the implicit subject of the poem: the young lover "borrows" the god's spouse, just as Pushkin "borrows" the subject "Proserpine." The rivalry with authority is enacted on both the level of the erotic plot and the metapoetic level of literary competition. At the same time, that rivalry is in itself a jest: Parny's short, unmelodious verses as little suggest a revered literary ancestor as the god-husband's authority is inviolable. The "pygmy" stature of the one extends to the other—a joke Pushkin would repeat.[73]

Thus, under the double disguise of an "imitation" and a polemical taunt, "Proserpine" furnished a covert form for Pushkin's first public response to the Vorontsov debacle, occupying a transitional place between the necessarily unpublished anti-Vorontsov epigrams of 1824 and the spate of retrospective elegies of 1825–26 mourning his loss of Vorontsova. Pushkin turns a gracefully outdated "empire-style" pastoral into a mockingly personal allegory, with the despised Vorontsov in the role of cuckolded god of the underworld, incarcerating his spouse against her will, and the speaker in his familiar position of youthful supplication before the goddess. Beyond this limited topical meaning, however, I would like to explore the way Pushkin uses the neoclassically conventional and playful plot of "Proserpine" to allegorize the darkly archetypal structure of erotic experience for himself.

Pushkin's first act of interpretation is, as usual, one of selection and demarcation. Parny's entire cycle of *tableaux* had dramatized a single playful "moral," disclosed by Venus to her pastoral lover at the end: that the individual women with whom he has consorted throughout the poem were merely "disguises for Venus," to whom he has thus ultimately been faithful.

> Je t'aimai long-temps en secret.
> Tout est facile à ma puissance;
> Et Vénus de ton inconstance
> Fut toujours la cause et l'objet.[74]
>
> I loved you for a long time in secret.
> Everything is easy for my power;
> And Venus, of your unfaithfulness,
> Was always the cause and the object.

Proserpine is just one of the many faces of Venus, and "Tableau XXVII" ends on a buoyant note as the shepherd emerges from Hades with "happy thoughts." By isolating the episode depicting the underworld rendezvous of the mortal youth with the goddess Proserpine, Pushkin has redrawn the borders of his allegory.[75]

How does Pushkin use Parny's feather-light creation to explore his own preoccupations? Let us examine the texts side by side:

Le sombre Pluton sur la terre	Плещут волны Флегетона,
Etait monté furtivement.	Своды Тартара дрожат,
De quelque Nymphe solitaire	Кони бледного Плутона
Il méditait l'enlèvement.	Быстро к нимфам Пелиона
De loin le suivait son épouse:	Из Аида бога мчат.
Son indifférence est jalouse.	Вдоль пустынного залива,
Sa main encor cueillait la fleur	Прозерпина вслед за ним,
Qui jadis causa son malheur:	Равнодушна и ревнива,
Il renaissait dans sa pensée.	Потекла путем одним.
Myrtis passe: il voit ses attraits,	Пред богинею колена
Et la couronne de cyprès	Робко юноша склонил.
A ses cheveux entrelacée.	И богиням льстит измена:
Il se prosterne; d'une main	Прозерпине смертный мил.
Elle fait un signe; et soudain	Ада гордая царица
Remonte sur son char d'ebène.	Взором юношу зовет,
Près d'elle est assis le berger.	Обняла—и колесница
Les coursiers noirs d'un saut léger	Уж к Аиду их несет:

Ont déjà traversé la plaine.
Ils volent; des sentiers déserts
Les conduisent dans les enfers.
Du Styx ils franchissent les ondes:
Caron murmurait vainement;
Et Cerbère sans aboiment
Ouvrait ses trois gueules profondes.
Le berger ne voit point Minos,
Du Destin l'urne redoutable,
D'Alecton le fouet implacable,
Ni l'affreux ciseau d'Atropos.
Avec prudence Proserpine
Le conduit dans un lieu secret,
Ou Pluton, admis à regret,
Partage sa couche divine.
Myrtis baise ses blanches mains:
La presse d'une voix émue,
Et la déesse demi-nue
Se penche sur de noirs coussins.
    Elle craint un époux barbare:
Le berger quitte le Tartare.
Par de longs sentiers ténébreux
Il remonte, et sa main profane
Ouvre la porte diaphane
D'où sortent les Songes heureux.[76]

Мчатся, облаком одеты;
Видят вечные луга,
Елизей и томной Леты
Усыпленные брега.
Там бессмертье, там забвенье,
Там утехам нет конца.
Прозерпина в упоенье,
Без порфиры и венца,
Повинуется желаньям,
Предает его лобзаньям
Сокровенные красы,
В сладострастной неге тонет
И молчит, и томно стонет...
Но бегут любви часы;
Плещут волны Флегетона,
Своды Тартара дрожат:
Кони бледного Плутона
Быстро мчат его назад.
И Кереры дочь уходит,
И счастливца за собой
Из Елизия выводит
Потаенною тропой;
И счастливца отпирает
Осторожною рукой
Дверь, откуда вылетает
Сновидений ложный рой.
(2.2, 319–20)

PARNY: Dark Pluto had mounted furtively to the earth. Of some solitary nymph he was meditating the abduction. His spouse followed him at a distance: her indifference is jealous. Her hand still picked the flower which had once caused her unhappiness: it was being reborn in her thoughts. Myrthis passes: he sees her attractions, and the crown of cypress woven into her hair. He prostrates himself; with one hand she makes a sign; and suddenly remounts her ebony carriage. Near her sits a shepherd. The black coursers with a light leap have already traversed the plain. They are flying; deserted paths conduct them into hell. They crossed the waves of the Styx: Charon murmured in vain; and Cerberus without barking opened his three profound throats. The shepherd does not see Minos, the redoubtable urn of Destiny, the implacable lash of Alecton, nor the horrifying scissor of Atropos. With prudence Proserpine conducts him into the secret place, where Pluto, admitted reluctantly, shares her divine couch. Myrthis kisses her white hands: urges her with an agitated voice, and the half-nude goddess leans back on black cushions. She fears a barbarous spouse: the shepherd leaves Tartarus. By long murky paths he climbs back, and his profane hand opens the diaphanous door from which happy thoughts emerge.

PUSHKIN: The waves of the Phlegethon splash, the vaults of Tartarus tremble, pale Pluto's horses quickly whisk the god out of Hades to the nymphs of Peleus. Along the deserted bay, indifferent and jealous, Proserpine passed after him on a certain path. Before the goddess a youth timidly bent his knee. Even goddesses are gratified by betrayal: the mortal appeals to Proserpine. The proud tsaritsa of hell summons the youth with her gaze, embraces him—and the chariot is already carrying them to Hades: they fly, clothed in cloud; they see the eternal meadows, Elysium and the lulled shores of the languid Lethe. *There* is immortality, there oblivion, there no end to pleasures. In ecstasy, without porphyry and wreath, Proserpine obeys his desires, yields her secret beauties to his kisses, drowns in sensual delight, now is mute, now languidly moans. . . . But the hours of love fly; the waves of the Phlegethon splash, the vaults of Tartarus tremble: pale Pluto's horses quickly whisk him back. And Ceres's daughter leaves, and behind her out of Elysium by a secret path she leads the lucky man; and with a careful hand the lucky one opens the door, out of which flies a false swarm of dreams.

The first thing I would point out is the accurate, even hypertrophied quality of the translation's formal features. It is as if Pushkin has deliberately set himself the task of re-creating the poem's delightfully "pygmy," singsong poetics both metrically and syntactically. He opens more dramatically, however, with a sustained five-line crescendo, full of acoustic effects and motion; the slow, furtive climb and meditation of Parny's god is amplified into a precipitous arrival, closer in fact to Ovid's original account of Proserpine's abduction:

Pluto, Saturn's son, contained his wrath no longer, but urged on his grim steeds, and with his strong arm hurled his royal sceptre into the depths of the pool. Where it struck the bottom, the ground opened up to afford a road into Tartarus, and the yawning crater received his chariot as it hurtled down.[77]

The more Pushkin accentuates the mythological pomp of Pluto's "grand entrance," the more its sublimity trembles on the verge of the ridiculous. Pushkin reproduces Parny's trademark clausules and colons only at semantically marked junctures: in the epigrammatic formulation "I boginiam l'stit izmena: / Prozerpine smertnyi mil," or to mark the repetitive phrases that warn of Pluto's return:

Плещут волны Флегетона,
Своды Тартара дрожат:
Кони бледного Плутона
Быстро мчат его назад.

The waves of the Phlegethon splash, the vaults of Tartarus tremble: pale Pluto's horses quickly whisk him back.

Reduced to a refrain, the identical repetition of Pluto's grand (but belated) entrance now unmistakably marks him as comical, as fixed features—like the twice-repeated epithet "pale Pluto"—often do.

The description of the youth's descent into the underworld is also quite differently proportioned. Whereas Parny lingers over the many frightening mythological creatures and obstacles passing slowly by the shepherd on his path to Hades, Pushkin's adulterous travelers are whisked through a landscape that promises forgetfulness and immortality: the eternal fields of Elysium, the "sleeping shores" of the languid Lethe. Its most salient characteristic is its wateriness, ubiquitous in Ovid's accounts of abduction and condensed by Pushkin into a few liquid words and sounds (*pleshchut*, *volny*, *zaliv*, *potekla*, and the names of various rivers), which heighten the aura of mythological and psychological dream space. Whereas Parny's goddess never loses her hieratic status (in fact her husband's presence is constantly invoked), Pushkin's Proserpine stands before him without her regalia, obedient to his desires, as though they had momentarily traded places. Whereas Parny's narrative trails off tactfully just as the half-naked goddess leans back on black cushions, Pushkin devotes a full ten lines to the sensuous delights of the goddess and her young lover, trailing off in his turn ("No begut liubvi chasy") only after everything has been said. The counterpoint between the *mchat* of Pluto and the *nesut*, *mchatsia*, *begut* of the lovers has a farcical effect: Pluto's rumbling arrival is ineffectually late. Pluto's original abduction of Proserpine from the earth to the underworld has been mockingly reenacted, and avenged, by her symmetrical abduction of a mortal to the underworld.

Pushkin's poem, unlike Parny's, hinges on the structural opposition between acceleration and timelessness. Pluto's comings and goings are, as Sacks has suggested, associated with the exigency of time. The furthest reach of Hades is described as a place that is above all exempt from the rule of time: "Tam bessmert'e, tam zabven'e / Tam utekham net kontsa" (*There* is immortality, there oblivion, there no end to delights). It is also a place exempt from differentiation: the goddess, stripped of her "porphyry and wreath," is obedient to the youth's desires; in other words, equal. Pushkin accentuates the tension between the blissful timelessness of the union with Proserpine and the accelerated time and separation enforced by the husband's approach. Expelled from the underworld into the world of time and death, Pushkin's youth emerges not with the "happy thoughts" of Parny's shepherd, but with a phrase that diverges strikingly from the original:

> И счастливец отпирает
> Осторожною рукой
> Дверь откуда вылетает
> *Сновидений ложный рой.*
> (2.1, 320) [emphasis mine]

And the lucky one opens with a cautious hand the door, out of which flies *a false swarm of dreams.*

The phrase probably derives from Ovid, who populates the cave from which the river Lethe flows with "voiceless quiet and empty dreams . . . indistinguishable from the real shapes they imitate, . . . as many as the corn ears in the harvest, as leaves on the woodland trees, or sands scattered on the shore."[78] To account for this phrase, which I believe contains the crux of Pushkin's difference from Parny, I will elaborate some of the implications of the Persephone myth, implications that could quite plausibly have been discussed in the classical circles influenced by German scholarship of the late 1810's and the 1820's.[79]

The story of Pluto/Hades' rape and abduction of Proserpine/Persephone, the maiden daughter of Demeter, goddess of the fertile earth, was well known to Pushkin, at least in the Ovidian version. The myth unambiguously identifies sexuality with death: in raping Persephone, Hades separates her from her maiden self and her bond with her mother, consigning her to the realm of nonbeing. In the end Persephone is shared equally by the two powers, her mother and her husband, thus acquiring a double identity: the underside of her love is the separation and death of the self. An innocent victim of Hades' rapacity, Persephone nevertheless acquires his attributes: the deadly powers of the Homeric underworld, such as the power of the Gorgon's head to turn the viewer to stone, are identified with her and her duplicity. (Compare again Ovid: "While I was gliding through the Stygian pool beneath the earth, there I saw your Proserpine, with my own eyes. She was sad, certainly, and her face still showed signs of fear: none the less, she was a queen, the greatest in that world of shadows, the powerful consort of the tyrant of the underworld.")[80] Hence on a votive tablet Persephone is depicted both as the goddess of love and beauty and as the goddess of tombs and the dead.[81]

In fact, Hades is a relatively late addition to the original matriarchal myth of a cyclical chthonic goddess whose violent death originally made the land fertile, and who in primitive societies is propitiated by ritual reenactments of her suffering and rebirth. The equation of marriage with death, bridal chamber with grave, and cycle of fertility with death of self seem to be universal features of matriarchal vegetation myths. Sexuality itself (not just sexual failure or loss) and mourning are indissolubly fused. Hence the origins of the world are always represented, in Joseph Campbell's words, as a "ritual love-death": "death and sex come into the world as the basic correlates of temporality." The fleeting nature of the universe's forms was often represented by the swastika, an "emanation of dreamlike forms" from the whirlwind of creation.[82]

The Greek myths and cults surrounding Persephone are clearly similar in essence. Persephone herself is worshiped under a triple aspect, as fertile and mourning mother (Demeter), as lost and then recovered maiden (Kore), and as moon goddess (Hecate). Various figures in Greek mythology (Demeter, Orpheus, Dionysus, the mortal Pirithous) attempt heroic descents into the underworld to reclaim the dead; or as Jung puts it, "the hero's main feat is to overcome the monster of darkness," to enact the triumph of consciousness over the unconscious.[83] Orpheus's effort to bring Eurydice back from the underworld fails finally because underworld "shades" cannot be looked at in the light of day. The myth of the descent into the underworld and the dismemberment of the vegetation god became recurrent motifs in elegiac poetry, signaling the poet's descent into mortal sorrow and his ascent with consolation for others and poetic power and immortality for himself.[84] Persephone's underworld of undying "shades" or "images" (eidola) is thus a treasure house of poetic images as well, into which the poet descends at great risk to his conscious, lucid self.[85]

Jennifer Hixon has found in the story of Pirithous a possible psychological motivation for Pushkin's choice of mythological narrative.[86] Pirithous, inconsolable in his mournng for his dead wife, descends into the underworld in order to marry Persephone—in other words, death itself. With the aid of Theseus he makes his descent, but Hades seats him in the Chairs of Forgetfulness, where he remains permanently fastened. Pirithous thus epitomizes what Sacks has described as "unsuccessful mourning . . . the imprisonment of his affective energies, the locking up within himself of impulses previously directed toward or attached to the deceased."[87] It is possible to reinterpret Pushkin's "Proserpine" in light of this model as precisely such a descent into "forgetfulness" (*zabvenie*), a willing immolation of himself in the undying image of what he has lost. All he can bring back with him from the depths of his immersion are pale simulacra of that original experience—"a false swarm of dreams."

The Parny-Pushkin plot is not really a story of heroic descent, though; the youth is rather a sacrificial victim, "of whom [the goddess] indifferently makes use."[88] Perhaps the greatest resemblance can be found with the rites consecrated to Persephone, the Eleusinian mysteries, which, Homer wrote, "the poet may not disclose," while maintaining, "He who has seen the unutterable works of Demeter is fortunate: the uninitiate will enjoy no such lot in the darkness of death."[89] In these rites a priestess of Persephone accepted the "sacrifice" of the initiant, which consisted in a ritual reenactment of the goddess's own passive surrender to rape and violence.

The role of the "culture hero" is to transmute that ecstatic experience and knowledge into language. To enter the underworld is to reduce the three-dimensional world of nature to the two-dimensional world of mirrorlike psychic images, eidola, a transformation that is experienced as both loss and gain, as the death of the natural self in exchange for shamanistic empowerment.[90] The Orphic mysteries explicitly issued "passports" to the "fountain Mnemosyne" rather than the river Lethe, enjoining not forgetfulness but remembrance. The role of the male only later introduced into the vegetation mysteries appears to be the recovery for consciousness of wordless (feminine-vegetative) knowledge. In "Proserpine" it is in fact Hades / Pluto who forces the lover out of his blissful experience of timeless and wordless union, undifferentiation, back into the day world of lucidity, consciousness, and *substitutive language*. It is Pluto, the god of the "unseen," of "nourishment and riches," who ejects the youth (twice called "schastlivets") out of paradise and back into the world with his frail substitutive cargo: "Snovidenii lozhnyi roi."

It is perhaps worth emphasizing that this wordless knowledge is the subject's own, albeit unconscious and inaccessible. What is in fact a single "hermaphroditic" human nature is allegorized in mythological narrative as polar (gender) opposites: the conscious self as "child-hero" and the unconscious as the supraordinate, demonic personality of the two-faced mother/maiden. "Much of the fear which the female sex arouses in men is due to the . . . illusions that swarm in the male Eros," illusions naively identified with certain women.[91] In other words, living women are perceived as masks, a "false swarm of dreams" substituting for the *same* underlying chthonic goddess. The maiden is forced into prostitution and death in order to reveal her true chthonic nature, her terrifying multiplicity-in-oneness. Each individual sexual experience is a visit to the goddess—not Venus, as Parny's jollier allegory would have it, but the goddess of death.

Sexual experience can thus be mythologized as the means of transformation, self-immolation, the dangerous source of poetry. The beloved is the goddess who can bestow that oblivion, that descent into the unconscious, which is the opposite of everyday life and hence akin to a death of self. Erotic elegy thus simultaneously celebrates sensual love and mourns the death of a lucid, human, articulate, or male self. If male reason is the victim of what is experienced as "sacrifice," undifferentiation, muteness, even emasculation or castration, then the "initiant" of the goddess eventually emerges from his sacrifice invested with compensatory prophetic powers and inspired speech: both less and more than a man.[92]

Like so many elegies, "Proserpine" is in essence meta-elegiac: it dramatizes "the elegist's reluctant submission to language itself."[93]

Pushkin goes beyond expressing or exorcising his anger and grief over separation by allegorizing and mocking the participants. I will quote Hixon's well-formulated conclusions in full:

> By turning his grief into a poem which expresses that grief, the elegist joins a tradition with roots deep in both culture and psychology "by which interruption and loss is followed by a figurative or aesthetic compensation." The mourner relinquishes his instinctual desire for union with the dead in exchange for his reintegration into the symbolic order of which language is a part. In choosing to base his poem on a translation, Pushkin makes especially clear this bargain—he submits himself not only to language in general, but forces his grief into the form of another person's (literally foreign) language. Although this might suggest that the poet is so fully reconciled to the need to substitute language for desire that he can do so even within the especially strict confines of translation, on the other hand it makes clear that the accommodation is far from complete—the act of substitution is marked as exactly *foreign* to inner emotion.[94]

The more foreign the better. "To write about oneself," Pushkin said in 1825 apropos of his own memoirs, "is impossible."[95] The inherited forms of the mythological/neoclassical world turn out to be a mirror for his underworld of psychic demons, enabling Pushkin to name and explore his fear and ritual propitiation of the power of the erotic, as well as his conviction that in self-immolation in the "foreign," mute, timeless, female element (of a woman's desires? of his own psyche?) lay the key to artistic fecundity: the counterfeit swarm of dreams that—unlike the mourned beloved—do reach linguistic daylight. It is only thanks to the "eternal return" of Hades / Pluto, the Oedipal figure of separation and temporality, that "the happy mortal" is forced to take the "hidden path" back up to the surface, and language.

It is quite possible that the psychological-anthropological background I have adduced may seem out of all proportion to the modest intentions and frivolous neoclassical tone of "Proserpine." This reflects my belief that in "Proserpine" Pushkin was attracted by a narrative both sufficiently distanced from and remarkably close to the repetitive structure of erotic-elegiac experience. Whereas "Proserpine" can be considered in the grand scheme of Pushkin's oeuvre a minor poem, "Kleopatra," written three months later, forces itself on our attention both because of its startling quality and because of Pushkin's own intermittent twelve-year preoccupation with it. "Kleopatra" can also be seen as the pinnacle of Pushkin's "Orientalism,"[96] but in the following chapter I will try to show just how complex that readily available and yet perhaps not fully comprehended system of images was. Precisely the conventionality of Orientalism made it another safely disguised framework for dramatizing the unresolved, "impossible" aspects of himself. What I will try eventually to show is that in the peculiar form of "Kleopatra" Pushkin stumbled on a mode beyond the lyrical, a mode that apparently rejected the narrow interior world for the objective realm of history and yet found in selected segments of history precisely the images of its own psychic drama. Because Pushkin circled back to "Kleopatra" again and again at the end of his life, I will postpone my discussion of the entire sequence of texts until the last chapter, hoping that the reader will bear in mind the sacrificial-ritual framework I have used to elucidate the latent meanings in "Proserpine," as well as the self-perpetuating alternation of erotic experience and elegiac language that has been the subject of this chapter.

Chapter 3

The Foreign Fountain: Self as Other in the Oriental Poem

Had Pushkin been exiled to Siberia, inward into the Russian heartland, his poetic development would have taken a different course. In fact, in his imaginary conversation with Alexander I, written just after the close of the southern episode of his existence, he teased himself with that very eventuality: "But here Pushkin would have flared up and would have blurted out a whole lot of unnecessary remarks, and I [Alexander] would have banished him to Siberia, where he would have written a poem called *Yermak* or *Kochum* in various rhyming measures."[1] The commutation of his sentence had taken him instead to the southern border of the Russian empire, a locus both of increased contact with other cultures and a shakier sense of Russian identity.

Edward Said considers France and Britain, the principal nineteenth-century colonial powers, to be the primary elaborators and practitioners of Orientalist discourse; "less so Germany and Russia."[2] In the case of Russia he is incorrect. Even the word *south* is loaded: what was east to Europe was south from the vantage point of St. Petersburg. Russia's military-political frontier to the south and east was a constant policy issue for the European powers. Chronic warfare on the southern front in the eighteenth century had paved the way for General A. P. Ermolov's takeover of the Caucasus, which served him and his army almost as an alternative power base to St. Petersburg.[3] A place of congregation for soldiers returning from the peace talks in Paris, it soon became a hotbed of Decembrism. Meanwhile, Russian military strength in the south threatened not only the native populations of Circassians, Kalmyks, and others, but also the Turkish Empire, against which Russia went to war in 1829, and above all the colonial interests of France and England in the Middle East.[4] Napoleon understood this so well that, as a justification for European "defensive" measures, he commissioned C. L. Lesur to fabricate the so-called last testament of Peter the Great, in which the dying tsar allegedly willed to Russia a manifest destiny of Middle Eastern conquest.[5] It was here, on the southern border, that Russia defined her identity vis-à-vis both Europe and the Asian territories she incorporated into her empire. In a sense, it was here that Russia determined where that all-important border between east and west lay, and whether Russia belonged to Asia or, as a *practitioner* of Orientalist discourse, to Europe.[6]

The Southern Poems, written in quick succession between 1821 and 1823, principally in Kishinev and Odessa, can be read as meditations on that problematic Russian identity. "The Prisoner of the Caucasus" (1821), "The Robber Brothers" (1821–22, unfinished), "The Fountain of Bakhchisarai" (1821–23), and "The Gypsies" (1823–24) were Byronic études that explored themes of (preeminently male) Russian identity in different cultural contexts. Although the specific cultural setting changes, each of the three completed Southern Poems enacts a basic nuclear plot: a love affair with a "native girl," framed by distant rumbles of Russian political domination. The interior world of the Russian outcast, which he attempts to redefine outside his own culture through an immersion in a "foreign" passion, is always reclaimed by the advancing border of his own culture: hence the unpopular, apparently empire-glorifying epilogues of "The Prisoner" and "The Gypsies," which put their respective tales of passion into historical and rational perspective. "The Fountain of Bakhchisarai" provides the most interesting test case because it seems at first glance to lack the paradigmatic western/Oriental love affair. We shall see how a purely Oriental tale on the model of Byron's "Bride of Abydos" could nevertheless limn the borders of Russian identity.

In fact, Russian Orientalist discourse developed in much the same stages as did European Orientalism: (1) military-diplomatic policy; (2) academic institutionalization; (3) poetic-artistic fashion;

(4) travel literature. Pushkin's acquaintance with Byron in the south was extremely timely. Precisely at the time that Russia's involvement in post-Napoleonic realpolitik reached a peak, Romanticism provided a system of images to transcribe it.

It is probably no accident that the career eventually chosen by Friedrich Schlegel, that barometer of cultural enthusiasms, was Oriental linguistics. His main contribution to the rapidly proliferating field of Orientalism, *On the Language and Wisdom of India* (*Über die Sprache und Weisheit der Inder*, 1810), coincided with the codification of information by French scholars in the wake of Napoleon's conquest of Egypt in 1798. What is interesting for our purposes is the way Orientalism and the literary genres that flourished under its aegis (the poetic "tale," the *Arabian Nights* structure of inset narratives, the travelogue, the chrestomathy of fragments) replay many of the Athenaeum's cherished theories; already in 1800 Schlegel was predicting, "It is the Orient that we must search for the highest Romanticism."[7]

Particularly in the work of the second-generation Romantics, the fragment as often as not would appear in Oriental dress: Byron's Turkish Tales, referred to in his correspondence as "foolish fragments," emerged in quick succession in 1814–19, Coleridge's "Kubla Khan," framed in a triptych of fragments, was finally published in 1816, Goethe's *West-East Divan* (*West-östlicher Diwan*) appeared in 1819, Pushkin's Southern Poems followed in 1821–23, and Victor Hugo's *Les Orientales* was published in 1829. Raymond Schwab, summarizing the evolution of "the Oriental Renaissance" from 1765 to 1850, called the Orientalist taste quite simply "a later transposition eastwards of a similar enthusiasm in Europe for Greek and Latin antiquity during the High Renaissance,"[8] a point Victor Hugo made more epigrammatically and with an almost visible Gallic shrug: "In the century of Louis XIV one was a Hellenist, now one is an Orientalist."[9] In Michel Foucault's eyes, European culture was "inventing for itself a depth in which what matters is no longer identities, distinctive characteristics, permanent tables . . . but great hidden forces developed on the basis of their primitive and inaccessible nucleus, origin, causality, and history."[10]

There is, however, an important qualitative difference in the position of the modern European vis-à-vis ancient Greece, which entailed, as we have seen, a profound sense of his own insufficiency and fragmentation, and that same European's position vis-à-vis any culture of "the Orient," which was a stance of knowledgeable expertise. A modern writer like Friedrich Schlegel, who could scarcely speak about himself or his own society without ironic self-interruption and fragmentation, encountered no difficulty in summarizing his knowledge, in telling the whole story, of "the East." The encyclopedic scope of the innumerable works Orientalism spawned is in a sense the last vestige of the old European mission of enlightenment: the encyclopedic encirclement of knowledge. History, which had been so thoroughly demystified by eighteenth-century philosophical historians, could, after all, be told as an epic whole. The old Aristotelian narrative with a beginning, middle, and end could be applied to a part of the world that was regarded as having run its course, whose development was "arrested," and that could therefore be anatomized and represented systematically and completely. Orientalism was the last complete system of knowledge, spared by the asymmetry between subject and object the modern complexes that beset any account of Europe to itself. Transfixing the Orient as the barely animate object of an immense network of knowledge conferred on the European a new self-image. In that scholarly portrait of Oriental cultures' antiquity, disorder, and boundlessness, the European created a portrait of his own coherence and power.[11]

Napoleon's invasion of Egypt, conducted under the slogan "Nous sommes les vrais musulmans," would be the prototype for innumerable western campaigns to liberate the classical Orient of the scholars from its degenerate modern inhabitants. Preceded and flanked by an army of Oriental specialists, Napoleon conquered Egypt in the name of the Koran and an earlier greatness laboriously reconstructed and guarded by scholars, who in a very real way owed their own prestige and livelihood to a sustained sense of the Orient's threatening foreignness and uninterpretability. The philologist's glamorous ability to decode inscriptions preserved on ancient ruins (the Rosetta stone was decoded in 1822) was tantamount to a legacy, authorizing him to repossess and salvage Oriental antiquity from and for modernity.

"The Orient, in short, existed as a set of values attached not to its modern realities, but to a series of valorized contacts it had had with a distant European past," with "world history."[12]

Moreover, and this is one of Edward Said's acutest formal observations, the classic Orientalist form of textual and taxonomical display—the anthology or chrestomathy, the museum exhibition, the philologist's set of quotations—embodied certain discursive presuppositions: the Orient's delapidation, its fragmentation into specimens, and the concomitant power of the specialist who assembled and presented them to view. The nineteenth-century anthological format exemplified by such works as Sylvestre de Sacy's *Chrestomatie arabe*, Joseph Renan's *On the Origin of Language*, and Edgar Quinet's *The Genius of Religions* was, indeed, agglutinative, embodying "a systematic discipline of *accumulation*, both philological and imperial."

> Since the Orient is old and distant the teacher's display is a restoration, a revision of what has disappeared from the wider ken. . . . From being lost it is found, even if its missing parts have been made to drop away from it in the process. . . . Oriental writing itself ought not to be taken in whole. . . . The special value of linguistics . . . is not that natural science resembles it, but rather that it treats words as natural, otherwise silent objects, which are made to give up their secrets. . . . Philology embodies a peculiar condition of being modern and European . . . of setting oneself off, as great artists do, from one's time and an immediate past, even as, paradoxically and antinomically, one actually characterizes one's modernity by doing so.[13]

Russia, the conqueror in turn of Napoleon, hastened to identify herself with modern expertise. The minister of education, S. S. Uvarov, conducted a correspondence with Goethe about Russia's role as mediatrix between east and west that resulted in Uvarov's "Project for an Asian Academy" (1810), which paved the way for the founding of the departments of Oriental languages at the universities of Moscow and St. Petersburg. Another typical "eastern career" was Józef Sękowski's phenomenal rise as academic Arabist to become the editor of the most successful Russian periodical, *Biblioteka dlia chtenia* (Library for reading), where he kept Russian readers abreast of European travel writing on Central Asia and helped foster an explosion of Russian *puteshestvia* (literary journeys) to Astrakhan, India, Turkey, and the Biblical lands.[14]

Clearly, the process is reciprocal: if Orientalist discourse consists of a system of binary oppositions in which the naming subject always figures as the diametric opposite of the named object, both participants are transfixed by the transaction; or, as Said says, "the Orient has [in turn] helped to define Europe (or the West) as its contrasting image, idea, personality, experience."[15] Although poets like Byron, Chateaubriand, Pushkin, Lermontov, Nerval, and Juliusz Słowacki traveled extensively in the regions they described, specific information about individual "eastern" cultures tended to reinforce an invariable schema of paradigmatic oppositions, or, as Said says, "an observation about a tenth-century Arab poet multiplied itself into a policy towards (and about) the Oriental mentality in Egypt, Iraq, and Arabia."[16] For convenient reference, I have further schematized Said's observations into a set of binary oppositions:

EAST	WEST
Old	New
Spiritual "origins," undifferentiated wholeness	Materialist "ends," analysis and synthesis
Irrational, atomistic	Rational and systematic
Prophecy, poetry	Science, history, the military
Passive, sensual body; fecundity	Active mind; seminality
Female, mother; or rigid patriarchy	Dynamic male
Death and decay, arrested development, ahistory	Dynamic growth, historical teleology
Time reverts to space	Space incorporated into European "destiny," historical meaning
Pure spectacle	"Eye of European"
Silence and unintelligibility	Speech, meaning

Clearly, the "positive" features with which the west confronted the Oriental "enigma," an "other" whose threat seemed less military or political than ontological, were precisely those about which western culture had betrayed ambivalence since the Enlightenment: every step of rational or civilized progress had begotten an antithetical longing for nature, emotion, the past, or mystical truth; for every encyclopedic, totalizing discourse there had appeared a subversive, fragmenting dialogue. It is difficult to avoid surmising that much of what Europe "lost" or suppressed in its own culture in the process of becoming rational, civilized, and powerful was projected onto the distant and forbidden Orient, whence it exerted an attraction for the European imagination that would otherwise be difficult to account for.

For precisely as long as European Orientalism produced its encyclopedic surveys, linguistic histories, societies, and travel literature as an accompaniment to its territorial appropriations, the Orient served as the most powerful metaphor for the European's ambivalence about and displacement in his own society.[17] Most Romantic poets claimed to draw their inspiration from, and sided overtly in their subject matter with, the Orient, *against* the social, political, or imaginative constrictions of their own societies. In the very process of associating himself with the Oriental half of the paradigm (passionate, lawless, inspired, prophetic) in apparent opposition to the prevailing European-imperial discourse, the Romantic Orientalizing writer tended to perpetuate the terms of the opposition. Indeed, the writer was, in a different way and for his own purposes, enacting his own appropriation of the Orient.

Byron and the Eye of the European

Literary Orientalism can thus be easily identified by a cluster of constant features that migrated quite predictably from text to text, almost in direct proportion to the degree of originality claimed by the Orientalizing writer. Perhaps the most obvious and popular features were luxury and sensuality, reflected both in decor and in violent and erotic plots; if in popular tales the Orient provided local color and a pretext for openly sexual and often sadomasochistic thrills,[18] in "high" literature luxury and sensuality could signify "love of liberty" and often accompanied a radical and iconoclastic political message. A virtuoso like Byron combined both.

Together with the exotic "color" and "passion" went Oriental design—that famous "atomism and discreteness of the Arab imagination."[19] For the western conception of completeness, narrative logic, and causality, Orientalizing fictions substituted fragmentary and cumulative designs: disparate poems or tales strung together in a pure, "ornamental," and potentially limitless sequence, or embedded concentrically in a "Chinese box" structure also implying infinity. Thus the fascination with fragments that we have repeatedly observed found a new allegorical motivation. The Oriental prophet, ejaculating his often unintelligible truths in a desert, furnished a commonly invoked prototype for the European poet's sacred, nonfunctional discourse. The Oriental fragment's cultivated unintelligibility and "inspired nonsense" testified to its provenance from some other natural or sacred linguistic stratum than modern civilized intercourse. The poet donned the Orient's "difference" as his own mantle:

> And all who heard should see them there,
> And all should cry, Beware! Beware!
> His flashing eyes, his floating hair!
> Weave a circle round him thrice,
> And close your eyes with holy dread,
> For he on honey-dew hath fed,
> And drunk the milk of paradise.[20]

It is no accident that the friend who urged Coleridge to publish his fragmentary poems "as is" was Lord Byron. Although "Kubla Khan" may be considered the "ur-fragment" of English Romanticism,[21] if there is one poet who drew fragmentation, Orientalism and modern poetry into one instantly recognizable cluster, it was Byron. While the fragments of the first-generation Romantics, whether German or English, derived their resonance primarily from the grandiosity of their original and collective conception and only secondarily from the accidents of autobiography, Byron from the beginning made fragmentariness a personal quirk, his nonchalant and increasingly self-parodying trademark. In his correspondence he cultivated the image of the casual gentleman-amateur who composed while he shaved and never revised anything (although the drafts for *Don Juan*, at least, contradict him), whose improvised fragments never added up to a whole work but accurately portrayed the inimitable divagations of his mind: "The Bride such as it is is my first *entire* composition of any length, . . . for the G[iaour] is but a string of passages—and C[hil]d Ha[rol]d is & I think always will be unconcluded. . . . The Giaour [has been added to] but still in foolish fragments . . . it is no wonder that I wrote one—my mind is a fragment."[22] Again, about *Don Juan* he wrote to his publisher, "Don't ask me for the plan of Donny

Johnny. I *have* no plan. I *had* no plan; but I had or have materials. . . . Why, man, the soul of such writing is in its licence."[23] Byron consistently accounts for his fragments in an anti-sublime[24] way—as signs of aristocratic negligence and freedom; as eighteenth-century exercises, akin to Sterne's and Diderot's, in the "license" of associative mental operations; as an ongoing improvisation. The flippant tone of his prefaces and notes always dissociates him from the voices of pathos within the poems themselves.

At the same time, like Sterne, Byron continued to feed the insatiable appetite of Romantic readers for literature in process. He jealously guarded his poems' potential for further accretion and completion. Thus *Childe Harold*, which emerged in installments and changed drastically during the interrupted course of its composition, and *Don Juan*, which Byron predicted would stretch to one hundred cantos, but broke off at Byron's death on the sixteenth, were homologous with the processes of life and thought. Byron hinted that when he had lived a little more, new cantos of *Childe Harold* might emerge.

What struck readers most forcefully was the suppletive relation between the poem's ostensible hero, the shadowy Harold, and the passionate narrator, whose voluble tirades in the first person increasingly interrupt and eventually upstage the third-person plot. That plot is more and more clearly a construct, around the edges of which Byron peeks and establishes his collusive relationship with the reader. In many ways the Byronic "tirade," often provoked by a scene from Childe Harold's travels, resembles a Winckelmannian "rhapsody" before a silent sculpture. The scene, excerpted from its native context, provides a mute pretext around which to weave his political, aesthetic, and autobiographical associations, to "speak for" not only the silent, damaged Harold but also the oppressed cultures he visits and the vicariously passionate, suppressed reader.

The formula operated most clearly and successfully in the series of narrative poems that went under the collective title Turkish Tales and made Byron the best-selling author of his generation. The formula for the Byronic narrative poem has been most precisely and dismissively described by B. M. Zhirmunsky, in his comparative study of Pushkin and Byron. Byron himself dismissed his own invention as a composite of the age's ready-made styles, "all of them trashy and bombastic."

In "Beppo," he airily mocked the vogue to which his own tales had lent prestige:

> Oh that I had the art of easy writing
> . . .
> How quickly would I print (the world delighting)
> A Grecian, Syrian, or Assyrian tale;
> And sell you, mix'd with Western sentimentalism
> Some samples of the finest Orientalism.
>
> (St. 51)

Nevertheless Pushkin, freshly transplanted to the south in 1821, lost no time in adapting not just any Orientalist model, but precisely Byron's, for reasons that he specifies.

> The Eastern style was a model for me, insofar as it is possible for us, rational, cold Europeans. Apropos again, do you know why I dislike Moore? Because he is excessively Eastern. He imitates childishly and in an ugly manner the childishness and ugliness of Saadi, Hafiz, and Mohammed. A European, even in the rapture of Oriental splendor, must preserve the taste and eye of a European. That is why Byron is charming in *The Giaour*, *The Bride of Abydos*, etc.[25]

I will consider first a few of the formal features by which Byron maintained an ironic tension between his Oriental subject matter and his "European eye." Using "The Bride of Abydos" as a point of comparison for "The Fountain of Bakhchisarai," I will then show how the Oriental formulas Pushkin borrowed from Byron reshaped his thinking on subjects erotic, political, and poetic.

Pushkin's Southern Poems not only imitated the exotic subject matter of Byron's Turkish Tales but reproduced their format, with its conspicuous stylistic breaks and discontinuities. Each poem reproduced approximately the following sequence of frames: (1) title; (2) subtitle; (3) dedication; (4) prologue; (5) narrative poem full of interruptions, chronological gaps, and inserted songs or internal monologues; (6) epilogue; (7) prose annotations. The resulting poem appeared to be a collage of separate parts, addressed to different audiences, in different meters and styles, and flaunting, rather than attempting to disguise, its discontinuities, obscurities, apparent planlessness, and general aura of improvisation. The hidden and explosive creative sources of the imagination could be effectively identified with the Orient, its feminine and sensual fecundity, its commingled sensuality and spirituality, its infinitely unfolding chains of stories, and its illogical but vivid fragmentation.

On the other hand, the concentric frames surrounding the nucleus of the Turkish tale provide opportunities for stylistic disengagement. The subtitle is a way of classifying the title, of calling attention to the form of its narrative. The letter to the publisher forces the reader to take cognizance of the poem he is about to read as a written text, an item of transaction, a part of Byron's career. The dedicatory poem, in sharp contrast, suddenly turns its back, as it were, on the public, narrowing its address to a single, intimately known audience, yet leaving the public privy to this intimate aside. Each frame, in other words, is a performance, displaying a different facet of Byron. The dangling ending and epilogue reinforce this sense of a story that continues although the performance has been abruptly terminated. And finally, in the annotations the reader meets a quite different, unbuttoned, and genial host, who takes him behind the scenes and shows him the real travels, exotic and familiar, from which the poem was made. Byron over and over steps outside the style of the previous frame, each time revealing himself to be different, less limited, ironic. At the same time, the fact that these styles could be cannibalized, eclectically juxtaposed, meant that they had been detached from any unified world of value. They were the stylistic vestiges of ruined worlds, out of which the "postmodern" scavenger constructed a disturbingly relativistic, uncentered, and idiosyncratic collage.

The practice of framing the Romantic poem with prose prefaces and annotations[26] was an established feature of the Byronic genre, deriving, most probably, from its affiliation with (Orientalist) travel writing. The motivation for these scholarly—often pseudoscholarly and even incorrect—annotations was the unfamiliarity to European readers of the exotic settings, customs, and terminology that were a major source of the Romantic and "poetic" quality of the genre. To the extent, then, that the Byronic poem departed from European norms of intelligibility in its poetic language and exoticism, it restored them in its prose. In his prose annotations Byron explicitly interposes himself as a kind of interpreter and guide, the "European eye" that Pushkin found so necessary a component of literary Orientalism. That the Orient is above all a literary theme is underscored by both Byron and Pushkin, in Byron's dedication of "The Corsair" to Moore and Pushkin's citation in "The Prisoner" of Derzhavin's and Zhukovsky's earlier verses on the theme of the Caucasus. At the same time, both poets emphasize their personal acquaintance with the terrain and customs that serve as the colorful backdrop to their poems. Byron footnotes the foreign words liberally sprinkled throughout his text (*hibouque*, *Dervis*, *Galane*), uses rhymes to highlight the unpronounceability of "The Giaour," explains unfamiliar customs as an eyewitness, and cites exotic literary or oral sources for some of his incidents. Byron's annotations are often extended and personable commentaries that evoke the contrasting persona of Byron the gentleman traveler, the salon wit and raconteur—a genial and ironic voice, which, pace Lotman, is as different as can be from the tragic masks of the Byronic heroes within the tales themselves. For example, the footnote to line 734 of "The Giaour" gives the exotic details in the poetic text a familiar and habitual air:

> "Alla Hu!" The concluding words of the Muezzin's call to prayer from the highest gallery on the exterior of the Minaret. On a still evening, when the Muezzin has a fine voice, which is frequently the case, the effect is solemn and beautiful beyond all the bells in Christendom.

while the note to line 782 at once mocks both Byron's own melodrama and the genre of "eyewitness" testimonial:

> The freshness of the face and the wetness of the lip with blood are never-failing signs of a vampire. The stories told in Hungary and Greece of these foul feeders are singular, and some of them most *incredibly* attested.

and the note to line 479 brilliantly parodies the philological footnote:

> The celebrated famous ruby of Sultan Giamschad, the embellisher of Istakhar; from its splendour, named Schlebgercy, "the torch of night;" also "the cup of the sun," etc. In the First Edition, "Giamschad" was written as a word of three syllables; so D'Herbelot has it; but I am told Richardson reduces it to a disyllable, and writes "Jamschad." I have left in the text the orthography of the one with the pronunciation of the other.

Pushkin's format follows suit, but his annotations to "The Prisoner," for example, are infinitely drier and less funny than Byron's colorful footnotes, and only distantly allude to the writer's personal experiences as a traveler:

> *Kumys* is made from mare's milk; this beverage is in great use among all the mountain and migratory peoples of Asia. It is rather pleasant in taste and is considered quite healthful. (4, 115)

Pushkin's prose notes oppose to the lyricism of his poetic descriptions of the Caucasus the deliberately "cold" and unenthused "eye of a European." How important this structural contrast of frame to tale was becomes clear in "The Fountain of Bakhchisarai," to which Pushkin appended a particularly elaborate and detached prose frame, as though in compensation for its lack of an internal western viewpoint.

Pushkin appears immediately to have remarked on this innovative feature of the "Bride of Abydos": the fact that it conspicuously lacked a Childe Harold or Giaour figure, a western hero. Instead, the "eastern" plot itself serves to dramatize the poet's lyrical concerns. The only marker of an east/west cultural divide is the prefatory poem set off in ternary meter, "Know ye the land," which introduces the east as the land where all norms are violated, while the very brevity of the poem testifies to the fact that this "knowledge" is pure convention: everybody knows the code.

The tale opens strikingly, with a view of the Oriental potentate on his throne, immobile in thought, flanked by a court that hangs on the absolute power of his glance and word: "Deep thought was in his aged eye." Power in the "land" of this poem depends on the ability to see, to conceal, and to reveal. Old Giaffir, it turns out, has many secrets: he has brought Selim up in the belief that he is his own unworthy effeminate son, rather than the disinherited son of Giaffir's brother, murdered by Giaffir's own hand, and hence also in the belief that he is the brother of Giaffir's daughter Zuleika. Effectively disinherited, Selim is in addition castigated for being "Greek in soul" and "less than a woman"; Giaffir "fails to see aught that beseems a man" in him. The concealment of the secret of Selim's birth, that is, his paternal origin, effectively bars him from manhood. He is essentially equated with Zuleika, whose fate as a woman—with "fairy form," "fairy fingers, my weaker will"—is not to be seen, or to be veiled and unveiled at her "father's will."

(Woe to the head whose eye beheld
My child Zuleika's face unveil'd!)

. . .

Nay, Father, rage not—nor forget
That none can pierce that secret bower
But those who watch the women's tower.
(Can. 1, st. 3)

Concomitantly, where concealment of secrets is a source of power, seeing is a transgression, a violation, an act of "piercing" denied to all but the usurping father. There is an analogy between Zuleika's concealment and Giaffir's secrets—his poisoning of his brother, his plans for marrying his daughter off to an aged ally, "his and my united power." To see "Zuleika's face unveiled" would be the structural equivalent of unveiling Selim's hidden identity, his manhood. Both would represent a diminution of the power Giaffir has arrogated to himself.

Sympathetic though Byron may be to the plight of his dispossessed characters, his own poetic system conforms to the patriarch's. Zuleika is unveiled to the reader as a spectacle for the eye, her emotions interesting insofar as they alter her skin color and the aesthetic effect of her appearance:

In silence bow'd the virgin's head;
And if her eye was fill'd with tears
That stifled feeling dare not shed,
And changed her cheek from pale to red,
And red to pale, as through her ears
Those winged words like arrows sped.
(Can. 1, st. 8)

At the moment of her rebellion, Byron substitutes for a description of the thoughts or emotions beating under her "timid breast" a description of the exotic objects that fill her room:

Yes! there is light in that lone chamber,
And o'er her silken ottoman
Are thrown the fragrant beads of amber,
O'er which her fairy fingers ran;
Near these, with emerald rays beset,
(How could she thus that gem forget?)

Her mother's sainted amulet,
Whereon engraved the Koorsee text,
Could smooth this life, and win the next;
And by her comboloio lies
A Koran of illumined dyes

. . .

All that can eye or sense delight
  Are gather'd in that gorgeous room:
  But yet it hath an air of gloom.
She, of this Peri cell the sprite,
What doth she hence, and on so rude a night?

(Can. 2, st. 5)

A room full of mute and markedly exotic cultural artifacts is as good a metonymic representation as any of Zuleika's human absence; so, as a matter of fact, are the other descriptions: "fairy fingers," "fairy form," "sprite." There are no secrets here, but an infinite regress of colorful surfaces.

Contrast Selim's false appearance with the hidden depths of his secret identity. Not only in Giaffir's court, but in the poem itself the main source of power is the concealing and speaking of secrets: "I am not, love! what I appear" (can. 1, st. 14). "And how my birth disclosed to me, / Whate'er beside it makes, hath made me free" (can. 2, st. 13). In a poem full of intimations of epic activity and mortal danger, the heroic act is the act of speaking, intensified by the patently sexual metaphors surrounding the word "tongue":

All this, Zuleika, harshly sounds;
  But harsher still my tale must be:
Howe'er my tongue thy softness wounds,
  Yet I must prove all truth to thee.

. . .

He [Giaffir] ever went to war alone,
And pent me here untried—unknown;
To Haroun's care with women left,
By hope unblest, of fame bereft

. . .

'Tis vain—my tongue cannot impart
My almost drunkenness of heart,
When first this liberated eye
Survey'd Earth, Ocean, Sun, and Sky,

As if my spirit pierced them through,
And all their inmost wonders knew!
One word alone can paint to thee
That more than feeling—I was Free!
E'en for thy presence ceased to pine;
The World—nay, Heaven itself was mine!
(Can. 2, st. 17–18)

From "one word" to "the World" is but a step. Selim has experienced the silence, enclosure, veiling, "unmanning" of the woman's world; indeed, Zuleika's "softness," her one defining characteristic, has "unmann'd him" as much as Giaffir's tyranny. Like the veils that swathe her, preventing her from looking out as much as being looked upon, her muffled softness must be "wounded," "pierced through," and left behind if he is to be free. Enclosed in a world of surfaces and luxurious pleasures, she becomes herself an enclosure for the "piercing" spirit; all he has to do is abjure her and his newly sharpened eye will be able to pierce and claim not only "Earth, Ocean, Sun and Sky," but "their inmost wonders," too; "The World—nay, Heaven itself was mine!"

The web of "unnatural relationships," including Selim's "Greek" emasculation and the breath of incest that hovers over his and Zuleika's attachment, all proliferate from Giaffir's original unnatural act, the murder of his brother. It is possible, however, to look at the convoluted plot rather as a dramatization of dangerous desires: not just the autobiographical incestuous incident with Byron's half-sister Augusta, but the underlying desire for a return to childhood unity, the perfect harmony of androgyny that incest longs to recreate. The poem is haunted—and the reader constantly titillated—by the shadow of incest, which so energizes Byron's style that it seems almost to be the raison d'être of the plot. If the patriarch has unmanned him, he has also enabled Selim not to leave childhood, to live on in the paradise of incestuous fantasy. All sorts of narrative energy accumulates from this proximity to taboo. In the end, Giaffir, with his own appropriative designs on his daughter's sexuality, enacts the Oedipal role of the paternal principal, forcing Selim to utter the word that will make him free. Interestingly, that word is in fact a recognition of kinship with the old patriarch. Selim recovers his "manhood"—that is, his exclusive power of sight, thought, and language. Its price is the abandonment of the dream of (divine) union with one's sister / one's "Greek" self for mere (mortal) sexuality.

Zuleika in fact responds to the barely latent import of this speech as to a mortal wound:

> Oh! not my brother!—yet unsay—
> God! am I left alone on earth
> To mourn—I dare not curse—the day
> That saw my solitary birth?
> Oh! thou wilt love me now no more!
> My sinking heart foreboded ill;
> But know *me* all I was before,
> Thy sister—friend—Zuleika still.
> Thou led'st me here perchance to kill
> If thou hast cause for vengeance, see!
> My breast is offer'd—take thy fill!
> Far better with the dead to be
> Than live thus nothing now to thee!
> (Can. 2, st. 11)

The same "secret" that restores to Selim his identity as a man reveals to her her true identity: "dead" and "nothing." Although Selim insists at great length on their unbreakable bond and heroically tries to rescue her, the denouement of the poem confirms the original verdict: the sexual bond means separation and death. "Ah, wherefore did he turn to look" (can. 2, st. 25). Like Orpheus's, Selim's transgression is specular: the dead (woman) must not be looked at, cannot be brought out of the underworld into the light. She, transformed from a "sister" into a sexual object, reverts to her natural "original" state, death. She is transformed back into the eternally seductive, eternally death-oriented narcissus flower with which the Persephone myth began.

Both lovers die, but they leave instructively different traces. Zuleika's name is heard repeated—at least by imaginative listeners—by a nightingale, a "natural" singer:

> That note so piercing and profound
> Will shape and syllable its sound
> Into Zuleika's name.

'Tis from her cypress summit heard,
That melts in air the liquid word:
'Tis from her lowly virgin earth
That white rose takes its tender birth.
(Can. 2, st. 28)

The spot where Selim fell is marked neither by vegetation nor by melting, liquid sound, but by a "marble stone," placed by "no mortal arm" (can. 2, st. 28). Although it is incessantly washed by the waves, the trace left by Selim is permanent, cultural, inscribed in stone.

"The Fountain of Bakhchisarai"

Pushkin's second Southern Poem, "The Fountain of Bakhchisarai," quickly establishes its serial connection to "The Prisoner of the Caucasus" not only as another Oriental tale, but also as a further exploration of the Byronic equation east = passion = freedom. What did the east offer the westerner, or the south the Russian, that contributed to this trope? "The Prisoner of the Caucasus" quite clearly displayed the "epic life" of the natives as an attractively masculine code. The Russian's travels in space took him back in time to a precivilized era and values that offered him relief from the claustrophobic demands of salon and court. Many Russians became "Caucasianized," borrowing the vivid representation of "manhood" in horses, weapons, and violent mores of the natives they ostensibly had conquered.[27] The east moreover represented the opportunity to "indulge passions" proscribed by western society, to cross borders of class, gender, or "decency." The plot of the Oriental tale thus almost always hinges on cross-cultural sex, with the western/eastern distribution of values superimposed on the male/female relationship. On the passion of the Oriental beauty was inscribed her double submission to her lover's male and western authority. The great attraction of her passion was that it was nonbinding.

If the political implications are clear when we equate the Orient with a woman, we must also take into account the sexual-psychological implications of equating woman with the Orient—in other words, with "Orientalizing" sex. In the Oriental tale, the danger posed by a woman's unleashed sensuality was already contained by the eastern culture's patriarchal structures—for example, by the ubiquitous harem. The preoccupation with harems that runs through the popular and pornographic fictions of the nineteenth century reveals its true basis in sexual anxiety: the more feminine sexuality must be contained, mechanized, and surveyed before it can be approached, much less enjoyed, the more it is revealed as something alien and extremely dangerous to the male psyche.[28]

Pushkin took pains partly to conceal, partly to reveal the origins of his improbable story. The orally transmitted "legend of Bakhchisarai" related to Pushkin by Sofia Kiseleva (née Poniatowska) had connected the "Fountain of Tears" with a Polish captive, although all the documentary evidence pointed to a Christian Georgian girl.[29] Pushkin keeps both suppletive heroines. Of course the opposition of dark/light, passionate/spiritual, and "native"/European heroines was a cliché of Gothic and historical fiction; Scott, Byron's fictional mentor, often projects the conflicting cultural identities (archaic-Scottish versus modern-English) of his wavering hero onto two contrastive heroines, with predictable results.[30] The captive Georgian and Polish girls appear similarly to represent the two frontiers of Russian power and identity. The "south" is, canonically, where a Russian finds out if he is European or, after all, Asian, while Poland logically marks the boundary of a Russian's westernness.[31] The sexual encounter of Polish woman and Russian man is one of the places where the mutual relations of the two cultures might define themselves. Yet in "The Fountain of Bakhchisarai," as in the "Bride of Abydos," there is no such encounter. Or is there?

The world of Bakhchisarai is at first glance a closed Oriental system. Yet from the beginning Pushkin seems to invoke Byron's clichés only to question them. The poem opens as the "Bride of Abydos" did, with a description of the immobile tyrant bending his court to the least expression of his eyes, thought, and will:

> Гирей сидел, потупя взор;
> Янтарь в устах его дымился;
> Безмолвно раболепный двор
> Вкруг хана грозного теснился.
> Все было тихо во дворце;

Благоговея, все читали
Приметы гнева и печали
На сумрачном его лице.
(4, 155)

Girei sat, with downcast eyes; the amber in his mouth smoked; mutely the slavish court pressed around the terrible khan. All was still in the palace; reverently all read the signs of anger and sadness on his overcast face.

The silence and lowered eyes, mingled anger and sadness are so unusual, make the tyrant so illegible to his anxious court, that they literally "read" his face for signs of his intentions. All glances, actions, events are supposed to issue from him. Yet, as the poem opens, the tyrant is strangely paralyzed, a "spectacle"—or perhaps more accurately, an illegible text—to his court. What is his secret, the narrator asks. Is he planning a new war, á la Giaffir, or angered by the incursion of a giaour into his harem? The Byronic clichés are brushed aside. Yet there has been an incursion; the image of patriarchal power has been undermined from within.

Typically, the harem is the place from which all thought, desire, events, and time itself have been evacuated. The women within its precincts must live veiled—"utaeny ikh krasoty" (4, 156)—yet open to eternal inspection. The harem is defined, by contrast with the khan, as the place that has no secrets, that is all spectacle. Here, too, Pushkin's treatment of the Oriental women has a nuance different from Byron's, which treats the shades of Zuleika's skin and the luxurious objects in her room as quite adequate descriptions of Zuleika herself; her life of enclosure and childish luxury fits her like a glove. Pushkin's harem is a prison strictly patrolled by the eunuch, a place where not only thought and will but even pleasure are sniffed out and punished, where life by means of unchanging order is supposed to be transmuted into inanimate matter, a still life. Yet in Pushkin's harem, life resists; even in the poem's genre scenes—girls bathing in a fountain, and so on—the scene's purely specular aesthetics is constantly undermined by internal tension. The situation of perpetual surveillance, the constant effort to ferret out invisible psychological movements and turn them into legible signs and motionless spectacle, is nicely captured in the typical Orientalist conceit of the goldfish bowl:[32]

Беспечно ожидая хана,
Вокруг игривого фонтана
На шелковых коврах оне
Толпою резвою сидели
И с детской радостью глядели,
Как рыба в ясной глубине
На мраморном ходила дне.
Нарочно к ней на дно иные
Роняли серьги золотые.
(4, 158)

Carelessly awaiting the khan, around the playful fountain on silken carpets they sat, in a lively crowd, and with childish joy gazed as the fish moved in the bright depths on the marble bottom. Others deliberately tossed their golden earrings to it [her] at the bottom.

The concentric specular structure of this scene is clear: the fish is watched by the girls, who are perpetually surveyed by the eunuch, who is in turn "motionless and not daring to breathe," constantly awaiting "a sign" from the khan (4, 158). The cycle should end here: before the khan, all doors are, in theory, "wide open" (*nastezh'*). One place only is excluded from the universal system of surveillance:

И между тем, как все вокруг
В безумной неге утопает,
Святыню строгую скрывает
Спасенный чудом уголок.
(4, 162)

Meanwhile, as everything around drowns in mad luxury, a little corner, miraculously saved, conceals a strict shrine.

The enumeration of mute, luxurious objects in Zuleika's room in every way confirmed the poem's "Orientalist" structures of value, particularly its evaluation of women as soft, sensual, empty-headed, and specular. The room in which the Polish girl Maria is held captive is instead an oasis of spirituality that exerts a powerful negative effect on the space of the harem:

Угрюмый сторож ханских жен
Ни днем, ни ночью к ней не входит:
Рукой заботливой не он

На ложе сна ее возводит;
Не смеет устремиться к ней
Обидный взор его очей; . . .
Сам хан боится девы пленной
Печальный возмущать покой;
Гарема в дальнем отделенье

Позволено ей жить одной:
И, мнится, в том уединенье
Сокрылся некто неземной.
Там день и ночь горит лампада
Пред ликом девы пресвятой.
(4, 162)

The gloomy guard of the khan's wives enters neither night nor day: not he with a solicitous hand leads her to the bed of sleep; nor does he dare to cast on her the offensive gaze of his eyes; . . . The khan himself fears to disturb the sad peace of the imprisoned girl; in a distant part of the harem she is permitted to live alone; and, it seems, in that solitude is concealed someone unearthly. There day and night a lamp burns before the visage of the blessed virgin.

Here all the rules of the harem are negated: a light shines perpetually, yet tolerates no observation; solitude and individuality replace the inevitable plural anonymity of the "light throng" of harem girls; a single religious icon takes the place of luxurious objects and pleasures; and personal memory is opposed to the timeless, historyless monotony of the harem. Above all, the spiritual power of an otherwise weak and inexperienced girl forces physical and political strength to respect it.

If criticism has had a kind word to say about "The Fountain of Bakhchisarai," it has been praise for the passionate character of Zarema, permitted by Pushkin to aggressively articulate her desires. This, however, is the one thing the Oriental woman is permitted to do without inhibition: to express passionate and sensuous desire for a man. If Zarema somewhat exceeds her traditional role, it is in ferociously claiming possession of him:

Отдай мне пржнего Гирея...
Не возражай мне ничего;
Он мой! он ослеплен тобою.
Презреньем, просьбою, тоскою,

Чем хочешь, отврати его;
Клянись . . .
Но слушай: если я должна
Тебе... кинжалом я владею,
Я близ Кавказа рождена.
(4, 166–67)

Give me back Girei as he was... Don't argue with me; he is mine! He is blinded by you. Use contempt, prayers, grief, whatever you want, to turn him away; swear. . . . But listen: if I have to... I know how to use a dagger, I was born near the Caucasus.

The ferocity of Zarema's physical desire essentially justifies the structures devised to contain it, to seal off the man's world of thought and action from the woman's world of "mad sensuality" (*bezumnaia nega*), undifferentiated fusion, and death.

Pushkin has been praised for the progressive humanization of his passionate heroines, for "giving them a voice." In each of the Southern Poems a "native girl" goes a little further in asserting her passion, escaping male enclosure into individualism and language. In each of them she dies. In fact, in "The Prisoner" and "The Fountain" she dies an elliptical, hidden death that returns her to water, silence, and undifferentiation without a trace. Only in "The Gypsies," where the male/female roles are most sharply (and threateningly) reversed, does Zemphira die defiantly before our eyes, shouting "Umiraiu liubia!" (I die loving!). The two words could not be jammed more closely together. In "The Fountain of Bakhchisarai," Zarema must die for two reasons: because she represents the Orient and because her cry "On moi!" (He's mine!) has articulated the danger of uncontrolled female passion. The Oriental woman—that is, feminine sexuality as the dangerous "other"—must be put down.

Is Maria's fate essentially the same? It has been suggested in a recent study that "the scandal" of Pushkin's poem is the secret "equality" of the two seemingly opposed women. They are both prisoners, they both rebel against their fate, they both die, and their deaths are mysteriously hidden from view.[33] I would suggest, nevertheless, that Pushkin's plot has interesting but firmly Orientalist implications. It shakes certain expectations in order to confirm others.

It begins with an omnipotent Oriental tyrant, only to reveal him as paralyzed, emasculated by passion. It begins with a harem full of passive, mute, and anonymous women-objects, only to cede the role of actor, aggressor, and speaker to two highly individualized women. It begins with a closed Oriental society—not a giaour, not a westerner in sight—and yet depicts the conquest from within of that society. It begins with a male conqueror and a woman captive, and shows the reversal of their roles: the conqueror "unmanned" by his captive, not because she is more beautiful, more passionate, more determined, but because she is the bearer of western values. Her culture conquers.

Zarema admits that she has forgotten her mother's religion, her childhood, and the circumstances of her abduction. She has no memory or past values to act as a restraint on her passions. Byron's Zuleika, defying her father's authority to unite with her brother, leaves behind in her room several comparable objects:

> Near these, with emerald rays beset,
> (How could she thus that gem forget?)
> Her mother's sainted amulet,
> Whereon engraved the Koorsee text,
> Could smooth this life, and win the next;
> And by her comboloio lies
> A Koran of illumined dyes;
> And many a bright emblazon'd rhyme
> By Persian scribes redeem'd from time.
> (Can. 2, st. 5)

The "Koorsee (throne) verse in the second cap. of the Koran," Byron explains in a footnote, "describes the attributes of the Most High, and is engraved in this manner, and worn by the pious, as the most esteemed and sublime of all sentences"; while "comboloio" is "a Turkish rosary." Like Zarema, Zuleika has forgotten the inscriptions, the patriarchal writings that would keep her, like her mother, in her place, in her room, protected from this life for the sake of "the next." When Zarema and Zuleika leave their rooms, forget where they came from, reach out (and speak out) for their passion, they die.

What a contrast, then, Maria is. Instead of trying to get out, she escapes inward; instead of forgetting, she remembers, and forces others to remember where she came from; far from forgetting her religious icons, she sets the Virgin Mary in the middle of her bare little room and tends the flame. Notably, her memories are of a childhood of purity, in which she was protected and pampered by her father. Not surprisingly, she is frightened most by Zarema's articulate and all-too-womanly outburst:

Невинной деве непонятен
Язык мучительных страстей,
Но голос их ей смутно внятен,
Он странен, он ужасен ей.
(4, 167)

To the innocent maiden the language of passions is incomprehensible, but their voice is faintly audible, strange and terrible to her.

Almost without passing through a bodily death, Maria disappears from the face of the earth, called back "like a new angel" to her "native heaven." Contrast—on the same night—the equally mysterious disappearance of Zarema downward into "the chaos of the waters." Were these two fully realized women, or two parables about the two halves of feminine or even human "nature," each with its own exemplary denouement? Zuleika's name, we saw, is preserved in the syllables uttered by the nightingale, as opposed to the marble pillar that enshrines Selim's memory. Zarema's body and voice leave no trace at all. Maria has also disappeared into silence, but her memory has left an indelible mark on the khan's will, so on history itself, and finally, through his inscription, on stone, on legend, and on art:

... В Тавриду возвратился хан
И в память горестной Марии
Воздвигнул мраморный фонтан,
В углу дворца уединенный.
Над ним крестом осенена
Магометанская луна
(Символ, конечно, дерзновенный,
Незнанья жалкая вина).
Есть надпись: едкими годами
Еще не сгладилась она.
За чуждыми ее чертами
Журчит во мраморе вода

И каплет хладными слезами,
Не умолкая никогда.

(4, 169)

The khan returned to Tavrida and in memory of grieving Maria he erected a marble fountain in a secluded corner of the palace. Over it the Mohammedan moon is shielded by a cross (a brazen symbol, of course, the fault of pitiful ignorance). There is an inscription: the corrosive years have not yet worn it away. Behind its (her) foreign features the water bubbles in the marble and drips cold tears, never falling silent.

Her name itself is almost effaced, yet it continues to give rise to legend, art, culture, while Zarema's passion reverted to nature, leaving no trace.

What are the implications of this conclusion? Pushkin himself calls (his own) symbol of the overshadowing of the Moslem crescent moon by the Christian cross "brazen," but this is indeed one of the stories he has told: the story of one culture infiltrated from within by the values of another. Precisely because in Maria sexuality does not have to be contained by the physical walls of a harem, but is culturally restrained, sublimated into "spirit," she is enshrined, culturally inscribed. Meanwhile, the passionate heroines who give voice not to the sacred texts of their culture but to their individual bodies and desires die in silence. The "fountain of tears" is the perfect mediating symbol for the woman's story, shaping as it does the elemental chaos and perpetual flow of water into a permanent cultural form. Its language is not the lucid language of reason, but the foreign babble of hidden, underground emotions, silent women's stories.

But that is not all the fountain of Bakhchisarai implies. Every Turkish Tale refers somehow to the sources of Byron's own creativity. Indeed, travel to Oriental lands is commensurate with the culture's search, the poet's search for origins, unconscious springs. In its last two pages Pushkin steps outside his own tale and essentially interprets its allegory for the reader. He tells us that at the time of his visit to the dead, silent ruins of Bakhchisarai, he was preoccupied with "forgetting" his own past life in the north. Banished from the feasts of the capital, he filled the dead shell of the ruined palace with memories, visions, and finally language: "I visited . . . I wandered . . . I saw. . . I saw." Foreign feasts spring up, "the harem's women breathe again," the silent stone monuments speak "in audible language." "Where have the khans disappeared, where is the harem?" (4, 169–70), Pushkin asks, but then dismisses his own question. He was never interested in the history itself, which is why he diverged so freely from its factual basis. In the conclusion of the poem Pushkin encourages his reader to view his story as Byron's readers viewed his Turkish Tales, as an allegorical representation of the poet's otherwise hidden and unspeakable psychic underworld.

> Все изменилось... но не тем
> В то время сердце полно было:
> Дыханием роз, фонтанов шум
> Влекли к невольному забвенью,
> Невольно предавался ум
> Неизъяснимому волненью,
> И по дворцу летучей тенью
> Мелькала дева предо мной!..
> . . . .
> Чью тень, о други видел я?
> (4, 170)

Everything had changed... but that is not what my heart was then full of; the breath of the roses, the rush of the fountains induced an involuntary oblivion, involuntarily my mind submitted to an ineffable agitation, and around the palace like a flying shade the maiden flitted before me!.. Whose shade, O friends, did I see?

As willed language dissolves into the involuntary bubbling of the unconscious, a figure coalesces, a shade. The stories of Bakhchisarai emerged, the poet implies, from an underground source of memory, pain, and "madness" that can only be gestured at: the underground part of the poet's own memories that cannot be transcribed directly into legible text but can only flow involuntarily into the "foreign" language of an Oriental woman's tale. Here, at the end of "The Fountain of Bakhchisarai," Pushkin appears to articulate to himself the substitutive function of "historical imagination" for lyrical memory.

Then *opomnis'*, Pushkin orders himself: not "remember" but "stop remembering," push memory back down, out of language and into the underground. And he closes the poem with a rejection of the underground feminine psyche he has inadvertently, as it were, revealed to the reader, for the freedom of insatiable sight, the pure and masculine spectacle of the south:

> О, скоро вас увижу вновь,
> Брега веселые Салгира! . . .
> Волшебный край, очей отрада! . . .
> Когда, в час утра безмятежный,
> В горах, дорогою прибрежнои,
> Привычный конь его бежит
> И зеленеющая влага
> Пред ним и блещет, и шумит
> Вокруг утесов Аю-дага...
>
> (4, 171)

O will I soon see you again, gay banks of the Salgir! . . . Magical land, delight of the eyes! . . . When at an untroubled morning hour, along a mountain path beside the shore, his accustomed horse runs and the moisture turns green and sparkles before him, and roars around the cliffs of Aiu-Dag...

In the last, rather puzzling lines of the poem Pushkin performs a series of dismissive gestures: he reveals that the historical story he has told is just a substitutive projection of his own secret memories; then he dismisses the backward-turned elegiac imagination for the present tense of the masculine body in space, no longer an "I" troubled by internal demons but a liberated "he." Our last image of Pushkin, in contrast to the downcast, paralyzed, and obsessed Girei of the opening stanza, is a figure of bold and masculine freedom, unencumbered again by either sexuality (Zarema) or memory (Maria). As soon as the troubled psyche has bodied forth its energies in these exotic feminine forms, they become expendable, can be killed. The (feminine) source is left behind, the strange (masculine) inscription remains, and the reader is tantalized by the erased track between the two. "When will I return to immerse myself in those streams?" Pushkin asks, then projects his feeling of cathartic liberation from his *poema* into one last enviable image of "himself," galloping away.

Pushkin was ambivalent about "The Fountain of Bakhchisarai," alternately rejoicing that it was "making a splash," worrying that it exposed his secrets,[34] and calling it trash. "Between ourselves," he confided to Viazemsky, "the Fountain of Bakhchisarai is rotten, but its epigraph is delightful"; and "I modelled myself on the Eastern style of speech, as far as that is possible for us rational, cold Europeans."[35] This did not prevent him from requesting Viazemsky's full participation:

Here, my dear and worthy Asmodaeus, is my latest poem for you. I have thrown out what the censors would have thrown out for me, and also what I did not wish to expose before the public. If these disconnected fragments strike you as being worth printing then have them published; but do me a favour, don't give in to that bitch of a censorship, bare your teeth over every verse and, should it prove possible, tear her to pieces for my sake. Except for you I have no protector *there*. One further request: write a foreword or a postscript to Bakhchisarai... I am enclosing a police report as source material, glean some facts from it (but obviously don't mention the source). Also look up the article on Bakhchisarai in Apostol-Muraviev's Travels and copy out the more tolerable passages—and then cast the spell of your prose over it all.[36]

When Pushkin decided to reprint the poem in 1830, he did not forget about the sine qua non of a "European eye," but he created it himself from a collage of framing documents. "Fragment from a Letter to D.," a casual description of Pushkin's impressions of his travels in 1820, written in 1824 for Anton Del'vig's almanac *Northern Flowers*, was now paired contrapuntally with an excerpt from I. M. Murav'ev-Apostol's learned *Journey in Tavrida*. The attachment of the two consecutive afterwords fulfills among other things precisely this function: it encloses Pushkin's Oriental gem in a cold, rational, "European" frame.

I immediately left for the so-called tomb of Mithridates (the ruins of some tower); there I picked a flower as a souvenir and lost it the next day without any regret at all. The ruins of Pantikapea acted no more forcefully on my imagination. I saw traces of streets, a half-overgrown ditch, old bricks and nothing more . . . "That's Chatyrdag"—the captain told me. I couldn't make it out, nor was I curious to. (8.1, 437)

Even a visit to Bakhchisarai evokes the same alienation:

K** had poetically described it to me, calling it *la fontaine des larmes*. Entering the palace, I saw a broken fountain; from a rusty iron pipe water dripped drop by drop. I walked around the palace greatly irritated by the neglect in which it is decaying, and by the half-European alterations to some of the rooms. I.I. led me almost by force down the decrepit staircase to the ruins of the harem and to the khan's cemetery:

But not with this
Was my heart at that time filled:

I was tormented with fever. (8.1, 438–39)

As Iu. M. Lotman points out, the world of poetry is presented as foreign—indeed illegible—to the author.[37] He quotes his own lines sarcastically and out of context. It is worth pointing out that Pushkin actually left out the more poetic sections of the original letter, the verses to Chaadaev that "visited him" at the temple of Diana, and the last paragraph, whose meditation on the elegiac logic of his psyche would have significantly softened the letter's function as a coldly prosaic, even amnesiac, contrasting frame: "Now explain this to me: Why do the southern shore and Bakhchisarai have such an ineffable charm for me? Why is the desire so strong in me to visit places, left by me with such indifference? Or is memory the strongest capability of our soul, bewitching everything in its domain?" (8.2, 435). Pushkin deliberately designed his notes in prose as the negation or marked absence of poetry and lyrical inspiration. Deprived of the lyrical energy he had invested in the fictional image of his loss, his description disintegrates into a series of separate, meaningless details, compared with which even Murav'ev-Apostol's travel notes seem poetic.

Pushkin's appendix thus transforms his poem. Its composition covers about ten years of his life, from the initial trip with Raevsky to the notes dated 1830, and completes the Romantic theme of ruins in an unexpected way: not only the poetic legends but even the poet's own eyewitness reports conflict. The contrast between poetry and prose is used to portray the erosion by time not only of the architectural ruin, but also of the lyrical sensibility through which it was filtered. In an elegy Pushkin might simply have lamented his lost youth and freshness of perception; but, as he himself remarked, "Our literature will not go far on memories of departed youth."[38] The effect here is more piquant and complex because it is dramatized through an ironic juxtaposition of styles. The final format of "The Fountain" thus has something in common with the sophisticated structure of "Journey to

Arzrum," which embeds reminiscences of his first Romantic poems in the mature Pushkin's dispassionate account of his recent travels. Both turn out to be lyrical self-portraits, with overt irony and covert poignancy contrasting the style and the mind of Pushkin in 1820 and 1830.

Not only the Romantic setting of "The Fountain of Bakhchisarai" but Pushkin himself become objects of a "dialogized" vision. What is curious is that the addition of some rather ungainly and disharmonious appendixes in 1830 actually did "assure the fate of his verses,"[39] rescuing their fragile lyricism from the stale exoticism of his second Byronic tale. Pushkin understood that on its own, in the present, "The Fountain" was already an anachronism; yet set back in the past and virtually disowned by its author, it became, like an inscription in a forgotten language, a miraculously preserved fragment of an irretrievably vanished vision.

Pushkin's "Journey to Arzrum": The Poet at the Border

"Who needs travel? I do all my traveling in my head," said Pushkin, not quite ingenuously, toward the end of his life (13, 280).[40] In fact, Pushkin's chronic desire for travel had so often been frustrated or deflected that his loudly lamented exile in the early 1820's to the Caucasus, Crimea, Bessarabia, and Odessa in retrospect came to represent the peripatetic freedom of his youth. When in 1829 Pushkin and Viazemsky were refused permission to travel to Paris, Pushkin embarked instead on the illicit trip south that would become the basis for his literary "Journey to Arzrum" six years later. In 1836, with a rueful backward glance at the Orientalist fashion he himself had helped to launch in Russian poetry, Pushkin wrote, "I plead guilty: I would give everything which has been written here in imitation of Lord Byron for the following spontaneous and unimpassioned lines in which the poet makes his hero exclaim to his friends, 'Friends! sisters! I'm in Paris! I have begun to live as well as breathe!'"[41]

And perhaps the exuberant first words of an unfinished drama, "In a week I'll definitely be in Paris!" represent a vestige of that never-to-be-realized desire.[42] In short, if the south served as an escape valve for dreams of uninhibited motion and adventure, it was also a surrogate, marking the boundaries rather than the fulfillment of that freedom. Not surprisingly, then, the theme of the seductive border crossing is central to the "Journey to Arzrum": "Arpachai! Our border! I galloped toward it with an inexpressible feeling. I had never yet seen foreign soil. The border had something mysterious for me; since childhood, travel had been my favorite dream. Later I led a nomadic life, wandering now around the south, now the north, and had never yet broken beyond the bounds of unencompassable Russia" (8.1, 463).

"Journey to Arzrum," written by Pushkin in 1835, was a revision of his Caucasian travel diary of 1829,[43] which itself represented a revisitation of the southern landscapes first witnessed during his earlier exile in 1820–23. This embedded structure reinforces Pushkin's nostalgic comparison of the Caucasus then, "nine years ago," and now;[44] space becomes a marker of time. Simultaneously, the embedded structure forces the reader to recognize space as textual space, as a product of descriptive fashion. The reader who juxtaposes the "south" of Pushkin's Southern Poems with the same geographical regions traversed by his traveler discovers that they are systematically inverted.[45] In the early 1820's Pushkin had used the place of his enforced exile to incarnate the Romantic trope of imprisonment as spiritual freedom.[46] Thus in the opening lines of the epilogue to "The Prisoner of the Caucasus," Pushkin clearly appropriated the wild freedom of the native tribes and the plummeting mountain landscape to fashion his own poetic persona:

> Так Муза, легкий друг мечты,
> К пределам Азии летала
> И для венка себе срывала
> Кавказа дикие цветы.
> Ее пленял наряд суровый
> Племен возросших на войне,
> И часто в сей одежде новой
> Волшебница являлась мне.
>
> (4, 113)

Thus the muse, light friend of dream, flew to the borders of Asia and plucked for her wreath the wild flowers of the Caucasus. She was captivated by the rough garb of tribes raised on war, and often in this new outfit the enchantress would appear to me.

Turning the tables on the space of his imprisonment, the poet converted his central image of captivity into *captivation*—a punning emblem of his inventive freedom.

In 1829 the situation was reversed. Willfully tearing through the net of restrictions that had tightened around his professional and personal life since his return to the capital, Pushkin bolted.[47] With one motion he exchanged political surveillance, literary pressures, and multiple romantic commitments for an interlude of adventure in the geographically distant, un-Russian, and largely male theater of war in the south. The escape was enacted in space, yet, as Pushkin implied in an unpublished fragment, it masked a different quest:

Желал я душу освежить,
Бывалой жизнью пожить
В забвенье сладком близ друзей
Минувшей юности моей.
Я ехал в дальние края
Ни шумных... жаждал я,
Искал ни злата, ни честей
В пыли средь копий и мечей.
(3.1, 468)

I wanted to refresh my soul, live the old life awhile, in sweet oblivion near the friends of my evanescent youth. I was traveling to distant lands, I had no desire for loud... I sought neither gold nor honor in the dust amid the spears and swords.

As in "Journey to Arzrum," the object of his quest is defined by negations and omissions, absences. Pushkin seeks in this return to the spaces he had traversed and described "nine years ago" a respite from contemporaneity, from the impetus of time itself: "to refresh his soul" is "to live the old life." One might say that the trip to Arzrum creates the same structural escape hatch that Eugene Onegin's journey, the excised penultimate chapter, does in Pushkin's novel: by means of a detour into purely spatial narrative, the journey postpones the impending temporal denouement, the plot's end.

In undertaking the trip illicitly, without the permission of A. K.

Benckendorff (the head of the secret police) and without a travel pass, Pushkin was also laying claim to one of the gentlemanly prerogatives of which he had been systematically stripped: that freedom to travel that in Russia was one of the marks of differentiation between the land-bound peasant, the legally restricted merchant, and the "unmarked" landowner.[48] Like his famous predecessor in passportless, gentlemanly travel, Sterne's Yorick,[49] Pushkin bolted from Russia in order to experience at least the negative freedom of nationlessness, namelessness, or, to use Victor Turner's well-known term, liminality:

> The attributes of liminality or of liminal *personae* ("threshold people") are necessarily ambiguous since this condition and these persons elude or slip through the network of classifications that normally locate states and positions in cultural space. . . . Their ambiguous and indeterminate attributes are expressed by a rich variety of symbols in the many societies that ritualize social and cultural transitions.[50]

Common attributes of the threshold figure or group cited by Turner are anonymity, invisibility, nakedness, silence (the state of being a blank slate), sexlessness (or symbolic hermaphroditism), twinning, sexual continence, acceptance of pain and danger, and laughter. If Pushkin's journey in some ways mimics a "rite of passage" from a state of separation to a new, stable state of social reincorporation, that victory, as we shall see, will be a hollow one. However, the intervening liminal or marginal period, the immersion in unstructured *communitas* described by Turner, does correspond in many points to Pushkin's experiences on the margins of the Arzrum campaign.

Throughout his journey confusion surrounds his name and profession: Ermolov doesn't remember Pushkin's full name, he travels in the convoy of a nominal double, Count Pushkin, from whom he periodically detaches himself, he is regularly mistaken for a Frenchman, a doctor, and a dervish. Like Yorick, he penetrates into all manner of forbidden enclosures: the four walls of Ermolov's house arrest, the tent-like enclosure with a single aperture at the top in which Pushkin encounters the Kalmyk Circe, the Ossetian funeral, the women's baths in Tiflis, the Turkish harem, the Moslem citadel of Arzrum, even the "sanctuary" of nature, encircled by its Caucasian peaks. His incongruous outfits (the top hat he sports among the military uniforms, the Turkish fez recollected by his contemporaries in their memoirs)[51] serve as disguises, *shapki nevidimki*, guaranteeing his incognito as a nameless gentleman but also disqualifying him as a male (to the women at the baths where he has been admitted on "women's day" he is invisible, not a man).[52] Unlike Yorick, he has no faith in the traveler's ability to negotiate his way—sexually, monetarily, sentimentally, or verbally—around the various borders that divide cultures, classes, and genders, to go, in Sterne's memorable phrase, "translating all the way."

Borders in Pushkin's travel diary are neither readily translatable nor negotiable. In the comical encounter with the Kalmyk girl, there is finally no common denominator even of sexuality to bridge the barriers of language, food, and differently articulated gender roles. Cultural differences actually invert gender roles, as Pushkin makes clear in their brief comic exchange: "A young Kalmyk girl, not bad looking at all, sat sewing and smoking tobacco. 'What's your name?'—'***.' —'How old are you?' 'Ten and eight.'—'What are you sewing?'—'Britches.'—'For whom?'—'Myself.'—She handed me her pipe and started breakfast" (8.1, 447).

The poem he eventually addresses to her ("To a Kalmyk Girl") may be a Sternean tribute to the permeability of cultural barriers to desire, but it will never be read by its addressee. Instead Pushkin will reemphasize its noncommunicative status by letting it serve, at a Turkish identity check, as his missing travel pass: "Judging by the Asiatic features of his face, I did not think it necessary to search through my papers, and pulled out of my pocket the first scrap I came across. The officer, inspecting it importantly, ordered horses to be brought for his honor at once and returned my paper to me: it was the epistle to a Kalmyk girl, scribbled by me at one of the Caucasian stations" (8.1, 465). The implication is a mockingly Sternean one: Pushkin writes his own identity, but that identity is illegible.

Conversely, at an Ossetian funeral Pushkin carefully notes down the external customs he is witnessing, appends an "appropriate" quotation from the Irish poet Charles Wolfe,[53] but then admits, "No one could explain these rites to me" (8.1, 450). For Pushkin the various cultural enclosures are impregnable, attempts at communication turn to misunderstanding, and sentiment offers a conduit not to the "other," across the border, but back to oneself. The most important border is not geographical, but temporal, the underlying journey a personal search for time past.

That Pushkin presents in a prosaic ("realistic") light locales and incidents described or experienced more poetically in his earlier works has been pointed out by many.[54] But Pushkin not only "demystifies" the Romantic clichés of his youth, he is also attracted to them. For example, he nostalgically compares the hot springs with their more primitive aspect "in my time":

> I admit that the Caucasian waters are now more convenient, but I missed their former wild state; I missed the steep rocky paths, shrubs, and unguarded precipices over which I used to clamber. . . . Soon night fell. The pure sky was scattered with millions of stars. . . . Here, in the olden days, A. Raevsky used to sit with me, listening to the melody of the waters. (8.1, 447)

Slightly less explicitly, Pushkin alludes in passing to the locales and subjects of his Southern Poems: "The mountains stretched above us. On their peaks crawled barely visible herds, like insects. We distinguished a shepherd, perhaps a Russian, once captured and aged in slavery" (8.1, 448). Two pages later, Pushkin finds a blotched copy of "The Prisoner of the Caucasus" itself and "reads it with great satisfaction. It was all weak, youthful, incomplete; but a great deal was discerned and expressed correctly" (8.1, 451).[55] Soon after that, Pushkin verifies his original feeling of indifference on witnessing dramatic Caucasian landscapes in the past: "I rode by Kazbek as indifferently as I once floated past Chatyrdag. It's true that the rainy and cloudy weather prevented me from seeing its snowy pile, as a poet put it, *propping up the horizon*" (8.1, 452).

The point is not only that Pushkin fails to respond to a poetic cliché, but that he is also *repeating* the earlier moment recorded in his travel account "A Fragment from a Letter to D." That apparently anti-Romantic piece had in fact ended with an unexpected tribute to the inspirational power of nostalgia. "Why do the southern shore and Bakhchisarai have such an ineffable charm for me?" (8.1, 439). Accordingly, Pushkin's second glimpse of Kazbek, on his return from Arzrum to Russia, does yield a poetic "epiphany" in prose as well as the lyric "Monastery on Kazbek":

In the morning, riding by Kazbek, I witnessed a miraculous sight: torn white clouds stretched across the peak of the mountain, and a solitary monastery, illuminated by the rays of the sun, appeared to float in the air, borne by the clouds. The raging Balka also manifested itself to me in all its greatness. (8.1, 482)

It is a poem that is *not* included in the "Journey" that translates this landscape of isolation and unleashed rage back into a Romantic image of escape:

Высоко над семьею гор,
Казбек, твой царственный шатер
Сияет вечными лучами.
Твой монастырь за облаками,
Как в небе реющий ковчег,
Парит, чуть видный, над горами.
Далекий, вожделенный брег!
Туда б, сказав прости ущелью,
Подняться к вольной вышине!
Туда б, в заоблачную келью,
В соседство бога скрыться мне![56]
(3.1, 200)

High above the family of mountains, Kazbek, your regal tent radiates eternal rays. Your monastery beyond the clouds, like an ark soaring in the sky, floats barely visible above the mountains. Distant, longed for shore! Thither, bidding farewell to the gorge, would that I could rise to the free heights! Thither, in a cell beyond the clouds, to hide myself near God!

One way of looking at the peculiar alienated space of Pushkin's "Journey to Arzrum," which has attracted the attention of so many Modernist critics,[57] is as the iconic representation of the absence of the poet's "I" (and eye) from his text. Pushkin insisted in his preface to the "Journey" on its essential privacy: it was not an ode or epic, not a satire, not a quest for poetic inspiration, but simply the notes of a gentleman.[58] By 1835, however, journals and newspapers were bursting with a new kind of travelogue, the Oriental journey, often undertaken by professional commercial travelers and specialists. They generated their own conventions of landscape description and spatial symbolism, which I will discuss in the following pages. Rewriting his "Journey" in 1835 for publication in his recently approved journal, *The Contemporary*,[59] Pushkin had to clear a space for himself in the overgrown forest of European and Russian Orientalist writing. When Józef Sękowski crammed the pages of his own best-selling publication, *The Library for Reading*, with translations and reviews of European journeys to the east and Middle East ("Jerusalem in 1831," "England and China," "Egypt in 1833") and explicitly drew the Russian public's attention to the international commercial rivalry underlying European travelers' journeys to Central Asia,[60] he was encouraging Russians to follow Napoleon's path-breaking strategy in Egypt in 1798: "Describe and conquer."[61]

Pushkin was by no means oblivious to this frame of reference. He sandwiches his own "Journey to Arzrum" between two French texts. In his preface he scathingly polemicizes with Victor Fontané's recent *Voyages to the Orient Undertaken by Order of the French Government*, while the elaborate anthropological findings of a six-page "Notice on the Yezidis," appended to his own "Journey" in full and in French, are casually contradicted by his own account (8.1, 468). Traces of a polemic with other travelers' "learned associations" are scattered throughout "Journey to Arzrum"; for example, Pushkin wryly comments on the historical background he has just provided for the Darial post: "See the travels of Count J. Potocki, whose learned investigations are as entertaining as Spanish novels" (8.1, 452). As he alerts the reader to the national interests that lie behind the anthropological, linguistic, geographical, and religious masks of the travelogue, Pushkin calls attention to the collision of European and Russian Orientalist discourses in the "south."

In describing Asia, Russian travelers were not only inventing and propagating their version of "eastern" geography but establishing Russia's right to be identified with the practitioners of Orientalism. As Chaadaev wrote in his *Philosophical Letter* of 1836, whether Russia belonged to Europe's historical destiny was still a moot point.[62] And as Pushkin warned, "Ancient history is the history of Egypt, Persia, Greece, and Rome. Modern history is the history of Christianity. Woe to the country that finds itself outside of the European system!"[63] The purpose of Russia's Orientalist policy was to assure her place within the European system, as an equal and a contemporary. When Russia's expanding space became interpretable as a western-Orientalist mission to civilize Asia, Russia would annex for herself a place in European and global history.

This brings us to the final substitution so germinal for the discourse of travel: the transformation of space, and space-as-history, into textual space. Oriental travel was preeminently a system of citation from other textual authorities; a typical traveler collated his own experiences with those of his predecessors, hence the enormous apparatus of footnotes and appendixes that attached itself to the genre. Knowledge was a survey of a civilization from its origins to its decline, an anthologist's display of specimens severed from their native context, in essence, an autopsy. For the purposes of the investigation the culture was assumed to be "dead," in a state of arrested development, no longer capable of knowing or naming itself. Hence the recurrent emphasis on ancient inscriptions, obsolete and illegible testimony to the muteness and deadness of their cultures, yet restored to meaningful participation in the history of civilization by western decipherment and display.[64]

Poets, while claiming for themselves a different status and relationship to the East from that of ordinary travelers, often contributed in a significant way to the reshaping of Oriental space in the popular perception. As Said shows, Byron, Chateaubriand, Alphonse de Lamartine, and Hugo undertook their literary travels as misfits, political or moral exiles from their native societies, in the name of greater personal and imaginative freedom. Nevertheless, over the course of his poetic/religious *Itinerary*, Chateaubriand manages to reiterate many clichés of Orientalist discourse, from comparing his pilgrimage to Napoleon's last crusade to concluding that the West must bring the enslaved Asians true liberty by conquering them. Lamartine, declaring his *Voyage en Orient*, published in 1835, to be "a great act of my inner life," resolves to become the Dante of the Jews, Egyptians, and Hindus against Rome and the West. He is, nevertheless, quite incapable of viewing an Oriental landscape without inserting into it Circe, Biblical poetry, and comparisons to the paintings of Nicolas Poussin and Claude Lorrain.[65] Byron's tales might speak of political rebellion, exotic sexual and moral crimes, and unspeakable wounds, but their annotations offer a very different perspective and persona: that of the chatty, expert, insatiably curious and intrepid European, penetrator and describer of other cultures' secrets. As a result, from Portugal to St. Petersburg, from Albania to Asia Minor, Byronic verses became the inscriptions that humanized, Europeanized, the foreign landscape, inscribing it indelibly on the traveler's and reader's map as a "Byronic place."[66] Pushkin's own Southern Poems had performed this same inscribing function for the territories on the southern border of the Russian empire.

Thus travel to the Orient always took place in a densely populated textual space, in constant reference to the crisscrossing tracks of other travelers. Often described overtly as a desert, a place of solitary exploration and private reality, the Oriental space was also a meeting ground for Europeans, a space densely coated with descriptive writing to which each new traveler tipped his hat as he went. Pushkin's "Journey" both acknowledges the commentaries of previous travelers and wryly questions the convention. His "notes of a gentleman" represent an attempt to disengage himself from Orientalist discourse, both professional and poetic, and clear a space for his own journey in the overpopulated space of literary travel. Yet his sympathetic and ironic review of A. N. Murav'ev's *Journey to the Holy Land*, written in 1832, had already suggested his awareness of the difficulty of such an endeavor:

> With fondness and involuntary envy we read the book of Mr. Murav'ev. . . . Our young countryman was drawn there [to Jerusalem] not by the vain desire to seek colors for a poetic novel, nor by agitated curiosity, to find forceful impressions for a tired, deadened heart. He visited the holy places as a believer, as a humble Christian, as a simple cross bearer thirsting to prostrate himself in the dust before the grave of Christ the Savior.—He traverses Greece, preoccupied by one great thought, he does not strive, like Ch[ateaubriand], to exploit the opposed mythologies of the Bible and the Odyssey. He does not pause, he hurries . . . he penetrates into the depths of the pyramids, sets off into the desert, enlivened by the black tents of the Bedouins and caravans of camels, enters the promised land, and finally from on high suddenly sees Jerusalem. (11, 217)

Let us set this touchingly straightforward model of travel writing, unhindered by any awareness of the clichés of its own discourse, against Pushkin's own re-vision of the South three years later.

Pushkin had ended his panegyric epilogue to "The Prisoner of the

Caucasus" with a contrast between the oblivion into which Kotlarevsky, the former "scourge of the Caucasus," had fallen, and Ermolov's current glory: "Smiris', Kavkaz, idet Ermolov!" (Submit, Caucasus, here comes Ermolov!) (4, 114). Pushkin must have had these verses in mind when he opened his journey to the Caucasus with a depiction of Ermolov's ironically identical fate less than a decade later, when even to mention Ermolov's name in print was forbidden (the passage was in fact excised before publication). General Ermolov, before whom the entire Caucasus had once quailed, is now a "prisoner of the Caucasus," confined in the four walls of his own house. His great historical adventure over, he is reduced to exchanging innuendoes with Pushkin ("about politics—not a word") and worrying how he will be treated in the history books (8.1, 446). The grand space of his domain has contracted to a tiny enclosure, his life is congealing into a historical text even as he lives. Meanwhile, his bitter rival, Count Paskevich, has inherited Ermolov's territorial imperative, and Pushkin will see him realize Ermolov's mocking nickname, the "Count of Jericho," by taking Arzrum with good timing and a civilized minimum of bloodshed, to the tune of French phrases and a marching band.[67] The juxtaposed fates of the two generals symbolically bracket the space of "Journey to Arzrum": the tigerish Ermolov has become the patron of confined enclosure, while the courtly Paskevich advances over a relentlessly unfolding space.

Thus in Pushkin's second journey, Russia's imperial imperative in the South has shifted from the epilogue of a Southern Poem squarely to the center of the reader's attention. Pushkin, in the company of the Russian convoy and later the Russian army, passes through a landscape consisting of a series of enclosures, cultural enclaves that are ethnically, historically, and linguistically isolated from each other. Pushkin notes every border crossing, every change of terrain and fertility; he gives thumbnail sketches of each tribe's cultural features, primarily as they affect Russian military policy in the area—the guerilla warfare of the Circassians, the decadence of the Moslems—while not placing great credence in a westerner's ability to interpret alien customs. With an ironic glance over his shoulder at other missionary travelogues, he recommends the introduction of the Bible and the samovar as more subtle instruments of cultural assimilation (8.1,

450). Indeed, his meeting with the Persian poet Fazil Khan, who answers Pushkin's high-flown Oriental rhetoric with a polite European phrase, is eloquent testimony to the spread of western civilization.

As in so many Oriental journeys, the landscape through which Pushkin passes is repeatedly characterized as deserted, a land of silent ruins, plague-filled cemeteries, and dried-up fountains. Amid the burial mounds, all that remains of a minaret is a spiral staircase, bearing ghostly witness to a decayed spiritual authority. Like Chateaubriand and Lamartine, Pushkin frequently stresses the muteness of these cultures—on the one hand the native tribes' ignorance of the language spoken just across their border, on the other the illegibility of ancient inscriptions, the senselessness of their poetry.[68] Unlike Chateaubriand, Lamartine, and Hugo, he makes no claim to speak on their behalf; nor does he "bring landscapes to life" for his western readers by inserting Biblical or classical associations, except with pointed parodistic intent (his "Circe of the steppe," the shopworn quotations from Horace) (8.1, 447, 466). The numerous poems and journeys of others (Chateaubriand, Murav'ev, Potocki, Gamba) to which Pushkin alludes in his own text have already coated the landscape with their names, descriptions, cultural associations, and itineraries.

Meanwhile, the intercultural erotic tale so symbolically central to Pushkin's Southern Poems has been pushed to the edge, or out of the narrative altogether. "The Prisoner of the Caucasus" had exploited most typically the Byronic topos of the sexually passionate, exotic beauty whose love for a civilized westerner leads to her demise, a parable of sexuality and power consonant with the fate of her culture. Early in "Journey to Arzrum," as we have seen, Pushkin flirts with the Kalmyk girl but finds that "exotic" differences pose an insuperable barrier to sexuality. One might say that the surface of the erotic tale has dissolved to reveal its allegory of power. The "desire to possess" is no longer dramatized in the erotic plot, but rather metaphorically shapes the landscape Pushkin so impatiently crosses.

Pushkin repeatedly penetrates feminized enclosures reminiscent of the locales of his Southern Poems, reputed bastions of cultural impregnability: the women's baths in Tiflis, the khan's labyrinthine palace in Arzrum, the pasha's harem, with its bribable guards and flirtatious women, the city of Arzrum itself, eagerly offering Paskevich its keys. All these enclosures belie their names and are easily transgressed, witnessed. Pushkin mocks the notion that an Oriental erotic tale—*vostochnyi roman*—could still be used to dramatize the myth of enclosed east and penetrating west. His account of his easy access to the pasha's harem concludes provocatively, "Thus I got to see a harem: that rarely happens to a European. There you have the basis for an Oriental novel" (8.1, 480–81). His "Journey" confirms instead what the Oriental poem "The Giaours now glorify Stambul" ("Stambul Giaoury nynche slaviat"), inserted at its end, denies: that the east is wide open, not desirable, but debased in its exposure.

At the same time, the Russian military thrust has become a matter of cultural inertia and seepage, not a masculine epic of conquest, as in the epilogues to the Southern Poems, but a highly civilized, operatic and faintly effeminate appropriation:

> The troops [answered] the Turkish fire with a drum roll and music. The Turks ran away, and Top-dag was occupied. . . . On the abandoned battery we found Count Paskevich with his entire retinue [so vsei svoei svitoiu]. From the hilltop, Arzrum opened itself to view with its citadel, its minarets, its green roofs pasted one on top of the other. The count was on horseback. Before him on the ground sat the Turkish deputies, who had arrived with the keys to the city. (8.1, 474)

The inhabitants of Arzrum put up little more resistance than do the chickens mistakenly attacked by the Russian soldiers, and the pasha "so vsei svoei svitoiu" surrenders with alacrity to Paskevich "so vsei svoei svitoiu"[69] so that he can drink his coffee. Both sides are clearly posing for a historical portrait.

The exotic "other" is already riddled with sameness. The landscape of male adventure and open spaces to which Pushkin had hoped to escape strangely resembles the confined "city of life."[70] That "demon of impatience"[71] so often pointed out by critics as one of the surrealistic elements of the "Journey to Arzrum" thus has a rather precise psychological motivation: Pushkin's fantasy of escape has collided with the crowded, metaphorically predictable landscape of Russia's Oriental mission. No sooner does he reach the impatiently desired goal of his journey than he ricochets homeward, refusing Paskevich's invitation to further pursue Russia's inevitably expanding border. Even in a poem composed to celebrate the Treaty of Adrianople, signed by Russia, Greece, and Turkey in 1829, Pushkin's underlying metaphors betray his ambivalence:

> Опять увенчаны мы славой,
> Опять кичливый враг сражен,
> Решен в Арзруме спор кровавый,
> В Едырне мир провозглашен.
> И дале двинулась Россия,
> И юг державно облегла,
> И пол-Евксина вовлекла
> В свои объятия тугие.
>
> (3.1, 168)

Again we are wreathed in glory, again the strutting enemy has been crushed, the bloody quarrel has been decided in Arzrum, and peace proclaimed in Edyrna. And on moved Russia, and enshrouded the south in her supremacy, and drew half the Euxine into her tight embrace.

The first stanza's masculine, military tone is undercut by the clumsily rhymed image of Russia's lumbering momentum and tight, motherly embrace.

If no enclosure really resists Russian engulfment, Pushkin finds it equally impossible to penetrate to "the other side." Over and over he eagerly approaches a border—a river with a dangerous reputation, a famous mountain, the citadel of Arzrum—only to discover that the border dissolves or recedes before him.

> Before us gleamed a little river, which we were supposed to cross. "There is Arpachai," a Cossack told me. Arpachai! Our border! This was worthy of Ararat. I galloped to the river with an inexpressible feeling... I had never yet broken beyond the borders of unencompassable Russia [neob"iatnoi Rossii]. I gaily rode into the river of my dreams and my good horse bore me out onto the Turkish bank. But this bank had already been conquered: I was still in Russia. (8.1, 463)

Open space is transformed into a vast receptacle, Russia into an ineluctable embrace.

In "Journey to Arzrum," even the traditionally liberating mountains take on attributes of enclosure: "The Caucasus receives him into its sanctuary"; "The deeper we penetrated into the mountains, the narrower grew the ravine." The crowded Terek ("stesnennyi Terek") breaks a furious vertical path between the "tesnye stseny" of the mountain cliffs, and licks the "soles of their feet" with a hungry wave. Precisely at this point a soldier cries out to Pushkin, "Don't stop, your Honor, they [the natives] will kill you," completing the association of the Terek with a river of death (8.1, 451). Most striking of all is Pushkin's description of a mountain pass:

> Seven versts from Lars is the Darial post. The ravine bears the same name. Cliffs stand on both sides in parallel walls. Here it is so narrow, so narrow, writes one traveler, that you not only see but seem to feel the closeness. A scrap of sky shows like a blue ribbon over your head. Streams, falling from the mountain heights in tiny splashing rivulets, reminded me of the abduction of Ganymede, Rembrandt's strange painting. Moreover, the ravine is illuminated absolutely in his style . . . Darial in ancient Persian means gates. (8.1, 451–52)

The passage represents an especially dense accumulation of parodistic moments from the Oriental travel genre: the quotation from "one traveler," the "learned" translation of a Persian word, the comparison of the landscape to "Rembrandt's strange painting" with its inserted classical figures and theatrical lighting—an analogy that becomes comical if we realize that the Terek's little splashing streams bring to mind Rembrandt's plump infant Ganymede because he is urinating with terror, still clutching two cherries as he is borne upward to Paradise in the claws of Zeus's eagle. The image originated in Ovid's *Metamorphoses* but was daringly adapted by Dante in his *Purgatorio* and may perhaps retain overtones of these literary contexts for Pushkin. (Dante falls asleep after his emergence from hell and dreams that, like Ganymede, the mortal boy abducted by an eagle to be Zeus's cupbearer on Mount Olympus, he himself has been seized by an eagle and transported to the gates of Purgatory, from where the gate of the "true city" can already be seen.)[72] This parody of a poetic epiphany is all that remains of the vision "from on high . . . of Jerusalem" with which, for example, Murav'ev's Oriental journey had rewarded its reader.

If Pushkin's gentlemanly mask allows him to absent himself, as a poet, from his journey, to occupy a liminal "moment in and out of time,"[73] his narrative contains meetings with poet-figures living in fatal proximity to the border where time and space intersect. The conquered pasha's "timeless" greeting to Pushkin ("Blessed is the hour when we meet a poet") is quickly undercut by his harsh treatment of the dervish,[74] whom he calls Pushkin's "brother": "Emerging from his tent I saw a young man, half-naked, in a sheepskin cap, with a stick in his hand and a skin over his shoulder. He was shouting at the top of his voice. I was told that this was my brother, the dervish, come to greet the conquerors. They could barely drive him away" (8.1, 477). The dervish is quite probably shouting anathema, not greetings, at the victors; but his utterances are obsolete in the new historical and diplomatic circumstances, so this "equal with the powerful of the earth" is chased away (8.1, 477). Moreover, the dervish finds himself suddenly on the other side of the linguistic border, his inspired expostulations unintelligible. A more scathing exposé of the contingency of the poet's position could scarcely be devised.

Perhaps most telling, in view of the prominent opposition of Oriental versus European and mute versus articulate, is the fate of Pushkin's own poems within the text. "To a Kalmyk Girl," his poem about the unimportance of the culture gap between him and the Circe of the steppe, is so unintelligible to the natives that Pushkin uses it, "the first scrap of paper he comes across," in lieu of a travel pass. "The Prisoner of the Caucasus" is reduced to a soiled manuscript found along the roadside. A certain analogy is intimated between Pushkin's ironic demotion of his old poems to tattered physical objects, samples of Russian writing, rather than meaningful messages, and the illegible inscriptions left on the Moslem ruins: "a few unknown names, scratched on the bricks" (8.1, 448). Both types of message have lost their historical context and been turned into archaeological artifacts. On the other hand, the inscrutable Russian inscription now wields political power.

If Pushkin's journey has failed to release him into the "other" space of adventure, if it has equally failed to return him to the familiar spaces of "nine years ago," it does produce a powerful encounter with himself as "other." On a mountain pass, Pushkin unexpectedly encounters the coffin of another poet and a namesake, Aleksandr Sergeevich Griboedov, whose mangled remains are being shipped back from a Persian diplomatic mission that ended in literally Dionysian violence. Griboedov's body had been torn apart, to the point of unrecognizability, by an angry mob.[75] In reply to Pushkin's inquiry, "What are you carrying?" the carters of the coffin appropriately mutilate the name ("Griboed"), truncating its humanizing suffix; and Pushkin, full of "strange forebodings," hastens to jot down his *zapiski* (notes) of the living Griboedov and reclaim him from linguistic and historical oblivion. Griboedov, caught between Asia and Europe, poetry and politics, has been literally sacrificed to the Russian border, yet Pushkin envies him his "instantaneous and beautiful," adventurous death. He worries rather about the amnesic oblivion that threatens to engulf Griboedov's name and reknown: "We are lazy and uninquisitive" (8.1, 462). This is the "Asiatic" aspect of Russia's tight embrace, loath to relinquish her object physically, in space, but indifferent to preserving its memory in time.

The encounter with Griboedov's dismembered corpse and already disintegrating name anticipates the end of the "Journey to Arzrum." In almost every travel narrative, the homecoming is the affective climax, the moment when the traveler brings home to his society the tale of his exotic travels and in doing so renews and reintegrates himself into that society:[76] "A Russian, having traversed many lands, must after all admit that it's better in Russia," concludes one traveler typically, while Murav'ev ends his *Journey to the Holy Land* with the following exclamation: "What moments of bliss can compare with the first instant of desired reunion with the fatherland, when it opens its hospitable embrace to the exhausted traveler."[77]

Pushkin, after his two-page race back across the same landscape, is greeted quite differently. He opens a literary journal only to find the critics engaged in their usual sport of Pushkin-bashing: "In every way possible my poems and I were attacked. . . . Such was my first welcome in our amiable fatherland" (8.1, 483). The "rite of passage" has been undertaken in vain. Once more Pushkin finds himself on this side of the boundary, trapped in the same vicious "little comedy" of Russia literary life from which he had sought to escape. Like the Spanish traveler in a prose fragment Pushkin wrote immediately after his return from Arzrum, he recognizes in Russia's embrace the "secret malevolence" of an Asiatically closed, mummified society.[78] "When I . . . see these mute, immobile mummies, reminding me of Egyptian burial grounds, some sort of chill pierces me. . . . Any man who does not belong to their little herd is received like an alien—not only the outsider, but even one's own kind" (8.2, 541). Pushkin's journey dissolves in the sound of his and I. I. Pushchin's laughter—not the shared laughter of *communitas*, but the alienated laughter of outsiders.

The spatial values of Pushkin's second journey to the south, have been, indeed, strangely inverted. The open spaces of adventure and personal reminiscence have been crowded out by the highly public and literarily overpopulated space of Orientalism. Attempting to escape from Russia and contemporaneity, he has discovered the impossibility of crossing over into another culture, another land, another state of mind: every border crossed evaporates, is not *the* border, while the ever-opening, unresisting space engenders its own peculiar claustrophobia. Meanwhile, if his Oriental journey has finally confronted Pushkin only with the ubiquity of the Russian border, then his return has brought him full circle, to a recognition of the killing Egyptian stagnation of St. Petersburg and his own permanent "otherness" within it.[79] For the Russian-Christian imperial mission the "Journey to Arzrum" narrates, the implicit historical irony is equally devastating: conquering the east in the name of western civilization, Russia may in fact be on the other side of the boundary, outside the modern European-Christian historical system, in "Egypt."

Like Pushkin, I am reminded of another "strange painting." Was it not the same claustrophobia that impelled Gogol to write *Dead Souls* in Rome, claiming he could see Russia as a whole only "from a beautiful distance," while his irrepressible Russian landowner Nozdrev, pointing to the vertiginously elastic borders of his estate, cries, "And that's mine. And that's mine, too"? The "Journey to Arzrum" purported to take the *Contemporary*'s readers to a foreign land, but in the margins of his travelogue Pushkin left an illicit portrait of his absent, inescapable subject, Russia.

Chapter 4

"What's in a Name?" The Rhetoric of Imposture in *Boris Godunov*

Shortly after his arrival in Mikhailovskoe in the autumn of 1824, Pushkin discovered that home was not what it seemed: the government surveillance and personal treachery to which he had been subjected in Odessa were to be continued by his father. A restrained note to his close friend Vera Fedorovna Viazemskaia gives us a glimpse of Pushkin's state of mind: "My father has had the weakness to accept an employment which in any case places him in a false position with regard to me; as a result, I spend on horseback and in the field all the time I am not in bed. All that reminds me of the sea saddens me—the noise of a fountain makes me literally ill." [1] A quarrel and the family's precipitous departure left Pushkin to his books,[2] the surveillance of a local priest, and exultant work on his "tragedy without love," [3] with which, he joked in *Eugene Onegin*, he was apt to "smother" provincial visitors:

> Да после скучного обеда
> Ко мне забредшего соседа,
> Поймав нежданно за полу,
> Душу трагедией в углу.[4]

After a dull dinner, having dragged in by the coattail a neighbor who has dropped by, I smother him in a corner with my tragedy.

Pushkin's playful tone was not reciprocated by his contemporaries when, after half a decade of censorial interference, the play finally reached an audience.[5] *Boris Godunov* was a bewildering "string of conversations," critics typically complained, "unconnected, in fragments" in which "everything takes places out of the spectator's or reader's view . . . [while] hidden from us offstage."[6] Pushkin seemed to have lost control of his devices of fragmentariness and allusion, and of his audience's response.[7] Indeed, the word "fragmentary" was used to describe Pushkin's compositional and imaginative failure to achieve the Shakespearean goal he had set himself, rather than his deliberate poetic strategy.

In this chapter I will show that the disorienting effect remarked on by *Boris Godunov*'s first critics successfully induces its audience to experience the same labile relationship to rhetorical language and historical "fact" that its characters enact.[8] At the same time, by filtering the historical material he had inherited from N. M. Karamzin through the dramaturgical and philosophical prism of Shakespeare's chronicle plays, through the skeptical "eye of a European," as it were, Pushkin created a convincing "Renaissance" portrait of Russian political and social history. It was a portrait that, far more than Karamzin's faux-naïf, medieval-providential interpretation of the Time of Troubles, could be comprehended in the same terms as the political struggles and underlying discourses of power that shaped Tudor England, Machiavelli's Italy, or, for that matter, Romanov Russia. No one understood the importance of things "hidden from us offstage" better than Pushkin.

This emerges clearly if we examine the complementarity of Pushkin's instincts as a *reader* and his practice as a *writer*. The more a piece of writing claimed to be nonfiction, authentic memoir, "dry fact," the more Pushkin's skepticism and inventiveness were aroused. The truth was what was missing, what had to be deduced. This was not just an accusation he leveled at less truthful writers; it was in the nature of writing itself. In his letter to Zhukovsky about his quarrel with his father, for example, the one thing missing from his report is exactly what Pushkin said, or wanted to say, to his father.[9] The letter is a fragment, not "initial" or "terminal," but with the center torn out. Pushkin writes for the kind of reader he is, or reads as the kind of writer he is. His burrowing into documents was not just a search for the "unadorned facts" behind historical narrative; it was a skeptical pursuit of the "pretender" in every "chronicler," the missing truth or fragmentariness of every allegedly complete and impartial record.

Compare the following letter, in which Pushkin delightedly critiques one of the hot-off-the-press Napoleonic memoirs:

> You don't send me *Conversations de Byron*—oh well, all right; but, my dear, if it is at all possible, beg, borrow, or steal Fouché's Memoirs, and send them to me here. I would give the whole of Shakespeare for them; you cannot imagine what a man Fouché is! In my opinion he is more fascinating than Byron. These memoirs should prove to be a hundred times more instructive, more intriguing, more vivid than those of Napoleon, i.e. from a political point of view, because I don't understand a damned thing about war. Napoleon grew stupid on his rock (God forgive me!). In the first place he lies like a child (i.e. obviously); 2) he judges people not like a Napoleon, but like a Parisian pamphleteer, some Pradt or Guizot. Somehow I have a very, very shrewd suspicion that Bertrand and Montholon were bribed! *Especially as it is precisely the most important information that is missing*. Have you read Napoleon's memoirs? If not, read them: apart from everything else they read like a splendid novel, mais tout ce qui est politique n'est fait que pour la canaille.[10]

Pushkin seeks in written documents not authoritative "truth," but the competing voices of various interested participants, liars, improvisors, each telling his own version at a given moment to a given audience, each casting a different, peripheral light on the center stage of so-called historical events. Needless to say, Pushkin did not invent this demystified view of history; it was the product of eighteenth-century historiography, and the intellectual basis of the Scott novels Pushkin was so busily devouring. Scott's historical heroes are always illuminated from the perspective of a "peripheral hero"[11] whose path has accidentally crossed theirs, a perspective that gradually exposes history as something *made*, not so much by deliberate or heroic actions as by accidents and the pieces of paper that happen to record, interpret, and survive them.

Moreover, the very act of assembling all the contradictory evidence and projecting a new historical interpretation demands an equivalent suppleness and wiliness of imagination on the reader's part. Notice that Pushkin does not merely present his brother with the final conclusions of his deductions; he conveys the intellectual excitement of the skeptical pursuit of inconsistencies, the delight in taking realpolitik apart to see how it is made. His purpose is not to substitute his own truth, but to awaken a kindred ironic activity of mind in his reader. This pleasure is definitely for the elite; only the populace actually believes what it is told.

When Pushkin proudly advertised to his friends that he was writing "a Romantic tragedy," he was, of course, signaling the change in direction his friends were all waiting for: from the repetitive personal concerns of elegy to a subject of historical, national, and philosophical import. They assumed that Pushkin would begin, in a sense, where Karamzin as monarchical historian had necessarily left off: that he would reveal the truth behind the official history of Boris Godunov. Instead, *Boris Godunov* was to many critics the final proof of Pushkin's lack of staying power, his fatal intellectual fragmentariness. A "chain of scenes" stretching over a period of seven years and hopping all over the continent had been assembled under the deceptive title *Boris Godunov*. What Pushkin served up to his readers conformed neither to the climactic five-act structure of a tragedy nor to the revelational mission of Romantic historiography.

> What sort of nonsense is this? . . . Neither a comedy, nor a tragedy, nor the devil knows what! . . . So it's *historical scenes*! . . . Is there the slightest shadow of unity in this string of conversations, which is drawn together under a single cover under the name of *Boris Godunov*? . . . He—*Boris Godunov*—should constitute its subject, should be its hero! And what happens? *Boris Godunov* dies, and these *historical scenes* drag on and strain your patience.[12]

What did Pushkin have in mind? In his retrospective prefaces he points, like many European playwrights of the 1820's, to Shakespeare as his inspiration.[13] The distinctions he draws between French classical or court tragedy and Shakespeare's "national" drama were precisely those being articulated in the latest French debates—in François Pierre Guillaume Guizot's introduction to the multivolume P. Letourneur translation of Shakespeare of 1821, for example, or in

Stendhal's *Racine et Shakespeare* of 1824. It is not difficult to see how the prescribed forms of French tragedy implied a certain theory, or emplotment, of history.[14] The "unity of space" meant in practice the constriction of space to a few important interiors, where the talk of the powerful resonated. The "unity of time and action" created an impression of tight, clear, relentless causality, precisely the theory later historians were to question. An overemphasis on decision and speech banished crude action offstage as the redundant physical enactment of what had already been represented verbally. The "unity of style," which required that everyone speak the same declamatory language, effectively banished from the historical stage anyone but the elite. The formal, static staging reproduced the poses and perspective of classical historical painting, with its clear perspectival demarcation of historical heroes versus background. Generic purity ensured that tragedy and comedy were socially segregated. If history was promoted to the status of a tragic subject, then it was meant to be a cathartic spectacle to be watched in passive awe.

By the same token, a transformation of dramatic convention must imply a different theory of history. When modern French playwrights jettisoned the unities, however, they did not decentralize their historical perspective: the Romantic hero merely stepped into the causal center of an (admittedly more tumultuous) painting. By 1827 the allegedly Shakespearean tragicomedy, with its action spread out all over Europe, had become the vehicle for Romantic revolutionary heroes transforming their respective nations' destinies[15]—often an unsubtle form of political allegory masquerading as history, for which Pushkin had nothing but contempt.

An entirely different tradition of Shakespeare scholarship had flourished in Germany since Gotthold Ephraim Lessing.[16] Virtually every major writer produced an essay on Shakespeare (Goethe, Schiller, both Schlegels); in fact, Schiller had anticipated Karamzin's treatment of the False Dmitri theme in his own dramatic fragment *Demetrius*. Although Pushkin was notoriously oblivious to most developments in Germany, one of the books he particularly requested during his preparation for *Boris Godunov* was August Schlegel's *Course Lectures on Dramatic Art and Literature*. In the lengthy chapter on Shakespeare, Pushkin would have found a great deal to catch his eye: a discussion of Shakespeare's "organic" relationship to Elizabethan society and Renaissance discourses of power, above all Machiavelli's,[17] as well as a suggestive analysis of specific dramatic innovations. Schlegel pointed out the mobility and semiotic economy of Elizabethan stage sets, the semantic importance of the offstage dimension, whose unwitnessed actions did not necessarily coincide with characters' onstage reports; the function of Shakespearean "double time," with its superimposition of a fast-moving plot and narrative suspense that apparently take only a few weeks on the actual several years' worth of chronicle events; ensemble characterization, in which each character serves economically to reveal aspects of the others; and diversity of language, encompassing not only different classes and regional dialects, but stylistic modulations within the speech of a single character according to circumstance—familiar, ceremonial, or psychologically pressured. Shakespeare's famous punning was interpreted not just as "low humor" but precisely as a symptom of tension and compression of thought, and his irony not just as a rhetorical device on the surface of the characters' language but as a manifestation of the play's radical ambivalence about its subject.

Most useful for Pushkin's purposes was Schlegel's very clear interpretation of the individual and cyclical meaning of Shakespeare's chronicle plays. He pointed out not only the overarching idea of a providential design in the Tudors' ultimate accession to the throne, à la Karamzin, but also the equivocal role of chance in the establishment of their fortunes. In Herbert Lindenberger's striking formulation, the audience of the entire cycle of chronicle plays experiences an "intellectual suspension" between its pattern- and law-deducing urge and its sense of the ultimate *irreducibility* of historical particulars to any generalizable principle. If classical drama with its tight *liaisons de scènes* suggests a system of causality verging on determinism, Shakespeare's chronicle plays shape a more "organic" conception of a slow-moving and inscrutable historical process, which manages to incorporate even the seemingly extraneous or peripheral actions of less-than-central figures of society. The playwright treads a fine line between imposing a too-clear providential meaning on his tapestry of events and risking or even inviting the audience's sense of semantic entropy. Shakespeare's chronicle plays can have it both ways: they can verge on radical disorder within an individual play without entirely giving up the perspective of the whole historical cycle.[18] The various cases of despotic misrule, internecine violence, and social disorder can be viewed teleologically as peripeteia or instructively tragic failures preparing for the ultimate establishment of the Tudors' legitimate rule; *or* the whole notion of legitimacy may be ironically eviscerated along the way by the bloody history, conflicting claims, lies, and sheer accidents retrospectively ennobled by it. The chronicle play thus dramatizes (and makes its audience experience) the historian's struggle to wrest meaning from mere "chronicle."

It is perhaps something like this that Pushkin had in mind when he later called Karamzin, to whose memory *Boris Godunov* was dedicated, "our first historian and our last chronicler."[19] Karamzin was treading the same dangerous territory as Shakespeare: both had to refashion disparate chronicle accounts into the coherent prehistory of the current ruling house without totally sacrificing accuracy and drama. Nancy Anderson has shown that Karamzin synthesized his chronicle sources in very much the same way that Shakespeare reworked Raphael Holinshed's *Chronicles* in his history plays.[20] Caryl Emerson suggests that Karamzin invests his retrospective providential narrative with drama by giving his tsars full-dress tragic treatment, yet preserves the sometimes contradictory accounts of contemporary chroniclers undiluted in his footnotes.[21] In this way he also lays claim to the aura of authenticity that surrounded the "simple" chronicler.

Karamzin, perhaps providentially, never lived to complete his history, that is, to bring his chronicle up to the time of the Romanovs. It breaks off in fact with the disintegration of Russia in the *Smuta*, or Time of Troubles, a clear consequence, in his telling, of the fatal impostures of Boris Godunov and the False Dmitri. One is a tragically conscientious and effective ruler, the other a medieval demon, but both are doomed by the illegitimate origins of their reigns. Any pragmatic connection between competent rule and national prosperity is denied; civil disorder becomes the visible manifestation of metaphysical disorder. Ivan the Terrible may have been a violent ruler, but he was a legitimate one; therefore the Russian people's experiences can be characterized as "suffering," hard but not meaningless. Boris Godunov would have been an effective Renaissance ruler, but his violation of natural and divine law plunged the Russian people into a disintegration of authority and identity, a potentially infinite proliferation of substitutes, and a consequently endless cycle of violence. In one case the suffering is a Job-like "trial," divinely imposed for the finite period of the ruler's life, and tempering the people's sense of identity in fire; in the other the destruction of the integrity of the "king's body" leads to the wholesale loss of identity and meaning in the *Smuta*. As Karamzin's "last word" it sounded more like a double-edged warning than a ringing endorsement of the present monarchy. It relied, to some extent, on the reader to extrapolate his own conclusion. Nevertheless, it ultimately led him to associate civil order and a firm sense of national identity with the principle of dynastic continuity, irrespective of the defects of specific reigns.

Why, then, was *Boris Godunov* not assimilated to the legible structure of the Shakespeare / Karamzin chronicle cycle? In fact, the young Germanophile philosophical critic, Ivan Kireevsky, did just that. He leapt to Pushkin's defense by identifying the principle of organic unity underlying the play's apparent fragmentation. Essentially as in Karamzin, he traces the society's phenomenological disintegration back to the sick secret at its heart. But because the Romantic mystery play conveys its meaning in a series of metonymic glimpses, the audience must essentially narrate its own gloss, perform the synthesizing role of the Karamzinian narrator for itself. Nevertheless, for an imaginative reader like Kireevsky, the chaotic interlude of the *Smuta* actually confirms the underlying metaphysical connectedness of phenomena, the wholeness of Pushkin's philosophical vision.

The shadow of the murdered Dmitri reigns over the tragedy from beginning to end, governs the progression of events, serves as link between all the characters and scenes, disposes in a single perspective the separate groups, and to the various colors gives a single general tone, a single bloody hue. . . . The majority of tragedies, especially recent ones, are concerned with an action that is taking place or is about to take place. Pushkin's tragedy develops the consequences of an act already completed, and the crime of Boris is presented not as an *action*, but as a force, as a thought, which reveals itself little by little now in the whisper of a courtier, now in the quiet reminiscences of a monk, now in the lonely daydreams of Gregory, now in the strength and success of the Pretender . . . now in the agitation of the people, now finally in the collapse of the unjustly reigning dynasty. This gradual burgeoning of a radical thought in events various but connected by a single source, gives it a tragic character and thus permits it to take the place of a main character, or passion, or action. Such a tragic incarnation of a thought is more characteristic of the ancients than the moderns.[22]

Curiously, Pushkin's contemporaries all agreed on one thing: that the fact of Boris's crime was unequivocally established in the play. Even this, as we shall see, is debatable.

Sympathetic as Kireevsky is to Pushkin's project, I actually find that the much-maligned Romantic historian N. A. Polevoy more accurately conveys the play's immediate effect on the viewer or reader:

Is it not the general opinion that when you read Pushkin's drama, in your memory lingers much that is good, beautiful, but unconnected, in fragments, so that you can come to no complete conclusions? . . . Everything takes place out of the spectator's or reader's view; scarcely has the action been initiated, scarcely have we become acquainted with the personages, when everything again disappears, and we know neither the action, nor the characters, until they return to relate what happened while they were hidden from us offstage.[23]

Polevoy does not try to explain away the disorientation the play's scenic structure engenders. He errs, in my view, only in assuming that this effect was inadvertent.

Pushkin was enthusiastic about Karamzin's work for an unexpected reason: "It's palpitating, like yesterday's newspaper,"[24] in other words, immediate, unsynthesized, *lacking* in "historical perspective." Pushkin deliberately outdoes Karamzin and Shakespeare in creating a scenic equivalent for the linear but nonretrospective time and space of chronicle. The twenty-three scenes of *Boris Godunov* are not subordinated to any five-act or other cumulative structure. Extending over the period 1598–1605, they fail to coincide with any particular biography, reign, or point of view, certainly not that of the eponymous hero. No two adjacent scenes occur in the same place. Space is represented as a series of interiors and outdoor encampments scattered over an immense geographical area, from Moscow to Lithuania and Kraków, and includes a heterogeneous assortment of enclosures, from palace to monastery to inn to battlefield. This is what Lotman would call *tochechnoe prostranstvo*, a field of equivalent points not distributed around a center, linked by a trajectory, or selected according to any hierarchical principle. It is a space thinly populated, impermanently demarcated, ready to revert to "pure space" at any time.[25]

Through his shifts of scene, Pushkin forces his audience to experience the non-omniscient, temporally and geographically restricted point of view of the chronicler. The chronicler's perspective on history is limited to what he himself has seen in the present and recent past, what he has been told or has overheard, and what he has gleaned from previous chronicles. Rather than present the viewer-reader with a finished representation of his own conclusions, Pushkin forces his audience to experience both the blindness of a contemporary vis-à-vis the events swirling around him, in which he takes part, if at all, only by hearsay, and the historian's vertiginous immersion in a cacophony of documents. Ordinarily the contemporary eyewitness or participant and the retrospective, objective historian are regarded as opposite poles of the historical process. Pushkin forces his audience to experience the two positions as essentially identical: each as an interpreter working on the basis of very partial evidence, fatally exiled by geography, time, the sources he has access to, and the "blind spots" of his subjectivity from a clear view of the events themselves.

I think that Pushkin's removal to provincial exile, from which he could participate as a "contemporary" in his own time only through hearsay, conflicting epistolary messages, official and smuggled newspapers, and his own reconstructive imagination, made him acutely aware of the contingency of human knowledge. He places his audience in the same uncomfortable position. In the same way that Pushkin had to collate the partial information and hearsay from his correspondence into a coherent picture of the life from which he had been exiled, the play forces the viewer-reader to glean understanding from a sequence of fragmentary glimpses and distorted reports. As we have seen, Pushkin's account of his quarrel with his father shared a crucial feature with Joseph Fouché's memoirs about Napoleon: "It is precisely the most important information that is missing." He makes Zhukovsky deduce, from his father's reported speech after he came out, what Pushkin felt, said, and did in the room with his parents. In the same way, Pushkin preserves the essential unknowability of the event at Uglich; it is the black hole in the text from which all the play's language is generated.

Pushkin constructs a position for his audience from which it never ceases to be aware that its view is profoundly obstructed. The staging of the opening scene is iconic in this regard. The first words of the play are *nariazheny my*—"we are costumed." Shuisky and Vorotynsky appear on the stage dressed up for surveillance, but there is no one to watch: the crowd has moved to a monastery visible in the distance, leaving center stage empty. Pushkin uses the ordinarily decorative background set in a strikingly innovative way: to focus the audience's attention on events that are neither offstage, geographically or temporally removed, nor available to direct perception. They are present, but must be deduced. The entire space of the theater is thus organized into a series of concentric circles, the play's audience watching Shuisky and Vorotynsky peering into the distance (upstage) at the crowd, which in turn strains to catch a glimpse of the ceremony taking place inside the walls of the monastery. Boris Godunov is, vividly, the vanishing point of all these sight lines.

Of course physical obstacles to perception are only the beginning of the audience's problems. The two characters onstage are sure they know exactly what is happening in the distance, and are happy to provide the audience with a synopsis. Interestingly, Shuisky's cynical interpretation of what the invisible event means, and how it will all end, *precedes* any description of what is taking place. It is not a real event, he explains, it is a highly formulaic piece of theater with a definite sequence and duration (as the perfective verb form *po* indicates): the people will "wail for awhile, and cry for awhile, Boris will furrow his brow a bit longer, like a drunkard before a goblet of wine, and then at last he 'will humbly deign' to accept the crown. But in reality he will continue to rule us as before" (7, 5). Shuisky's words drip with a skeptical irony directed toward the very formulas he is using. The audience is handed the "signified" before it even knows what the signifier is, so that it is skeptically ready to see straight through Vorotynsky's naive description to its propagandistic core. What Shuisky tells us is not to trust our eyes.

For if we could see over that wall into the monastery, the infinite play-within-a-play regress would only continue. Boris would pretend not to heed the people, who would pretend to entreat him not to retire to the monastery, where he would pretend to wait for a sign from God—which everyone knows is a re-creation of Ivan IV's well-known ritual of monastic abdication and "divine election," with which he forced the people to participate in and ratify the theater of his power.[26] Boris has chosen—one might almost say plagiarized—the most semiotically charged ritual of the most fearful of Russia's tyrants in order to legitimize his own appropriation of power. Even while breaking bodily into the dynastic lineage, Godunov scrupulously preserves its weird *forms*. One might say that through this ritual of quasi-elegiac tribute he projects for himself the father he needs.

At this point the audience has registered Vorotynsky's dull-wittedness and Shuisky's *shustrost'*, or cleverness. A certain portion of it has probably accepted Shuisky as the deconstructive *raisonneur* of the play and is then likely to accept as a further true revelation Shuisky's next thought, "If Boris's charade doesn't turn out the way I have predicted, then Dmitri-tsarevich died in vain." (It is perhaps from this moment that Polevoy felt he was watching the unsuspenseful "last days of a condemned man.")[27] Notice, however, that Shuisky's pseudological and lawyer-like sentence creates only the illusion of verifiable causality. He posits a transparent equivalence between (present) sign and (historical) signified: if Boris's charade of abdication ends as Shuisky has predicted, with his reinstated rule, then (this means that) Boris killed Dmitry. Like the lawyer who posed the pseudoquestion Have you stopped beating your wife? Shuisky cannot be contradicted. Boris indubitably will or will not be crowned. If he is, his bid for power went as planned. If Boris is not crowned, he murdered in vain.

When Vorotynsky asks point-blank whether Boris did away with the tsarevich, Shuisky's answer is a masterpiece of circumstantial framing. He answers with the implied answers to his own questions, "Who then? Who bribed Chepchugov in vain? Who sent up the Bitiagovskys, Kachalov, and Shuisky himself to report on the fresh traces of the crime?" (7, 6). These questions pretend to be the same question as "Who killed the tsarevich?" but are not. They also allow Shuisky to present his own role as investigating prosecutor in 1592 in a double light: as a mere instrument of his lord's will, a passive repeater of Godunov's own stage-whispered lie; and simultaneously as an eyewitness who saw more than he was able to say.

Notice Shuisky's profound understanding of the way words' proximity illogically contaminates their meaning. For example, to be present on the spot where a crime had taken place is certainly not to be a witness; no matter how "fresh" the traces are, they can only be speculated upon. Yet Shuisky does not give up the valuable word *witness*; he merely postpones it until the next sentence, justifying its use with a persuasive substitution: "The whole town was the witness of the crime, all the citizens pointed in unison." The one who wrote and signed the report did not witness the crime. In fact, no individual testified to it either. By grammatical substitution, however, Shuisky creates a singular subject, *ves' gorod*, to stand in fictional apposition to "witness." At the same time, this multiple subject cannot actually speak; its frenzied gestures and noise must be interpreted by one nobleman into intelligible language. He is merely the inarticulate crowd's translator. But here again his antecedent is hazy: their gestures as they point to the *place* where the crime was committed are translated by him into the *name* of the perpetrator.

Vorotynsky pays no attention to the series of suppletions on which Shuisky's claim of "witness" is founded. Why didn't Shuisky then make his accusation? Because, Shuisky answers hazily, he suddenly realized that his own role was already scripted by Boris. "It's not the time to remember," he will later explain; it is not always safe or expedient to put the truth into words. Shuisky is taking a risk; in revising his own documentary testimony of 1592 now in retrospect, he is calling himself at least a onetime liar. If he gets away with it, he will have succeeded in planting a new and eventually more useful version of his "memory." It will not be long, of course, before even Vorotynsky recognizes Shuisky's expedient duplicity. Yet his description of events is likely to stick in the audience's memory.

This brings up another difficulty for viewers of *Boris Godunov*. With such scenic velocity, the audience tends to look to characters to confirm or articulate its developing understanding of the action. But Vorotynsky is quickly exposed as a gullible idiot, and Shuisky as an expedient liar. The audience is on its own. It has to remember the speaker along with the speech; not to reduce words to their abstract information, but to be able to deduce—even in retrospect, as things unfold—what lay behind their being spoken. Obviously, scenes on a stage and in real life, unlike scenes on a page, cannot be reread. The version of events planted by Shuisky in the beginning will continue to color the audience's interpretation unless it learns to revise its hypotheses in retrospect.

For example, the next scene in Red Square, which shows "the people coming back, all scattered," sheds an unexpected light both backward and forward on the very concept of *ves' gorod* invoked by Shuisky. We see with our own eyes that there is no such thing as "the whole city," "the whole people," with a single shared experience and voice. First we see "one," "another," "a third" intoning in pure Church Slavic their learned *pravoslavnye* (orthodox) roles, led by the deacon: "Neumolim!" "O bozhe moi, kto budet nami pravit'?" (Immovable! My God, who will rule us?) (7, 10). Then we hear "odin," "drugoi," "tretii" speculating among themselves in much more colloquial Russian about the outcome of the affair—"Chto slyshno?" "Vse esche upriamitsia" (What's the news? He's still balking)—much like an audience rather than participants in a historical event ("ne nam cheta") (7, 12–13). It is only when the distant roar sweeps toward them that these individual peasants throw themselves to their knees, joining the wave of collective demonstration as it engulfs them. We still hear them, asking each other for onion to make themselves cry, even as, visually, they become part of the spectacle of the united "people":

> Послушай! Что за шум?
> Народ завыл, там падают, что волны,
> За рядом ряд... еще... еще... Ну, брат,
> Дошло до нас; скорее! на колени!
>
> (7, 13)

Listen! What's that uproar? The people have sent up a cry, they're falling like waves, row after row... another... another... Well, brother, here it comes; quick! down on your knees!

This scene proleptically devalues any claim in the play based on a unitary "people's" witness or will. Not only does such an entity not exist as a conscious, singular subject, but "the people" we meet in the play are as prone to duplicity and manipulation of appearances as the other classes. The individual scenes must be mentally juxtaposed to allow us to glimpse the fundamental irony of the whole spectacle: Boris waits for "a sign" from the "whole people" on which to base his suprapersonal claim to the throne, while "the people" wait for "a sign" from inside the wall as to when and what they should demonstrate (the clergy acting, of course, as cheerleaders). Everyone knows the sign system so well that the most important thing need never be said: "The power is mine/yours." Nothing is said or done in one's own name, only in the name of others.

The audience finally comes face-to-face with Boris in the fourth scene. The strangely feminine, even erotically submissive metaphor Boris uses to proclaim his sincerity, "My soul is unclothed before you" (7, 15), calls attention to his entire performance. In what way is his speech like a striptease? Precisely in the way certain conventions of address/dress are calculated to put the audience in a position of simultaneous arousal and self-denial. "Vy videli, chto ia priemliu vlast' / Velikuiu so strakhom i smiren'em" (You have seen that I accept great power with fear and humility) (7, 15). He veils his will to dominate in highly conventional wisps of medieval Christian rhetoric. Prostrating himself femininely before God's will, Boris calls himself "the one you wondrously raised, the one you loved," whom the boyars in their common bondage to God are now bound to serve. Having claimed a special filial relationship with a certain "you, O my kingly father" as a replacement for his actual unmentionable paternity, he quickly completes the last grammatical substitution before we realize that we are not quite sure what the antecedent of "you," and now "him," is: "Serve me as you served him, before I was elected by the people's will" (7, 15).

Is he talking about God or the previous "angel tsar"? Has he been elected by divine or by popular will? Are his metaphors familial or erotic? It has been suggested that Boris's style is a hodgepodge of discourses because his sense of identity is uncertain.[28] Actually, Boris mixes together the religious, the erotic, and the political no more outrageously than did his contemporary, Elizabeth I. He uses the medieval formulas for transfer of power to clothe a modern political coup in the name of the people. He presents his audience with a hybrid discourse, surreptitiously transplanting a new basis for legitimacy directly into the old medieval doctrine of the king's body. The bits and pieces of the old theocratic language are like a bikini; far from stripping his soul, they make the nakedness of his will to power palatable. Boris's final words have a ring of Biblical reconciliation:

> Теперь пойдем, поклонимся гробам
> Почиющих властителей России,
> А там—сзывать весь наш народ на пир,
> Всех, от вельмож до нищего слепца;
> Всем вольный вход, все гости дорогие.
> (7, 15–16)

Now we shall go and bow down to the graves of the deceased rulers of Russia, but later—let the whole of our people be summoned for a feast, let all be welcomed, all are dear guests.

The gesture of piety toward ancestral graves is at the same time an appropriation of their authority and a fraudulent claim of kinship; the egalitarian call to feast imperfectly masks a brutal leveling of distinction; boyar and beggar are reduced to the same silent anonymity in the name of "our entire people."

This is not the first time, nor will it be the last, that a political figure in *Boris Godunov* speaks in the name of the people. We have seen that in the first few scenes the phrases "ves' narod" and "ves' gorod" are bandied about, at the same time that the dramatic scenes themselves cast a humorously dubious light on any such entity. Here again Pushkin both hews close to Karamzin and ultimately questions the metaphors that shaped his telling of history. For it is Karamzin, writing in the monarchist aftermath of the French Revolution, who grafted onto his providential-dynastic historical plot an important but counterrevolutionary role for the "will of the people."[29] When imposture is rife in the institutions of power, when language itself has been usurped, the truth will out in other ways: the "ruins of Uglich" cry out repeatedly, "bezmolvie naroda" (the muteness of the people) refuses to ratify the imposture, and the secret truth is eventually bodied forth by history. In Karamzin the people, like graves, nature, and other things not corrupted by language, have a mystical intuition of their nation's true destiny;[30] and their unbroken silence can be interpreted as a form of Christian expression and action. Karamzin's historical narrative is thus a hybrid discourse not unlike Boris's in that it boldly assimilates to its monarchical conservatism the liberal historians' trump card—the "will of the people."

It has been suggested that the most famous line of Pushkin's play, the final stage direction "narod bezmolvstvuet" (the people remain silent), is a direct citation of that oft-repeated phrase from Karamzin, making, in the eyes of many commentators, the people's mysterious will the secret moving force of the play.[31] According to this view, Pushkin has accepted the essentially Romantic *narod* fashioned by Karamzin as one of the principal dramatis personae of Russian history. In my view, Pushkin instead reveals to us the constructedness and expediency of the concept "ves' narod." Migrating from mouth to mouth, it is used by various political leaders as the basis for their claims to power. What Karamzin tries to portray as an authentic and legitimate force in Russian history, Pushkin exposes as a very powerful *legitimating* trope—and one that had been used with tremendous effectiveness only recently (in the American Revolution, in the French Revolution, and by Napoleon).[32]

Where did Pushkin get the idea for the shape of these opening scenes? In view of his eagerness to associate his dramatic debut with Shakespeare, it was natural to go to a source readily recognizable to all—to what has been called "the granddaddy of conspiracy plays," *Julius Caesar*.[33] It is the first play Shakespeare wrote after the completion of his chronicle cycle. Perhaps capitalizing on the relative safety of Roman over Tudor history, it makes explicit what was only intimated in the chronicle plays: that "legitimacy" represents language's completion of the bloody conquest of many centers of power by one. It unleashes a much more corrosive analysis of the relation between centralized political power and language, a relation that enables the alliance of monarch and "the people" against the nobility. I suggest that it was precisely the opening scenes of *Julius Caesar* that gave Pushkin a way to refashion Karamzin's faux-naïf, even Romantic, portrayal of "the will of the people" into a Machiavellian study of charisma and the crowd.

Julius Caesar begins with a vulgar, prosaic, punning altercation between two aristocrats and several commoners who use every trick of popular guile and obfuscation to evade the condescending questioning of their "betters." This little scene of mutual mockery and misunderstanding sets the tone for the next. "What means this shouting? I do fear the people / Choose Caesar for their king" (act 1, sc. 2, lines 79–80). Three times, the audience learns from a sarcastic aristocrat, the crown has been offered to Caesar, three times he has rejected it—a transparent demagogic spectacle put on for an infantile, manipulable crowd. To the aristocrats, the crowd is a single entity, "tongue-tied in its guiltiness" (act 1, sc. 1, line 62); they are deaf to the shifty cleverness of the individual tradesmen's answers to their interrogation. At the same time, at least one of them is uncomfortably aware of the demoralization of the republican aristocracy: "He [Caesar] were no lion, were not Romans hinds" (act 1, sc. 3, line 106), an opinion expressed much less epigrammatically by Vorotynsky to Shuisky at a similar juncture:

> Народ отвык в нас видеть древню отрасль
> Воинственных властителей своих.
> Уже давно лишились мы уделов,
> Давно царям подручниками служим,
>   А он умел и страхом и любовью
> И славою народ очаровать.
>
> (7, 8)

The people have become unaccustomed to seeing in us an ancient branch of their warlike rulers. We long ago were deprived of our estates, we have long served the tsars as assistants, while he knew how to charm the people with fear and love and glory.

Caesar's theatrical manipulation of the crowd depends also on the monumental separation of his name, and the grammatical third person he habitually uses, from his physically frail, human "I." Throughout the play, the republicans' attempts to expose Caesar's human frailties founder on the grammatical separability of his proper name. Caesar speaks of himself chronically in the third person, even, most famously, at the moment of his death:

> I could be well moved, if I were as you;
> If I could pray to move, prayers would move me:
> But I am constant as the Northern Star,
> Of whose true-fixed and resting quality
> There is no fellow in the firmament.

. . .

> So in the world: 'tis furnished well with men.
> And men are flesh and blood, and apprehensive;
> Yet in the number I do know but one
> That unassailable holds on his rank,
> Unshaked of motion. And that I am he.
>
> . . .
>
> *Et tu, Brute?*—Then fall, Caesar.
>
> (Act 3, sc. 1, lines 58–77)

Caesar is killed at the midpoint of the play, yet not only does his killing not restore "liberty, freedom, and enfranchisement" (act 3, sc. 1, line 81), as the republicans proclaim, but the disembodied power of his name, and indeed of names in general, continues to drive the growing violence of the action to the end. Antony's slippery, improvisational funeral oration, in which he consolidates his own power by establishing himself as chief mourner for the dead body at his feet, giving voice to each wound's "gaping mouth," is a masterpiece of substitutive illogic: from Caesar's silenced body is extrapolated Caesar's "will," a bogus document whose subtleties are entirely lost on the plebeian audience. Correctly enough, they understand Caesar to be an empty category, demanding to be filled: "Let him be Caesar" (act 3, sc. 2, line 50). By the same token, the connection of individual to name is dissolved: the mob kills Cinna the poet because his name overlaps with Cinna the assassin's; another man called Brutus is captured in Brutus's place. As Kevin Moss has pointed out about *Boris Godunov*, proper names have lost their quality of "propriety," of defining nothing but the individual that wears them.[34] In *Julius Caesar* proper names exceed the boundaries of mere civilized identification and revert to magical qualitative categories. Even the formerly rational and secular republican assassins come to believe that the "ghost of Caesar" is luring them one by one to their self-destruction, in a Rome suddenly medieval and miracle-ridden.

The play ends with the triumph of "Caesar" after all, in the shape of Octavius; the self-immolation of republican individualism; and the emergence of the formerly comical and easily manipulable crowd as a volatile political force. What has changed? Apparently everything. Not only is Caesar dead, but all of his republican enemies as well; indeed the very mentality of the Roman Republic has disappeared.

But from another point of view, the only thing that has survived immutably is the *name*, or rather the category, "Caesar." And this was the work less of Julius Caesar himself than of his successors, who proved unable to express their own will to power and individuality except in his language.

In *Boris Godunov* we encounter a world something like the Roman society imagined by Shakespeare, poised between a "medieval" mythical mentality and a Renaissance belief in human will and ingenuity.[35] The strong leader is the one who, *Prince*-like, harnesses the former for his own ends. We have already seen how cannily the secular and shrewd Shuisky and Godunov disguise their modern, Machiavellian strategies with traditional rhetoric and ritual. Godunov faithfully reproduces Ivan the Terrible's idiosyncratic gestures of self-doubt and divine election. Why does he copy precisely this moment?

Pushkin has isolated the most ambiguous moment in Ivan's career, when the medieval Russian tsar crossed over into what Stephen Greenblatt has called the Renaissance prince's strategy of "displacement and absorption." In sixteenth-century England, for example, "the Anglican Church, and the monarch who was its Supreme Head did not, as radical Protestants demanded, eradicate Catholic ritual but rather improvised within it an attempt to assume its power." Thus in Elizabeth I's Accession Day celebration of 1590, three "virgins" emerged from a white taffeta pavilion, arched like a church and complete with altar, candles, and celestial music, to present her with princely gifts. Greenblatt uses this incident to illustrate a general Renaissance strategy for "fashioning" popular power, no longer by brute force or a hierarchy of fealty, but by symbolic spectacle:

> This secular epiphany permits us to identify two of the characteristic operations of improvisation: displacement and absorption. By displacement I mean the process whereby a prior symbolic structure is compelled to coexist with other centers of attention that do not necessarily conflict with the original structure but are not swept up in its gravitational pull; indeed, as here, the sacred may find itself serving as an adornment, a backdrop, an occasion for a quite secular phenomenon. By absorption I mean the process whereby a symbolic structure is taken into the ego so completely that it ceases to exist as an external phenomenon; in the Accession Day ceremony, instead of the secular prince humbling herself before the sacred, the sacred seems only to

enhance the ruler's identity, to express her power. Both displacement and absorption are possible here because the religious symbolism was already charged with the celebration of power.[36]

As we have seen, Boris's accession ceremony is more subtle: he turns the very act of "humbling himself before the sacred" into an incontestable assertion of his power. He does this by inserting himself into Ivan's "original" tradition of "displacement and absorption," whereby the "sacred space" of the monastery, including even its rituals of repentance and redemption, was used to sanctify seizure of power. Although the brutally centralized "autocracy" bequeathed by Ivan IV was a completely different institution from the Muscovite "monarchy" he had inherited, now, scarcely two generations later, he is invoked as the symbol of tradition, not revolution; his slyest or maddest acts of "pretending"—the famous scenes of repentance and abdication—have become the identifying sign of divinely bestowed authority. In short, the "let him be Caesar" scenario was prepared long before the appearance of Boris Godunov by Ivan's original *tsarist* usurpation of power.[37]

Did Ivan have "the right" to do this because he was a "legitimate" Muscovite monarch? No, like Julius Caesar he had not the right, but what Machiavelli would call the *virtù* to master or exploit the occasions *fortuna* meted out to him. I have so far used the word Machiavellian in its common adjectival meaning, but now I would like to restore its proper specificity. It is of course only an interesting coincidence that one year after the publication of Machiavelli's *The Prince* (1532) was born a ruler who instinctively acted out its most radical doctrines—Ivan IV. This was not at all the light in which Karamzin presented Russia's tyrant. Karamzin uses a medieval terminology of "sin and suffering" to explain behavior that the twentieth century prefers to call psychotic. Pushkin, however, appears to have recognized in Ivan's behavior an example of what Machiavelli called the prince's necessary "rhetoric of imposture."[38]

Whether or not Pushkin had actually read Machiavelli by the time he embarked on *Boris Godunov*, he had certainly been exposed to him via Shakespeare, whose political vision, like that of many Elizabethans, was saturated with Machiavellian analysis.[39] That Pushkin was intrigued precisely by the way Shakespeare represented the realpolitik of historical events is suggested to me by his odd reaction to Fouché's memoirs on Napoleon: "I would give all of Shakespeare for them!"[40] He reads Fouché through Shakespeare, and Karamzin's Boris Godunov through Fouché. In other words, Pushkin's insights into the workings of realpolitik and political imposture in his own time suggested a demystified, and at the same time appropriately Renaissance, outlook on the strange careers of three of Russia's sixteenth-century tsars.

Neither legitimacy nor sin is accorded much importance by Machiavelli. He divides governments into principalities and republics, dealing with each in a different treatise; principalities are in turn subdivided into hereditary and "new," the former having the advantage of stability but the disadvantage of inept heirs. The "new prince" is not castigated for the means of his accession to power but is given extra advice on how to maintain it. The violence of a reign's origins is of no significance as long as it is finite. "To possess them securely, it is only necessary to have extinguished the family line of the prince who ruled them, because in so far as other things are concerned, men live peacefully as long as their old way of life is maintained and there is no change in customs."[41] The prince must decide which of the "two humours found in every body politic," the nobility and the common people, he will ally himself with.

> He who attains the principality with the aid of the nobility maintains it with more difficulty than he who becomes prince with the assistance of the common people, for he finds himself a prince amidst many who feel themselves to be his equals, and because of this can neither govern nor manage them as he wishes. . . . The nobles should be considered chiefly in two ways: either they conduct themselves in such a way that they commit themselves completely to your cause or they do not. (34)

If not, the response must be decisive. Machiavelli differentiates between "cruelty" as a characteristic, that is, enjoyment in the perpetration of cruelty, and "those cruelties that are carried out in a single stroke, done out of necessity to protect oneself, and are not continued but are instead converted into the greatest possible benefits for the subjects" (32). Indeed, cruel acts are useful if they eradicate potential enemies and instill the habit of silence in "those that remain unharmed." "One must either pamper or do away with men. . . . Anyone who believes that new benefits make men of high station forget old injuries is deceiving himself. . . . Any harm done to a man must be the kind that removes any fear of revenge" (10–11, 29). If human beings were good, cruelty would always be evil; but since human beings are treacherous and bestial, only the rational and preemptive use of cruelty and fear can save them from their own disorder. "And it is essential to understand this: that a prince, and especially a new prince, cannot observe all those things for which men are considered good. . . . He should know how to enter into evil when necessity commands" (59–60)—and to "exit" from it untarnished and unobserved. Notice the theatrical metaphors; evil and good are stages, not states of being.

But the people must remain unaware of these entrances and exits. Without the support of the people, the ruler cannot create stability; he must fabricate a seductive mirror image of himself to keep the people enamored of him while he conducts the real business of ruling behind it. A prince's appearance must reflect back to his people their traditional values, the fixed rules they live (or are supposed to live) by.

> It is not necessary for the prince to have all of the above-mentioned qualities [mercy, faithfulness, integrity, kindness, above all, religion] but it is very necessary for him to appear to have them. Furthermore, I shall be so bold as to assert this: that having them and practising them at all times is harmful; and appearing to have them is useful; . . . his mind should be disposed in such a way that should it become necessary not to be so, he will be able and know how to change to the contrary. (59)

No standard of ethical conduct, no oath can stand in all situations; the circumstances determine which promises should be kept and which are no longer true. The successful ruler is the improvisor, who tailors his conduct to the occasions offered by Fortuna ("It is better to be impetuous than cautious, because fortune is a woman" [84]) while scrupulously avoiding the *appearance* of changeability, effeminacy, irresoluteness, or lying. Human nature makes this not too difficult to do. "Men in general judge more by their eyes than their hands; for everyone can see but few can feel" (60).

Even this cursory synopsis gives us, I think, a different way of evaluating the actions of the various "new princes," the rival aristocrats, and "the people" in *Boris Godunov* besides the theocratic-moral lens interposed by Karamzin. Although Vorotynsky may dismiss Shuisky as a "cringing courtier" at the end of Boris's coronation scene, we recognize the aristocratic insubordination and wily self-masking that will eventually bring this "equal among princes" to power (and which Boris should have preempted). In the light of Machiavelli, Ivan IV's medieval ceremonies acquire a strategic rationale; Karamzin's moral diagnosis of the causes for Boris's downfall can be contested; and Dmitry's improbable successes can be related to a Renaissance "rhetoric of imposture." Perhaps most striking of all is our discovery that there is no oasis in the world of *Boris Godunov* for non-"princely" values. Both in the humble monastery and in the romantic garden, where we least expect to find it, the spirit of Machiavelli is alive and well.

The scene of Boris's coronation ends with Shuisky's politic warning to Vorotynsky, "Now's not the time for remembering," and Vorotynsky's hissed retort, "Cringing courtier!" (7, 16). Suddenly we are transported to the dark cell of a diligent monastic chronicler and his "spiritual son." Pimen claims no special identity for himself; he is the nameless vessel of divine authority, and his chronicle nothing but a few words that have survived the encroaching forgetfulness of old age and the endemic amnesia of his society.

> На старости я сызнова живу,
> Минувшее проходит предо мною—
> Давно ль оно неслось, событий полно,
> Волнуяся, как море-окиян?
> Теперь оно безмолвно и спокойно,
> Немного лиц мне память сохранила,
> Немного слов доходит до меня,
> А прочее погибло невозвратно...
> Но близок день, лампада догорает—
> Еще одно, последнее сказанье *(Пишет.)*
> (8, 17–18)

In old age I live anew, the past passes before me—was it so long ago that it rushed on, full of events, choppy like the ocean? Now it is speechless and calm, few faces has my memory preserved, few words reach me, while the rest have perished irrevocably... But the day approaches, the lamp burns down—just one more, one last story. (*He writes.*)

The rhetoric is modest, but the action is not. Pimen's first speech begins and ends with the same words, "Eshche odno, poslednee ska-zan'e," yet how different they sound the second time. He has with-drawn from the world, few of its tumultuous voices reach him, and yet it is only those that get through to him that will count. In his old age he lives (somewhat ghoulishly) anew; the very dimness and selec-tivity of his memory give him untold power to decide what will live on in language and what will perish. Suddenly the previous scenes with their wily intrigues and historic speeches seem positively weightless compared to the "last word" of this sequestered monk; he, not they, is "making history."

And rightly so, the consensus has been; having withdrawn from the world, he has earned the right to be its "impartial" judge. Indeed, in one of his later draft articles on *Boris Godunov* (1828) Pushkin wrote about Pimen so protectively as to make my reading difficult to sustain:

> The scene of the chronicler—the character of Pimen is not my invention. In him I drew together those characteristics in our ancient chronicles which captivated me: the innocence of soul, the disarming humility, the almost child-like quality which is at the same time combined with wisdom, the pious devotion to the Divine Right of the Tsar, the complete absence of self-regard and partiality, which breathe in these precious memorials of bygone days, among which the embittered chronicle of Prince Kurbsky differs from the others as the stormy life of this exile from Ivan differed from the humble lives of tranquil monks.[42]

All I can say in defense of my skepticism is that no one could give diametrically opposed versions with a straighter face than Pushkin. In fact, it is precisely when Pushkin waxes sincere that we should watch out; isn't his emphasis on the "childlike innocence" of the monks rather too insistent? Is a "childlike" and "pious devotion to the Divine Right of the Tsar" a preferable response to Ivan the Terrible's abuses than Kurbsky's "embitterment"? I think that what Pushkin as archivist appreciates is the utter distinctness of his documentary sources' points of view and ideology. That their piety enabled the monks to weather Ivan's storm in comparative "tranquility" is a point Pushkin makes with his usual subtlety; the reader chooses how to weight these words. Perhaps the fact that in an early draft Pushkin had a Mephistophelian "evil monk" plant the idea for Grigory's imposture represents a trace of Pushkin's real ambivalence about the figure.[43]

Let us look at the scene in the "miraculous monastery" more closely. During their conversation about Grigory's wild dreams, Pimen divulges that he was not always so detached from the world: he was once an habitué in Ivan IV's violent and luxurious court. But there is a world of difference between what Pimen remembers and speaks—"oral history"—and what he actually writes down. Like Boris, he could say "on the exhausted memory lies much evil," but this dimension of his experience goes no further than his nightmares; it doesn't make it into the official version. The stories that he chooses to relate about Ivan are quite selective: not about battles, feasts, murders, but precisely about the moment Ivan, "exhausted from anger and executions," fled from his own power to the higher authority of the monastery. Pimen's language reveals his awareness of the theatricality of this transformation; it is described literally as a change of stage set:

> Царь Иоанн искал успокоения
> В подобии монашеских трудов.
> Его дворец, любимцев гордых полный,
> Монастыря вид новый принимал:
> Кромешники в тафьях и власяницах[44]
> Послушными являлись чернецами,
> А грозный царь игуменом смиренным.
> (7, 20)

Tsar Ivan was seeking comfort in the semblance of monastic labors. His palace, full of proud favorites, took on the new guise of a monastery: *oprichniki* [Ivan's secret police], in hoods and hair shirts, appeared as obedient monks, and the tsar as a humble Father.

When Ivan addresses his courtier / "monks" as "my fathers," Pimen for one understands where he must place himself to be the recipient of that projected authority—in the monastery. With lightning flexibility, he steps into the safer and ultimately more powerful "father's" role that has opened up to him.

Just where we would least expect to find it, in a medieval Russian monk's retreat from the world, I think Pushkin gives us a classic example of the mode of behavior Stephen Greenblatt has identified as distinctively western and distinctively Renaissance: improvisation.

> In his influential study of modernization in the Middle East, *The Passing of Traditional Society*, the sociologist Daniel Lerner defines the West as a "mobile society," a society characterized not only by certain enlightened and rational public practices but also by the inculcation in its people of a "*mobile sensibility* so adaptive to change that rearrangement of the self-system is its distinctive mode." While traditional society, Professor Lerner argues, functions on the basis of a "highly constrictive personality", one that resists change and is incapable of grasping the situation of another, the mobile personality of Western society "is distinguished by a high capacity for identification with new aspects of his environment, for he comes equipped with the mechanisms needed to incorporate new demands upon himself that arise outside of his habitual experience." Those mechanisms Professor Lerner subsumes under the single term *empathy*, which he defines as "the capacity to see oneself in the other fellow's situation."[45]

Tracing its development to the Renaissance man's need for quick and appropriative penetration into other (especially "native") cultures, and his rhetorical training in either-side argumentation, Greenblatt reinterprets Lerner's "mobile sensibility" and "empathy" as a darker and more complex ability to insinuate oneself into any structure of belief and divert its benefits to oneself; in short, as "*improvisation*, by which I mean the ability to capitalize on the unforeseen and to transform given materials into one's own scenario. The spur-of-the-moment quality is not as critical here as the opportunistic grasp of that which seems fixed and established."[46]

The chronicler's account of Feodor, Ivan's weak and possibly weak-minded son, becomes the story of Feodor's lifelong monastic vocation and his death, sanctified by a holy vision perceptible to the tsar alone, yet which Pimen is able to describe in some detail. His monk's-eye view of history omits virtually everything that doesn't pertain to the greater glory of the monastic profession. "Never again will we see such a tsar," he exclaims, nostalgic for what must have been a politically disastrous reign but one very good for monks. Conversely, Boris's ascent to the throne is called "an unheard-of calamity," and we must recall what Shuisky said earlier about the young Tsar Feodor "seeing everything with the eyes of Godunov, hearing everything with the ears of Godunov" (7, 7) to comprehend the depth of Pimen's resentment at this outsider's infiltration into his sphere of influence. Godunov's ascent has obviously spelled disaster for monastic court politics, perhaps necessitating Pimen's pious withdrawal from worldly affairs. Godunov's masterful "absorption and displacement" of the sacred discourse has made Pimen's location in the monastery obsolete.

But Pimen has one more improvisation up his sleeve. When Grigory presses him, the "honest father," to talk about Uglich, Pimen bases his right to remember on having been an eyewitness: "Privel menia bog videt' zloe delo, / Krovavyi grekh" (God brought me there to see the evil deed, the bloody sin) (7, 22). What Pimen saw in his life determines what his readers will know. But is the relationship between eyesight and knowledge so uncomplicated? A number of scenes have demonstrated that this is not the case; a number of phrases ("za gorodom vedat'," "vid novyi prinimal," "takogo tsaria nam ne vidat'," "privel menia bog videt' ") sharpen our awareness of the mediating concept of *spectacle*—a "sight" organized in order to foster a certain kind of knowledge. Curiously, Pimen has almost always been exempted from any accusation of "interest." Yet this very fact testifies to his success in getting his eventual readers to "see" history through his eyes without even being aware of his "point of view."

Pimen's description of the event at Uglich deserves to be compared to Shuisky's. He avoids saying why he happened to be there; the fact that he arrived on some assignment at night is trivial compared to the real reason for his presence: God sent him. He switches at this point to a very vivid present tense:

> Крик, шум. Бегут на двор царицы. Я
> Спешу туда ж—а там уж весь город.
> Гляжу: лежит зарезанный царевич.
> (7, 22)

Cries, uproar. Everyone runs to the tsaritsa's courtyard. I hurry there—and the whole town is already there. I look: there lies the slain tsarevich.

The present tense effectively mutes the fact that, like Shuisky, he came too late; he saw nothing but the dead body. The criminals are identified in retrospect, on the evidence of their pallor and agitation and the mob's hysteria. We hear the accusatory epithets, "mamka predatel'nitsa" (nurse-traitor) and "Judas Bitiagovsky" before we hear any evidence for them. "Vot, vot zlodei!—razdalsia obshchii vopl', / I vmig ego ne stalo" (There he is, the criminal!—resounded the general howl, and in an instant there was nothing left of him) (7, 22).

To name is to execute. Three men running are immediately chased down as "murderers" and brought before the body, which emits one last shudder. "Repent!" translates the mob, and "in horror"—at the "miracle"?[47] at the hysterical mob? at the axes hanging over their heads?—the "criminals" name Boris. The conventions of "miraculous" narrative disguise the fact that Pimen *saw* nothing but a dead body and the hysteria of the mob, which instantly created the scapegoats it needed—in fact, a few extra—to account for the fact of the body. Pimen appears not to notice that the panic-stricken mob is understandably eager to deflect suspicion from itself and therefore has a stake in its own testimony, or that the "confession" of the "criminals" was obtained by extortion.

On this sad note he will close his chronicle, for no special reason except that he has lost touch with worldly affairs since then; and he tries to bequeath his vocation to chronicle "everything, everything to which you will be witness" (7, 23) to Grigory, his spiritual son. Grigory knows the medieval code well enough to recognize in the unworldly chronicler's "last word" a blistering political denunciation with the power not only to rewrite history, but to challenge present power and shape the future. What he accepts from his spiritual father's hand is the bequest not of his genre, but of his wily will to power, his talent for finding a niche for himself in the apparently inhospitable conditions of the given world.

A son's role is born not from Pimen's vocational example, but from the poetically hazy spot in his story, the very gap in his "witnessed" facts that has been evocatively papered over by a traditional hagiographic "miracle." Grigory recognizes his moment. If the dead tsarevich could be miraculously resurrected once, why not again? If there has been a crime against the divine order of things, won't there equally be an instrument of divine vengeance? "I ne uidesh' ty ot suda mirskogo, / Kak ne uidesh' ot bozh'ego suda" (And you will not elude earthly judgement, as you will not elude divine judgement) (7, 23). There is a role in Pimen's narrative waiting to be filled. What Grigory finally inherits from his spiritual father is the power of language—the empty word—to remake reality, the princely gift of improvisation.

Why, then, does Boris Godunov's "new princedom" fail? He has shown his mastery in copying, in inserting himself into a ready-made scenario. But he proves to be too literal, too responsible, too determined to *be* the image he has created for others.

> Мне счастья нет. Я думал свой народ
> В довольствии, во славе успокоить,
> Щедротами любовь его снискать . . . .
> Бог насылал на землю нашу глад,
> Народ завыл, в мученьях погибая;
> Я отворил им новые жилища.
> Они ж меня пожаром упрекали!
> Вот черни суд: ищи ж ее любви.
> В семье моей я мнил найти отраду,
> Я дочь мою мнил осчастливить браком—
> Как буря, смерть уносит жениха...
> И тут молва лукаво нарекает
> Виновником дочернего вдовства—
> Меня, меня, несчастного отца!...
> Кто не умрет, я всех убийца тайный:
> Я ускорил Феодора кончину,
> Я отравил свою сестру царицу—
> Монахиню смиренную... все я!
>
> (7, 26)

There is no happiness for me. I thought to comfort my people in prosperity and glory, to win their love with munificence. . . . God sent down upon our earth a famine, the people cried out, perishing in torments; I established for them new habitations, they blamed me for fires! That's the mob's judgment for you: just try to seek its love. In my family I hoped to find consolation, I thought to make my daughter happy with a marriage—like a storm, death carries off the bridegroom... Even here gossip cunningly blames for his daughter's widowhood—me, me, the wretched father!.. Whoever dies, I am everyone's secret murderer: I hastened Feodor's end, I poisoned my sister the tsaritsa—a humble nun... always I!

Boris's coup in the name of the people has backfired. The silent *narod*, in whose fictional name he acted, becomes in his eyes a dangerous and grammatically feminine *chern'* (mob) the moment it speaks. His attempt to be the only instigator of every policy, the only subject of every sentence has been turned logically against him: just as Machiavelli predicted, he is held responsible for every action in the kingdom, good or bad. Boris is swallowed up by a grammatical subject that has outgrown any plausible predicate, any realistic principle of causality. By the end of the speech, he is fleeing the pronoun "I." His body is only a place where various independent agents struggle: the single conscience, the single blot, the soul, the reproach. The subject is abandoned as a kind of demonic pregnancy overtakes him:

> И все тошнит, и голова кружится,
> И мальчики кровавые в глазах...
> И рад бежать, да некуда... ужасно!
> Да, жалок тот, в ком совесть нечиста.
> (7, 27)

And it's sickening, and my head is spinning, and bloody boys [are dancing] in my eyes... And [I'd] gladly run, but there's nowhere... horrible! Yes, pitiful is he in whom the conscience is unclean.

As we have seen so many times in this chapter, the most feared accusation—that *he killed Dmitry*—is omitted, leaving a nightmarish residue of images, fractured syntax, and avoidance of the first-person predicate altogether. Boris imagines himself instead as "tot, v kom": not the subject of his actions, but a receptacle for inimical forces. Whether the "bloody boys in his eyes" are induced by his own memory or contagious public hysteria remains unclear. The audience's conclusion depends on its evaluation of what this soliloquy is: an unwilling and fragmentary confession of the secret truth, which happens to be overheard by the audience, or a mad scene, in which what we witness is the hysterical disintegration of the tsar's mind.[48] We literally don't know what is before our eyes.

Here again, I suspect that Shakespeare provided the model. In *Julius Caesar* and *Henry IV, Part I* the relatively small domains of Roman Italy and fifteenth-century England quickly revert to chaos when their political centers are removed. Or does it only seem so to the guilt-stricken rebels? The rational Roman republicans, who had thought to restore civil liberty with a single justified act of violence, realize with horror that no end to the violence is in sight. Their beloved republic has been transformed overnight into a chaotic war zone where even the battle lines have disappeared, where the "empty names" of the dead practice guerilla warfare on the living. The republicans end up attributing their military and political failure to "the ghost of Caesar," turning "our swords in our own proper entrails" (act 5, sc. 3, lines 95–96). Similarly, Boris:

> Кто на меня? Пустое имя—тень—
> Ужели тень сорвет с меня порфиру,
> Иль звук лишит детей моих наследства?
> Безумец я!
>
> (7, 49)

Who's attacking me? An empty name—a shadow—surely a shadow will not tear off my purple, nor a sound deprive my children of their inheritance? I am a madman!

Is Boris's failure caused by the "spot on his conscience," or perhaps vice versa? Isn't it equally possible to say that he comes to personify his insoluble political problems as demons? Pushkin's fragmentary scenic technique makes palpable the sheer geographical dispersion of Boris's Russian domain. This Russian boundlessness breeds the lack of information and the rumors that make the modern, competent rule Boris strives for such a chimera. It makes it impossible for him to follow one of Machiavelli's first rules for the new prince of a "mixed principality": live in your domain, "because by being on the spot, one sees trouble at its birth and one can quickly remedy it; not being there, one hears about it after it has grown and there is no longer any remedy" (10). If that is impossible, send colonies to outlying regions; maintain their loyalty, so that a "powerful foreigner" cannot win over malcontents; and above all, "either pamper or do away with men, because they will avenge themselves for minor offences while for more serious ones they cannot" (11). By failing to make a preemptive, "cruel" strike against potentially disloyal nobles, Boris allows himself to be drawn into the self-fulfilling pursuit of conspiracy and the public impression of growing chaos. Once this has happened, all his efforts to help the populace, as he complains so bitterly, fall on deaf ears. This, too, Machiavelli has predicted:

A prince should, above all, live with his subjects in such a way that no unforeseen event, either good or bad, may make him alter his course; for when emergencies arise in adverse conditions, you are not in time to resort to cruelty, and that good you do will help you little, since it will be judged a forced measure and you will earn from it no thanks whatsoever. (33)

In short, by the time of his famous soliloquy, Boris has committed so many cardinal errors of princely rule that nothing remains for him but to resort to the old terminology of sin and conscience to account for his failure as a Renaissance prince.

In Shakespeare's political plays, as in Machiavelli's *The Prince*, there is no such thing as a ruler with a pure conscience. The one who reestablishes order after a civil war is not the one with a spotless conscience but the one who, like Octavius or Henry V, can wade through rivers of blood and betrayal and emerge with his name untainted. Boris's problem is not that he once killed, but that he has let it paralyze him; the prince's duty is to use prophylactic "cruelties" in order to avoid the far worse evil of civil chaos. Behind the debate about legitimacy in Shakespeare's history of the English monarchy lies a more cynical lesson: that extraordinary power is begotten *and maintained* by the readiness to commit violence and then call it by another name. Indeed, parts I and II of *Henry IV* as well as *Henry V* can be seen as the making of a *Prince*, English-style.

Of all of Shakespeare's pretenders, the post-Napoleonic generation was most attracted to the charismatic figure of Prince Hal in *I Henry IV*. This favorite of Walter Scott's left his imprint on Scott's many pretenders,[49] and, it seems to me, on Grigory's transformation into Samozvanets (Pretender, or, literally, "self-namer") in Pushkin's scenes on or near the Russian-Lithuanian-Polish border. Both Hal and Dmitry are improvisors who convert a talent for speaking every man's language, for regarding language as essentially empty and nonbinding, into the source of their charismatic power.

In the scenes at the inn, at the court of the Polish king, and on the battlefield, Grigory / Dmitry repeatedly demonstrates Prince Hal's self-proclaimed talent for "drink[ing] with any tinker in his own language during my life."[50] Later that same talent will enable the English prince to unite around himself the comical, mutually incomprehensible border dialects of his Welsh, Irish, and Scotch allies. Grigory / Dmitry amasses his power on the periphery of the Russian territory and the Russian language, precisely the borderlands where the imposed unity of the imperial language fades out. The Russian language becomes contaminated with dialectal forms, shading eventually into the comical and mutually incomprehensible foreign languages (Polish, French, German) of Dmitry's motley allies. Compare these two battle scenes from *Henry V* and *Boris Godunov*:

Macmorris. It is no time to discourse, so Chrish save me! The day is hot, and the weather, and the wars, and the king, and the dukes. It is no time to discourse. The town is beseeched, and the trompet call us to the breach, and we talk, and, be Chrish, do nothing.
Jamy. By the mess, ere theise eyes of mine take themselves to slomber, ay'll do gud service, or ay'll lig i' th' grund for it! ay, or go to death! And ay'll pay't as valorously as I may, that sall i suerly do, that is the breff and the long. Mary, I wad full fain heard some question 'tween you tway.
Fluellan. Captain Macmorris, I think, look you, under your correction there is not many of your nation—
Macmorris. Of my nation? What ish my nation? Ish a villain and a bastard, a knave, and a rascal! What ish my nation? Who talks of my nation?
Fluellan. Look you, if you take the matter otherwise than is meant, Captain Macmorris, peradventure I shall think you do not use me with that affability as in discretion you ought to use me, look you, being as good a man as yourself, poth in the disciplines of war, and in the derivation of my pirth, and other particularities.
Macmorris. I do not know you so good a man as myself. So Chrish save me, I will cut off your head!
Gower. Gentlemen both, you will mistake each other.

(Act 3, sc. 2, lines 97–124)

Войны (бегут в беспорядке). Беда! беда! Царевич! Ляхи! Вот они, вот они!
Маржерет. Куда? куда? Allons... poshol' nazad!
Один из беглецов. Сам *poshol'*, коли есть охота, проклятый басурман.
Маржерет. Quoi? Quoi?
Другой. Ква! ква! тебе любо, лягушка заморская, квакать на русского царевича; а мы ведь православные.
Маржерет. Qu'est-ce à dire *pravoslavni*?.. Sacrés gueux, maudite canaille! Mordieu, mein herr, j'enrage: on dirait que ça n'a pas des bras pour frapper, ça n'a que des jambes pour foutre le camp.
В. Розен. Es ist Schande...
Маржерет. Ha, ha! voici nos Allemands.—Messieurs!.. Mein herr, dites-leur donc de se rallier et, sacrebleu, chargeons!
В. Розен. Sehr gut. Halt! *(Немцы строятся.)*Marsch!
Немцы (идут). Hilf Gott! *(Сражение. Русские снова бегут.)*

Ляхи. Победа! Победа! Слава царю Димитрию.
Димитрий (верхом). Ударить отбой! мы победили. Довольно; щадите русскую кровь. Отбой!

(7, 73–75)

Warriors (running in disorder). Trouble! trouble! Tsarevich! Polaks! There they are!
Marzheret. Which way? Which way? Allons... get back!
One of the fugitives. Back up yourself, if you've got the urge, damned Basurman.
Marzheret. Quoi? Quoi?
Another. Kva! kva! you may feel like quacking at the Russian Tsarevich, you foreign frog; but we're Orthodox Russians [*pravoslavnye*].
Marzheret. What do you mean by that—*pravoslavni*?.. Damned fools, cursed rabble! By God, mein herr, I'm in a rage: it seems it has no arms for striking, it has nothing but legs for getting the hell out.
V. Rozen. That is shameful.
Marzheret. Ha, ha! here are our Germans!—Messieurs!.. Mein herr, tell them to rally and, goddamn it, let's charge!
V. Rozen. Very good. Halt! *(The Germans line up.)* March!
Germans (advancing). Hilf Gott! *(Battle. The Russians again flee.)*
Polaks. Victory! Victory! Glory to Tsar Dmitry.
Dmitry (mounted). Sound the retreat! We've won. That's enough; spare Russian blood. Retreat!

Clearly, Pushkin has understood the comical effect of such macaronic attempts at communication, and in particular the impression of "Bergsonian" psychological rigidity linguistic tics create:[51] the pompously wordy Welshman, the crude and touchy Irishman, the laconic Scottish man of action find their counterparts in Pushkin's garrulous Frenchman, cowardly bragging Poles, and monosyllabic German fighters (whose lines probably exhausted all the German Pushkin knew). As Greenblatt points out,

> By yoking together diverse peoples—represented in the play by the Welshman Fluellan, the Irishman Macmorris, and the Scotsman Jamy, who fight at Agincourt alongside the loyal Englishmen—Hal symbolically tames the last wild areas in the British Isles, areas that in the sixteenth century represented . . . the doomed outposts of a vanishing tribalism. . . . The verbal tics of such characters interest us because they represent not what is alien but what is predictable and automatic. They give pleasure because they persuade an audience of its own mobility and complexity; even a spectator gaping passively at the play's sights and manipulated by its rhetoric is freer than these puppets jerked on the strings of their own absurd accents.[52]

Prince Hal's verbal virtuosity will help incorporate all of these defective dialects and peripheral populations into the complex and eloquent English identity of Henry V.

Pushkin's scene is constructed on similar lines, but sheds a more ambivalent light on Dmitry's synthesizing move. What the audience sees with its own eyes is total chaos: soldiers running and shouting "Beda, beda!" to their "leaders," the tsarevich and the Poles, who are nowhere to be seen. In complete ignorance of what is going on, and despite the lack of a common language, the French and German captains march some German battalions into the fight. Again Russians run past, followed this time by their "leaders," the Poles as usual bragging "pobeda!" and Dmitry, on horseback, chalking up whatever just happened as a victory. Who is to say what just happened? But the addition of one tiny syllable (and a shift in stress) turns *bedá* (calamity) into *pobéda* (victory), and *samozvanstvo* (self-naming) continues to "make history."

Pushkin said that he used the historical character of the French king Henry IV to flesh out the skeletal Dmitry he had found in Karamzin: "He is like him bold, generous, and a Gascon, like him indifferent to religion."[53] But Dmitry Samozvanets owes his improvisational self-creation to Prince Hal. Throughout *I Henry IV* Hal's slumming, the unprincely company he keeps and slang he affects, and his constant role playing cast doubt on his fitness to assume his father's hard-won (usurped) crown. One of the funniest scenes is a play within a play in which Hal and Falstaff burlesque Hal and his father, the king, and then exchange roles, earning from their audience the compliment "As like one of these harlotry players as ever I see!" Parodically anticipating the actual tête-à-tête with his father that will ensue, Hal appears to be incurably alienated from the high seriousness his father expects of him:

> Yet let me wonder, Harry,
> At thy affections, which do hold a wing
> Quite from the flight of all thy ancestors.
>
> . . .
>
> The hope and expectation of thy time
> Is ruined, and the soul of every man
> Prophetically do forethink thy fall.
>
> (Act 3, sc. 2, lines 29–38)

Henry IV would like a princely son to legitimate *him*, to represent the next step in their dynasty: Henry V. As it is, "Hal" seems to be a walking refutation of his father's monarchical claim.

The more the king lectures his son about proper behavior in public life, however, the more we recognize Henry IV's kindred theatrical talent:

> By being seldom seen, I could not stir
> But, like a comet, I was wond'red at;
> That men would tell their children, "This is he!"
> Others would say, "Where? Which is Bolingbroke?"
> And then I stole all courtesy from heaven,
> And dressed myself in such humility
> That I did pluck allegiance from men's hearts,
> Loud shouts and salutations from their mouths
> Even in the presence of the crowned king.
> Thus did I keep my person fresh and new,
> My presence, like a robe pontifical,
> Ne'er seen but wond'red at.
>
> (Act 3, sc. 2, lines 46–57)

In the context of this paternal example, Prince Hal's promise, "I shall hereafter, my thrice-gracious lord, / Be more myself" (act 3, sc. 2, lines 91–92), sounds more than a little ironic. Later, when the king's emissary bids Harry Hotspur to "name his griefs" against the king, these all turn, not surprisingly, on Henry IV's many-facedness:

> The king is kind, and well we know the king
> Knows at what time to promise, when to pay.
>
> . . .
>
> He came but to be Duke of Lancaster,
> To sue his livery and beg his peace,
> With tears of innocency and terms of zeal,
>
> . . .
>
> He presently, as greatness knows itself,
> Steps me a little higher than his vow
>
> . . .
>
> And now, forsooth, takes on him to reform
>
> . . .
>
> Cries out upon abuses, seems to weep
> Over his country's wrongs; and by this face,
> This seeming brow of justice, did he win

The hearts of all that he did angle for—

. . .

Broke oath on oath, committed wrong on wrong.
(Act 4, sc. 3, lines 52–99)

If the king can rival Hal in theatricality, Hal, it turns out, can match his father for calculation; the "juggler's" persona he has adopted is a deliberate disguise, a discardable foil for the future:

So when this loose behavior I throw off
And pay the debt I never promised,
By how much better than my word I am,
By so much shall I falsify men's hopes;

. . .

I'll so offend to make offense a skill,
Redeeming time when men think least I will.
(Act 1, sc. 2, lines 196–205)

Hal's playacting does not disqualify him for his father's position, but is an apprenticeship in "one of power's essential modes."[54] Another of these modes is the princely assumption that everything is as counterfeit as his own behavior. The one relationship where we feel we are seeing the real Hal, without a mask, is in his candid, bantering friendship with the irrepressible fat man. Falstaff's casual purging will be only one of many "broken oaths" along Prince Hal's path to power: "Out of the squalid betrayals that preserve the state emerges the 'formal majesty' into which Hal at the close, through a final, definitive betrayal—the rejection of Falstaff—merges himself."[55] Falstaff is the price Hal has to pay for the impeccable princely image of Henry V.

Indeed, the instability of his name—Hal, Harry, Harry Monmouth—in a play populated with Henrys and Harrys suggests a playful avoidance of the single identity being pressed on him. Shakespeare went so far as to tamper with history when he arranged for Prince Hal/Harry to enter manhood by killing his dashing young rival, Harry Hotspur (Percy)[56]—killing, in a sense, his own multiplicity:

Hotspur. If I mistake not, thou art Harry Monmouth.
Prince. Thou speak'st as if I would deny my name.
Hotspur. My name is Harry Percy.

Prince. Why, then I see
A very valiant rebel of the name.
I am the Prince of Wales, and think not, Percy,
To share with me in glory any more.
Two stars keep not their motion in one sphere,
Nor can one England brook a double reign
Of Harry Percy and the Prince of Wales.
(Act 5, sc. 4, lines 58–66)

Even while Hal is moving toward an assumption of his monarchical identity, Shakespeare undermines the latter with a memorable image: when the rebels close in to kill his father, they discover that they have killed one of many decoys dressed in the king's costume, while the "real" Henry, if such a thing exists, has gotten away.

We can now pinpoint where Grigory/Dmitry most resembles Hal, and where Pushkin significantly modifies his model. The scene in the Lithuanian tavern serves as a similar apprenticeship in "drinking with any tinker in his language in my lifetime." As in Shakespeare, the pentameter gives way to prose, but a prose organized (as is that of Hal's drinking companions) by its own poetics: "Litva li, Rus' li, chto gudok, chto gusli, / Vse nam ravno, bylo by vino, da vot i ono!" (Who cares if it's Lithuania or Russia, a pipe is as good as a banjo, it's all the same to us as long as there's wine, and here it is!) (7, 28).

We are, palpably, at a linguistic border, where the spoken Russian is interlarded with so much dialect, punning, and riddling that it becomes almost unintelligible. It is, in fact, an oral idiom designed to elude official comprehension. What we learn about Grigory when a police document almost succeeds in reattaching him to his old identity is that he is willing to collude with the underclass when it is expedient, but has no scruples about using his literacy to frame a fat and jolly monk in his place. He could easily have read aloud a physical description that incriminated no one in the room, but judged it safer to provide the police with a sacrificial body. There is no boundary that contains or defines his behavior. When lying fails, he breaks through the window physically to escape—not simply into a different identity (Dmitry), but into freedom from identity, *samozvanstvo*, the freedom to name his own reality.

For this is of course the essence of Dmitry's imposture. Like Hal, he wears an assortment of names: Grigory, Otrep'ev, Samozvanets, Dmitry. He pays little attention to the verisimilitude of his impersonation. Instead, he finds for each interlocutor the phrase the latter wants to hear:

> Не странно ли?—сын Курбского ведет
> На трон, кого? да—сына Иоанна...
> Все за меня: и люди и судьба.
>
> (7, 52)

Isn't it strange?—Kurbsky's son leads to the throne whom? Yes—the son of Ivan... Everything is on my side: both people and fate.

For Kurbsky's son he creates a reentry into Russian history, precisely what his exiled father had forfeited. He flatters the Polish nobleman Sobański's illusions about his independence:[57] "Khvala i chest' tebe, svobody chado!" (Praise and honor to you, freedom's child!) (7, 52). Then, like Napoleon, he quickly cements the flattery with a bribe. He actually makes no effort to sculpt a closed, coherent representation for his entire audience, but makes sure to address each interlocutor's interests and tastes at the moment he is talking to him. When Hal speaks, we hear a master strategist; but Pushkin gives Dmitry the quality he had noticed in the Napoleon memoirs: he "lies like a child (that is, obviously)." Hal's allies believe in him; Dmitry's certainly don't. Dmitry is more effective as a blank screen, available for their projections, talented at echoing their own phrases. He seems to know that while people will aggressively unmask an imposter, they will be loath to part with their own invested illusions and desires.

This is exactly what Boris cannot fathom: the emptier the word, the more insubstantial the rumor, the less explicit the discourse, the more space it creates for other people's roles; fragmentariness, in politics as well as poetry, "is the secret of entertainment."[58] While Boris's attempt to forge an effective monarchy founders on the impossibility of policing his subjects' minds, Dmitry's "resurrected name" feeds on the crowd's secret thoughts. He lives out everyone's fairy tale, the fantasy of freedom from assigned names and destinies, the fantasy of pure self-invention: "Budu Tsarem na Moskve" (I will be tsar in Moscow). Unlike Henry V and Boris Godunov, Dmitry never assumes the burden of authority, never loses a moment's sleep under the weight of his pretend crown. The last time we see him, shortly after the play's midpoint, he has dropped asleep on the battlefield. He disappears from the stage, but his name marches on to take Moscow.

Boris might well ask in perplexity, "Who besieges me? An empty name—a shadow" (7, 49). Samozvanets's career could be summed up in the saucy induction that opens *II Henry IV*:

> *(Enter Rumor, painted full of tongues.)*
> *Rumor.* Open your ears, for which of you will stop
> The vent of hearing when loud Rumor speaks?
> I, from the orient to the drooping west,
> Making the wind my post-horse, still unfold
> The acts commenced on this ball of earth.
> Upon my tongues continual slanders ride,
> The which in every language I pronounce,
> Stuffing the ears of men with false reports.
> . . .
> Rumor is a pipe
> Blown by surmises, jealousies, conjectures,
> And of so easy and so plain a stop
> That the blunt monster with uncounted heads,
> . . .
> Can play upon it.
> ("Induction," lines 1–20)

There is one scene in *Boris Godunov* that cannot be derived from Shakespeare's political or chronicle plays: the thirteenth, Dmitry's courtship of the Polish nobleman Mniszek's daughter Marina, only briefly touched on in Karamzin's *History*. J. Thomas Shaw first noticed that *Romeo and Juliet* may have furnished the external Renaissance color (including the courtly manners and setting, the rhyming couplets and interpolated sonnet) for Pushkin's Polish scenes.[59] It seems to me that Pushkin's dialogue with Shakespeare and exploration of Renaissance discourses go deeper than that. Dmitry and Marina's "scene at the fountain" is not only a parody of Romeo and Juliet's balcony scene, as I will show in some detail, but it is also a meditation on the central question Juliet (and so many of Shakespeare's characters) pose, "What's in a name?" Pushkin's Marina is no Juliet, though, and her answer to the question will be startlingly different.

According to Pushkin, the scene actually violated his original intentions for his play. He explains its inclusion in this way:

A tragedy without love appealed to my imagination. But apart from the fact that love entered greatly into the romantic and passionate character of my adventurer, I have rendered Dimitry enamored of Marina in order the better to throw into relief the strange character of the latter. It is still no more than sketched out in Karamzin. But most certainly she was a strange, beautiful woman [une drôle de jolie femme]. She had only one passion and that was ambition, but to such a degree of energy, of frenzy that one can scarcely imagine it. After having tasted of royalty, watch her, drunk of a chimera, prostitute herself with one adventurer after another—share now the disgusting bed of a Jew, now the tent of a Cossack, always ready to give herself to anyone who could present her the feeble hope of a throne which no longer existed. Watch her boldly face war, destitution, shame, and at the same time negotiate with the king of Poland as one crowned head with another—and end miserably a most stormy and most extraordinary life. I have only one scene for her, but I shall return to her, if God grants me life. She troubles me like a passion. She is horribly Polish, as the cousin of Mme Lubomirska used to say.[60]

We have seen that Polish-born mistresses played a key role in Pushkin's salon, amorous, and elegiac activities in Odessa; that a Polish heroine had already been woven into another "scene with a fountain," in another context fraught with power and promiscuity.[61] When Pushkin promises to return to the story of Marina, if God grant him life, we believe him. He has been here before, and he apparently cannot resist returning. Compare just one elegy, "Desire for fame" ("Zhelanie slavy"), written in 1825:

Когда, любовью и негой упоенный
Безмолвно пред тобой коленопреклоненный,
Я на тебя глядел и думал: ты моя,—
Ты знаешь, милая, желал ли славы я;
Ты знаешь: удален от ветреного света,
Скучая суетным прозванием поэта,
Устав от долгих бурь, я вовсе не внимал
Жужанью дальному упреков и похвал . . .
... Что я, где я? Стою,
Как путник, молнией постигнутый в пустыне,
И все передо мной затмилося! И ныне
Я новым для меня желанием томим:

Желаю славы я, чтоб *именем моим*
Твой слух был поражен всечасно, чтоб ты мною
Окружена была, чтоб громкою молвою
Все, все вокруг тебя звучало обо мне,
Чтоб, гласу верному внимая в тишине,
Ты помнила мои последние моленья
В саду, во тьме ночной, в минуту разлученья.
(2.1, 392–93)

When, drunk with love and pleasure, speechlessly kneeling before you, I gazed at you and thought: you are mine—you know, darling, whether I desired glory; you know: removed from the frivolous world, tired of the empty nickname of poet, exhausted by long storms, I paid no attention to the distant buzzing of reproaches and praise. . . . What am I, where am I? I stand, like a traveler struck by lightning in the desert, and all before me has misted over! And now I am tortured by a desire new to me: I desire fame, so that by my name your hearing will be perpetually stricken, so that you will be surrounded by me, so that everything around you will resound with noisy rumor about me, so that, listening in the silence to the true voice, you will remember my last prayers in the garden, in the misty night, at the moment of parting.

We recognize this same elegiac configuration, used now to flesh out the character of his young adventurer, in the historical play that Pushkin advertised as "a tragedy without love."

Samozvanets walks onstage with his script planned. He has named himself, now he plans how he will name her: "Kak obol'shchu ee nadmennyi um, / Kak nazovu moskovskoiu tsaritsei" (How I will seduce her proud mind / how I will name her tsaritsa of Moscow) (7, 58). But like all of Pushkin's lovers before him, in her presence he loses his head, forgets his lines ("ne nakhozhu zatverzhennykh rechei"). It is actually she who names him—"Tsarevich! Dmitry!"—and stubbornly refuses to let him step off the public stage into a lover's role, elegiac language, or ahistorical time. "Chasy begut . . . Slova ne nuzhny" (the hours fly . . . words are unnecessary), she censors him, and inverting some famous lines from Baratynsky's "The Admission" ("Priznanie," 1823), she nips his elegiac afflatus in the bud.

Марина. Верю,
Что любишь ты. Но слушай: я решилась

> С твоей судьбой, и бурной и неверной,
> Соединить судьбу мою.
>
> (7, 59)

I believe that you're in love. But listen: I have decided to unite my destiny with your stormy and uncertain destiny.

> Баратынский, «Признание»:
> Верь, жалок я один.
> Душа любви желает,
> Но я любить не буду вновь . . .
> Мы не сердца под брачными венцами
> Мы жребии свои соединим.

Believe, I'm pitiful alone. The soul longs for love, but I will not love again. . . . Not our hearts under the bridal wreaths, but our lots we will unite.

Preempting the erotic-elegiac language that would put her in the fixed and silent role of its addressee, his "nalozhnitsa bezmolvnaia" (mute mistress), she seeks to replace erotic inequality with political partnership.

"Let me forget myself," he begs, "let me express everything that fills my heart"; femininity arouses in him a desire for oblivion, for an escape from historical action and functional language into pure stream of consciousness. Circling hypnotically around the talismanic phrase "tvoia liubov'" (your love), his language disintegrates grammatically. She refuses to play her "timeless" role of conduit to his psychic underworld, and pitilessly returns him to the real world of historical action and ticking time. If we have Romeo and Juliet's balcony scene whispering in the backs of our minds, the contrast is indeed poignant:

> *Juliet.* I have forgot why I did call thee back.
> *Romeo.* Let me stand here till thou remember it.
> *Juliet.* I shall forget, to have thee still stand there,
> Rememb'ring how I love thy company.
> *Romeo.* And I'll still stay, to have thee still forget,
> Forgetting any other home but this.
>
> (Act 2, sc. 2, lines 171–76)

No such "home," no such forgetfulness is permitted Dmitry.

Why does Marina refuse the traditional lovers' scenario, fight so bitterly over the language in which they conduct their dialogue? Because, I have suggested, she understands that discourses contain an inherent distribution of roles; a woman inserted into an erotic discourse, no matter how idolatrous, has been removed from the world of action and power into the world of passion and nature, where a man is free to take holidays, but a woman is immured. This ferocious, unfeminine pursuit of power only faintly disguised as love is what attracted Pushkin to Marina in the first place.

Whereas in "Proserpine" the fatal banishment from "timelessness" back into time is enforced by the husband-rival, in "Kleopatra" and in Marina's scene the woman herself counts out the hours in paradise, then ejects her young lover-victim into death, or history. Kleopatra's language is an unheard-of synthesis of erotic proposition and death sentence, words of power so strange that they guarantee her immortality. For Marina, the erotic dimension fades still further into the background, and she maneuvers "like a snake" to banish altogether Dmitry's "unnecessary words" of love from the discourse of power she longs to enter. Even as one by one she destroys the clichés of the balcony scene, though, she is forced to confront its most important question: "What's in a name?"

Juliet, in her innocence, reasons with herself thus:

> O Romeo, Romeo! wherefore art thou Romeo?
> Deny thy father and refuse thy name;
> Or, if thou wilt not, be but sworn my love,
> And I'll no longer be a Capulet.
> 'Tis but thy name that is my enemy.
> Thou art thyself, though, not a Montague.
> What's Montague? It is nor hand, nor foot,
> Nor arm, nor face, nor any other part
> Belonging to a man. O, be some other name!
> What's in a name? That which we call a rose
> By any other name would smell as sweet.
> So Romeo would, were he not Romeo called,
> Retain that dear perfection which he owes
> Without that title. Romeo, doff thy name;
> And for that name, which is no part of thee
> Take all myself.
>
> (Act 2, sc. 2, lines 32–49)

Romeo, of course, immediately accepts her proposition:

> I take thee at thy word.
> Call me but love, and I'll be new baptized;
> Henceforth I never will be Romeo.
> (Act 2, sc. 2, lines 49–51)

The paradox that shapes the whole scene is that even while the lovers reject names in favor of the wordless truth of their experience, they hasten to offer each other different names, such as "love," which must be backed up by an exchange of "vows," which are in turn guaranteed by "the moon" or "thyself," which brings them back full circle in their search for nonverbal collateral. If, as they would like to convince themselves, their names are powerless to determine their fate, then no less so are the words (including the secret wedding vows) they lavish on each other in their attempt to break the hold of language. Every moment of their love, to the last words of the play, will be shaped inescapably by their names, "Juliet and her Romeo." When Dmitry begs her to forget his name for the moment, Marina retorts with a perverse inversion of Juliet's declaration of love. She substitutes for Juliet's rhapsodic "all myself" a metonymic formality (her hand in marriage), and offers it in exchange not for him, but for his name:

> Не юноше кипящему, безумно
> Плененному моею красотой,
> Знай: отдаю торжественно я руку
> Наследнику московского престола,
> Царевичу, спасенному судьбой . . .
> Димитрий ты и быть иным не можешь;
> Другого мне любить нельзя.
> (7, 60–61)

Not to a feverish youth, madly captivated by my beauty, know: I give my hand triumphantly to the heir apparent of the Moscow throne, to the tsarevich saved by fate. You are Dmitry and can be no other; I am allowed to love no other.

Taking his cue from Romeo, but also in reverse, Dmitry "takes her at her word." You love my name, he says, then know it is only a name, a fiction. For him, to be wedded to the name Dmitry is to be diminished. It means to be loved for a single impersonation, rather than for his improvisational freedom to name and from names—his *samozvanstvo*. He will not let himself be upstaged by a dead man. When Marina sarcastically asks why she should believe him, what will back up his oath—"No chem, nel'zia l'uznat', klianesh'sia ty?" (7, 64) (again echoing Juliet in reverse: "O swear not by the moon. . . . Swear by thy sweet self, which is the god of my idolatry, and I'll believe thee")—she plays right into his hand. There *is* no referential basis for Dmitry's language. It is precisely at the moment Marina reminds him of his nothingness that he regains his power over her.

"Dmitry" exists only if Samozvanets chooses to make him exist. It turns out that the one thing Marina cannot do without is his "words." His pure verbal invention is their entrée into history. It is precisely at the moment she utterly doubts his word that Dmitry breaks free of her logic. Switching to rhyming verse at the same time he switches to pure lies, he haughtily asserts the absolute power of pure language:

> Тень Грозного меня усыновила,
> Димитрием из гроба нарекла,
> Вокруг меня народы возмутила
> И в жертву мне Бориса обрекла—
> Царевич я.
>
> (7, 64)

The shade of the Terrible adopted me as a son, named me Dmitry from the grave, swirled up nations around me, and condemned Boris to be my victim—I am the tsarevich.

It is his understanding of the contingency of his being, his availability as a pretext, rather than his true identity as Dmitry, that makes him immune to her threats to expose him. Not his charismatic fiction, but her unpopular truth will be silenced.

Marina at last hears the language she wanted to hear—the language of power. It turns out that it is possible to win her in the same way that the *narod* can be bewitched: "with terror and love and fame." After all, her only means of escaping from silence into history is by accepting a part in his play. He almost met his downfall when he tried to strip himself of language, to "tell the truth." Yet that confession brought him no closer to the truth than his lies; he is no more the poor monk Grigory than he is the tsarevich Dmitry; that was just his preceding role. The truth about him is *samozvanstvo*, which makes all of history potentially his story and him the true heir of Ivan's rhetoric of imposture.

When in the balcony scene Juliet asks, "What's in a name?" Romeo promises to unname himself—"Call me but love and I'll be new baptized." But *Romeo and Juliet* will block the lovers' every attempt to escape the aegis of language. The scene at the fountain closes on Marina's appropriately contrapuntal retort: "Name yourself tsar, and then I'll let you speak of love." In *Boris Godunov*, nothing is more powerful than the "empty word."

Compare in the mind's eye the last scene of *Boris Godunov* with the first. What has changed? Tragically, a great deal: the whole Godunov family has been wiped out. Yet the scene should be staged to stress its structural similarity with the opening scene. The audience watches the *narod* watch the Godunov house in the distance, just as it watched the monastery where he was crowned: from the outside. Again, fateful decisions (such as the killing of the children) are made "inside," visible neither to contemporaries nor to us, the later audience. Again, the historical hero (Dmitry) is nowhere to be seen, but the action is being carried out in his name. Again, the people cheer opaquely, or just as opaquely, remain silent. Pushkin's play has given us nothing on which to base an interpretation of their motives. If the ending retains some relation to *Julius Caesar*, it could be that Pushkin's main intention was to preserve a sense of the *narod*'s opacity and volatility—an apt warning, despite Pushkin's antipathy to political allegory, to the Decembrist "republicans," who were preparing their own coup d'état and speaking in the borrowed phrases of Brutus and Cassius even as he wrote. Or, when the word has been shown to be so powerful and so empty, when, as Kevin Moss puts it, "the semiotic process is undermined to such an extent, there is only one solution—escaping signification altogether—precisely the solution found by the people at the end of the play. . . . The zero ending may function as an absence—as a refusal to signify, a rejection of verbal signification altogether as inherently dangerous."[62]

The play ends in an ironic shimmer. I will postpone a more thorough characterization of Pushkin's irony until the next chapter, but will conclude with this comment. Pushkin leaves his audience in a much less comfortable position than does the traditional device of dramatic irony, in which the audience is rewarded for its attentiveness by a more complete understanding of the cumulative shape of events than any single character in the play possesses. The more one sees, presumably, the more one knows. Just the opposite is the case in *Boris Godunov*. To expect from Pushkin's play a reconstruction of true historical events is, as Stephanie Sandler has said, to invite frustration.[63] *Boris Godunov* is a dramatization of their utter unavailability, not just to later historians but to contemporary chroniclers, historical figures, participants, and even "eyewitnesses." Instead, *Boris Godunov* shows us that a gripping tale, devoid of factual basis and even the barest verisimilitude, can hijack history.[64] Ultimately, history is made by those daring enough to lie, to inhabit any available story, to invent themselves and their fathers as well. It was, for a twenty-five-year-old virtuoso who had been sequestered by the combined efforts of his Polish mistress, his father, a priest, and his namesake the tsar, a satisfying story to tell.

Chapter 5

The Sense of Not Ending: Romantic Irony in *Eugene Onegin*

Eugene Onegin as Fragment

Hamlet is finished not only because the Danish prince dies, but also because those whom his ghost might haunt have died, too. *Madame Bovary* is finished not only because Emma has killed herself, but because Homais has at last got his decoration. *Ulysses* is finished because everybody in it has fallen asleep (although the good reader wonders where Stephen is going to spend the rest of the night). *Anna Karenina* is finished not only because Anna has been crushed by a backing freight train but because Lyovin has found his God. But *Onegin* is not finished.

> To Captain Medwin, Byron said one day
> (October, eighteen twenty-one, at Pisa):
> "Poor Juan will be guillotined—*has been*—
> In the French Revolution..."
> ... but Eugene?[1]

The evidence Nabokov offers for regarding *Eugene Onegin* as unfinished is, however, biographical or apocryphal, rather than internal—a fact he spoofs, but does nothing to alter. "To Captain Yuzefovich, Pushkin said one day, June 1829, in the Caucasus: 'Onegin will either perish in the Caucasus or join the Decembrist movement.' "[2]

Other critics have developed convincing "finalizing" interpretations of *Eugene Onegin*'s internal structure. Jan M. Meijer suggests a satisfying way of reading the novel: as a form that so changes the array of forms out of which it grew, and which it outgrows, that it cannot continue. It has made its own matrix of lyrical poetic forms obsolete and can only lead beyond itself to something new.[3] This is a developmental model in both *fabula* and form: in fact, the plot thematizes the same forward-moving development that the form displays. The characters—or at least Tatiana, who has become the main character by the end—mature, shed their illusions; even more, as William Mills Todd III points out, Tatiana becomes a creative artist within her own sphere of possibilities, harmonizing the diverse materials of her culture.[4] The form of the novel, and the poet himself, move irrevocably from an orientation to the system of lyric poetry, excluding what it cannot poeticize, to a narrative form that encompasses a richer diversity of life and literature. One might say that the polarities contained in the subtitle *A Novel in Verse* are resolved by a dialectical reconciliation of the values of the latter with the former. The novel does not need to sound the traditional wedding bells or death knell because it has traced a change of form, of mind, of values that are equally conclusive. The story of Eugene Onegin turns out to be the story not of his career, marriage, or death, but of Tatiana's—and the poet-narrator's—*Bildung*. Leaving Eugene trapped in exitless solipsism, Tatiana and the poet move together into psychological and creative maturity.

In this chapter I will show why I believe that *Eugene Onegin* should be considered a deliberately fabricated Romantic fragment poem,[5] which reserves for itself the possibility of a different lyrical and heuristic closure precisely by ending, or not ending, as it does. The external rupture of its form actually dramatizes the internal dynamic of its language, a language that incites the reader to build and constantly modify his understanding of the poem's meaning out of partial, temporary, and—at some later point, almost always—ironically counterpointed perspectives. Woe to the critic who quotes any one sententious passage as a formulation of the wisdom arrived at through the process of *Bildung* enacted by the characters or by the Pushkinian narrator himself. The stripping away of veils of illusion does not unveil a final, absolute truth, in the way of a Wordsworth. Even the most definite sounding statements in *Eugene Onegin* can be thought of as having invisible quotation marks—that is, as representing a partial point of view, belonging to this or that character, or even more importantly, to particular moments in a single life. The limitation of each single viewpoint is often exposed by its juxtaposition to a broader, more experienced, or more disenchanted one. But sooner or later the latter "wisdom" will find itself ironically framed in turn by a different and apparently more valid perspective.

For Wordsworth, the task lies in stripping away false habitual modes of perception and linguistic expression to reveal the eye of the child and the language of man, purified of literary artifice and with their intrinsic access to the truth intact. For Pushkin, as for a series of writers one might call Romantic ironists, some of them *avant la lettre* (Sterne, Diderot, Byron, Friedrich Schlegel, Stendhal, Hoffmann, Kierkegaard, Baudelaire, Flaubert), perception is determined by the inherent limitations of the subject's position, spatial and temporal, and by the language that determines the very categories of his thought.[6] As I will show in my analysis of the plot movement of *Eugene Onegin*, there is no consistent, dialectical development from an illusory, partial language to a privileged, authentic one. Anyone who expects to arrive at a point of stable wisdom from which the rest of the novel resolves into uniperspectival sense is reading the wrong author.

The function of irony is not to unmask and unveil, but to exercise the faculty of evaluation, to chart the mind's movement among alternatives and language's "hovering"—to use Schlegel's word—among alternative possibilities of meaning. I would like finally to show that the plot of *Eugene Onegin*, far from dramatizing the evolution of selected characters and the poet figure toward a mature, demystified perspective and language, actually allegorizes irony's refusal to give up, to synthesize, to privilege one perspective over the other. Pushkin's ironic plot keeps all the balls in the air to the end. No viewpoint is definitively discarded; every partial viewpoint implies the existence, just around the corner or over the page, of another. Perhaps most notably, Pushkin avoids privileging even a mature, ironic viewpoint over the others. (Compare his poet-narrator to the worldly-wise narrators of a Fielding or a Thackeray, safely bemused by the vagaries of other people's illusions.) The trick is to prevent the reader from preempting the discomfort of ironic "hovering" by giving in to the temptation of drawing a conclusion.

I will begin by showing how Pushkin maintained the formal appearance of unfinishedness as he approached the end of his work. Then I will show how the plot of *Eugene Onegin* dramatically mirrors the ironic irresolution of its language.

> Вы за «Онегина» советуете, други,
> Опять приняться мне в осенние досуги.
> Вы говорите мне: он жив и не женат.
> Итак, еще роман не кончен—это клад:
> Вставляй в просторную, вместительную раму
> Картины новые—открой нам диораму:
> Привалит публика, платя тебе за вход—
> (Что даст еще тебе и славу и доход).
> Пожалуй—я бы рад—так некогда поэт
>
> (3.1, 396)

You advise me, friends, to take up Onegin again in my autumn leisure. You tell me: he's alive and unmarried. Therefore, the novel is still unfinished—it's a gold mine. Insert new pictures into a spacious, commodious frame—show us a diorama: the public will come flocking, paying you to get in (which will bring you fame and an income). Certainly—I'd be glad to—thus did a poet once

Toward the end of his penultimate sojourn in Mikhailovskoe in the autumn of 1835, a season he could usually count on for his annual creative surge, Pushkin complained that nothing was coming—he couldn't write.[7] This was not strictly true; the revised "Journey to Arzrum" and the several attempts to construct a prose tale around his much earlier poem "Kleopatra" are the fruits of that summer and fall. In other words, Pushkin, perhaps for lack of fresh inspiration, was turning back to earlier projects with the intention of completing them. In the stanzas addressed to his publisher P. A. Pletnev, he toyed with assimilating *Eugene Onegin* into this set of uncompleted projects, although its last chapter had been announced as its final one five years before, and its text republished in its entirety in 1833.

What would constitute a recognizable ending? By the standards of the novel of manners or adventure, no end point had been reached: the hero was neither married nor dead and therefore still capable of story-worthy adventures. On the other hand, if *Onegin* belonged to the agglutinative narrative of the *Childe Harold* or *Don Juan* type, whose final shape and dimensions ("one hundred cantos or so") would be dictated by the author's whim, stamina, desire to resume, and ultimately, his longevity, *Onegin* need not be considered finished at all: after all, Pushkin was still alive, and still in need of a livelihood. Why waste, Pushkin has his friends say with varying degrees of crassness, such a tried-and-true, profitable vehicle?

Four times Pushkin revised his stanzas, recasting them in octaves and alexandrines before settling back into the best-known version, "In my autumn leisure" ("V moi osennie dosugi"), proving, if nothing else, how difficult it was to give up the familiar shape, "the marvelous machinery," as Nabokov puts it, of the Onegin stanza.[8] Pushkin never actually discloses what his own criteria for closure are, and, perhaps symptomatically, the end of the stanza peters out on the backward-looking phrase "tak nekogda poet," suggesting a willingness to resume a nostalgic discourse with his readers, rather than any definite compositional intentions. Not Eugene's narrative future but the poet's past appears to be the subject of the last phrase as it tapers off—or, in other versions, a wryly exact calculation of the price that might be charged the audience for "entry." The alternate versions evoke two different relationships between the author and his envisioned readers: the faintly archaic rapport he enjoys with his friends and colleagues ("friends," "you, my stern rival," "amiable Pletnev"), and the favor of the broader public, which he must now attract. The last two chapters of *Onegin* had in fact enjoyed nowhere near the critical acclaim of the first six, provoking gleeful commentary in certain journalistic circles about Pushkin's poetic demise.[9] In each version of his epistle, the arch poetic idiom of the 1820's in which Pushkin addresses his sympathetic reader repeatedly degenerates into the commercial terminology of the "iron age of calculation."[10]

For all their joking good humor, the stanzas suggest the same image of poet as circus performer, and of his poetic product and even process as commodity, that we find in "Egyptian Nights." The vulgar note Pushkin puts in the mouths of his "friends" makes one wonder about the quality of their advice: are they correct in assuming that Pushkin's creative "leisure" will respond to market forces, the broad public's appetite for entertainment? Is *Eugene Onegin* nothing but an "expandable frame" into which can be inserted an indeterminate number of "dioramas" (Pushkin's mention of a modern new technology of entertainment geared for the broad masses is not accidental or innocent) until the audience's appetite for new adventures is sated and its rather straightforward formal expectations met? Can another batch of chapters be put on order without destroying the internal integrity of "our novel," or did his friends discern none? In my view, with each successive version of the imaginary dialogue the supposed rapport and well-meaning literary advice of friends and publisher expose themselves increasingly as crass misunderstanding and distance. I would like for the moment simply to draw attention to the possibility of an ironic reading of these stanzas, and therefore to the possible irony of Pushkin's never-to-be-acted-on suggestion that *Eugene Onegin* might still be completed.

Another piece of evidence, the "missing" chapter 10, of which eighteen stanzas survived in cryptographic form, has been adequately discussed in the scholarship.[11] It is quite possible that in 1829, under the fresh impression of his encounters with exiled Decembrists in the southern army, Pushkin seriously considered a much longer biographical trajectory for his hero. Chapter 10 does read like a ringing rebuttal of all the criticisms that had accumulated around *Eugene Onegin*, from the Decembrists' early disillusionment with its "triviality" to Bulgarin's sarcastic send-up of the seventh chapter, published immediately after Pushkin's return from Arzrum: "Renowned lyres have remained mute, and in the desert of our literature has once again appeared Onegin, pale, weak."[12]

Chapter 10 *would* have changed the work's final form. Even if its scathingly incisive chronicle of political events had eventually linked up with Eugene's story, it would have introduced a dimension completely absent in *Onegin*, political history—belatedly turning Eugene into a Walter Scott–style hero in verse.[13] The poetic style of chapter 10 is jarringly different, something between the accusatory (*oblichitel'nyi*) diction of "A guard dozed motionless on the Tsar's threshold" ("Nedvizhnyi strazh dremal") and "André Chénier" and the dry density of Pushkin's mature historical prose. In fact a number of the details about Alexander I's balding and dandified appearance, as well as their sharply derogatory tone, can be traced to Byron's last satirical works, *Don Juan* and *The Age of Bronze* (1823), the officially censored but ubiquitously read and quoted subtexts that invisibly shaped the pre-Decembrist intellectual climate.[14]

We do know that in the 1830's Pushkin was gripped by an increasing sense of obligation to record for posterity contemporary events about which he and his generation had been forced to keep silent: "I absolutely will write a history of Peter I, but of Alexander—*with the pen of Kurbsky*. . . . It is absolutely necessary to describe contemporary events so that (in the future) we can be referred to. It is already possible now to write about the reign of Nicholas and about the fourteenth of December."[15] In fact, of course, the history of Pushkin's own time would remain unspeakable, the urge to bear witness deflected into other forms or more distant times. Nevertheless, Pushkin would continue to try to tell the political history of his own class,[16] and on at least one other occasion, in "Ezersky" or "My Genealogy," chose the old familiar bottles of the Onegin stanza for his dangerous new wine. Chapter 10, I believe, marks the overlap: it was still ostensibly—at least by metrical inertia—part of the old structure, but in retrospect clearly marks the first step on the road to "The Bronze Horseman," Pugachev, and "Journey to Arzrum." By severing the umbilical cord where he did, Pushkin preserved the historical atmosphere and stylistic integrity of the 1820's world of *Eugene Onegin*: a world characterized by the ironic innuendo and habitual elisions of Alexander's theatrical court society.[17] The burning of chapter 10 does not violate, but rather preserves, that subtle harmony of spoken (social) and unspoken (historical-political) dimensions.

I would conjecture that it was in fact the destruction of chapter 10 that suggested to Pushkin the poem's final shape. Originally, Pushkin's plan appears to have been a symmetrical arrangement of three parts, each containing three chapters, with "Onegin's Journey" inserted into the penultimate slot before the return to St. Petersburg. It was only in 1831, a year after the burning, that Pushkin excluded the "Journey" and made the "Grand Monde" the eighth and final chapter. When *Eugene Onegin* was published in its final form in 1833, it was with the dangling appendage of this "omitted" journey chapter, or at least its fragments.

It is worth noting that the "Fragments of Onegin's Journey," unlike chapter 10, do not alter the outer circumference, the *end* of the narrative. They create, instead, a structural escape hatch, an interlude of potentially endless lyrical reminiscence, which looks back to and foregrounds the Byronic forms, themes, and above all the fragmentary improvisational monologue from which *Eugene Onegin* had originally sprung. In the rough draft of the "Introduction" to what was planned as chapter 8, Pushkin drew attention to this Byronic stylistic level:

> I deliberated with myself if I should not destroy this chapter, being tempted to do so by the fear that a playful parody might be regarded as an expression of disrespect toward a great and sacred memory. *Childe Harold*, however, stands on such a height that, whatever the tone adopted in speaking of it, I could not have harbored the thought of any possibility of insult existing there.[18]

Since "Onegin's Journey" retraced both Pushkin's original 1820 itinerary in the Caucasus and Crimea and his 1829 revisit, it is logical that he should revert imaginatively to the Byronic style associated with the south, if only in playful palimpsest. But I believe that Pushkin toward the end of his long poem also chose to foreground an original affinity with Byron that was deeply structural.

From the beginning, after all, *Eugene Onegin* was destined to be apprehended as a fragment, if only by its inevitable analogy with *Don Juan*. It was not just that Byron had died, leaving fourteen stanzas of a new canto behind; the "one hundred cantos" predicted by Byron at the outset would never, it seems safe to say, have been achieved, and were not meant to be (compare Pushkin's analogous promise to write "a *poema* of twenty-five cantos or so" [1, 59, 14]).[19]

> In that Byron prominently dramatizes throughout the poem his improvisational method, the piecemeal construction would, to the most naive reader, seem to reflect an epistemological imperative. . . . The irresolution which characterizes *Don Juan* describes neither the relation of one canto to its successor, nor the terminal condition of the work as a whole. The poem's (in)famous irresolution occurs within each canto and through the author's digressions and his disruptive posturings. The subject of *Don Juan* is, we see, its methods: acts of interpretation and uses of context. One does not care about the whole Byron has, or pretends he has, or promises. One cannot even believe in such wholes by the end of the poem.[20]

The "whole" narrative exists for the sake of interruption, ironic challenge—or as Pushkin's first readers understood it, for the sake of

Byronic "satire." Pushkin hastily denied any connection with the explicitly political term,[21] yet retained the covert radicality of the fragmentary narrative form.

Although there is a practical reason for the fragmentary form of "Onegin's Journey," namely Pushkin's prophylactic excision of stanzas that explored such politically forbidden spaces as Arakcheev's penal settlements, its ultimate effect is of a different order. Pace Nabokov, who maintains that the "Journey" bears no resemblance whatsoever to the Childe's pilgrimage, it seems to me quite clear that the "Journey" parodies the suppletive relationship between shadowy Childe Harold and garrulous author that was the distinctive feature of the work.[22] In much the same way, Eugene Onegin is made to repeat his author's travels, his refrain of "Skuka, skuka" (boredom, boredom) recalling the Childe's catatonia while serving similarly as a catalyst for the author's lively political and lyrical counterpoint. Most notably, of course, Eugene's "Journey" is usurped by Pushkin's reminiscences of Odessa, replacing the forward-moving spatial and temporal momentum of the journey by an elegiac loop back into the past: "Itak ia zhil togda v Odesse..." (And so I lived then in Odessa...) (6, 205).

Neither Onegin's journey nor the author's reminiscences of Odessa are represented fully; rather, as in E. T. A. Hoffmann's *Tomcat Murr*, each interrupts and fragments the other. This suppletive relationship between the two narratives places at the center of the reader's attention precisely the suture between what is told and what is not told. The fragmentary chapter appended to *Eugene Onegin* draws attention once more to the ontological status of omission in the work. The omitted stanza or fragmentary chapter acts in much the same way that the anthological fragment, the epitaph, or the fragmentary hoax poem did on the imaginations of early Romantic readers. As Marjorie Levinson puts it, factual context was no longer used to explain text; instead, context was extrapolated by the sympathetic imagination to make sense of text.[23] The hole left by the omitted stanzas in the "whole" fabric of the poem reminds us of what is missing in any piece of language. Something is said only because something else is not said; the omission designates the presence of what has not been spoken or recorded, while the existing text acquires a dimension of absence: it represents only a part of what was once there, of what was possible.

A similar dialectical relationship might be diagnosed between the "mimetic" portion of the novel (Eugene's travels) and the "lyrical" portion (Pushkin in Odessa). Which is the central narrative, which the digression? Ostensibly the former is a third-person fiction, the latter an autobiographical tangent, yet the way the two journeys are superimposed on each other blurs the border between the two. The description of Pushkin's haunts in Odessa repeats Eugene's day in St. Petersburg in chapter 1, while, as Nabokov has established, Eugene's journey retraces Pushkin's footsteps in the Caucasus.[24] The distinction between "he" and "I" creates a figure for two different moments in a continuum: the joie de vivre and elegiac élan of the Odessa passage, written in his new exile at Mikhailovskoe, can be attributed to Pushkin's intense nostalgia for the south in 1825, while *skuka*, as I outlined in Chapter 3, was the predominant ambience of his journey to Arzrum, embarked on in 1829 with expectations of spiritual renewal. One might say that the "he" and "I" narratives are allegorizations of different emotional moments, and it is the contrast between the 1823 and 1829 sojourns in the south, or more precisely, between Pushkin's elegiac enthusiasm for the absent south in 1825 and the disillusionment in its presence in 1829, that Pushkin wished to render. Each is in a fragmentary relationship to the whole experience of psychological discontinuity.[25]

In fact, in many ways the "Fragments of a Journey" recreate the originally "open" format of *Onegin*, now through an elegiac lens. It is conceivable that the lukewarm reception that greeted the Moscow chapter provoked Pushkin to try to recapture that ambience of openness. It was by now commonplace for a Romantic poet to publish an uncompleted draft as a "Romantic fragment poem," whose defective form fostered "the transformational *act* (his own and the reader's), as opposed to the *product*, as the essential literary fact." "The Romantic Fragment Poem, like all other literary forms, contains a latent imagination of a reader, one who is capable of a particular response to the work's irresolution."[26] It aims, in other words, to construct a reader who will in turn construct it. Claiming deliberately to disdain the "false finality of the material object or completed work" for the sake of preserving the accidental form left by "divine visitation, . . . irresolution—a valorizing sign—confers upon the fragmentary work the character of the infinite, inexhaustible semiotic event. . . . Irresolution has become a marked quality, a sign of aesthetic intentionality. . . . A form originally offered as the most natural and spontaneous now looks like a most artificial, ironic and literary construction."[27] Pushkin's closural strategy makes sense in this context. Drawing toward the close of his seven-year work, he sought to preserve its original openness of structure, and thereby perhaps to reengage his readers' waning interest. Indeed, I would suggest that the double journeys inscribed by Pushkin in this penultimate chapter capture the ambivalence of the writer's attitude to his work: one journey moves forward, apparently in space, but also toward the unavoidable end of the story; the other, rushing joyously backward to the work's lyrical source, creates a deliberately unresolved structural counterpoint.

From this perspective, then, Nabokov is wrong: *Eugene Onegin* is finished, although (or perhaps because) its plot is interrupted, part of a chapter and the hero's biography damaged, and questions of what happened next left unanswered. "If poetry is defined as an interruption of the linear, diachronic flow of language from a referent, through a code or grammar, to a listener (the communicative circuit), the fragment poem not only performs, it dramatizes the poetic function."[28] Far from breaking off, *Eugene Onegin* completes its demonstration, indeed its allegorization, of the fragmentary nature of subjectivity and language.

The "Double Lorgnette" of Irony

What kind of author-reader rapport did "the motley stanzas of a romantic *poema*," as Pushkin once referred to *Eugene Onegin*, create?[29] In Levinson's view, "The way the Romantic Fragment Poem sought to construct a reader who would in turn construct *it*" should be demystified as a kind of hoax, willingly entered into by author and reader. The author's refusal, or inability, to completely render his conception in language implicitly denigrated the complete artifact produced by mere workmanship, while celebrating even the fragmentary by-products of authentic divine visitation, to which it thus laid claim. Around the ruptured edges of the fragment hovered "the figure of the poet as the presence of an eternal, chameleon authorial energy."[30] Concomitantly, this formal rupture opened up a space for the reader, who constructed as much context as he needed to make the fragment meaningful to him. Therefore, every reading of the fragment was unique, bearing the imprint of his narrative intuition, his own "inspiration." As Diderot had insisted, "One must be almost in a state to create art in order to feel it strongly."[31]

Eugene Onegin does not disdain this form of audience engagement. The omitted stanzas and ellipses in the first chapter are rather specific nudges to the reader to reconstruct their absent contents. Thus, for example, stanza 8 serves as a kind of runway for the omitted innuendos of stanza 9:

> Но в чем он истинный был гений,
> Что знал он тверже всех наук . . .
> Была наука страсти нежной,
> Которую воспел Назон,
> За что страдальцем кончил он
> Свой век блестящий и мятежный
> В Молдавии, в глуши степей,
> Вдали Италии своей.
>
> (1, 8, 3–14)

But where he was a veritable genius, what he knew more firmly than all the arts . . . was the art of soft passion which Naso sang, for which he ended his brilliant and tumultuous span a sufferer in Moldavia, in the wild depth of steppes, far from his Italy.[32]

Pushkin's elegies and letters of the eventful Odessa fall of 1823 furnish a fund from which to extrapolate the possible contents of the missing stanza: the habitual analogy between his own and Ovid's overlapping exiles, developed fully in "To Ovid" that same year, with perhaps an associative evocation of his Italian mistress Amalia Riznich. Stanzas 10–12 read like an ironic retelling of the incidents told in an elegiac key in "The Demon," "Proserpine," and the erotic elegies of 1823–25, suggesting in what specific direction the omitted stanzas 13 and 14 might have developed the all-purpose image of the cuckolded husband with which stanza 12 provocatively concludes:

И рогоносец величавой,
Всегда довольный сам собой,
Своим обедом и женой.
(1, 12, 10–12)

And the majestic cuckold, always pleased with himself, his dinner, and his wife.

Indeed, at the end of the chapter Pushkin gives the reader more or less explicit instructions as to how textual fragmentariness can be interpreted:

Пишу, и сердце не тоскует,
Перо забывшись, не рисует,
Близ неоконченных стихов,
Ни женских ножек, ни голов.
(1, 59, 5–8)

I write, and the heart does not fret; the pen, forgetting itself, draws next to unfinished lines neither feminine feet nor heads.

Notice the complementary relationship implied between (erotic) life and text: only closure of the experience enables closure of expression. Passionate life expresses itself in interrupted writing; the pen "forgets itself" to supplement imaginatively the inadequacy of language with silent pictures. Thus, reading backward, we understand the fragment to be a *sign* of ongoing passion; in Diderot's words again, "A man . . . utters a cry. . . . Nevertheless, I've understood everything."[33]

Throughout chapter 1 Pushkin engages his reader with casual innuendo, inciting him to draw on his reading of other Pushkin poems or awareness of other information to reconstruct a common anterior context, around which author and reader can establish the beginnings of a sympathetic consensus.

Онегин, добрый мой приятель,
Родился на брегах Невы,
Где, может быть, родились вы
Или блистали, мой читатель;
Там некогда гулял и я:
Но вреден север для меня.
(1, 2, 9–14)

Onegin, a good pal of mine, was born upon the Neva's banks, where maybe you were born, or used to shine, my reader! I used to take a stroll there, too: but the north is harmful to me.

The double entendre is a simple one, but engages the reader in a pleasurable reading beyond the literal meaning. The reader becomes, or fails to become, the "moi chitatel'" who understands what kind of threat to his health Pushkin has in mind. Beyond that, we recognize Pushkin's first of many exercises in parabasis, which Friedrich Schlegel called "the essence of irony." *Eugene Onegin*, like *Tristram Shandy* and *Don Juan*, is full of those moments when the process of writing is represented as occluding the fiction being made.

ничего
Не вышло из пера его,
И не попал он в цех задорный
Людей, о коих не сужу,
Затем, что к ним принадлежу.
(1, 43, 10–14)

Nothing issued from his pen, nor did he get into the cocky guild of people upon whom I pass no judgment—since I belong to them.

Gary Handwerk's interpretation of Schlegel's aphorism sheds considerable light on the way the omitted stanzas and semantic elisions mold the reader's relationship to the text from chapter 1 of *Onegin* on: "Parabasis is not the core of irony, but merely literalizes what always occurs in the ironic interchange. Its essence is not the interruption of illusion, but the opening up of a space for the response of the audience and their inclusion in the communicative act."[34] Thus another form of Pushkinian parabasis is the way he includes and exercises his readers' literary expertise. One reader may recognize Viazemsky's "First Snow" ("Pervyi sneg") as the source of the chapter's epigraph, another may be able to supply the missing subject of the phrase "I zhit' toropitsia i chuvstvovat' speshit" (and to live it hurries and to feel it hastes): namely, youth (*molodost'*). One reader may recognize with pleasure the allusion to Pushkin's earlier work "Ruslan and Liudmila," another may savor his playful re-creation of its mock-epic diction, or rather the jarring incompatibility of certain colloquial or prosaic idioms in the mock-epic, neoclassical context that frames them:

Так думал молодой повеса,
Летя в пыли на почтовых,

Всевышней волею Зевеса
Наследник всех своих родных.
(1, 2, 1–4)

Thus a young scapegrace thought, flying in the dust with post horses, by the lofty will of Zeus the heir of all his kin.

From the beginning Pushkin solicits and develops his reader's awareness of words' auras of stylistic, discoursive, and humorous implication. Our first glimpse of Eugene is a quoted text, which immediately thematizes the distinction between overt and latent content, and from which we extrapolate its missing speaker:

Какое низкое коварство
Полуживого забавлять,
Ему подушки поправлять,
Печально подносить лекарство,
Вздыхать и думать про себя:
Когда же черт возьмет тебя!
(1, 1, 9–14)

What base perfidiousness the half-alive one to amuse, adjust for him the pillows, sadly present the medicine, sigh—and think to oneself when *will* the devil take you?

The outrageousness of the lines was multiplied if the reader recognized that Pushkin had substituted "my uncle" for the "ass" of Krylov's well-known fable "An ass of most honest principles" ("Osel samykh chestnykh pravil")[35] and deduced a further layer of outrageous innuendo at the expense of Pushkin's famous uncle V. L. Pushkin. Two "young scamps" are characterized by the same stanza: the one who attends his dying uncle in the barely disguised expectation of a fortune, and the one who uses this opportunity to play a poetic trick on his own uncle.

Eugene's childhood, boyhood, and youth take a mere two stanzas to describe. What enables this compactness? Again, Pushkin's exploitation of an ironic shorthand: he uses a fixed phrase, then exposes its ironically contrasting content. The notion of ironic "mention" developed by linguists Dan Sperber and Deirdre Wilson helps clarify Pushkin's linguistic operations. What characterizes an ironic statement is the distinction between "use" and "mention." An ironic statement "mentions" an expression that might be appropriate in a different context but is incongruous in the given one.[36]

Thus in stanza three the formula "Sluzhiv otlichno-blagorodno" (having served outstandingly) entitles the subject in practice to a ruinously extravagant lifestyle subsidized by the tsarist court—which casts a whole new light on the "services" rendered. *Madame* and *Monsieur* are metonyms for the eternal French governesses and tutors of dubious provenance employed by the Russian aristocracy to "educate" their children. We don't need to know exactly what happened; Pushkin uses a series of elegiac formulas whose euphemistic sentimentality contrasts ludicrously with their sexual implications, and with their abrupt and crude consequences:

> Когда же юности мятежной
> Пришла Евгению пора,
> Пора надежд и грусти нежной,
> Monsieur прогнали со двора.
> (1, 4, 1–4)

Then, when tumultuous youth's season for Eugene arrived, season of hopes and tender melancholy, Monsieur was chased off the property.

By the time it ends its career as the direct object of an unceremonious and colloquial Russian expulsion, whatever conventionally refined aura the French epithet *Monsieur* may have had has been destroyed. The rest of the stanza develops the same strategy. "Vot moi Onegin na svobode" (Now my Onegin's at liberty)—the apparently casual formula "na svobode" is then filled out in ironic detail. To be free in Russian society means to be dressed according to the latest London fashion, speak and write French, dance the Polish mazurka, and bow with cosmopolitan grace. Eugene's mastery of the details of a fashionable exterior then leads to an ingenuous deduction of his inner qualities—"Chego zh vam bol'she? Svet reshil, / Chto on umen i ochen' mil" ("What would you more? The World decided he was clever and very nice") (1, 4, 13–14)—and it is up to the reader to notice the lapse in logic.

In the first two pages Pushkin's narrative has not exceeded the bounds of Wayne Booth's classical definition of irony: a statement that means something other than it says. To arrive at the nonliteral meaning, the reader must perform what Gary Handwerk calls "contextual loading": thus, in a straightforward example such as "No vreden Sever dlia menia," *vreden* can signify both physical and political harm, *Sever* can refer to both the meteorological and the political climate of the capital, while the entire sentence masks a threat with solicitous concern for the poet's well-being. Some of the other examples we have looked at are subtler in that they rely on the reader's ability to detect a stylistic and semantic relation of incongruity between ostensibly separate segments.

What, then, is the purpose of such an "intricate intellectual dance," with a well-established leader and follower?[37] Denser, more economical, and trickier than ordinary communication, it confirms tacitly what "we" already know. The purpose of engendering momentary perplexity is precisely to establish "amiable communities of interpretation": "[Irony's] complexities are, after all, shared; the whole thing cannot work at all unless both parties to the exchange have confidence that they are moving in identical patterns."[38] Such a concept of irony, Handwerk comments, "enacts and relies upon accepted human values within a clearly defined context; it is essentially normative."[39] By short-circuiting literal or surface meanings, the rhetorical trope of irony locates a basis for intersubjective agreement; it creates a shortcut, for the author and his selected audience, to intellectual intimacy.

If we picture Pushkin's position in May 1823, as he began to write *Onegin* at a great distance from the capital yet *for* it as an audience, it becomes clear why it was important that he strongly engage his distant, forgetful, or ambivalent audience in an "amiable community of interpretation" in the first two pages. The simultaneous double meanings of irony perfectly conveyed both Pushkin's mastery of the oral and literary idioms of the capital and his slight distance from them. He is no longer an unconscious user of the discourses furnished by his culture, and he arouses in his readers a corresponding awareness of the strange incongruities of their language. His purpose is to focus the reader's attention on the potential variability of seemingly automatic uses of language, and on his own acts of interpretation.

The difference between the traditional use of rhetorical irony, the notion of aesthetic irony commonly called "Romantic," and Schlegel's version of Romantic or "Socratic" irony is the degree to which the ironist himself is implicated in the language he "mentions" and obliquely questions. As Handwerk explains, Schlegel's Romantic irony is not just a celebration of the artist's omnipotence, his "godlike self-unmasking" amid his creation.[40] The act of self-distancing and reframing makes of *every* ironist an artist, a self-creator. An ironic speaker steps outside the particulars of his own situation, much as the chorus steps away from the tragic action, and observes it as he might a third-person event. By reframing his situation from another's perspective, the ironist "not only juxtaposes beliefs within a given and stable context, but constantly juxtaposes competing contexts, none of which is dominant."[41]

Elaborating on Schlegel's aphorisms, Handwerk has defined Romantic or ethical irony as the product of linking irony and the problem of the subject in German idealism. To solve the problem Schlegel adopted the conception of *Ich* as a process, discovering itself / selves through its own unexpectedly witty and self-distancing utterances to other subjects. In other words, to Schlegel, with his insistence "upon the provisional and fragmentary nature of the individual subject," can be traced the first theoretical formulation of the modern "decentered self."[42] In the eyes of the German Romantics, however, ironic *Unverständlichkeit* became a power for unifying humanity through a continual questioning and reshaping, rather than finalizing and mythologizing, of the social consensus and the ever-evolving self. Irony solves the problem of representing the self

> by fragmenting, rather than hypostasizing, the individual subject. . . . Irony is a linguistic act used to define the place and *movements* of the subject. . . . Romantic narratives explore the nature of an ironically limited subject with devices such as roles and role-exchange. . . . The subject-object split is internalized as the difference between a demystified absolute subject and an illusion-bound empirical subject.[43]

The most suggestive formulation of what I believe to be taking place in *Onegin* appears in Paul de Man's analysis of Baudelaire's notion of *dédoublement*. In "On the essence of laughter," Baudelaire describes the ironist / philosopher as someone "in the habit of doubling himself and observing disinterestedly the phenomena of his 'I,' " thus demonstrating the peculiarly human power to be self and other at the same time.

> The nature of this duplication is essential for an understanding of irony. It is a relation, within consciousness, between two selves, yet it is not an intersubjective relation. Baudelaire distinguishes between a simple sense of comedy that is oriented toward others, and thus exists on the necessarily empirical level of interpersonal relationship, and what he calls "le comique absolu" [or irony], where the relationship is not between man and man, two entities that are in essence similar, but between man and what he calls nature, that is two entities that are in essence different. . . . The dédoublement thus designates the activity of a consciousness by which a man differentiates himself from the non-human world—a rare capacity which belongs to those who deal in language. . . . Language thus conceived divides the subject into an empirical self, immersed in the world, and a self that becomes like a sign in its attempt at differentiation and self-definition.[44]

Until now I have focused on the way Pushkin uses "normative" ironic strategies to project the kind of reading and reader he wants. Nabokov and Lotman alike have tended to treat Pushkin's irony as the expression of the detached aesthetic subject interested ultimately in characterizing its own Olympian creative processes.[45] I believe we can move beyond this line of inquiry by showing in what ways *Eugene Onegin* realizes the more radical conception of epistemological irony I have outlined above. If we examine the central Petersburg section of chapter 1, with its brilliantly artistic and symptomatic "hanging back and catching up" motif,[46] we will recognize in it precisely an allegorical representation of Pushkin's own "hovering" between different selves. In de Man's words, "the fundamental structure of allegory reappears here in the tendency of the language toward narrative, the spreading out along the axis of an imaginary time in order to give duration to what is, in fact, simultaneous within the subject."[47]

The first thing we notice in Pushkin's day in the life of Eugene is the peculiarity of its temporal structure. "Byvalo," the first word of the stanza, sets the action in an indefinite, habitual, repetitive past. From then on a frenzied whirl of activities is related in the present tense, with future and past used only to denote sequence:

> Уж темно: в санки он садится.
> «Пади, пади»!—раздался крик;

Морозной пылью серебрится
Его бобровый воротник.
К *Talon* помчался: он уверен,
Что там уж ждет его Каверин.
Вошел: и пробка в потолок,
Вина кометы брызнул ток,
Пред ним *roast-beef* окровавленный,
И трюфли, роскошь юных лет,
Французской кухни лучший цвет,
И Стразбурга пирог нетленный
Меж сыром лимбургским живым
И ананасом золотым.

(1, 16, 1–14)

It's already dark. He gets into a sleigh. The cry "Way, way!" resounds. His beaver collar turns silver with frost dust. To Talon's he has dashed off; he is certain that Kaverin is already waiting for him. He's entered—and the cork hits the ceiling, the flow of comet-vintage wine has spurted, a bloody roast beef is before him, and truffles, luxury of youthful years, the best flower of French cuisine, and an imperishable Strasbourg pie between a living Limburg cheese and a golden pineapple.

Of course words like "uzh," "pomchalsia," "Padi, padi," "zhdet," and "bryznet" intrinsically express temporal pressure. So does the rapid fire of the syntactic units: an average of one or even two predicates per line. In effect, the scene unfolds before the reader as he rushes into it at breakneck speed. Each successive detail is given from the moving perspective of the passenger. The departure of the carriage is not precisely described at all; Pushkin "cuts" cinematically[48] to its effect on the passenger: the shout "Padi, padi!" behind him, the sudden dusting of his beaver collar with snow (and here again, an adjective's promotion to predicate ["serebritsia"] volatilizes an epithet into an action). The moment Eugene enters the restaurant ("Voshel:"), the action speeds up so much that even the verb drops out, leaving only the perceptible consequence of the action: "i probka v potolok."

Before Eugene and the reader, Pushkin then unfolds a painterly spectacle of foods, but here it is the epithets attached to the epic list of substantives that are saturated with temporal significance: "vina *komety*," "roast-beef *okrovavlennyi*," "triufli, roskosh' *iunykh let*," "luchshii tsvet," "Strazburga pirog *netlennyi*," "syrom limburgskim *zhivym*," "ananasom *zolotym*." Each food is presented at its peak of freshness, rareness, ripeness, or vintage, at a moment hovering between perfection and decay, as is the moment seized out of time by Pushkin. Pushkin seems deliberately to evoke the traditional juxtaposition of food and mortality that is the distinctive structural feature of the still life as a genre.[49] One would like to prolong the moment of plenitude amidst this tenuously perfect still life, but the momentum of the verbs reasserts itself and destroys the scene's aesthetic harmony:

Еще бокалов жажда просит
Залить горячий жир котлет,
Но звон брегета им доносит
Что новый начался балет.
(1, 17, 1–4)

Thirst still begs for goblets to quench the hot fat of the cutlets; but Breguet's chime reports to them that a new ballet has begun.

Most clearly emblematic of the passage's mortal pressure is the recurrent ringing of the sleepless, efficient, foreign watch—the metronome that regulates the *perpetuum mobile* of Onegin's dandified existence.

The visit to the theater (st. 21) dramatizes a similar contrast of perspectives. Eugene rushes ("poletel") to the theater to play his prescribed role of "law-giver" of the theater's highly ritualized etiquette.[50] With Pushkin's cinematic switch to Eugene's point of view, the scene is rendered as an undifferentiated blur of perceptions—"Vsio khlopaet"; "Vse iarusy okinul vzorom, / Vsio videl: litsami, uborom / Uzhasno nedovolen on"; "S muzhchinami so vsekh storon"; "Vsekh pora na smenu / /Balety dolgo ia terpel, /No i Didlo mne nadoel" (All clap as one; he cast a glance at all the tiers: saw it all; is terribly dissatisfied with faces and outfits; with men on all sides; to all comes a time for change; I've stood for ballets a long time, but I'm sick even of Didlo)—the key word in the passage obviously being *vsio/vse* (all), the stylistic symptom of Eugene's penchant for blasé generalization.

For the narrator, on the other hand, the name Didlo is a ticket to the otherworld of the past. Already the theater has been described as an enchanted land, brimming with the highly differentiated shades of past playwrights, performances, and idols. Eugene's characteristic forward motion ("voshel," "poletel," "idet mezh kresel po nogam" [1, 21, 1–2]) is replaced by Pushkin's equally characteristic ebbing back, out of this world into an absent one ("Tam, tam pod seniiu kulis / Mladye dni moi neslis')." (Notice the delightfully inappropriate completion of the elegiac nature trope "my young days flowed by in the shade of" by the unlikely "the backstage.") The narrator's experience of the theater contains the same words, but wearing a different associative aureole. Eugene goes to the theater in search of constant change ("Vsekh pora na smenu"); his lorgnette searches the loges of unknown ladies for novelty, but he finds "everything" the same. Pushkin is faithful to his old goddesses (in the plural); *his* lorgnette is disillusioned by novelty, while a familiar face is the mnemonic path to the lyrical past. Pushkin goes to the theater not to see the new, but to experience more acutely the absence of the old. His language both invests his subject with poignancy and disengages itself in a gracefully self-conscious parabasis, a display of the poet's own sensibility as it works itself up to an elegiac pitch:

> Мои богини! что вы? где вы?
> Внемлите мой печальный глас.
> Все те ж ль вы? другие ль девы,
> Сменив, не заменили вас?
> (1, 19, 1–4)

My goddesses! What has become of you? Where are you? Hark my sad voice; Are you still the same? Are other maidens substituting for you without taking your place?

Notice the typical elegiac sleight of hand: the presence of the theater and its intrinsic change (*smena*) are necessary in order to elicit mnemonically the desired anterior image, which it has only brought into acuter focus, *not* replaced. A complex play with connotations of change, exchange, and betrayal is involved.

To arrive by this route at the famous Istomina stanza is to cast its ontological status into doubt. Is it a vivid description of a performance that takes place in the narrative present, right before Eugene's entrance? Or is it the imaginary climax of Pushkin's elegiac tribute to his past goddesses, an unfolding in sensuous slow motion, without the benefit of binoculars and only through the lens of elegiac desire, of an ecstatic image of balletic movement that Eugene, in the very thick of things, is oblivious of? Whether we take Istomina's dance as a moment literally missed by Onegin because of his fashionably late arrival, or as a vision of aesthetic perfection intrinsically inaccessible to a man of the world in medias res, its allegorical significance is more or less the same. To be in life's presence is to be Eugene, blinded by his own momentum; to be absent is to see clearly, past life's ever-changing sameness, to the image's eternal difference. This philosophical theme emerges, however, only from the juxtaposition of the two perspectives.

It might be objected that this is only "aesthetic irony" of the most legible kind, valorizing at the expense of a mere myopic mortal the broader and deeper vision of the Romantic artist. Yet the narrator's allegiance to the past and aversion to novelty are in turn distanced by Pushkin's clear awareness of the quotation marks around his elegiac phrases, and by the mocking novelty of his rhymes ("k teatru" and "Kleopatru," "vol'nost'iu dysha" [elegiac fixed phrase] and "entrechat"). If the narrator's unhurried, elegiac fidelity of vision ironically frames Eugene's blasé and cursory attention only to matters of external form, a third viewpoint emerges that treats both the elegiac discourse and the *mondain* discourse as fair game, material to be detached and rearranged into new poetic patterns. Thus is the elegiac perspective privileged and ironized in turn by Pushkin's "representation of the act of representation."[51]

Let us turn to the well-known description of Eugene's "study" in stanzas 23–26 for an even less readily interpretable balance of power. The narrator begins on an epic intake of breath, as though praying for inspiration: "Izobrazhu l' v kartine vernoi . . ." In an epic it would already be incongruous to "portray" in such high style anything as trivial as a "lonely study." However, Romanticism was making the poet's and even the dandy's "study" a subject for potentially serious treatment. After showing us the externals of Onegin's life, Pushkin prepares to penetrate its "interior," spatially and psychologically. The trouble is that for Eugene's room, *study* is a misnomer; it is actually a dandy's boudoir or dressing room, with distinctly feminine and theatrical associations. (The phrase "Odet, razdet, i vnov' odet" [dressed, undressed, and dressed again] slyly echoes the recent description of Istomina: "To stan sov'et, to razov'et" [now her waist winds, now unwinds].) In fact, the metonymic description of a room's furnishings as attributes of their absent inhabitant is a trope employed largely for women, rather than men, as we have seen in the Oriental tales. When the narrator develops an extended epic digression on the merchandise that has made its way from around the world to decorate the "study" of the eighteen-year-old "philosopher," an ironic gap yawns between both the epic diction and its mercantile referent and the massive operation of world trade and its trivial end (a dandy's comfort).[52]

The following stanza performs an even quicker slide into bathos; beginning archaically with "amber on pipes from Tsaregrad," the narrator's list passes quickly from porcelain and bronzes through perfumes to "little combs, little files, straight scissors and curved, thirty sorts of brushes, for the nails and for the teeth" (1, 24, 5–8). We have moved with unseemly modern rapidity from external decor to the most intimate details of personal toilette and physiology. Teeth certainly belong to an "interior," but not perhaps the one we had in mind. So far the passage has set up a series of ironic displacements: for the epic world, a room; for a spiritual or psychological "interior," a physical one; for a "philosopher's" studies, a dandy's vain habits. The second half of the stanza surveys the opposition of "philosophy" to "nails" and "teeth" from a new angle. Pushkin presides over a delightful cameo appearance by two authentic Enlightenment philosophes who are arguing precisely over the issue of manicure etiquette. Moreover, Rousseau, who might be called not only the "defender of human freedom and rights" (1, 24, 13), but also the inventor of the psychological interior, emerges as the heated defender of social propriety ("Rousseau could not understand how pompous Grimm dared clean his nails before him, the eloquent crackpot"). The noble afflatus of Rousseau's epithet "Zashchitnik vol'nosti i prav" is speedily undercut by the colloquially anticlimactic line terminating on a poor (punning) rhyme that clinches the couplet: "v sem sluchae sovsem ne prav" (is in this case not right at all).[53] When the meeting of the famous philosophes degenerates into an argument between a haughty dandy and a touchy orator, it gives a whole new meaning to the word "philosopher."

We are not allowed to rest in this new position for very long.

Stanza 25 appears to continue in the same vein, but the assertion of the right of any "man of action" to concern himself with the beauty of his nails somehow turns into a passive acquiescence to the despotism of habit. By the time the narrator calls Eugene "a second Chaadaev," not only are we not sure which famous aspect of Chaadaev's personality Pushkin is referring to, his dandyism or his reputation for deep thinking,[54] but we wonder how we are to rank the categories "dandy" and "philosopher." If Rousseau looked like a crackpot in the dandy's presence, Eugene's dandyism now rhymes unflatteringly with pedantry ("V svoei odezhde byl pedant, / I to chto my nazvali frant"). By the end of the third stanza all we have learned about Eugene's interior life is that he spends three hours a day in front of the looking glass, preparing his exterior for public view. When at the end of the stanza he slips past the author and reader in his new costume, he has in effect eluded every descriptive category the author had set up for him:

> Подобный ветреной Венере,
> Когда, надев мужской наряд
> Богиня едет в маскарад.
> (1, 25, 11–14)

Akin to giddy Venus when, having donned a masculine attire, the goddess drives to a masquerade.

We manage to glimpse Eugene only when he is doubly disguised, as Venus attending a masquerade, in her turn disguised as a man; in effect, each mask cancels the other. If we recognize the source of Pushkin's literary simile as a borrowing from Parny's allegorical *The Disguises of Venus*, then even Eugene's physical appearance dissolves. The more truly language attempts to portray its subject, the more it reveals its own *mise en abîme*, language referring to other language. But perhaps the unveiling of an apparently vivid simile as traditional allegory is revealing after all: the image of love on which Eugene is fixated is his own reflected image in the looking glass, the image that has been created for others. Under the masks of the Ovidian lover, the master of erotic disguise, the god(dess) of love herself, hovers the face of Narcissus—the one whose love is doubled back on himself.[55]

Double disguise, "double lorgnette," the double carriage lanterns painting rainbows on the snow on the way to the ball: Eugene is accompanied by images of doubleness, in fact, by images that double for himself. His character is structured like language: a visible signifying surface/text, and the absent signified/interior to which it refers. We are given his room, his appurtenances, his reflection in the mirror, his gestures, samples of his language, and out of these fragments we extrapolate a presence, the place behind the scenes where they all intersect.

By contrast, the narrator, "ia," is only too happy to launch into a confession. His most famous lyrical digression, "dve nozhki," appears in the context of the ball, where he claims he has given up his own practice of erotic conquest but still enjoys the sight of girls' flying feet. The digression has often been taken as a passionate tribute to the owner of a particular pair of feet. In fact, however, the word "nozhki" is grammatically ambiguous, implying either one pair of feet or many. "Nozhki" thus acts as a shifter, moving the narrator through a series of associative vignettes—flying feet pursued across the dance floor by guardsmen's spurs, the fat feet of all but three Russian women, two beloved feet that left their light print on the elegiac meadows and oriental carpets of his memory, the "conventional beauty" of the balletic foot, the flirtatious foot under a long tablecloth, the foot reflected in the mirror-like parquet of the ballroom, and the feet kissed by southern waves at the base of a granite cliff.

The associative dithyramb is both a bravura display of his own elegiac depth of feeling and a deeply ironic deconstruction of its allegorical basis. "Dve nozhki" purport to be a metaphor for his fixation, a symbol of his undying secret love. Not to name them, however, is to leave them available for unbridled fantasy, unlimited displacement into allegorical language. In fact, the feet serve as a mnemonic device, shifting him from memory to memory, attachment to attachment, each reminiscent of an anterior one. The metonymic relationship of the two feet to the unnamed woman they stand for is exactly the same substitutive relationship in which each woman stands to every other. The subject of the lyric is no one nameless love, but rather the narrator's "faithfulness" to the underlying erotic essence, for which each woman and each pair of feet is only a sign, a transferable fetish.[56]

Thus the last stanza begins with yet another memory, yet another elegiac incarnation of the same fixed erotic experience:

Мне памятно другое время.
В заветных иногда мечтах
Держу я счастливое стремя...
И ножку чувствую в руках.
(1, 34, 1–4)

I remember another time: now and then in fateful dreams I hold the happy stirrup and in my hands I feel a little foot.

The mention of feet evokes another time, which contains another image of feet, in endless relay. In this stanza language has clearly become saturated with substitution. The two lovers disintegrate into metonymic attributes—her foot, her touch, the "happy stirrup"; his hands, his seething imagination, his withered heart at last kindled to full erotic and linguistic release by the longed for *repetition* of the familiar (and completely imaginary) scenario:

Опять кипит воображение,
Опять ее прикосновение
Зажгло в увядшем сердце кровь,
Опять тоска, опять любовь!
(1, 34, 5–8)

Again imagination seethes, again that touch has fired the blood within my withered heart, again the ache, again the love!

Here we might recognize what de Man calls "the recurring process of totalization":

The subject uses language to convert a world structured by the contingency of metonymic connections into one dominated by metaphoric necessity. One can therefore always trace a metaphoric chain of substitutions, by which the world is unified, back to an illicit equivalence at its origin, a leap from metonym to metaphor. This original leap is the source of the incompatibilities that generate allegorical deconstruction. . . . The meaning constituted by the allegorical sign can then consist only in the *repetition* of a previous sign with which it can never coincide, since it is of the essence of this previous sign to be pure anteriority. . . . Allegory can only blindly repeat its earlier model without final understanding.[57]

"The feet," then, are not a part of some beloved woman or women at all, but the image of his desire the narrator has created out of their bodies. Treated as the "true sign" of erotic fulfillment at the beginning of the digression, the feet turn out to be "deceitful" in the end, and at its end. The disillusionment that quickly ensues leaves to the reader's imagination in exactly what way reality failed to meet expectations. Underneath the frivolous innuendo, however, lies a stark assertion of every erotic encounter's partiality. Each is only a metonym awakening a tremendous hunger for the lost referent, a hunger it can never satisfy. "Invoked to fill the absence of a prior signifier, each new signifier in turn reveals itself as incomplete, as necessarily calling up yet another signifier to supplement its own absence."[58]

Paradoxically, however, precisely the fetishistic repetition of this *obman* enables the self to experience the stable, *retrievable* sense of an interior self—in other words, the self created by elegy. The real object is the recognition of the subject in his own experiences, hence the repetitive insistence on certain marked forms recognizable as his own. The "end" of the hunger is not love, but the subject's recovery of his lost impulse toward language. The imaginary subject comes into being when, as Lacan puts it, "a mnemic element of a privileged anterior situation is taken up again in order to articulate the current situation, that is to say, that it is employed there unconsciously as a signifying element with the effect of molding the indeterminacy of experience into a tendacious signification."[59] Read in this way, I believe that the "little feet" digression, which presents a lyrical picture of the poet-narrator's interior life in apparent contrast with Eugene's dispassionate methodology of display and seduction, begins to reveal the common psychological substratum shared by elegiac repetition and erotic repetition compulsion.

Pushkin quite openly foregrounds and then dismisses the issue of fictional alter egos, in a stanza frequently quoted to prove Pushkin's allegiance to the principles of "realistic," or non-Romantic, characterization:

> Всегда я рад заметить разность
> Между Онегиным и мной,
> Чтобы насмешливый читатель . . .
> Не повторял потом безбожно,
> Что намарял я свой портрет,
> Как Байрон, гордости поэт,
> Как будто нам уж невозможно

Писать поэмы о другом,
Как только о себе самом.
(1, 56, 3–12)

I'm always glad to mark the difference between Onegin and myself, lest a mocking reader . . . afterward shamelessly repeat that I have scrawled my own portrait like Byron, the poet of pride—as if it were no longer possible for us to write long poems about anything but ourselves!

Authorial disclaimers notwithstanding, the question of Pushkin and Eugene's relationship continues to obtrude. Any reader moderately informed on Pushkin's habits in St. Petersburg and Odessa would have no trouble matching them ("Slichaia zdes' moi cherty") to Eugene's dandified existence, marked as they were by exaggerated sartorial display, including the fatuous fingernails, hobnobbing with the aristocracy, and an eighteenth-century conception of erotic conquest, together with its inevitable aphoristic precipitate.[60] More importantly, the frequent protestations of affinity or difference within the text, the ambiguous opening monologue with its double applicability to hero and author, and Pushkin's well-known sketch for an illustration of the poet and Eugene leaning together on the parapet of the Neva embankment keep the relationship between the two at the center of the reader's attention.[61] This "hovering" between likeness and unlikeness is formulated most clearly at the end of the chapter, where several of the ironic strategies we have been identifying come into play.

Stanza 45 begins with a complex parabasis that locates the poet within the boundary of his fiction, elaborately citing a whole series of resemblances to account for his and Eugene's friendship. What unites them is their common rejection of "the burden of worldly conventions," their "freedom-loving" eccentricity. From the middle of the stanza, however, the phrase "both of us" becomes obtrusively repetitive, and their common features increasingly formulaic:

Страстей игру мы знали оба:
Томила жизнь обоих нас,
В обоих *сердца жар угас*;
Обоих *ожидала злоба*
Слепой Фортуны и людей

На самом утре наших дней.
(1, 45, 9–14) [emphasis mine]

The *play of passions* we both knew; life oppressed us both; in both, the *heart's glow* had gone out; the *rancor of blind Fortuna* and of men awaited both at the *very morn of our days*.

What began as a bold claim of originality dwindles into a predictable list of elegiac complaints, the clichés of an entire generation. Unless the reader senses the invisible quotation marks, the ironic *mention* of those phrases, he will miss the semantic switch from one kind of statement to its opposite: the friends are coupled by their "originality," by the kind of thing callow young men tend to believe about themselves. Notice that in this way Pushkin places himself both inside and outside the frame. He is both enclosed within the category "both of us" and freed by his representation of the syndrome.

Thus, at the very moment Pushkin seems semantically to be urging the pair's Romantic affinity, his style intimates something rather different. The following stanza begins with what appear to be authorial sententia on the subject of disillusionment: "Kto zhil i myslil, tot ne mozhet / V dushe ne prezirat' liudei" ("He who has lived and thought can't help despising people in his soul") (1, 46, 1–2). But an ironic aside to the reader distances the speaker from the quoted discourse; it turns out that this was a sample of Onegin's speech, which at first grated on the narrator.

Все это часто придает
Большую прелесть разговору.
Сперва Онегина язык
Меня смущал.
(1, 46, 8–10)

All this often imparts great charm to conversation. At first Onegin's language embarrassed me.

Although Pushkin continues to attribute to Eugene the same lyrical emotions he experienced in his company on the Neva embankment ("We were silently intoxicated"; "thus we flew in dream"), the difference between "Onegin's language," dry and reductive, and Pushkin's lyricism mutely suggests itself, until Eugene drops out of the equation "we" altogether and only "I" and "the language of Petrarch and love" remain. Pushkin's "I" asserts itself more insistently against the background of their common experience on the Neva precisely to the extent that his language detaches itself from the literal situation. From the local nocturnal sounds of carriage wheels on Millionnaia Street and a rowboat's oars on the Neva, Pushkin makes a sudden associative leap to more Romantic waters—"Adriaticheskie volny, / O Brenta!"—a veritable barcarole in the Byronic idiom he has supposedly abjured.

> Придет ли час моей свободы?
> Пора, пора!—взываю к ней . . .
> Пора покинуть скучный брег
> Мне неприязненной стихии,
> И средь полуденных зыбей,
> Под небом Африки моей,
> Вздыхать о сумрачной России,
> Где я страдал, где я любил,
> Где сердце я похоронил.
> (1, 50, 1–14)

Will the hour of my freedom come? It's time, it's time! To it I call. . . . It's time to leave the dreary shore of the element inimical to me, and amid meridian ripples beneath the sky of my Africa, to sigh for somber Russia, where I suffered, where I loved, where I buried my heart.

As in the "dve nozhki" rhapsody, what precipitates an acute sense of self is precisely the repetition of that familiar sense of disjunction between the "not this" of present experience and the tantalizing anterior image to which it seems to refer. Notice what an infinite regress is set up by Pushkin's lyrical flight: Pushkin, writing in Odessa, pictures himself with Eugene, absentmindedly listening to the lapping of the waves on the Neva bank but apostrophizing the Adriatic waves he knows only from literature, which in turn evoke a Romantic image of himself standing on the Odessa shore, picturing his flight to a distant African shore, from whose beautiful distance, as Gogol put it, he could finally imagine Russia. The recovery of a sense of self is precipitated not by the experience of homecoming but by the familiar experience (and language) of separation and allegorical substitution.

In "The Rhetoric of Temporality," de Man shows that ironic self-displacement and elegiac allegory necessitate each other. "The temporal void that [irony] reveals is the same void we encountered when we found allegory always implying an unreachable anteriority. Allegory and irony are thus linked in their common discovery of a truly temporal predicament." Moreover, they share a fundamental psychic reflex: like allegory, "irony is not temporary, but repetitive, the recurrence of a self-escalating act of consciousness."[62] Differences in terminology aside, it is, I believe, something like this awareness that Pushkin reaches for in the last stanzas of chapter 1.

Whereas "dve nozhki" was both a bravura demonstration of elegiac art and an ironic (though perhaps not altogether conscious) deconstruction of its own figurative language, the last stanzas of chapter 1 abandon elegy per se for meta-elegy. Instead of depicting one or another individual erotic attachment, Pushkin instead analyzes the psychological pattern he has observed repeated in all of them: the invasion and silencing of the creative self by love's "madness."

> Любви безумную тревогу
> Я безотрадно испытал.
> Блажен, кто с нею сочетал
> Горячку рифм . . .
> Но я, любя, был глуп и нем.
> Прошла любовь, явилась муза,
> И прояснился темный ум.
> Свободен, вновь ищу союза
> Волшебных звуков, чувств и дум . . .
> И скоро, скоро бури след
> В душе моей совсем утихнет:
> Тогда-то я начну писать
> Поэму песен в двадцать пять.
> (1, 58–59)

Love's mad perturbation I joylessly experienced. Happy who united with it the fever of rhymes . . . but I, loving, was stupid and mute. Love passed, the Muse appeared, and the dark mind cleared up. Now free, I seek again the concord of magic sounds, feelings, and thoughts . . . and soon, soon the storm's trace will hush completely in my soul: *then* I shall start to write a poem of twenty-five cantos or so.

The analogy made earlier between the elegiac representation of loss and the initial trading of experience for controlling linguistic dramatization in the Freudian "fort/da" paradigm can now be expanded. It is not only that the mourning subject converts his own helpless position as object left behind into a powerful situation of willful and repeatable dramatization. Rather, as Lacan maintains, his psyche is imprinted with the structure of language.[63] Every presence (signifier) implies the simultaneous absence of the signified; to be aware of the image is already to have lost the indivisible thing. The illusory wholeness and presence of the image provoke a corresponding sense of fragmentation and absence, of self-loss or death, in the subject. By contrast, an elegy may mourn the loss of the beloved, but it simultaneously celebrates the subject's emergence from the silence and darkness of experience into the light of representation. To repeat the language of loss is, paradoxically, to recover the wholeness of the speaking self. To provoke life to assume the familiar forms of loss is to ensure the completion of the image. In fact, as the long series of Pushkin's repetitive elegies dramatizes, it is the image that begins to assume the role of the "original," and actual erotic experience that becomes its pale and always deficient copy.

Notice what has happened by the end of this passage. What began as a psychological analysis of the dynamics of the poet's creativity begins to congeal into the fixed formulas of elegiac confession. The "I" "fades from his own speech," leaving as it were the empty shells of a series of elegiac clichés, "mentioned" with increasing irony. By the end of the stanza the image of "I" as elegiac poet is fully detached and stylized, and his eventual liberation into different possibilities of language—notably a long, completed narrative poem, rather than passionate fragments or repetitive elegies—exultantly predicted. The elegiac "I" is suddenly a rather comical "other," soon to be outgrown.

The Duel: An Allegory

Clearly, what I am suggesting is that Pushkin is engaged in precisely the act of ironic self-representation described by de Man: by fragmenting rather than hypostasizing his subjectivity, he locates it in the hovering, now narrowing, now widening gap between various pairs of characters, or counterpointed perspectives. The counterpoint in chapter 1 lends itself readily to de Man's schematization, with Eugene representing the subject blindly immersed in empirical reality (*on*), the Pushkinian narrator the "absolute subject" (*ia*). The typical bildsungsroman would chart a progression from youthful subjectivity to ironic wisdom. The typical Romantic novel would refuse this developmental model and posit an absolute discontinuity between the imaginative-elegiac and the philistine world views. Does either of these patterns do justice to the peculiar way Pushkin flows into and ebbs from his own language, his own positions?

One of the fundamental structural ironies of *Onegin* is that Eugene *begins* as a demystified ironist, immersed in, and yet detached from, his role playing. It would not be excessive to recognize the phonemes *on* (he) and *ne* or *neg-* (negation) as being enciphered in his name—Onegin.[64] But a second, equally important structural irony has been uncovered in the poet's much more vivid, impassioned response to life: he is never responding to the life before him, only to the absence of another time that the present necessarily implies. Is not Onegin a figure for absence, precisely the poet's absence from his own world? Or to put it another way, isn't Onegin all that's left of the poet when his creative mind is otherwise occupied?

I hope to avoid reading *Eugene Onegin* as a work with a built-in class consciousness, so to speak, a romance constructed for the interests of the common reader, while the interpolated, digressive story of its own creation is addressed over his head to the "aesthete." There are no digressions; only the basis for linkage is not always obvious. Far from seeing in *Eugene Onegin* a mimetic, "realistic" narrative interrupted by metapoetic digressions, I propose to look at the plot as an allegory of the poet's life in time: Eugene's life is a product, an accurate expression of the poet's system of values. I would like to show that the plot and relationships between different pairs of characters are determined by, and indeed act out, Pushkin's ambivalence, which thus becomes nothing less than their fate.

William Mills Todd III has made a particularly strong case for viewing the writer's virtuosity within his own text as a reflection of, not an antithesis to, the possibilities for creative self-expression and adaptation available to the members of his culture. Somewhat analogously, I take elegy and irony to represent not just literary poles of the author's creative imagination but also modes of experience available in differing degrees to the characters within the book, and to its readers. Extrapolating from Erving Goffman's *Presentation of the Self in Everyday Life*, Todd shows that the characters within the book are engaged in essentially the same acts of writing and reading or misreading of each other's "texts," or surfaces, as are the author and reader.[65] By the same token, by engaging his reader in ever more subtle exercises in ironic thinking, the author fosters in the reader a habit of skeptical and mobile relationship to the phenomena of his own experience, of living consciously in the light of irony.

The necessity for interpretive skill, that is, for seeing and accounting for both the potential dissonances and the potential relationships between juxtaposed phenomena—for example, two juxtaposed texts, or two contradictory modes of behavior—is made manifest at the beginning of each chapter, in the enigmatic encounter of epigraphs and main text. For example, what are we to make of the juxtaposed epigraphs of chapter 2:

> O rus!
> Hor.
> О Русь!

What issues does the triple pun raise (I am assuming that "Horace" is meant to echo the phonemes of "O rus")? The train of thought provoked by this neat juxtaposition might be something like this: Is the happy eclogic sigh "O rus" (O countryside), uttered by the urbane Roman poet Horace in philosophical response to his rustication to the Sabine farm, a coincidentally appropriate response to "Rus'" (Old Russia)? Is the pun a happy macaronic coincidence or a grotesque case of mistranslation? Can the form of classical eclogue or pastoral, and more broadly the western myth of a "return to nature," adequately render the reality of Russian country life? It seems to me that the macaronic echo effect sets off complex associative and intonational dissonances, the relatively simple, domestic sigh of relief and plenitude contrasting with the various tones of voice in which the archaic phrase "O Rus'" might be uttered, from tones of epic pride or historic pathos to a more modern wry bemusement. Again one might say that Pushkin has marked the two poles between which his portrait of Russian life will hover.

It has long been noted that just as Pushkin talks a great deal about problems of translation, most obviously in his struggle with the terminology of foreign fashions, his characters are enmeshed in comparable problems of reading and misreading in their daily lives. As chapter 2 begins, Eugene appears to be enacting a version of the western myth of nature as it had developed from Horace to Rousseau and the European Romantics, namely man's restoration to his undistorted human nature by country life. A closer look at Eugene's "renewal," however, suggests that he has merely turned the Russian provinces into a convenient backdrop for Byronic gestures: the local creek in which he takes his morning swim becomes the Hellespont, freeing his serfs from the *obrok* (quitrent) and offending the local landowners is Eugene's version of revolutionary *engagement*, while he continues in a lordly manner to sample the sexual favors of the peasants, the "native girls." Having turned his novel surroundings into a familiar script, he discovers that the *tedium vitae* that is an obligatory accompaniment of the latter returns too, and necessitates the introduction of further Byronic plot motifs, which we will explore in a moment. The irony is of course manifest: by the very process of translating what is new and unfamiliar to him—namely, Russian country life—into the familiar "exotic" terms of Romantic landscape, Eugene has lost the opportunity to experience anything new, to be changed by his life. He leaves the imprint of his psychic structure on every experience as unmistakably as he leaves the indentation of his nail on the pages of his books, attracted immutably only by his own reflection.

Nor does Eugene have a monopoly on misreading: his neighbors can assimilate the foreign body in their midst only according to their own cultural constructs: since he drinks red wine and doesn't kiss ladies' hands, he must be one of those *farmazony* (Freemasons), dangerous radicals they have heard about. But it takes only a slight shift into a familiar category—that of suitor—to neutralize his eccentricities. Again, any possibility for observation and evaluation is destroyed by an overly easy translation into familiar notions.

It is not an exaggeration to say that *all* the characters' actions amount to good or bad acts of reading. We are constantly made aware of the charged boundary between text and nontext and various characters' more or less creative negotiations of it. Larina at first prefers the titillating texts of her beloved Samuel Richardson to what she perceives to be the nontext of Russian country life. That life, however, then turns out to be too richly varied and humorous in Pushkin's telling for the awkward inscription hewn on Larin's tombstone to do justice to it. Instead, epitaphic space, religiosity, and rhyme dictate by absurd inertia the climactic characterization of Larin as "gospodnii rab i brigadir" (the Lord's slave and brigadier) in order to fit the obligatory end rhyme "mir" (peace). This early encounter with a text surreally unrelated to the life it was supposed to commemorate, and shaped instead by the formal difficulties of its genre, is delightfully emblematic of the relationship between most texts and their living "occasions" in *Eugene Onegin*.

It is no accident that Lensky's life is sandwiched, as it were, between two epitaphs: Larin's and his own. In the first case he is the (mis)reader, in the second the "subject" or "victim" of the epitaph. His encounter with the gravestone reads like a parody of the classic epitaph-reading scene from Wordsworth's "On Epitaphs," or any number of other graveyard verses, with their built-in "prosopopoeic" challenge to the poetic imagination. Lensky utterly fails to rise to the occasion. Unself-consciously imitating its simplest textual prototype, Hamlet's "poor Yorick" meditation, he seems oblivious to the rich notes of parody in that scene, already exploited by Sterne in *Tristram Shandy*. Moreover, the slide from text straight into text is too immediate:

> И полный искренней печалью
> Владимир тут же начертал
> Ему надгробный мадригал.
> (2, 37, 12–14)

And full of sincere sadness, Vladimir then and there inscribed a gravestone madrigal for him.

Virtually every word here has a flicker of irony for the reader already acquainted with Pushkin's "psychology of creativity." It is not fullness and sincerity of immediate feeling but a sense of incompleteness and confusion that impels the clarifying act of writing, and the translation of experience into language is always delayed, never "tut zhe." Otherwise the result is the automatic generation of text from text, "nadgrobnyi madrigal" from provincial epitaph, signifier from signifier. We should keep in mind Lensky's failure as an epitaph reader when we arrive at the later scene, where Pushkin will perform the same service for him.

In chapter 1 Pushkin the narrator described his and Eugene's originality in the first person, but in phrases so clichéd they suggested the opposite. Pushkin introduces Lensky by an analogous procedure. The phraseology of lyrical confession remains intact, but is incongruously displaced to the third person: "Akh, on liubil, kak v nashi leta / Uzhe ne liubiat" ("Ah, he loved as in our years one loves no more") (2, 20, 1–2). The apparently trivial transposition of "ia" to "on" exposes the comic fixity of each emotional elegiac phrase, its essential conformity to the banalities of a "discourse of the interior." Instead of a revelation of the interior life we are confronted with a series of "mentions," hyperbolic habits of language incongruously internalized as the self's "intimate feelings."

His prodigious poetic output of "gloomy elegies" culled from a cloudless love, and immediately fed back into the courtship as erotic communication with a distinctly practical function, creates a nagging contrast not only with Eugene and Tatiana's far more ambiguous relationship, but also with Pushkin's earlier elegiac model: "No ia, liubia, byl glup i nem." For Lensky the equivalence implied by his unconsciously paratactic construction "chto za grud', chto za dusha!" (What a bosom, what a soul! [4, 48, 7–8]) and between his shapely sweetheart and the fashionable word "ideal" with which his poetic career breaks off, is an uncomplicated one. He is blissfully unaware of any mistranslation on his part.

Meanwhile, however, the telltale gap or misalignment between "signifier" and "signified" will eventually act itself out in the plot. Poetic justice will not be served until the original mistranslation is ironically corrected: the anonymous biological imperative (and its attendant pleasures), which clothed itself in a standardized rhetoric of poetic uniqueness and idealism, will be revealed at the end, unchanged by its peregrination through literature. Olga will stand, with the same sweetly inscrutable smile and modestly downcast eyes, at a different wedding. The narrator's irony at Lensky's expense is so legible that it sets up expectations of just such a denouement very early. Clearly the reader is meant neither to experience Lensky's illusions as true, nor to experience their crumbling. Instead he observes from the outside a state of fatal blindness, leading to inevitable consequences.

> Он весел был. Чрез две недели
> Назначен был счастливый срок.
> И тайна брачныя постели
> И сладостной любви венок
> Его восторгов ожидали.
> Гимена хлопоты, печали,
> Зевоты хладная чреда
> Ему не снились никогда.
> Меж тем как мы, враги Гимена,
> В домашней жизни зрим один
> Ряд утомительных картин,
> Роман во вкусе Лафонтена . . .
> Мой бедный Ленский, сердцем он
> Для оной жизни был рожден.
> Он был любим... по крайней мере
> Так думал он, и был счастлив.
> Стократ блажен, кто предан вере,
> Кто хладный ум угомонив,
> Покоится в сердечной неге,
> Как пьяный путник на ночлеге,
> Или, нежней, как мотылек,
> В весенний впившийся цветок;
> Но жалок тот, кто все предвидит,
> Чья не кружится голова,
> Кто все движенья, все слова
> В их переводе ненавидит,
> Чье сердце опыт остудил
> И забываться запретил!
>
> (4, 50–51)

He was merry. A fortnight hence the happy date was set, and the nuptial bed's mystery and love's sweet crown awaited his transports. Hymen's chores, woes, yawnings' chill train, he never dreamed of. Whereas we, enemies of Hymen, see in home life nothing but a series of wearisome pictures, a novel in the genre of Lafontaine. My poor Lensky! He was at heart born for such a life. He was loved—or at least he thought so—and was happy. Blest hundredfold who is to faith devoted; who, having curbed cold intellect, luxuriates in heartfelt tenderness, like a drunken traveler staying the night, or, more sweetly, like a butterfly sucked onto a spring flower; but pitiful is he who foresees all, whose head never spins, who hates all movements, all words in their translation, whose heart experience has chilled and has forbidden to forget itself.

The irony is so legible that it scarcely bears explicating. "Taina brachnyia posteli," its archaic genetive "brachnyia" calling attention to the equally antiquated meaning of the phrase, is perfectly emblematic of the kind of fixed phrase uncritically assimilated into the tissue of Lensky's illusions; whereas for the narrator, and for the reader, each such phrase ("sladostnoi liubvi venok," etc.) wears quite obvious invisible quotation marks. Nor are the narrator's attempts to poeticize as "blessed" the youth's infatuated blindness terribly convincing. His supposedly poetic similes—"like a drunken traveler staying the night, or, more sweetly, like a butterfly sucked onto [*vpivshiisia*] a spring flower"—in fact continue the same ironic and naturalistic deconstruction of Lensky's youthful behavior. There will be no radical surprises in the unwinding of Lensky's destiny.

The dramatic irony in the passage applies instead to the second, unnamed object of the narrator's "pity," who foresees everything, hates all words and phenomena in their "true" translation, and is unable to forget himself in even momentary illusion. It is actually the "ironist" who will find himself the subject of an utterly unforeseen ironic transformation. Demystified clear-sightedness, which would seem to be the logical end of an ironic "sentimental education," is actually the starting point, which in retrospect will turn out to have been a form of blindness. Unforeseen psychological impulses and events will call into question the whole concept of "ironic understanding."

At this moment, it seems to me, several questions arise. What, for Pushkin, was the purpose of such an excessively vicious lampoon of Lensky? And why is Eugene, the demystified ironist par excellence, so willing in Lensky's case not to read between the lines? Why the divergence between the narrator and Eugene? Why the emphasis first on the friendship, then on the betrayal?

Specific candidates for the original of Lensky have of course been identified,[66] but it seems to me that this misses the point. It was not Pushkin's habit to turn on fellow poets who happened to be of weaker stature. More convincing, I think, is to see in the portrait of Lensky Pushkin's perhaps overly vehement response to Kiukhel'beker's powerful 1824 critique of the contemporary Russian elegy, with which the narrator openly polemicizes in chapter 4:

> Но тише! Слышишь? Критик строгий
> Повелевает сбросить нам
> Елегии венок убогий
> И нашей братье рифмачам
> Кричит: «Да перестаньте плакать,
> И все одно и то же квакать,
> Жалеть *о прежнем, о былом*:
> Довольно, пойте о другом!
>
> (4, 32, 1–8)

But hush! You hear? A stern critic commands us to throw off elegy's wretched wreath; and to our brotherhood of rhymesters cries: "Do stop whimpering and quacking the same old thing, regretting 'the foregone, the past'; enough! Sing about something else!"

Pushkin's tactic is not to argue his own side, but to take Kiukhel'beker's argument to an extreme. He reduces Kiukhel'beker's advice to colloquial common sense, but then applies the same standard to the ode, which Kiukhel'beker had treated with patriotic pathos. There is no qualitative difference between the elegy and the ode, only a difference of fashion. Had Lensky been born in an earlier generation, or had contemporary lady readers been fond of them, he would happily have written odes for his public. He is, essentially, its creation.

Lensky can be seen as a caricatural portrait of the type of elegiac poet Kiukhel'beker had challenged Pushkin to repudiate: an undiscriminating mimic of German fashions and a repetitious phrasemonger. To some extent, Pushkin is even willing to bequeath to him some of his own "youthful sins": Lensky dovetails nicely into the elegy versus irony polemic of chapter 1. There, as we have seen, Pushkin had already ironized, by dissecting into distinct "mentions," the elegiac phraseology of "I" 's own discourse. It remained only to embody this initial imaginative act of parabasis in a third-person representation of the elegiac poet, by which that youthful poetic self (shoulder-length black curls and all) might be exposed as "superannuated" and disowned.

From chapter 2 on, this tactic then liberates the narrator to define himself as everything Lensky is not. Thus while the Lensky-like elegist and odist write for the favor of the fair sex or for imperial snuff-boxes, Pushkin represents his own creative process as an essentially gratuitous one:

> Но я плоды моих мечтаний
> И гармонических затей
> Читаю только старой няне,
> Подруге юности моей,
> Да после скучного обеда
> Ко мне забредшего соседа,
> Поймав нежданно за полу,
> Душу трагедией в углу,
> Или (но это кроме шуток),
> Тоской и рифмами томим,
> Брожу над озером моим,
> Пугаю стадо диких уток:
> Вняв пенью сладкозвучных строф,
> Они слетают с берегов.
>
> (4, 35)

But I the products of my reveries and harmonious devices read only to my old nanny, companion of my youth; or after a dull dinner, catching a neighbor who has strayed my way abruptly by the coattail, I smother him in a corner with a tragedy, or else (joking aside), by yearnings and by rhymes oppressed, roaming along my lake, I scare a flock of wild ducks: harking to the chant of sweet-toned strophes, they fly off from the banks.

Pushkin preempts any ironic reaction to his pathos. The irony is already built into his language, into the self-mocking "mentions" of elegiac phrases ("garmonicheskikh zatei," "toskoi i rifmami tomim," "vniav pen'iu sladkozvuchnykh strof"). Pushkin actually took his own graduation to Shakespearean tragedy to be a very important step in his creative maturation, but this remains in the background of his self-deprecating caricature. The final vignette pretends to be serious, but again the joke is on the poet, whose sonorous verses merely startle his audience of ducks into flight (and at the same time the vignette rounds out the earlier quacking critic metaphor: the ducks' commentary is as relevant as his!).[67]

Pushkin's ironic self-portrait, scribbled in the margins of Lensky's, has accomplished what no amount of poetic pathos could:

it has created a highly Romantic image of the solitary genius, overflowing with an irrepressible, even gratuitous creative energy that forces itself unbidden through him into the world, and remains uncomprehended by it. This scene is paradigmatic for what will follow. Even as Lensky and his poetry are mocked and destroyed, he turns out to have been a decoy, a straw poet. Meanwhile, the "real" elegiac poet, whose image has been limned in the margins of the story, escapes unscathed.

Let us return to the question I asked earlier. What draws Eugene and Lensky, "ice and flame," "prose and poetry," the ironist and the elegist, together? What attracts Eugene, so unlikely to suffer fools gladly, to Lensky's poetic effusions, so different from his own epigrammatic skepticism? Why doesn't Eugene notice the tawdriness of Lensky's clichés in stanza 20?

> Мы любим слышать иногда
> Страстей чужих язык мятежный,
> И нам он сердце шевелит.
> Так точно старый инвалид
> Охотно клонит слух прилежный
> Рассказам юных усачей,
> Забытый в хижине своей.
> (2, 18, 8–14)

Sometimes we like to listen to the tumultuous language of another's passions, and it arouses our heart; exactly thus an old disabled soldier willingly bends an assiduous ear to the yarns of young swashbucklers, forgotten in his shack.

Quite simply, Lensky provides Eugene with a different mirror for his own face, a different interpretation of his own experience. Lensky represents to Eugene his own "lost youth," as in a narcissistic mirror, while Eugene symbolizes to Lensky his own "strangeness." What will break up the stability of this mutual narcissistic projection? Not rivalry over a woman, but rather rivalry over the feminine image.[68]

It is here, in fact, that Pushkin the narrator suddenly reappears as an explicit, even interrupting voice—and refuses further to condone the elegiac (once Batiushkovian, now dime-novelish) clichés of Lensky:

> Всегда скромна, всегда послушна,
> Всегда как утро весела,

> Как жизнь поэта простодушна,
> Как поцелуй любви мила . . .
> Все в Ольге... но любой роман
> Возьмите и найдете, верно,
> Ее портрет: он очень мил,
> Я прежде сам его любил,
> Но надоел он мне безмерно.
> (2, 23, 1–12)

Always modest, always obedient, always as merry as the morn, as simple-hearted as a poet's life, as sweet as love's kiss . . . everything in Olga... but take any novel, and you'll surely find her portrait; it is very sweet; I liked it once myself, but it has palled on me beyond measure.

The poet-narrator's impatience betrays itself in the same symptomatic use of the word *vsio*, which marked Eugene's bored and blurred glance around the St. Petersburg theater in chapter 1. The rhetorical superlatives with which Olga's description is laden lead inescapably to satiation, an unceremonious dismissal precisely of her predictable plenitude, the *lack* of a gap between matter and desire, without which imagination has no space to operate. If everything is *in* Olga (as the syntactic fragment, its epithets cut off, now reads), nothing needs to be supplied by language. Or conversely, any poetry inspired by her will be a stillborn reproduction, as Eugene's malicious similes imply:

> Точь-в-точь в Вандиковой Мадонне:
> Кругла, красна лицом она,
> Как эта глупая луна
> На этом глупом небосклоне.
> (3, 5, 9–12)

Just as in a Vandyke Madonna: she's round and fair of face like that silly moon up in that silly sky.

One ironic glance from Eugene's eyes suffices to kill Lensky's poetic "ideal," for the reader if not for Lensky. Olga, the Vandyke Madonna, and the moon form a predictable chain of metaphors linked not by their poetic "purity," but by their stupidly satisfied roundness. In what amounts to a dress rehearsal for their later duel, Eugene with one stroke destroys both tenor and vehicle, leaving only the carcass of Lensky's poetic language.

Perhaps most ominous for the elegist is the ironist's casual advice:

"Ia vybral by druguiu, kogda b ia byl, kak ty, poet" ("I'd have chosen the other, if I had been like you a poet") (3, 5, 7–8). The congested syntax of Eugene's comment reveals the basis for his friendship with Lensky, which is also the ground for their future conflict: he treats him like a second self. Lensky is allowed to be Eugene's erotic stand-in, the self who can feel and act on what the ironist, locked into his anesthetized indifference and emotional impotence, cannot. In compensation, he claims an authorial role, toying with the fantasy not of stealing Lensky's love, but of making Lensky's choices, substituting his own tastes and chosen images for Lensky's.

I would like, then, to look more closely at the figure of Tatiana. What is it about her that intrigues Eugene, that makes the narrator patronize her protectively as "My sweet Tatiana"? Why must the Olga "ideal" be not only mocked, but destroyed? Why must Tatiana be substituted? In order, finally, to rid the world of elegy and its hollow, repetitive stereotypes? Tatiana has so long been enshrined as the first positive and "real" Russian heroine that it is perhaps difficult to recognize what kind of image Pushkin has constructed in her.

Tatiana's portrait is actually a long series of negations. The lack of taste exhibited in her name, her lack of obvious sensual appeal, her alienation from family and childhood games, her preference for the substitutive pleasures of novels over life make her the symmetrical opposite of Olga's feminine "vsio," so threateningly *present*. Utterly shaped by the language of novels—*romany*—she sees life as a system of signs, and waits for them to take on the recognizable configuration of some textual "original." Hence, her first glimpse of Eugene is a recognition scene: "Eto on!" (That's him!) (3, 8, 2). Much of her time is spent in acts of interpretation. Tatiana is always the tense semiotician, parsing Eugene's gestures for his conformity to this or that literary type; conjuring over hot wax and mirrors; conning a book of symbolism to calculate the meaning of dream images unconsciously culled from it and other books; and able truly to begin perceiving Eugene only by "reading" the imprint of his thumbnail in the margins of his favorite books. She can "perceive" only another reader, can interpret only another act of reading.

In other words, if Pushkin has disowned "elegiac values" in the legibly ironic form of Lensky, he has reintroduced them in the covert form of his heroine. Like him, she inhabits a world of signs / surfaces and absent meanings; she corroborates the power of language to imprint on nature its own psychic structure of deprivation. Tatiana is constructed as the opposite of everyman's erotic ideal, the absence of her sister's obvious feminine presence. That very absence of an active feminine self, that melancholy hunger for the textual original to which her experience seems palely to refer, make her not the ideal Russian woman, as so many readers have maintained, but the outward incarnation of the elegist's own psyche. In Tatiana, Pushkin allegorizes and loves the structure of his poetic imagination. There is an underlying kinship between this act of ironic self-distancing and covert self-preservation and Eugene's transvestite double disguise in chapter 1 (Eugene masquerading as Venus masquerading in turn as a young man): the subject masquerades as its own love object, whose essential congruity with the subject may go unnoticed.

Thus on the empty spot left by Olga's discredited Vandyke Madonna, the narrator substitutes his own version of the same image:

> «Оставь меня: я влюблена.»
> И между тем луна сияла
> И томным светом озаряла
> Татяны бледные красы,
> И распущенные власы,
> И капли слез, и на скамейке
> Пред героиней молодой,
> С платком на голове седой,
> Старушку в длинной телогрейке;
> И все дремало в тишине
> При вдохновительной луне.
> (3, 20, 5–14)

"Leave me. I am in love." And meantime the moon beamed and with soft light suffused the pale charms of Tatiana, her loose hair and teardrops, and, on a bench, before the young heroine, a kerchief on her gray head, the little old woman in a long quilted vest; and in the stillness everything dozed by the inspirating moon.

What are the essential differences between Pushkin's "icon" and Lensky's? Pushkin's is Russian, not foreign; or, at any rate, the prototype of Juliet and her nanny has been so thoroughly assimilated that it is barely recognizable.[69] Just as there is a communication gap between Tatiana and her nanny (each misunderstands the meaning of the other, and tries to calque the experience described in her own idiom), Pushkin gives us an image we might or might not recognize as the aesthetic rebuttal to Lensky's imported Madonna.

Tatiana and her nanny compose a truly virginal image, implicitly opposed to the duplicitous virgin / mother, purity / fertility icon deconstructed by Eugene. The scene is presented as spontaneous, inadvertently glimpsed, not meant for an audience. Pushkin's sketch of Tatiana dreaming with her head propped on her hand and her nightgown slipping off her shoulder conforms very closely to the "natural" aesthetic of eighteenth-century genre painting.[70] It is in fact the girl's unawareness that is displayed for an audience; she is not in control of her presentation, yet it invites commentary, someone else's verbalization. Tatiana is pictured in an interval of wordlessness, the silence that divides one unsuccessful attempt to make herself understood from the next. What is being portrayed here? A girl in love? Yes, but also the act of inspired writing, or more precisely, the moment just before the mute psyche clothes itself in language: "No ia, liubia, byl glup i nem" (1, 58, 14).

Pushkin interposes as many obstacles as possible between this mute image of authentic feeling and its eventual articulation to the reader. There are many valid ways of accounting for Pushkin's protracted portrayal of a girl *writing* besides the one I am going to propose. Todd, in particular, has illuminated the specific sociohistorical context of a selectively bilingual culture in which the elite—and particularly upper-class women—certainly read and wrote but also spoke and thought about certain things only in a foreign language.[71] Paradoxically, Russian culture was so structured that the only language available for the expression of intimate, particularly sexual, feelings was a foreign one, French; or, alternatively, for certain highly educated men, Russian poetry, with its imported and controlled structures. I would like to suggest that we look at the relationship between Pushkin the narrator and his heroine not just as proof of Pushkin's empathetic ability to penetrate and articulate the psychology of a girl, but as a deliberately constructed antidote to the poet's own sexual experience, clothed in feminine form.

I have shown that Pushkin was repeatedly attracted in the Southern Poems to the trope of the passionate "native girl," for whom articulation is a difficult, and finally fatal, act. Tatiana, "Russian in her soul," seems to be a departure from this pattern; yet certain features of the Oriental feminine are preserved and even heightened: her defective language, her inability to speak for herself without male tutelage, which places the latter in a position of erotic as well as authorial control. Pushkin implies that Tatiana will be condemned for her spontaneity by prudish society ladies, but the violence of his metaphors suggests the more elemental threat posed to *him* by women in charge of their own bodies and language:

> Кокетка судит хладнокровно,
> Татьяна любит не шутя
> И предается безусловно
> Любви, как милое дитя.
> *Не говорит она*: отложим—
> Любви мы цену тем умножим,
> Вернее в сети заведем;
> Сперва тщеславие кольнем
> Надеждой, там недоуменьем
> Измучим сердце, а потом
> Ревнивым оживим огнем;
> А то, скучая наслажденьем,
> Невольник хитрый из оков
> Всечасно вырваться готов.
> (3, 25) [my emphasis]

The coquette reasons coolly; Tatiana loves in dead earnest and unconditionally yields to love like a sweet child. *She does not say:* Let's put it off; in this way we'll multiply love's value, ensnare more surely; let us first prick vainglory with hope; then with perplexity harass the heart, and then revive it with a jealous fire, for otherwise, cloyed with pleasure, the cunning captive is ready hourly to escape from his shackles.

The "coquette" is defined as a woman who has refused the erotic syndrome sketched in "The Prisoner of the Caucasus"; for to learn the Russian man's language of love in order, mistakenly, to assume the role of subject and express her own love is to destroy her power as *image*. The woman who speaks from the male position of "I" usurps his role and simultaneously turns herself from object of love into pursuer, or even more threateningly, into place of entrapment.

The "prisoner" of her presence can then only dream of escape into absence. The coquette is actually a female ironist who has taken possession of her own image, much as the classical girl studying her own effect in the mirror in Pushkin's 1821 fragment did. With the rhetorical deliberation of an author, she calculates her dosages: now a little hope, now a touch of incredulity, now jealousy are aroused in turn, forcing the hapless reader-lover to constantly reimagine the hypothetical behind-the-scenes "whole" from which these fragmentary and contradictory signs emanate. The coquette thus artistically ensures his continued captivation by the interpretive process. He curses her verbal and representational mastery, yet admits that without it he would be long gone.

Tatiana is of course quite different. Notice, in particular, how disempowered she is within her own culture, described as a helplessly emotional child or the "sweet object" of the poet's words, whose role is literally to serve as a mute or appealingly distorting medium for his language:

Она по-русски плохо знала,
Журналов наших не читала,
И выражалася с трудом
На языке своем родном,
Итак, писала по-французски...
Что делать! повторяю вновь:
Доныне дамская любовь
Не изъяснялася по-русски . . .
Я шлюсь на вас, мои поэты;
Не правда ль: милые предметы,
Которым, за свои грехи,
Писали втайне вы стихи,
Которым сердце посвящали,
Не все ли, русским языком
Владея слабо и с трудом,
Его так мило искажали,
И в их устах язык чужой
Не обратился ли в родной? . . .
Как уст румяных без улыбки,
Я русской речи не люблю . . .
Неправильный, небрежный лепет,
Неточный выговор речей

По-прежнему сердечный трепет
Произведут в груди моей.
(3, 26–29)

She knew Russian badly, did not read our reviews, and expressed herself with difficulty in her native tongue; hence wrote in French... What's to be done about it! I repeat again, as yet a lady's love has not expressed itself in Russian. . . . My poets, I appeal to you! Isn't it true that the amiable objects for whom, to expiate your sins, in secret you wrote verses, to whom your heart you dedicated—didn't they all, wielding the Russian tongue poorly and with difficulty, so sweetly garble it, and on their lips didn't a foreign tongue turn into a native one? . . . Like rosy lips without a smile, without a grammatical mistake I don't like Russian speech. . . . An incorrect, careless babble, an inexact delivery of words, as before produce a flutter of the heart in my breast.

Notice again the plethora of negations out of which his "positive" image of love is constructed: "liubit ne shutia," "bezuslovno," "ne govorit ona," "ne chitala," "vyrazhalasia s trudom," "ne vse li," "ne obratilsia," "bez ulybki," "bez gramaticheskoi oshibki," "ne liubliu," "nepravil'nyi, nebrezhnyi lepet," "netochnyi vygovor rechei." It appears to be of utmost importance that the object of love be a nonnative speaker of the (male) erotic discourse, a Circassian maiden trapped Pygmalion-like in her own inarticulateness.

Is a woman the "sweet child," the "sweet object" brought to full human life only by the man's words, his projection onto her of his imaginative structures? Or are linguistic structures actually devices of containment for her dangerous natural powers? At one point the narrator is ready to hand over the task of translating the letter to Baratynsky, more experienced in transmuting the "foreign words of a passionate girl" (3, 30, 6–7) into *magical incantations*, in other words, in safely appropriating her power for himself.[72] Clearly, in conflating the images of a young, sexually inexperienced girl and defective language, Pushkin has powerfully eroticized his own linguistic act. He has created an image of writing that divides it into female and male components, mute passion and expressive act, which must fuse quasi-sexually for authentic creation to take place.

Let us note one more divergence. The plot of "The Prisoner of the Caucasus" is Romantically paradigmatic in that the maiden's native Circassian represents a "naive," "poetic" language of passion, as beautiful in its unintelligibility as any "natural language";[73] but when expressed in a mutually intelligible, "civilized" tongue, her feelings reveal themselves to be a repetition of an all-too-familiar scenario from which the Russian wants only to escape. In the end she must revert to the mute language of action: she expresses her love precisely by freeing him from herself and her all-too-intelligible language. Her final gift to him is to disappear into the poetic nature from whence she came; his final gesture toward her is an "act" of silent understanding—"Vse ponial on" (4, 112). Their story is rescued from intelligible language for poetry.[74]

Notice how Pushkin elaborates the analogous moment in *Eugene Onegin*. At last, after ten stanzas of procrastination, Tatiana's "original" letter lies before Pushkin, but screened from the reader. The mysterious transmutation of passionate inspiration into a language that renders its every contradictory nuance has already taken place, apparently before the reader's eyes, and yet somehow in the gap between stanzas, just out of his view. We can judge it only by its effect on the narrator: he cannot understand ("ne mogu poniat' ") how her language can have *retained* the strange mixture of qualities (carelessness, nonsense, tenderness, madness, allure, harmfulness) characteristic of original, pre-analytical emotion:

Письмо Татьяны предо мною;
Его я свято берегу,
Читаю с тайною тоскою
И начитатся не могу.
Кто ей внушал и эту нежность,
И слов любезную небрежность?
Кто ей внушал умильный вздор,
Безумный сердца разговор,
И увлекательный и вредный?
Я не могу понять. Но вот
Неполный, слабый перевод,
С живой картины список бледный,
Или разыгранный Фрейшиц
Перстами робких учениц.

(3, 31)

Tatiana's letter is before me; religiously I keep it; I read it with a secret heartache and cannot get my fill of reading it. Who taught her both this tenderness

> and amiable carelessness of words? Who taught her all that winsome nonsense, the heart's mad conversation both fascinating and harmful? I cannot understand. But here's an incomplete, feeble translation, the pallid copy of a vivid picture, or *Freischütz* performed by timid (female) novices' fingers.

Most striking, perhaps, is the reversal of roles induced by the letter. In the presence of Tatiana's powerful originality, the narrator's own Russian poetry becomes a pale and defective copy. What does Pushkin mean to convey by this analogy, and by the whole passage's volatile mixture of sublimity and ironic anticlimax?

Although Tatiana's passionate state is identified with the "foreign passions" of native girls, the initial act of translation has already been performed by her: she writes her letter in French prose, the ultimately debased language of civilization. When Pushkin translates her letter into Russian poetry, he is intent on preserving her natural medium of a native / naive and poetic / passionate language. In place of the original binary paradigm, with its purity / corruption opposition, Pushkin subtly substitutes a ternary process that can easily be seen as an allegory for his own poetic achievement. The "tender babble" of passion passes through the clarifying prism of analytical, civilized language (French, western narrative forms), but is in fact *restored* to the sphere of passion and poetry by the final translatory act of the Russian poet. The final product, Russian poetry, is thus presented as a departure from the prosaic language of reason, a paradoxical recovery of the original poetic potency of language. Hence Pushkin's insistence on his fidelity to his feminine "original": "ego ia sviato beregu."

Pushkin's self-deprecating comparison of his translation to an amateurish performance of a great original piece of music can also be related to Romantic convention. Music represents the "natural language" of original inspiration, before it has been fragmented by "the machinery" of conceptual language. "Because the Romantic stereotype inevitably presents its naive speakers as singing, if possible with primitive instrumental accompaniment, the opposition naive/civilized can likewise be translated into the pair music/language."[75] Music is the only medium, for the Romantics, that conveys *intact* the simultaneous multifariousness of inspiration. Thus, for example, in E. T. A. Hoffmann's story "Don Juan," the singer of Donna Anna's role is, for the duration of her aria, actually infused with the original genius of Mozart. Pushkin appears to be tapping into the same associative system when he introduces his musical metaphor at the end of the translation passage. Instead of a legibly high-Romantic image of Mozart's genius being reconstituted in the inspired interpretation of the receiver, however, Pushkin gives us *Der Freischütz*, its anticlimactic effect heightened by its outlandish Russian transliteration and end-rhyme position.

Has Pushkin then glorified Tatiana's letter as "original music" only to ironize the whole trope? Can we read the image of "Freischutz" being played by lady amateurs as anything but a caricature of a Romantic cliché? Nabokov's footnote to the passage reveals the possibility of an underlying "original" lyrical memory, virtually undetectable under its double mask, of two beloved women—Vorontsova and Viazemskaia—bringing to fragile life in a Russian context the foreign musical score of *Der Freischütz*.[76] So, on closer inspection, the Romantic paradigm has been ironically inverted, and, precisely by this, renewed: the "original [German vocal] music" acquires a parodistic aura, while the reverent Russian act of interpretation creates a touching and aesthetic, indeed Romantically "naive," moment. The image hovers illegibly between an ironic and an elegiac intonation.

Notice that the whole protracted translation scene has permitted Pushkin to do what every Romantic aspired to do: represent his own process of creation in almost seamless mimetic disguise. In Pushkin's insistent subordination to Tatiana's "original," we might recognize a typical Romantic *mise en abîme*: the "origins" of the text, its "sponsoring source," are incorporated into the narrative but mysteriously hidden from view. Tatiana and the narrator essentially dramatize the two "moments" of verbal creation: the fiery and involuntary moment of imaginative conception, followed, to use Coleridge's terminology, by the cooler compositional work of "fancy."[77] Both are necessary, but to quote Shelley's formulation of the Romantic credo, "The most glorious poetry that has ever been communicated to the world is probably a feeble shadow of the original conception of the Poet."[78] By proposing an original, "prosopopoeic" source for his poetry, the poet seems to devalue, but actually mystifies, his own poetic artifacts. Completely characteristic, as we have seen, is the privileged access claimed by the male prophet-poet to the female / subterranean / mystical sources of creativity he manages to bring to light, often at the price of his own emasculation.[79] Hence, perhaps, the narrator's "ritual feminization" in the face of Tatiana's powerful, quasi-sacred text ("Ego ia sviato beregu").

With its many layers of translation, from the double enigma of Tatiana's girlish and Russian soul, through the French that is the only language she knows for representing—to herself as well as to anyone else—her emotions, to her ostensibly native language, which is actually the *male* province of Russian poetry, the entire process seems to me to be a deliberately protracted representation of the difficulty of the literary act, an allegory, comparable to though not as easily recognized as "Proserpine," of the perilous journey from the foreign country of the poet's psyche into the equally foreign country of legible language. The crossing of gender as well as linguistic borders in the translation process dramatizes the distance traveled to get from one pole of the poet's self to the other, as well as the risks involved.

If Tatiana's letter is the original, of which his own poetry is a pale copy, who taught her to speak? "Who [masculine] inspired in her these mad feelings and expressions?" When at the end of the *Paradiso* Dante recognizes Beatrice as his guide, she shields her smile and directs his gaze past herself to the true origin of the *Divine Comedy*, the blinding light of the Father. Here the grammatical gender used by Pushkin already implies a masculine antecedent, which could be Eugene, her beloved; or the male authors of her favorite novelistic narratives, out of which she has (mistakenly) constructed her subjectivity; or, finally, Pushkin himself. Whichever answer we choose, the implication is that Tatiana's words, her powerful self-expression, are not in fact her own.

Compare:

> И в это самое мгновенье
> Не ты ли, милое виденье,
> В прозрачной темноте мелькнул,
> Приникнул тихо к изголовью?
> Не ты ль, с отрадой и любовью,
> Слова надежды мне шепнул?
> Кто ты, мой ангел ли хранитель,

Или коварный искуситель:
Мои сомнения разреши.
(3, Письмо Татьяны)

Скажи, кто ты, пленитель безымянный?
С каких небес примчался ты ко мне?
Не ты ли, тот, который жизнь младую
Так сладостно мечтами усыплял
И в старину про гостью неземную—
Про милую надежду нашептал? . . .
Будь ангелом-хранителем души.

Хранитель бедный мой—любовью
В утеху дан разлуке он:
Засну ль? приникнет к изголовью
И усладит печальный сон.

TATIANA'S LETTER: And at the same instant wasn't it you, sweet vision, who flickered in the transparent darkness and bent softly over the head of my bed? Wasn't it you who with joy and love whispered words of hope to me? Who are you, my guardian angel or a treacherous tempter: resolve my doubts.

ZHUKOVSKY: Who are you, nameless captivator? From what heavens have you whisked down to me? Aren't you the one who with dreams so sweetly lulled my young life to sleep, and in old times about an unearthly—dear—guest whispered hope? . . . Be the guardian angel of my soul.

BATIUSHKOV: My guardian angel—by love was given to console parting: If I fall asleep? he will bend over the head of my bed and sweeten my sad dream.

The second extract is from Zhukovsky's "To the familiar genius just flown past" ("K mimoproletevshemu znakomomu geniiu," 1819), the third from Batiushkov's "My genius" ("Moi genii," 1815).[80] Many more could be quoted, including Pushkin's own "The Demon" ("On providenie iskushal" [He was tempting fate]); an elegiac subtext (and not, as Nabokov would have it, just Parny) could be found for virtually every line of Tatiana's letter. The effect, however, is the opposite of the ironic "mention" with which we have become familiar. Instead, familiar poetic phraseology acquires a renewed meaningfulness in the new context of Tatiana's daring declaration. "Ia k vam pishu—chego vam bole? . . . Do groba ty khranitel' moi" (I'm writing to you—what more do you want? . . . To the grave you are my guardian). Words that would have been trite or hyperbolic in a man's mouth in hers accurately characterize the risk and the degree of transformation.

What *is* original, then, is Tatiana's act of linguistic appropriation, her assumption in place of the customary feminine pronouns "she" and "you" of the subject's grammatical position: "I." Or perhaps we should say that what is original is the way Pushkin has found a new representation, a new speaker, a new occasion for the old elegiac language and insights. Moreover, he has placed that language in a new, Romantically marked position: not, as Kiukhel'beker had accused, at the faded end of a chain of foreign conventions and borrowings ("Who translates translators?"),[81] but at the origin: as the "natural music" of the spontaneous Russian psyche. One thing that Pushkin had learned from his Southern Poems was that a man who spoke in elegiac phrases was an imitator, a redundant poseur, a substitutor of words for actions, whereas when a girl used those same phrases, she was creating a new self, invading the male space of language, with explosive consequences. Pushkin hovers suggestively over the moment of closure: the pink seal drying on Tatiana's "inflamed tongue" suggests a double consecration: having transmuted her erotic passion into a linguistic act, she has sealed off her old self, created a new verbal self in its place. Like the heroines of the Southern Poems, she will suffer the consequences.

Viazemsky strenuously objected to the ending of "The Prisoner of the Caucasus": on the one hand to the elliptical and offhand phrase "Vse ponial on" (He understood everything), and on the other to the girl's abrupt and casual disappearance.[82] What to Viazemsky seemed unmotivated was in fact the basic dynamic of Pushkin's future narratives, bared: the girl's emergence into intelligible speech discloses her sameness, her inescapable presence, with its automatic *renvoi* to the missing elegiac love. Like "dve nozhki," she becomes a metonym for the absent original. The act of comprehension, with its telltale "vsio," simultaneously kills the individual experience. The captive returns to his internal prison / male freedom, as well as to the Russian empire, guarded by its bristling bayonets.

Does *Eugene Onegin* repeat or diverge from this pattern? Thanks to the doubling of "ia" (Pushkin) and "on" (Onegin), it does both at the same time. Perhaps the greatest tribute Pushkin can pay to

Tatiana's "spontaneous overflow of powerful feeling" is his incomprehension: not "vse ponial on," but "ne mogu poniat'" (I cannot understand). She retains her negative fascination for him as a text or an image to be interpreted, rather than as a redundant presence. Eugene's response to Tatiana's letter, on the other hand, is just an extended version of "Vsio ponial on." A more experienced reader of erotic narratives, he instantly categorizes it as a familiar pattern whose end can be foreseen, and therefore need not "be read to the end." Be glad, he tells Tatiana, that I'm no longer a fatal seducer, but just a decent, ironic guy—next time you may not get off so lightly. This is the civilized, ironic half of his response. The other half is delayed until Tatiana's name day party, when Eugene's destructive behavior moves him beyond irony into a strange orgy of mockery and psychological violence even further removed from the narrator's imaginative sympathy. Or is it?

There are many ways to explain what impels Eugene to wreck Tatiana's party. It seems to be a dandy's bored rebellion against the claustrophobia of the here and now; his refusal to accept the inertia even of his own "identity," to coincide with himself. He must always be *on*, unaccountable even to himself. Most obviously, he is intent on driving a rent between the beatific facade of Lensky and Olga's love and its reality. When Eugene with sinisterly unclear motives destroys Lensky and Olga's idyll and Tatiana's name day celebration, he is actually destroying the claustrophobic images of love and poetry they have erected, *restoring* the semiotic rift between surface and interior.

What has Tatiana done to deserve this retribution? Like the "Southern" heroines, she has assaulted the traditional differentiation of male writer / erotic subject and female reader / erotic object. More simply, she has aroused his fear. Generalizing unforgivably, one might say that the woman's passion will be found at the center of the narrative to the same extent that fear of passion underlies it; writing might be seen as the male exercise of retrospective or prophylactic control, giving passion a distinct, separate carrier and an appropriate fate. For example, Anna Karenina acts out the adulterous desires with which her whole society is saturated; her dramatic exorcism allows it to reaffirm its own principles of organization and morality. The heroine's role is to explore the limits of a dangerous passion, which by "inexorable logic" then contains her own punishment.[83]

Chapter 5 is the turning point of *Eugene Onegin*, a chapter of festive and violent transformations. The first change is in Pushkin's portrayal of the northern locale. Pushkin's descriptions of his surroundings in Mikhailovskoe in his letters and lyrics of 1824–25 conformed to the standard north / south opposition, as well as conveying his own frustration and boredom; northern nature is almost always perceived as the bleak absence of the color, sensuality, and art of the south.[84] Chapter 5 opens with winter's dramatic transformation of Russian nature into art:

> На стеклах легкие узоры,
> Деревья в зимнем серебре,
> Сорок веселых на дворе
> И мягко устланные горы
> Зимы блистательным ковром.
> Все ярко, все бело кругом.
> (5, 1, 9–14)

Delicate patterns on the panes; the trees in winter silver, gay magpies outside, and the hills softly blanketed over with the resplendent rug of winter. All's brilliant, all is white around.

In chapter 5 Pushkin's attitude to Russian life is closer to that of the little boy with the frozen finger: "Emu i bol'no i smeshno" (It hurts and it's funny too) (5, 2, 13). By giving up his personal "exile's view" of his surroundings and using Tatiana as his hypothetical subject, Pushkin enables himself to render the unexpected color, artistry, outlandishness, comedy, and grotesqueness of Russian country life. It is a mixture unlike any European one; "Thus has nature, inclined to contradiction, created us" (5, 7, 3–4). Like the peasant with his *kibitka*, he will cut a new path through the landscape ("obnovliaet put' "), even though it will bring him into conflict with his elegiac predecessors, Viazemsky and Baratynsky, and even with himself:

> Но я бороться не намерен
> Ни с ним покамест, ни с тобой,
> Певец финляндки молодой!
> (5, 3, 12–14)

But I have no intention of fighting either with him for the time being or with you, singer of the young Finnish Maid!

The possibility of a duel over poetry is jokingly brought up, but only temporarily postponed.

Through Tatiana, Pushkin is able to replay much of his own psychological material in a foreign, feminine key. The heavy superstitious dread described in such poems as "Portents" ("Primety") is detached from a lyrical "ia" and reassigned to Tatiana. In the context of her characterization, it is transfigured into a charmingly girlish and Russian characteristic:

> Ее тревожили приметы;
> Таинственно ей все предметы
> Провозглашали что-нибудь.
> (5, 5, 5–7)

Portents disturbed her: mysteriously all objects foretold her something.

What I have called the elegiac attitude to life, with its persistent and melancholy impoverishment of the present in favor of an absent signifier, becomes a source of imaginative enrichment. Tatiana's faithful scrutiny of the sign system she sees all around her makes every detail alive with meaning. Yet the elegiac point of view is not the final frame, nor should Tatiana's meaning be the final meaning for the reader. Her hermeneutic search fills the reader with bemusement and recognition.

Notice how many tonalities are mixed in the following stanza. Its first lines could easily be the beginning of a nature elegy:

> Морозна ночь, все небо ясно;
> Светил небесных дивный хор
> Течет так тихо, так согласно...
> (5, 9, 1–3)

The night is frosty; the whole sky is clear; the sublime choir of heavenly luminaries flows so softly, in such concord...

Such an elegy, if continued, would probably have evoked the poet's loneliness, his exclusion from or participation in nature's harmony, and an absent "other" to share and ratify this image of harmony.

But Pushkin breaks off the elegiac train of thought, or rather he has Tatiana act it out.

> Татьяна на широкий двор
> В открытом платьице выходит,
> На месяц зеркало наводит;
> Но в темном зеркале одна
> Дрожит печальная луна...
> Чу... снег хрустит... прохожий; дева
> К нему на цыпочках летит
> И голосок ее звучит
> Нежней свирельного напева:
> *Как ваше имя*? Смотрит он
> И отвечает: Агафон.
>
> (5, 9, 4–14)

Tatiana into the wide yard in low-cut frock comes out; she trains a mirror on the moon; but in the dark glass only the sad moon trembles... hark!... the snow crunches... a passer-by; the maiden flies up to him on tiptoe and her little voice sounds sweeter than a reed pipe's strain: "What is your name?" He looks, and answers: "Agafon."

Pushkin translates a complex interior response to the Russian countryside not into elegiac rhetoric, but into the visible, almost tactile world of Tatiana's play. So lightly dressed that "the moon trembles" in her mirror, she searches nature for a legible sign of her place in it, her destiny; nature gives her back only an inscrutable image of her own loneliness. If the scene of Tatiana attempting to read nature had ended here, it would have been touching, but Pushkin makes it "i bol'no i smeshno." When she politely attempts to elicit the fateful name of her destined "other" from a passing stranger, Russian reality leers incongruously through the fairy-tale decor: "Agafon" is not exactly the name of a "tainstvennyi posetitil'."

Through Tatiana, Pushkin finds a way of reclaiming and expressing elegiac emotion and of representing it as another's action, a body in space. Tatiana's elegiac expectations make nature more vivid *and* reveal their own comical incongruity: "Rus' " is not the fairy-tale realm she mistakes it for, but it does have its own inimitable magic. A reader who expects the ready-made "heavenly choir" effect of a Zhukovsky nature meditation will be deaf to Pushkin's music, which requires a much more mobile, do-it-yourself sensibility: "i bol'no i smeshno," the pipe and Agafon, tenderness and comedy must be perceived contrapuntally, or as dissonances in the service of an ultimately richer, more modern harmony. Pushkin doesn't depict himself trembling with fear, cold, emotion; he doesn't even say that Tatiana trembled, only that she was lightly dressed. The moon reflected in the dark mirror trembles for them. Instead of expressing rhetorically every shade of his own interior emotion, Pushkin invents an allegory that induces the reader to experience an emotional gamut as complex.

What is Tatiana searching for in the snow, in the wax designs at the bottom of the cup, in fatidic names? Some sign that what she desires is what is meant to be; that some force larger than herself is writing her narrative. Let's see what her dream tells her. Both the Freudian and folkloric interpretations concur in their basic view of the dream as an expression of the bride's fear of her imminent "deflowering," the death of her maidenly self.[85] The river crossing, the ambivalent bear / lackey, half savior and half destroyer, the wedding as "a wake" attended by monsters, all point us in the direction of Tatiana's traditional, subconscious, or prophetic fears of Eugene. But let us examine the landscape more carefully. We saw in the first stanzas of this chapter that winter has given nature a festive air, a frozen, artistic surface. Frost arrests change, turns nature into the semblance of a text in which human beings seek a message, a voice addressed to themselves. The yuletide rituals have exacerbated this air of masquerade, of nature turned into design, into sign; with the proper key, they suggest, its frozen *uzory* can be deciphered, a human message disclosed. We have already seen Tatiana trying to conjure a message for herself from the snowy landscape, then forgoing a spiritualist rendezvous at a midnight supper for two. In her dream, however, she continues her solitary interrogation of nature.

The first obstacle in her path is the foaming river, "ne skovannyi zimoi," over which two sticks, frozen together, form the semblance of a bridge.[86] The river still flows in its natural form, uninhibited by winter, and the frozen sticks only mimic a bridge, a crossing meant for humans. In fact, like the yuletide rituals, they create the semblance of a man-made structure where in fact there is only wild nature. Undissuaded by the obvious danger, Tatiana is dying to cross. Interestingly, the deserted landscape does yield a presence; a mound of snow stirs and turns into a bear. In spite of her fear, Tatiana chooses to interpret his outstretched paw as a hand helping her across to the other side. It is as if Dante, lost in a snowy version of his infernal landscape, had encountered a beast and mistaken it for his guide. However, Tatiana's bear, unlike Dante's beast, is difficult to classify. Grunting bestially, he pursues her through the pathless snow into a wood. But rather than blocking her path, he is following her inseparably, a "shaggy lackey" who is in some sense doing her bidding. The girl who had stood lightly dressed in the snowy night, as though eager to expose herself to the elements, now finds herself being literally undressed by nature, an implication Pushkin's language coquettishly suggests:

> то из ушей
> Златые серьги вырвет силой;
> То в хрупком снеге с ножки милой
> Увязнет мокрый башмачок . . .
> И даже трепетной рукой
> Одежды край поднять стыдится.
> (5, 14, 5–12)

Now out of her ears tears by force her golden earrings; now in the crusty snow, off her sweet little foot sticks fast her wet shoe . . . and she's even, with a tremulous hand, embarrassed to raise the border of her dress.

When she at last falls and is scooped up by the bear, Tatiana subsides fatalistically into stillness. Like a faithful servant, he is bringing her to her desired destination, a festively lit cabin in the wilderness. He deposits her, however, only on the threshold; she herself peeks secretly through a chink into the interior. Whose interior, if not her own?

Here again, what she sees and hears is ambiguous: monsters composed of fused halves of different creatures, yet seated around a festive table; beastly noise, yet human speech; and among the "guests," Eugene, half-beloved and half-terrifying, apparently unaware of her existence and yet surreptitiously ("ukradkoiu") glancing at the door. Tatiana's reaction to this scene is interesting; instead of rejecting the company he is keeping, she is relieved to see Eugene in charge, imposing on the monsters a human semblance:

> Он знак подаст: и все хлопочут;
> Он пьет: все пьют и все кричат;
> Он засмеется: все хохочут;
> Нахмурит брови: все молчат;
> Так он хозяин, это ясно.
> И Тане уж не так ужасно,
> И любопытная теперь
> Немного растворила дверь...
> (5, 18, 1–8)

He gives the signal—and all bustle; he drinks—all drink and all cry out; he laughs—all burst out laughing; knits his brows—all are silent; he is the master there, it's clear; and Tania is no longer so horrified, and being curious now opened the door a little...

Again, she chooses to go forward, heartened because he seems to be the master of the monsters; he has given formless or monstrous internal passions a human shape; amid the bedlam, he seems to give human signs. At his approach she feels fear, but is powerless to resist.

Significantly, the moment she is displayed by Eugene to the monsters is a moment of *recognition* and ridicule. They laugh wildly, and then point to her with various parts of their bodies and cry out, not "she's mine" but *moe*, "it's mine," as if referring to a thing: "Vsio ukazuet na nee, / I vse krichat: moe! moe!" (Everything points at her, and all cry: "Mine! Mine!") (5, 19, 13–14). The oscillation between singular and plural, as well as between feminine and neuter, draws attention grammatically to the passage, in a sense demanding that it be interpreted. *Everything* points to her, as though recognizing a kindred *thing*; all shout as though to amplify her own cry of self-recognition, self-possession. And that shout is telling her that this mixed animal and human nature, all of it, is hers.

It is precisely at the moment of recognition of her unity with the beasts that Eugene claims her/"it" ("*moe!*") and draws her unresisting toward consummation. But perhaps oddest of all is the last detail: Eugene lays his head on *her* shoulder, as if succumbing to her. Whose desire is about to be realized, what is the real object of fear? Both in Tatiana's dream and in the nightmare sequence from Zhukovsky's "Svetlana," on which it is modeled, the answer seems to be "the beast within": the compulsion of love, loss of human self and speech in "nature," loss of the human ability to make signs. At that very moment, Olga and Lensky walk in, a warning caricature of connubial bliss and fake poetry, and Eugene explodes in violence.

This is of course what will happen, first at Tatiana's name day party, then in the duel. Why has her dream predicted it? Because both the dream and the nightmarish party are connected at the root in Pushkin's psyche. After all, Eugene's destructive behavior only acts out the vicious irony with which Pushkin has surrounded Lensky and Olga from the start. With amusing pedantry, Tatiana consults the nineteenth-century equivalent of the *Interpretation of Dreams* in order to decode her nightmare's symbolism, but in vain. The reader, however, soon recognizes in the name day party not an idyllic country festivity, but a surreal repetition of the dream. In place of Lensky's pastoral idyll, Pushkin pretends to give us an epic feast, which turns instead into a Rabelaisian orgy of fleshly excess on the part of the guests and of scathingly angry, funny, and inventive caricature on the part of the narrator. Irony's destructive "double take" on life and spurious images is presented as the complementary sine qua non of poetic creation. Eugene's unaccountable violence kills Lensky as well as his banal and solipsistic version of the story, freeing the poet's "peripheral vision" to see and tell it in other ways.

I would like, at this point, to backtrack a little and suggest a source for the particular shape Pushkin's plot has assumed, although I may be verging on the sort of "vulgar biographism" Roman Jakobson and Nabokov claim to eschew.[87] The last stanza of chapter 4 (quoted above) contained a syntactic figure and a state of mind we have encountered before: "On byl liubim... po krainei mere / Tak dumal on, i byl schastliv" (He was loved—or at least he thought so—and was happy) (4, 51, 1–2). Recall the last truncated lines of the first poem addressed to Vorontsova from Pushkin's new "northern exile":

> Никто ее любви небесной не достоин.
> Не правда ль: ты одна... ты плачешь... я спокоен;
> . . . .
> Но если...
>
> (2.1, 348)

No one is worthy of her heavenly love. Isn't that true: you are alone... you are weeping... I am calm; but if...

I have already discussed this poem and this romance in the context of other "elegiac triangles" of the Odessa period. The cast of characters was more complicated than usual; not only was there a husband being duped by Pushkin, but Pushkin was simultaneously being duped by his "best friend" and rival for Vorontsova's favors, Alexander Raevsky, who may actually have colluded in delivering Pushkin into the hands of the irate husband and ultimately the political authorities.[88] Even at the time, Pushkin at least jokingly projected his creations onto his companions: the code name used by him and Raevsky to refer to Vorontsova was "Tatiana." Whatever the actual facts of the affair were, Pushkin's sense of betrayal infiltrated several poems, including of course "The Demon" and its earlier version:

Бывало, в сладком ослепленье
Я верил избранным душам . . .
Едва приблизился я к ним

Мое беспечное незнанье
Лукавый демон возмутил,
И он мое существование
С своим навек соединил.
Я стал взирать его глазами
Мне жизни дался бедный клад,
С его неясными словами
Моя душа звучала в лад.
Взглянул на мир я взором ясным
И изумился в тишине;
Ужели он казался мне
Столь величавым и прекрасным?
Чего, мечтатель молодой,
Ты в нем искал, к чему стремился,
Кого восторженной душой
Боготворить не устыдился.

(2.1, 294 and 293)

It used to be, in sweet blindness, I believed in select souls . . . scarcely had I drawn nearer [than] my naive ignorance a cunning demon disturbed, and he united my existence with his for eternity. I began to gaze with his eyes, life's poor treasure gave itself up to me, with his obscure words my soul sounded in unison. I glanced at the world with a clear gaze; how had it appeared to me so majestic and beautiful? What, young dreamer, did you seek in it, what did you aim for, whom with your exalted soul did you not blush to deify?

Notice that although Pushkin hints at a personal betrayal, he makes the focus of the poem a demonic vocational experience, similar in essence to "The Prophet" ("Prorok"). His encounter with the "malicious genius" drives a wedge between his previous childlike joy in life and the ruthless clarity with which he now pierces its surface to reveal its essence. One interesting difference between the earlier and the later, more finished and at the same time more elliptical, "Demon" is the use of pronouns. In the earlier poem the internalization of the demon's skeptical point of view is reflected in the progression of pronouns: the early harmonious beliefs of "ia" are corroded by and fused with the glance of "on," reflected in the way "he" finally addresses himself as "ty" (you) and refers to other people as "oni" (they). In "The Demon" the transformation has already occurred; "ia" appears only in the oblique case, while the subject of the entire poem is "on," "kakoi-to zlobnyi genii," who has split life into "names" and truth.

More than one commentator has noticed the "demonic" features shared by the "Demon" and Eugene, Pushkin's contemporary creations: "Ego ulybka, chudnyi vzgliad, Ego iazvitel'nye rechi" ("His smile, marvelous glance, his caustic words") (2, 1, 299). Eugene's mockery, skepticism, the very "third personness" of his name (Ego-genii On-neg-in), and of course his perversely destructive friendship with an idealistic young poet seem to be another legacy, or another representation, of the same experience. I am not trying to say that in Eugene Pushkin portrayed Alexander Raevsky and in Lensky himself. Lensky, one might say, is the product of Pushkin's self-alienation, the cathartic self-caricature that is left after the mocking glance of the demon has done its work. Never again will the subject experience itself so simply and rapturously. The happily unified subject "ia" and its naive, idyllic relationship to love and life can only be represented as an obsolete and alien form of life—Lensky—and his "izbrannaia dusha" as just a pretty girl.

Yet in *Eugene Onegin*, as in "The Demon," there is a poetic recompense: "Life's poor treasure gave itself up to me." Only the transformed, "poisoned" Pushkin could have written the poem "The Demon"; it is the direct product of that friendship / betrayal whose precipitate might be summarized in one word: irony. In other words, Pushkin assimilates the personal betrayal as a poetic catharsis. He might have contented himself with an elegiac response to the loss of Vorontsova; an epigrammatic response to the persecuting husband; and an indignant response to the man who betrayed him (as in "Treachery" ["Kovarnost' "]). But the ability to look at his own subjective experience through the angry, bemused, cool, and detached eyes of irony allowed Pushkin to find another form for the linked stories of his "betrayal" and his creative coming-of-age: chapters 5 and 6 of *Eugene Onegin*.

Tatiana may not recognize in her teeming houseful of barking, whistling, smacking, shouting guests the bedlam of the half-and-half monsters of her dream, but the reader does. The similarity is reflected not only in their behavior, but in their incongruously onomatopoetic names and characterizations: fat Pustiakov ("Mr. Trifle") and his weighty spouse ("tiazhelyi Pustiakov s svoei tiazheloi polovinoi"); Gvozdin ("Mr. Nail"), a landowner who thrives at the expense of impoverished peasants; the Skotinins ("Cattle"), a gray-haired but monstrously fertile pair with a family aged two to thirty; a series of spouses described as "halves" of one monstrously fertile organism. As if to keep up with the teeming proliferation of the guests and their appetites, Pushkin turns Tatiana's name day into a Rabelaisian orgy of names and epithets, as if the only thing that can balance such an excess of flesh is an explosion of signifiers. Thus, for example, a face in the crowd with the insubstantial name of "Flianov" is provided not only with a respectable rank ("retired counselor") but also with a cascade of unflattering epithets ("Ponderous gossip, old rogue, glutton, bribe-taker, and buffoon") (5, 26, 13–14). The effect is of verbal excess, of an angry yet pleasurable venting of pent-up verbal energy. Most scathing of all is Pushkin's send-up of the local rhymester, Monsieur Triquet, who makes Lensky look like a paragon of poetic originality:

> Остряк, недавно из Тамбова,
> В очках и в рыжом парике.
> Как истинный француз, в кармане
> Трике привез куплет Татьяне
> На голос, знаемый детьми:
> Réveillez-vous, belle endormie.
> Меж ветких песен альманаха

Был напечатан сей куплет;
Трике, догадливый поэт,
Его на свет явил из праха,
И смело вместо belle Nina
Поставил belle Tatiana.
(5, 27, 3–12)

A wit, recently from Tambov, in glasses and a ginger wig. Like a true Frenchman, in his pocket Triquet has brought a stanza written for Tatiana to a tune known to children. . . . Amid the time-worn songs of an almanac this stanza had been printed; Triquet—resourceful poet—out of the dust brought it to light and boldly in the place of "belle Nina" put "belle Tatiana."

The portrait of the not-too-tricky provincial plagiarist is particularly hilarious in the surrounding context of Pushkin's veritable verbal orgy.

At the noisiest moment of the feast, with Tatiana seated generically with the young ladies, opposite the men, and with the entire company "buzzing, shouting, laughing, whistling, not listening, raising a general alarm" obviously reminiscent of the din of the monsters, the door suddenly opens.

Вдруг двери настежь. Ленский входит,
И с ним Онегин. «Ах, творец!—
Кричит хозяйка:—Наконец!»
(5, 29, 9–11)

The door leaves suddenly fly open: Lensky enters, and with him Onegin. "Oh, Creator!" cries out the lady of the house, "—finally."

Enraged at finding himself in this ludicrous company, Eugene plots his revenge on Lensky ("poklialsia Lenskogo vz*bes*it'), meanwhile sketching ("stal *chert*it' v dushe svoei") mental caricatures of the guests. Clearly, he is represented as doing what Pushkin has in fact been doing all along, and Pushkin's buried metaphors give these imaginative activities a demonic tinge.[89] If the reader recognizes the homology between the narrator and the outsider at the provincial feast, he may also read in the hostess's exclamation a potentially punning meaning of which she, of course, is unaware: "Ah, Creator—at last."

It is precisely Eugene's seemingly gratuitous paroxysm of destructive irony that creates the story *Eugene Onegin*; each of the characters will be, as a result, liberated from a humdrum country idyll into a dramatic part. How does he accomplish this? In the same way that Pushkin has throughout this chapter: by introducing a rift between his surface presentation and his "interior," between his language and his meaning. Eugene introduces into this pleasurably mindless occasion, where everyone and everything is a solid "thing-in-itself," the necessity for reading, interpretation:

> Он молча поклонился ей,
> Но как-то взор его очей
> Был чудно нежен. Оттого ли,
> Что он и вправду тронут был,
> Иль он, кокетствуя, шалил,
> Невольно ль иль из доброй воли,
> Но взор сей нежность изъявил:
> Он сердце Тани оживил.
>
> (5, 34, 7–14)

He bowed to her in silence, but somehow the look of his eyes was marvelously tender. Whether because he truly was touched or he was flirting, playing games, whether involuntarily or by free will, that look expressed tenderness: it revived Tania's heart.

His "coquettish" creation of multiple and contradictory surfaces in this scene "enlivens" Tatiana's imagination precisely by turning her into his reader. His "coquettishness" is essentially a representation on the level of the narrative of Pushkin's mad verbal frolicking, in which metaphors shift us back and forth between the supposedly literal and the supposedly figurative levels until the dizzied reader can no longer tell which is which:

> За ним строй рюмок узких, длинных,
> Подобно талии твоей,
> Зизи, кристалл души моей,
> Предмет стихов моих невинных,
> Любви приманчивый фиал,
> Ты, от кого я пьян бывал!
>
> (5, 32, 9–14)

Followed by an array of glasses, narrow, long, similar to your waist, Zizi, crystal of my soul, the subject of my innocent verse, alluring vial of love, you, who used to make me drunk!

It is after this orgiastic outpouring of language drunk on its own images, its own referential untetheredness, that Pushkin unleashes his most wickedly merciless caricature of the "inspired poet":

> Освободясь от пробки влажной,
> Бутылка хлопнула; и вино
> Шипит; и вот с осанкой важной,
> Куплетом мучимый давно,
> Трике встает; пред ним собранье
> Хранит глубокое молчанье.
> Татьяна чуть жива; Трике,
> К ней обратясь с листком в руке,
> Запел, фальшивя. Плески, клики
> Его приветствуют. Она
> Певцу присесть принуждена;
> Поэт же скромный, хоть великий,
> Ее здоровье первый пьет
> И ей куплет передает.
>
> (5, 33)

Freeing itself of its damp stopper, the bottle popped; the wine fizzes; and now with a pompous bearing, long since tormented by his stanza, Triquet stands up; before him the assembly preserves a deep silence. Tatiana's barely alive; Triquet, addressing her, a slip of paper in his hand, proceeds to sing, off-key. Splashes of applause, accolades salute him. She must drop the bard a curtsy; the poet, modest although great, is first to drink to her health and hands her the stanza.

The scene's first level of irony is transparent: attaching the misnomer "poet," much less "modest but great poet," to Triquet is as absurd as his pretension of being a "Frenchman" from Tambov. Pushkin plays up with relish every possible absurd connotation of the Russified word *couplet*, whose formal meaning of alexandrine or rhyming couplet has been destroyed by Triquet's creative substitution of names. Because of the couplet's underlying etymological connection with the concept "little couple," it becomes the perfect parodistic point of intersection between the grossly fertile connubial and courting pairs (*cheta*) that populate the party and the diminutive product of the poet's solitary creative labors—his *kuplet*. Moreover, the relish with which Pushkin repeats the word *kuplet* in various markedly physical contexts ("v karmane Trike privez kuplet Tatiane," "kupletom muchimyi davno, Triket vstaet," "I ei kuplet peredaet") arouses in the reader's imagination an overly concrete, physical image that actually begins to compete with the word's literary meaning.[90] If, in addition, the etymological associations of the Slavic root *kup* are taken into account, it is hard to lay to rest the suspicion of scatological wordplay.[91] If this is indeed the case, it would only be a new version of a metaphor for poetic creation that Pushkin had always found irresistible.[92] The reader is tugged between the various simultaneous levels of the story, from identification or sympathy with Tatiana's plight, to a "structural" awareness of the scene's surreal or nightmare dimension, to a "Formalist" enjoyment of Pushkin's rollicking, unfettered flights of language.

What the narrator does to Triquet, to the whole provincial festivity, Eugene does to Lensky. The accelerating momentum of the images, from Homeric bees and heroes to the whirling waltz and stomping mazurka, overcomes the inertia and tedium of heavy provincial bodies and customs and levitates them through pure poetic energy into a bacchanal. By being mocked, they are set free. As the bacchanal reaches an intoxicated crescendo, Pushkin, instead of joining in with an elegiac rhapsody (for example, to feet), declares, "It's time for me to have more sense" (5, 40, 11). He draws away from the dance with a coolly rational simile, and just at that moment Onegin makes his perverse countermove:

> Однообразный и безумный,
> Как вихорь жизни молодой,
> Кружится вальса вихорь шумный,
> Чета мелькает за четой.
> К минуте мщенья приближаясь,
> Онегин, втайне усмехаясь,
> Подходит к Ольге.
>
> (5, 41, 1–7)

Monotonous and mad like young life's whirl, the waltz's noisy whirl revolves, pair after pair flicks by. Nearing the minute of revenge, Onegin, smiling to himself, goes up to Olga.

"If I were a poet," Eugene has already warned, "I would create a different story, name a different heroine; since I am not, I will at least destroy yours, create a space in matter for desire, imagination, language." The poisonous precipitate of ironic *dédoublement* has destroyed Pushkin's happiness and unity of subjectivity, but in compensation it allows him to represent his own humiliation in the third person, as the comical exposure and destruction of a foolish young poet and his vacuous ideal, and to represent his betrayal in a paradoxical way, as his poetic liberation.

Now, I think, we can approach the duel from a different perspective.[93] Certainly it can be seen as the culmination of the conflict set up between the two "selves" in chapter 1: the youthful elegiac poet-lover and the ironist in a fight to the death that the latter wins, or at least survives. Just as in the elegiac triangle, the goal of the love affair seems to be the lover's confrontation with his male rival; the duel is driven by the subject's need to ratify his image of life by vanquishing his own (other) self. Although the duel promises a climax in which their ultimate difference will finally define itself, it ironically performs the opposite function: at the last minute it strips the opponents down to their essential mirror-image resemblance.

The reader who quickly agrees with the overtly "humane," commonsense content of the narrator's address is, I believe, swallowing Pushkin's bait. The narrator's humane and sensible words betray a certain automatism of their own, for they utterly ignore the suppressed emotions that were part of the historical fabric of Eugene and Lensky's "friendship." One might say that the present epithet "vragi" (enemies) is just as much an oversimplification of their relationship as "druzia" (friends) was earlier; the relationship with each other ("drug druga") is full of unverbalized, and as Pushkin hints through his analogy to the "hereditary vendetta," historical or transferred, emotions, hence any number of contradictory potential dramas. The duel seems to be about nothing, about a trifle ("pustiak"), but in fact Eugene's gratuitous invasion of Lensky's "turf" has enacted visibly and a little absurdly the narcissistic dynamic that had drawn them to each other from the start. To attempt to ironize the term "enemies" by invoking the equally inaccurate term "friends" is to skate, Lensky-like, on the surface of reality and language, translating one name into another indiscriminately. The conventionality and awkwardness of the narrator's phrases give them away as "mentions": "Poka ne obagrilas' ikh ruka, / Ne razoitit'sia l' poliubovno" (As long as their hand has not been stained with blood, shouldn't they amicably go their separate ways?). Moralizing away blandly, the narrator concludes with the incontrovertible sententious couplet "No diko svetskaia vrazhda / Boitsia lozhnogo styda" (But wildly worldly enmity fears false shame) (6, 28, 10–14). Who will disagree that the social creature man is "wildly" fearful of exposure?

The key word is *diko*. Ostensibly a simple colloquial hyperbole meaning "extremely," it points us in the direction of a paradoxical truth: social man's fear of exposure, of loss of face, *is* "wild," elemental, aggressive, a deep-rooted force of human nature. That fear is arguably no less strong in the humane narrator and reader who would like to "laugh away" all conflicts and reduce the complexity of human bonds to the abstract phrases "friendship" and "pure love." The reader who too quickly sides with the narrator against the "false modesty" of "society" has missed the irony of Pushkin's possessive, "Zaretsky *nash*." Zaretsky, Onegin's cynical and scandal-mongering second, is "ours" because we all belong to society. The reader and narrator are not perched on a superior and somehow more natural ledge above the rest of society by virtue of their position as observers. The impulse to shoo the relationship of Eugene and Lensky back under the rubric of "friendship" is as much a symptom of "false shame" as is the duelist's adherence to the strict code of formalized enmity. Each point of view seeks to substitute an abstraction for the complexity of the relationship itself.

Whoever sees Eugene and Lensky merely as "friends" dragged from an "accidental" misunderstanding to purely contingent mutual destruction by the frozen social mechanism and technology of the duel has not recognized how much their mutual attraction was grounded in narcissistic projection and suppressed rivalry. "Enmity" is not just the artificial offspring of the dueling code; duels are a formal outlet for the elemental territorial conflicts that arise between people in close quarters, especially, perhaps, between "friends." A friend becomes an enemy when he impinges on my free space. Hence, perhaps, the virtually simultaneous descriptions of Onegin and Lensky as "friends" divided by the lines drawn in the snow and as "two enemies" forced by the rules of the duel to perform exactly the same actions:

Плащи бросают два врага.
Зарецкий тридцать два шага
Отмерил с точностью отменной,
Друзей развел по крайний след,
И каждый взял свой пистолет.
(6, 29, 10–14)

The two enemies throw off their cloaks. Zaretsky with eminent exactness has measured thirty-two paces, positioned the friends at opposite ends, and each has taken his pistol.

The duel clothes in visible form the simultaneous duality, the latent *bezumstvo* (madness) of human relationships.

Pushkin's tremendously effective tactic is to cease his commentary and let the pantomime, observed in clinical slow motion, speak for itself. Needless to say, one set of words merely replaces another, but the effect is that of replacing verbal eloquence with cold and precise actions. In fact, it is precisely the clinical, shiny, metallic description that works on our emotions like a mechanism; we react both to the cold precision of the dueling pistol and its loading and to the deadpan precision of the description. What is most striking about the pistol is its transitional position between art and nature: with its faceted "trunk," shiny surfaces, and clicking "toothy" parts it is a man-made instrument for controlling nature, just as the duel is a ritual artistically designed and paced (step by step, foot by foot, like poetry) for meting out death. Once a man has submitted to its rules, the mechanism is presumably responsible. Yet by giving us a slow-motion close-up of the participants' last actions, a view technically possible only in the post-dueling age of cinematography, Pushkin shows us how their last split-second decisions express character and affect consequences. Surrounded by snow as by a blank page, two black figures stand poised to write the denouement.

Eugene, unable not to prepare himself for any eventuality, raises his pistol, though without taking exact aim; Lensky, seeing the pistol raised, takes this for a sign on Eugene's part that he is, in fact, going to shoot it out, and he "also" begins to take aim. Eugene, seeing that Lensky is, after all, about to shoot, pulls the trigger in reflexive self-defense. The portrayal of the duel is ironically refined, choreographed as an almost exact mirror-image, but with one "leading" and the other, a split second behind, "following"; both merely defending themselves, neither attacking, each ever so slightly misreading the body language of the other. The first punning words of the description, "Now come together," thus suggest a different view of the duel: not as a separation of "friends," but as the fatal meeting with the only "other" that counts, the death of the self. I believe that Lensky's slightly more passive defensive reflex can be accounted for by his recent humiliation at Eugene's and Olga's hands. For him, to reconcile that reality with the "self" he has constructed, with his theory of life, is much more difficult than to acquiesce to death. Just as the chords of his poetic language peter out on the word "ideal," unable to integrate any dissonance, his inability to synthesize a new self in his own defense is acted out in the trance-like mirroring of the duel.

In spite of the elaborate cultural and technical devices with which the dueling ritual controls death, when it is unleashed, it breaks all human structures (including the boundary of the stanza); it is an avalanche that obliterates every human trace.

> . . . Туманный взор
> Изображает смерть, не муку.
> Так медленно по скату гор,
> На солнце искрами блистая,
> Спадает глыба снеговая.
> (6, 31, 2–6)

His misty gaze portrays death, not anguish. Thus, slowly, down the slope of hills, with sparks shining in the sun, a lump of snow descends.

Most noticeable is the dead face's lack of human expression, even pain, its inability to "portray" (*izobrazhat'*) anything but what it is—death. The strictly human distinction between the "interior" and the signifying surface, between the "snow" and the "design" has been lost; the blank snow has won. Eugene calls to Lensky; there is no answer. Then, as if to fill the empty silence, the space left until the end of the stanza, an elegy horribly, hilariously à la Lensky is intoned, confirming that he who lives a cliché, dies a cliché:

> . . . Младой певец
> Нашел безвременный конец!
> Дохнула буря, цвет прекрасный

Увял на утренней заре,
Потух огонь на алтаре!..
(6, 31, 10–14)

The youthful bard has met with an untimely end! The storm has blown; the beauteous bloom has withered at sunrise; the fire upon the altar has gone out!..

With this last, and rather vicious, "mention" of the *mladoi pevets* (death of the poet) genre,[94] it would seem that Lensky and the entire subject of elegy have been laid to rest, while irony grins over their remains.

Instead, in the crisp silence left by the superannuation of Lensky's limited language, Pushkin gives us a variegated feast of elegies, a one-man elegiac competition to prove, as it were, his own "right to inherit."[95] The elegies run the gamut of Pushkin's tonal system, beginning with the ostensibly prosaic, in fact powerfully musical and metaphorical description of the dead body as a deserted house, its windows shuttered and whitened over with chalk, every trace of its mistress gone.[96] Reaching back to the psyche/house metaphor adumbrated in Tatiana's dream, the unobtrusive power of the metaphor has transformed the natural corpse into an image, a human sign: at the very moment that Pushkin says "Propal i sled" (all trace has vanished), the human trace reappears. One after the other, the elegiac stanzas accumulate, painting different hypothetical images of Lensky in a dazzling sequence of key changes, elegiac sorrow becoming aware of its own formulaic phrases ("Chut' iz mladencheskikh odezhd/Uvial!"), modulating to irony ("Byt' mozhet, on dlia blaga mira/Il' khot' dlia slavy byl rozhden"), and then to an earthy satire ("A mozhet byt' i to") that dissolves Lensky in an eighteenth-century genre painting of Larin-like old age and human nature.[97] Last in the sequence, and circling back with legibly moralistic irony to Lensky's "poor Yorick" scene, is the repetition of the graveyard elegy à la Thomas Gray or Wordsworth, with Lensky no longer in the role of epitaph reader or writer, but in the role of its text.[98]

Much has been written about the stanza in which a Russian (Wordsworthian) peasant, weaving an authentic bast sandal as he sits on Lensky's gravestone, blends into a landscape teeming with pastoral life, full of intertwined streams and roots, natural images of a reconciliation "beyond language."[99] Even as Pushkin winds up his graveyard meditation with the peasant's spontaneous song, implying the possibility of a natural language of "truths instinctively ejaculated . . . exposed to all,"[100] a fashionably dressed city girl gallops up on horseback and interrupts him. Halting her horse before the gravestone, she raises the veil of her riding hat and runs her eyes rapidly ("beglymi glazami") over the final inscription, which is shielded from our sight, missing. By all the laws of graveyard poetry, the epitaph-reading scene should now conclude with the resurrection of Lensky's true image in the resonant imagination of a young girl. Instead, "What happened next?" is what this personification of the impatient reader wants to know:

> . . . «Что-то с Ольгой стало?
> В ней сердце долго ли страдало,
> Иль скоро слез прошла пора?
> И где теперь ее сестра?
> И где ж беглец людей и света,
> Красавиц модных модный враг,
> Где этот пасмурный чудак,
> Убийца юного поэта?»
> С временем отчет я вам
> Подробно обо всем отдам,
>
> Но не теперь.
>
> (6, 42, 4–14 and 43, 1)

"What has become of Olga? Did her heart suffer long? Or did the season for tears soon pass? And where's her sister now? And where's the fugitive from mankind and the world, of fashionable belles the fashionable foe, where's that overcast eccentric, the slayer of the youthful poet?" In due time I'll give you a detailed account of it all. But not now.

Not naming Eugene, but using the word *beglets* (fugitive, runner) to describe him, the same word the narrator uses to describe her eyes running over the young poet's epitaph, Pushkin creates an odd correspondence between them. The young poet's death has been in a sense signed, sealed, and delivered by the writer to his sophisticated, fast-moving, "beglyi" reader, who needs "other dreams" to keep her interest alive.

Appropriately, then, Pushkin's last elegy is on elegiac inspiration itself. His creative maturation is suddenly given the attributes of a nagging wife (prose), whose strictly referential interests have banished the wild play and gratuitous "dreams" of rhyme.

> Мечты, мечты! Где ваша сладость?
> Где, вечная к ней рифма, *младость* . . .
> Ужель и вправь и в самом деле
> Без элегических затей
> Весна моих промчалась дней
> (Что я шутя твердил доселе)?
> (6, 44, 4–12)

Dreams, dreams! Where is your sweetness? Where is its eternal rhyme, youth? Really and truly and in actual fact, without elegiac devices, has the springtime of my days whisked by (as I hitherto claimed in jest)?

Now the ironic process is reversed. Instead of exposing the banality of elegiac "mentions," Pushkin invests those very "mentions" with a lost glamor. They needed no other plot, no other narrative interest; the very repetition of a rhyme with its own history of contexts was a creative intoxicant, a metonymic fragment of the lost whole of the past. Pushkin simultaneously makes fun of "elegiac tricks," claims he is looking forward with a light heart to a life purged of the past-as-muse, and yet makes the last stanza of the chapter a backward glance and an incantation: Don't let irony, which liberated the mature poet from the young poet, now kill me altogether.

> Не дай остыть душе поэта,
> Ожесточиться, очерстветь
> И наконец окаменеть
> В мертвящем упоенье света,
> В сем омуте, где с вами я
> Купаюсь, милые друзья!
> (6, 46, 9–14)

Don't let a poet's soul grow cold, callous, stale, and finally petrify in social life's deadening intoxication, in that whirlpool where with you I bathe, dear friends!

Irony, which in chapter 5 was responsible for levitating prosaic provincial reality into a bacchanal, is, in the last few lines of this stanza, itself ironized, as Pushkin bids elegiac farewell to "ty," the solitary youthful inspiration of his love poetry, and wryly prepares to join "vy," the "consensual" world of irony, "realism," and the mature creativity soon to be represented by Tatiana in "the world." The duel thus marks a chiastic turning point in the narrative. Until now, poetic language has been mocked for being inadequate to the full reality of experience. From now on, reality will be unable to measure up to the memory of poetic images. The object of nostalgia will no longer be a "lost love" but its language.

The most satisfying interpretations of *Eugene Onegin* show that the characters act out the poet's metapoetic maturation, whereas Nabokov tends to notice only the symmetrical echoes that bind chapter 8 to chapter 1.[101] Meijer shows that by chapter 8 *Eugene Onegin* has outgrown its own poetic roots, the milieu and language of lyrical poetry, which the novel itself has made obsolete. Eugene would like to reinvent the past; he goes through the motions of reeducating himself as an elegiac lover-poet, but in vain. Eugene is left behind, *Eugene Onegin* is left behind, Pushkin goes forward. Todd has made a major contribution to our understanding of the novel's dynamic by showing that Tatiana's ability to evolve most closely approximates Pushkin's poetic development. Pushkin's creative fusion in poetry of all of the previously cacophonous languages of his culture is analogous to Tatiana's achievement in the salon, harmonizing the unpromising materials of her culture—gossipy guests, a fat elderly husband, the onerous obligations of court patronage—into a veritably European portrait of wit and natural refinement.

So has the hovering dialectic between "elegiac I" and "ironic he" finally been resolved, perhaps by a symbolic switch to a more integrated "she" and a virtuosically ventriloquistic "I"? What could be more satisfyingly closural and dramatically ironic than the chiastic trajectories on which Eugene and Tatiana have now been set? She is mistress of the salons he used to tyrannize; she now holds the dandyesque keys to her culture, virtuosically manipulating its conventions while he looks on. Meanwhile, the lovelorn Eugene is forced to follow in her old footsteps: he is reeducated as a reader, a letter writer, even an elegiac poet; he becomes the perpetual misfit in his own milieu that Tatiana had been at the outset. The ironic "he" reverts to an elegiac "I" right before our eyes; the theme of asynchrony that was the leitmotiv of Eugene and the narrator in chapter 1 is now replayed as the plot itself.

The ironist's inability to be fully engaged in his own life, which throughout the novel had been Eugene's trump card, reveals its essentially elegiac psychic structure. Why does Eugene now fall in love with Tatiana, obsessively and absurdly? The obvious answer is that she is now a social object to be coveted, a prestigious conquest; this is how Tatiana, by now a consummate ironist, in fact interprets his passion. Pushkin seems to urge the reader to join in the social consensus, which ironically dismisses Eugene's shenanigans as the same old attention-getting tricks of a self-styled eccentric:

> Чем ныне явится? Мельмотом,
> Космополитом, патриотом,
> Гарольдом, квакером, ханжой,
> Иль маской щегольнет иной,
> Иль просто будет добрый малой,
> Как вы да я, как целый свет?
> (8, 8, 5–10)

Now what will he appear as? A Melmoth, a cosmopolitan, a patriot, a Harold, a Quaker, a prude? Or will he strut in some other mask? Or else be simply a good fellow like you and me, like the whole world?

Precisely at this moment Pushkin turns the tables on us and nips our too-easy irony in the bud:

> —Зачем же так неблагосклонно
> Вы отзываетесь о нем?
> За то ль, что мы неугомонно
> Хлопочем, судим обо всем,
> Что пылких душ неосторожность
> Самолюбивую ничтожность
> Иль оскорбляет, иль смешит,
> Что ум, любя простор, теснит . . .
> И что посредственность одна
> Нам по плечу и не странна?
> (8, 9, 1–14)

—Why do you refer to him so unfavorably then? Because we indefatigably make a fuss, pass judgment on everything? Because the rashness of fiery souls is offensive or laughable to smug nonentity? Because, by liking room, wit crowds? . . . And mediocrity alone suits us and is not odd?

Notice that what seemed to be the narrator's rhetorical questions to himself or to the reader about Eugene turn out to be a gossipy conversation between two unknown voices in the salon. The first interprets Eugene's behavior in a way consonant with Tatiana's earlier reading of Eugene's marginalia, and therefore with the reader's, and invokes a collective consensus in which the reader feels implicated: "Il' prosto budet dobryi maloi, / Kak vy da ia, kak tselyi svet?" It is this assumed collective pronoun that provokes the other voice's withering scorn, which unexpectedly reinstates "on" as the victim of "our" leveling mediocrity. Notice then that the following well-nigh proverbial lines represent not mature wisdom, but the ironically "mentioned" common sense of the "collective": "Blazhen, kto smolodu byl molod, / Blazhen, kto vovremia sozrel" (Blest who was youthful in his youth, blest who matured on time) (8, 10, 1–2). Unexpectedly, the process of maturation, which until now seemed to have been positively associated with Tatiana and the poet's calm and catholic muse, is itself ironized as an attribute of the crowd into which "we" as readers have been integrated.

The narrator's viewpoint has "faded from his own speech," leaving the reader holding the bag. Meanwhile, an elegiac pathos hovers over the figure of the perpetually ironic misfit:

> Но грустно думать, что напрасно
> Была нам молодость дана,
> Что изменяли ей всечасно,
> Что обманула нас она.
>
> (8, 11, 1–4)

But it is sad to think that in vain was youth given to us, that we betrayed [her] hourly, that [she] duped us.

The dramatic plot of chapter 5, with its extroverted betrayal of one character by another "demonic" one, is now refigured as an internal experience, the self-betrayal of the psyche in time. Simply put, the metapoetic "success story" is simultaneously a psychological tragedy. It is this half of the poet's experience of life—the part visible to the world—that Eugene lives through without the secret justification of the poetry.

Eugene's first glimpse of Tatiana is a scene of recognition, as was hers of him. Just as she fell in love with him not for his mere presence but for his flickering resemblance to signs, to a language she had already encountered, Eugene is fascinated by the duality between Tatiana's present surface and apparently absent past self. The boudoir and mirror scene from chapter 1 turns out to have been a prophecy: Eugene can love only his mirror image, a being structured like himself, like language. Her hand may rest in his, but it must be "lifeless," a surface marking an absence, forever inaccessible. He cannot accept "vsio v nei" (everything in her), he must have deprivation. And Tatiana has become that ideal elegiac/ironic object of desire: her "true self" locked in the past, an object of her own nostalgia, while her visible self sleepwalks aesthetically and dispassionately through her present life.

It is not her harmony and her cultural mastery that have won Eugene's undivided love; it is her disunion, her fragmentation into a textual surface and a "lost original." However much we focus on Tatiana's newfound cultural power and popularity, this should not obscure their cost. The object of Pushkin's scrutiny is not just Eugene's outmoded fads or his hopelessly superficial egotism; it is the tragic structure of love, imagination, and language. Crudely, to get *vsio* is to lose yourself; to be deprived of some part of the total picture necessitates the imaginative work of love and language. It should not be overlooked, even as we take into account Tatiana's harmonizing power, Pushkin's creative maturity, and the obsolescence of the novel's lyrical matrix, that the final image on which Pushkin "freezes" his last frame is one we recognize. On the last page of the novel, Pushkin has his characters enact, as in a *tableau vivant*, the classic elegiac triangle, the lover kneeling before the goddess as the husband—time, death—approaches to eject him into language. There is no need to "read the novel to the end," because the plot's perpetual underlying structure has been laid bare: a tragic allegory of language's origins.

Chapter 6

How to Read an Epitaph: The "Kleopatra" Tales

The three major prose works of Pushkin's late period date from 1835: "Journey to Arzrum," "Egyptian Nights," and *The Captain's Daughter*. Yet as late in the year as October Pushkin complained to Pletnev from Mikhailovskoe, where he had sequestered himself in order to write: "I've never had such a fruitless autumn in my life. I'm writing, but bungling the job. For inspiration one must have spiritual tranquility, and I'm not at all tranquil."[1] "Egyptian Nights" had just been written, yet in some way it was not what Pushkin was looking for. What prompted Pushkin in 1835 to resurrect and rework his old travel notes and to open the first issue of his new journal *The Contemporary* with a piece that would only confirm his poetic decline in the eyes of the public? Why was Pushkin now so intent on framing in prose a poem he had never deemed fit for publication? What impelled him to write another account of the Pugachev rebellion, and in a genre that as early as 1830 had been pronounced outmoded by the leading writers in Europe?[2]

As different as they are in most respects, the three works share several common impulses: (1) Each circles back to an earlier period in Pushkin's life and to an earlier text. The impulse to express something "contemporary" by reworking an earlier text resembles the repetition compulsion we found to be the structural nucleus of Pushkin's lyrical poetry; it essentially arranges an encounter with an earlier hypostasis of himself. (2) Each work thematizes this fixed structure of Pushkin's imagination as a juxtaposition of history and contemporaneity: in "Journey to Arzrum" the Caucasus of 1829 and "nine years ago," in the "Kleopatra" tales Roman antiquity and nineteenth-century society, and in *The Captain's Daughter* the barbaric era of Catherine II, the narrator's "enlightened" era of Alexander I, the author and audience's present era of Nicholas I, and even the eventual reader's era are implicitly contrasted. This structure bears an obvious resemblance to the elegiac representation of "difference" or self-division as narrative "spread out over a temporal axis."[3] (3) Each prose work explicitly dramatizes the gap between poetry and prose. Much as elegy generates its own language from the repetition of erotic loss, Pushkin's late prose narrates the story of the loss of poetry, of its own deprivation.

It is possible, as we have seen, to read "Journey to Arzrum" as a journey to recover, through repetition, the sensation of lost time or a gap between different selves, and hence the necessary conditions for poetry. "Journey to Arzrum" then becomes not only a record of that journey's failure, but also a tragic and lyrical representation of life in the absence of poetry. The three prose frames of the "Kleopatra"[4] tales accomplish the same effect by different means. Each is in essence a "sham ruin" intent on creating a wide gap between the prosaic environment of historical, empirical reality and the inexplicable fragment of powerful language in its midst.

Pushkin's anxious comments on his work reflect the fact that "Journey to Arzrum," "Egyptian Nights," and the documentary *History of Pugachev*, which preceded *The Captain's Daughter*,[5] were the results of conscientious and financially pressured labor, rather than what Pushkin alternately called "inspiration," *drian'*, diarrhea —that is, an urgent and surprising outpouring of images. The correspondence of this period is littered with pathetic calculations of the finances of his family (which now included his mortally ill mother and destitute father), and nervous comments on his own inability to write: "I have already been in Boldino a whole week. I am sorting out my notes on Pugachev, but poetry is still dormant" (October 8, 1833). "I am working in a slipshod fashion. . . . I have embarked on a lot, but have no enthusiasm for anything; God knows what's the matter with me. I am growing old and weak-witted. . . . Do not expect Belkin" (October 30, 1833).[6] The style of these works is markedly "prosaic," not because, as Viazemsky put it, "the prose writer locked himself up tight in his prose, so that the poet could not even look in on him,"[7] but because, as Pushkin put it, "poetry was still dormant."

In 1833 Pushkin abandoned his plans for a novel about Pugachev, and decided to write up his archival materials in historical form instead.[8] He repeatedly insists that his "historical fragment" was merely a clear exposition of confusing documentary materials, written for himself alone and published only for the sake of badly needed profit. The reappearance of the Romantic label "fragment" in this context is noteworthy. Certainly, it is a reminder of the fact that since his archival research was conducted under severe censorial scrutiny and self-censorship, it could hardly be termed complete. Like *Eugene Onegin*, the label stimulates the reader's ironic awareness of the rhetorical layers and silences both in the documents' language and in Pushkin's. It is my impression, though, that the subtitle "Fragment" is also privately motivated. The history was a surrogate for the stillborn novelistic conception that Pushkin had been unable to bring to imaginative completion; the absence of poetry leaves the resulting work a fragment.

What I will suggest at the end of this chapter is that *The Captain's Daughter* both completes and perfectly transforms the series of fragmentary, ironic self-representations that began with "Kleopatra" in 1824 and appeared to elude or refuse completion in the sequence of prose fragments that culminated in "Egyptian Nights."

"Kleopatra" and Writer's Block

"Kleopatra," written between November 1 and 10 or 15, 1824, four months after Pushkin's arrival in Mikhailovskoe, was neither published nor mentioned by him in a correspondence otherwise peppered with plans for publication (of the second edition of "The Prisoner of the Caucasus" and of "Imitations of the Koran," "The Gypsies," and "The Robber Brothers"). Perhaps Pushkin simply realized that its erotic and / or political content were too risky to pass the censorship. But perhaps "Kleopatra" was unfinished in a more radical sense than was the kind of "fragment" Pushkin regularly published in the Romantic manner: he had in "Kleopatra" said more than he knew. It is Pushkin's own apparent inability to have done with it that draws our attention, for he returned to "Kleopatra" several times, in 1828 to recast it in four-foot iambs and between 1833 and 1835 to embed it in three different prose frames.[9] I will treat Pushkin's three frame tales as records of his attempts to read his own youthful poem, and by framing it each time in a different way, to highlight one strand of its complexly knotted meanings at the expense of others. I will recall the initial context in which "Kleopatra" appeared in order to show that, pace B. Tomashevsky,[10] the poem does represent the densest point of intersection of the many threads of Pushkin's creative life in 1824, and that it is no accident that he returned to it again and again as an emblem of not-quite-explicable poetic inspiration.

"Kleopatra" was one of the early products of Pushkin's new enforced solitude in Mikhailovskoe and of his oft-expressed frustration. Unlike the other narrative poems stamped with the unmistakable impress of Pushkin's Southern / Orientalist period (the first chapters of *Onegin*, the Southern Poems, "Gavriliada," "Imitations of the Koran"), it was not written in colorful Odessa; like the intimate elegies connected thematically with Odessa, it was written in retrospect. Its composition marks the moment Pushkin became aware just how violently his fortunes had altered. Not only had he been banished from the feasts of Odessa and its lively cultural and amorous life, but his own father had now stepped into the role (originally played by the cuckolded consorts Vorontsov and de Witt) of the tsar's eyes and ears, spying and reporting on his son's movements to the authorities. This must have been particularly galling because Pushkin's financially straitened and socially disadvantageous circumstances could plausibly be laid at the door of his profligate father. What cannot be doubted is that Pushkin's homecoming plunged him into an intolerable combination of familial turbulence, political pressure, lack of privacy, and intellectual boredom, a constant theme in his correspondence. It was during the climactic two weeks of this family crisis that Pushkin composed "Kleopatra." On November 19 his family left for St. Petersburg, abandoning Pushkin to solitude, provincial society, and the company of his nanny.

I would like to look at some of the traces this experience left in Pushkin's writing. In September the theme of literary commerce (*torg*) versus poetic inspiration surfaced for the first time in his poetry. "Conversation of a Bookseller and a Poet" conveys to what extent Pushkin experienced economic reality as yet another form of tyranny over his imaginative autonomy. The poem is cast as a dialogue between two "men of letters" who speak completely different languages: the lyrical poet, solipsistically engrossed in the stream of his internal images, and the bookseller, who tries various argumentative strategies and quite funny imitations of poetic rhetoric in order to persuade the poet to part with his *stizhki* (little verses), emphasizing the ease with which the poet produces them ("Nemnozhko stoit vam prisest' ") (2, 1, 324); fame; if not fame, then women's hearts; if women's hearts are worthless, then freedom, which—the bookseller at last finds his opening—can only be bought with the money the age is willing to pay for the very products of that "free inspiration." The *pointe* of the poem comes at the very end when the poet, at last agreeing to exchange his manuscripts for money, suddenly finds himself speaking prose.

For our purposes—that is, with an eye to "Kleopatra"—the most interesting passages come toward the end, when the bookseller asks whether not one woman is exempt from the poet's anathema. Unwilling to stir up memories, the poet hesitates, then cries out,

> Где та была, которой очи,
> Как небо, улыбались мне?
> Вся жизнь, одна, ли, две ли ночи?
> . . . .
> . . . Ах, мысль о той души завялой
> Могла бы юность оживить
> И сны поэзии бывалой
> Толпою снова возмутить!
> Она одна бы разумела
> Стихи неясные мои;
> Одна бы в сердце пламенела
> Лампадой чистою любви.
> Увы, напрасные желанья!
> Она отвергла заклинанья,
> Мольбы, тоску души моей:
> Земных восторгов излиянья,
> Как божеству, не нужно ей.
>
> (2.1, 328–29)

Where is she whose eyes, like the sky, smiled at me? Is all of life to be one or two nights? . . . Ah, the thought of that withered soul might yet enliven youth and rouse up dreams of past poetry in a crowd again! She alone would comprehend my obscure verse; alone would flame in my heart with the clear lamp of love. Alas, vain desire! She rejected the incantations, prayers, and anguish of my soul: like a divinity, she has no need of outpourings of earthly rapture.

A couple of weeks after the completion of "Proserpine," the image of a regal mistress divinely empowered to "bring back to life" "crowds" of "poetic dreams," but who bestowed life on him for only one or two nights, is embedded—buried?—in what at first seems an incongruous commercial context. The Vorontsova story is still recognizable in its transparent self-pity, clothed in predictable Christlike rhetoric, but not fully transformed. As the age bargains profanely for the products of the poet's sacred "strast' " (passion, and also suffering), the future themes of "Kleopatra" swim into view: "tiazhkii son," "sny poezii byvaloi," "tolpoiu ozhivit'," "bozhestvo," "torg," "vsia zhizn', odna li, dve li nochi?"

Pushkin's letter to Viazemsky of November 29, 1824 contains an amusingly different and certainly less ingenuous version of the "bargains" Pushkin had gotten himself mixed up in:

Your proposal regarding my elegies is unrealizable, and here is why: In 1820 I copied out my rubbish, and I intended to publish it by subscription; I printed tickets and disposed of about forty. Then I lost my manuscript at cards to Nikita Vsevolozhsky (of course, with a certain proviso). Meanwhile I have been compelled to flee from Mecca to Medina, my Koran started going from hand to hand, and the true believers are still awaiting it. Now I have given my brother the task of seeking out and buying back my manuscript, and then we shall proceed to the publication of the elegies, poetic epistles, and the miscellaneous things. It must be announced in the newspapers that, since the tickets may have been lost on account of the lengthy delay in publication, the name and address will suffice for the receipt of copies, for (let us tell a lie, to be on the safe side) the names of all the ladies and gentlemen subscribers are in the publisher's hands. If I incur losses and do lose several copies, there will be nobody to complain of; I myself am to blame (this must remain *between us*).[11]

In the demystified genre of familiar correspondence, Pushkin plays the role of his own crass bookseller. The form of the confession is delightfully disingenuous: Pushkin admits that he himself is to blame for his predicament, but is quite willing to lie and go to preposterous lengths to make sure that that truth remains a secret, "between us," from the public.

The family reunion resulted in a confrontation so violent that on October 31, 1824 Pushkin turned to Zhukovsky (yet another father figure) for mediation:

> Dear fellow, I resort to you. Judge of my position. When I came here I was met by all as well as could be, but soon everything changed. My father, frightened by my exile, has been constantly reiterating that the same fate awaits him. Peshchurov, appointed to have surveillance over me, had the shamelessness to offer my father the duty of unsealing my correspondence, in short, of being my spy. My father's hot temper and irritable touchiness would not permit me to have an explanation with him; I decided to be silent. My father began to reproach my brother to the effect that I was teaching him godlessness. I still kept silent. They received a document regarding me. Finally, desiring to remove myself from this painful position, I went to my father, asked his permission to explain my position frankly... My father flared up. I bowed, mounted my horse, and left. My father called my brother and ordered him to have nothing to do *avec ce monstre, ce fils dénaturé...* (Zhukovsky, think of my position and judge.) My head began to seethe. I went to my father, found him with my mother, and I blurted out everything that had been bothering me for three whole months. I ended by saying that I was talking to him for the last time. My father, taking advantage of the absence of witnesses, dashed out and declared to the whole household that "I had beat him, wanted to beat him, raised my hand threateningly, could have given him a thrashing..." I am not justifying myself to you. But just what does he want of me, accusing me of a felony? The mines of Siberia and the deprivation of honor? . . . To try to prove in court my father's slander would be horrible for me, but there is no court for me. I am *hors la loi.*[12]

To what extent Pushkin's letter to Zhukovsky was a histrionic performance is hard to say. Pushkin's style and preoccupations strikingly call to mind Waverley's conflict with his father (the reiterated anxiety over his "position," the choice of silence as the only honorable form of self-expression, the immediate imaginative leap to legal repercussions) and with astonishing precision look forward to the Oedipal fantasy of Grinev's dream in *The Captain's Daughter.*[13] Pushkin barely mentions his mother in passing, perhaps assimilating himself imaginatively to Waverley's stepson position, yet we tend to prick up our twentieth-century ears when we hear that Pushkin broke in on his father and mother's tête-à-tête in order to "blurt out" a rage that had been seething for "three whole months" and perhaps much longer. Pushkin has a child's intensified sense of drama about the dangerous power of his anger, so long withheld, now suddenly expressed.

True to the poetics of the Byronic *poema*, however, he elides from his narrative the truth that finally burst from him, leaving only his habitual suspension dots. Pushkin reports his father's quotation of his own speech, implying that it is a betrayal, but does not make absolutely clear whether the betrayal lies in misquotation or in publicizing and making legally binding what should have remained between them. Pushkin's father was clearly not wrong to hear the aggressive undertone in Pushkin's speech to him "for the last time," nor did Pushkin expect to get away without being punished. One almost feels that he is challenging his father to *face* him and recognize his anger. Instead, his father dissolved back into the St. Petersburg social life from which he had so briefly emerged to play his equivocal role, leaving Pushkin speechless.

Foiled, perhaps, in his desire for a decisive encounter with the power behind the masks that tyrannized him, perhaps even courting punishment, Pushkin poured out his pent-up self-justifications in a fantasy encounter. In his "Imaginary Conversation with Alexander I," written in December 1824, Pushkin continued to translate his predicament into the archetypal situations of Scott's novels (for example, Waverley's protection from a tyrannical father by the personal intercession of a benevolent monarch) and at the same time to court the punishment he feared.

Pushkin begins on a fairy-tale note that stresses the twinning of their names: "If I were the Tsar I would summon Alexander Pushkin and say to him: 'Alexander Sergeyevich, you write excellent poetry.' Alexander Pushkin would bow to me with a touch of embarrassed modesty, and I would continue."[14] Like a magnanimous father, the tsar engages Pushkin in a civilized analysis of his poems and his conduct, chiding him for his "irresponsible behavior," "rambling style," and "superficial opinions," but not holding him rigidly accountable for his youthful tangents. He allows Pushkin both to defend himself and to distance himself from past utterances ("Oh, your Majesty, why recall that infantile ode ["Freedom"]? . . . How can one judge a man by a letter written to a friend? Can one give a schoolboy's jest the weight of a crime, and judge two empty phrases as one would a public sermon?").[15] Pushkin substitutes for his father not only an ideally powerful and understanding ally, the tsar himself, but also turns the tsar into a second "Alexander," a second self who does not hold him accountable for his language but allows him to dart and improvise at will, fathering and refathering himself. Thus Pushkin is almost simultaneously a man, speaking man-to-man with the tsar, and an infantile schoolboy, his own disowned child. The tsar, by contrast, is strictly taken to task for acts inconsistent with his principles (such as Pushkin's exile). The tsar's retort to this suggests an element of self-knowledge on Pushkin's part: Pushkin would have pushed him until he found the limits of Alexander's magnanimity.

The conversation comes to an abrupt halt with a scene that clearly has its roots in the recent quarrel with his father: "But here Pushkin would have flared up and would have blurted out a whole lot of unnecessary remarks, and I would have grown angry and would have banished him to Siberia, where he would have written a poem called *Yermak* or *Kochum* in various rhyming measures."[16] The tsar reveals his true colors and deals out his most dreaded punishment, only to have it comically reduced to just another occasion for poetic improvisation. Pushkin appears to have realized by the end of the conversation that it was not a matter of disavowing this document or that peccadillo to this or that figure of authority. His own wellspring of "unnecessary remarks" was inexhaustible, and the impulse to challenge authority, responsibility, and the borders of his world a permanent condition. Even Siberia, the worst punishment and the most distant border, could be nonchalantly assimilated by Pushkin as just another occasion for poetry, another demonstration of his verbal power.

Zhukovsky tended to respond to Pushkin's complaints, whether of mistreatment or boredom or aneurysm, in the same way:

> To everything that has happened to you, and to all that you have brought on yourself, I have only one answer: POETRY. You have not got talent; you have genius. You are rich, you have an inalienable means to transcend undeserved

misfortune and to make good that which you have deserved; you above anybody can and must have moral dignity. You were born to be a great poet; be worthy of it. In this phrase lies your entire ethic, your entire happiness, your entire reward. The circumstances of life, both happy and unhappy, are its shell. You will say that I am preaching to a drowning man from the calm of the shore. No! I am standing on a deserted shore and I see an athlete struggling in the waves and I know he will not drown if he uses all his strength and I am only showing him the better shore that he will reach if he himself wishes it. Swim athlete! (November, 1824)[17]

To a young man intent on escaping the confines of his provincial cage, these encouraging words about the sacrifices he must make to his genius must have seemed yet another form of tyranny, particularly when not only his earthly pleasures but inspiration itself were flickering. Over and over Pushkin's letters of that fall sound the same pitiful theme:

I won't tell you anything about my life here. It's dull, that's all. . . . Talking of verse, today I finished the poem, *The Gipsies*. I don't know what to say of it. At the moment I am sick of it. . . . I am sending you a short intercession for the repose of the soul of God's servant Byron—I almost decided on a whole requiem, but it's dull writing for oneself. . . . Send me some poems, I am dying of boredom.[18]

I am in the best possible position to finish my poetic novel, but boredom is a cold Muse, and my poem makes no progress.[19]

Books, for God's sake some books. . . . Poetry, poetry, poetry! Conversations de Byron! Walter Scott! That is food for the soul. Do you know how I spend my time? Before dinner I write my Memoirs; I dine late; after dinner I go riding; in the evening I listen to fairy tales—and in this way compensate for the shortcomings of my cursed education. How delightful these tales are! Each one is like a poem![20]

I am expecting my brother and Delvig in a day or two, for the moment I am absolutely alone; . . . I lounge about in the ingle-nook and listen to old fairy tales and songs. Poetry doesn't come.[21]

Pushkin's brother, even more of a free spirit than Pushkin himself, was unfortunately slow to respond to repeated requests for the same texts: Byron's and Napoleon's posthumous documents, the Bible, Roman historians, Russian chronicles, Walter Scott. Initially as a pis aller until poetic inspiration returned, then increasingly as "food for the soul," Pushkin turned to nonfiction. Feeling spied upon, maligned, and misquoted, and seeing how quickly Byron was being "unmasked" after death by his own writings and even "conversations,"[22] Pushkin seems eager to record his own version of events, only to realize that to speak about oneself is impossible, as he expostulated to Viazemsky:

> Why do you regret the loss of Byron's notes? The devil with them! Thank God they are lost. He made his confession in his verses . . . in cool prose, he would have lied and acted crafty, now trying to sparkle with sincerity, now bedaubing his enemies. . . . We know Byron well enough. . . . To write one's memoirs is tempting and pleasant. There is no one you love, no one you know, so well as your own self. It's an inexhaustible subject. But it's difficult. Not to lie is possible, but to be sincere is a physical impossibility. The pen will sometimes stop, as from a running start before a chasm—on what an outsider would read with indifference. To condemn other people's judgement is not difficult; to condemn one's own judgement is impossible.[23]

If the fragments that survived Pushkin's auto-da-fé are any indication, his memoirs were anecdotal, perhaps politically incriminating, but strictly external.[24] It was particularly difficult to write them with a straight face when every autobiography or documental work he read confirmed the duplicity of the genre, the manifold opportunities it offered both for self-misrepresentation and for misreading. But this is precisely where the fascination lay. Pushkin's intellect came alive at the moment his skepticism was awakened in response to the imaginative challenge of reconciling contradictory or even false documents, finding precisely in their *nedoskazannosti* (ellipses), "dryness," and subterfuges a new stimulus to poetic imagination. In hindsight, of course, it is easy to recognize in the desultory reading Pushkin did as he waited for his muse to reappear precisely the new form it would take. In early November 1824, however, *Boris Godunov* was just a glimmer in its creator's eye, anticipated only by his interest in folk pretenders, lying memoirists, and his first "historical elegy," "Kleopatra."

One can identify the moment of creative realignment recorded in the letter written to his brother during that same two-week period in which Pushkin wrote "Kleopatra." Dividing his day between "breaking stallions"[25] and secluded storytelling sessions with his nurse, Pushkin's starved poetic imagination found itself rekindled and refocused by her ancient native stories. There is an archetypal quality to this scene that has not gone unnoticed. Betrayed by his father and a whole series of surrogate authority figures, betrayed (in his own view) by a series of powerful women, so neglected by his mother that he almost never mentions her, excluded from the high society life that was the very air he breathed, and perhaps his only privilege and patrimony, Pushkin received from his nurse both simple faithfulness and the belated motherly gift of her native Russian storytelling. An interlude of normally loving and loyal attachment released his blocked energies in the precise direction her genres suggested: fairy tale, historical legend, the multivoiced detritus of history.

But why Cleopatra? I will begin, as usual, with fashion. Cleopatra, always an eminent theatrical subject,[26] was at the time the focus of a Parisian succès de scandale. The opening of Alexandre Soumet's *Cléopâtre* in July 1824 had rekindled the old polemics about the propriety of casting Tacitus's *regina meretrix* as the heroine of a tragedy. (Pushkin's mentor La Harpe had attempted to ban her once and for all from serious drama in 1750, but to no avail.)[27] It is likely that Pushkin, an avid reader of foreign journals and newspapers, was aware of a theatrical debut that in the words of one journalist "marked the transition from Classicism to Romanticism": "By the pomp and dazzling beauty of his style, [Soumet] has disguised many of the defects inherent in the subject he had chosen, perhaps with temerity."[28]

What defects, what temerity? In the context of the "Racine ou Shakespeare" debate then raging in the French theater,[29] any dramatic allusion to Shakespeare was bound to be viewed as a controversial stand. At the same time, beneath the "literary scandals" that marked the opening nights of historical dramas such as Soumet's (and later Hugo's and Vigny's) lurked the more concrete danger of political allegory.[30] The Egyptian theme and setting made fashionable by the archaeological discoveries that accompanied Napoleon certainly had an aura of the forbidden; Egypt could be regarded as a code for the challenge to the old European order that had originated in Napoleon's Egyptian campaigns. Several years into the Bourbon restoration, to resuscitate the story of the passionate and anti-Roman lovers in a tragic key was to resuscitate the allegorical ghosts of political opposition. Octavius/Augustus represented Empire, the manly or authoritarian (depending on one's point of view) order of the ancien régime, while onto the eastern pleasure-loving pair could be grafted all of the accumulated implications of nineteenth-century Orientalism, either "positive" (passion, freedom, spirituality, poetry) or "negative" (sensuality, disorder, emasculation, ahistory). Knowing as we do how thoroughly intertwined with Augustan mythology was Alexander's imperial iconography, we might expect that the theme of Cleopatra, like that of "Oriental luxury" in general,[31] would have been automatically imbued with "freedom-loving" and subversive connotations. But the Romantic story of an empire defiantly lost for love is not the one Pushkin chooses to tell.

All European treatments of Cleopatra[32] until Pushkin's have one thing in common: like the contemporary accounts of Plutarch, Pliny the Younger, and Tacitus, they focus on Cleopatra's union with Antony, the fall of their empire, and their suicide. The concern of Roman historians was to establish the union of east and west threatened by Antony and Cleopatra as the opposite of Roman good government and self-government, as an engulfment of manly and rational rule by unrestrained female sensuality, self-indulgence, foreign ritual, and superstition. Antony was essentially eliminated as an independent political force in the victor's version of events; rather, he was depicted as the Egyptian queen's slave, robbed precisely by his own sensuality of his Roman virility. The battle over Rome by Julius Caesar's successors was transformed into a battle between true Roman principle and its feminine-Oriental inverse, even between the Olympian world order and the primitive and violent earth rituals of the east.[33] When Tacitus, with his famous epithet *regina meretrix*, and Horace echo the common Roman clichés about Cleopatra's voracious, decadent, and "un-Roman" promiscuity, they are touching on a whole system of associations connected with the prospect of Asian tyranny.

Although this Roman representation seems to coincide with the general tone of Pushkin's poem, the incident he describes is unique. It originates in a single evocative sentence from a dubious Roman source, *De viris illustribus urbis Romae*, in Pushkin's time still falsely attributed to the obscure fourth-century author of *De Caesaribus*, Aurelius Victor. Pushkin noted the name carefully in the margin of his notebook, although where he encountered this curiosity will probably never be ascertained.[34] Characteristically, Pushkin was attracted not by the "main line" of history, but by an insignificant and accidentally preserved anecdote, his favorite kind of source.[35]

Even more interesting is the fact that the anecdote achieves the reverse effect from the one intended by Cleopatra's muckraking memoirist. Later, in the second of his frame tales, Pushkin will have his raconteur Alexei Ivanovich explain why he had been so attracted to this subject:

> His little book [*On Illustrious Men of Rome*] is rather insignificant, but it contains the legend about Cleopatra that has so captured my imagination. And what is most remarkable, in this particular passage the dry and boring Aurelius Victor equals Tacitus in force of expression: "Haec tantae libidinis fuit ut saepe prostiretit; tantae pulchritudinis ut multi noctem illius morte emerint."[36]

Something analogous had happened to Pushkin in November 1824: killing his boredom and lack of inspiration by laboring over his own prose memoirs, he found himself visited by inspiration precisely in the form of "Kleopatra." Cleopatra emerges from Aurelius Victor's anecdote as so powerful a figure that she has managed for one moment to elevate even her prosaic Roman chronicler from his humdrum imperial propaganda to the level of poetry. A single sentence about Cleopatra not only casts the "illustrious Roman men" into shadow, it guarantees Aurelius Victor's immortality. Like the crowd in the first stanza, one of the faceless mob of Roman propagandists becomes quite inadvertently "inspired," "brought back to life," by the queen's vividly imagined proposition.

In what ways does "Kleopatra" represent a liberation of Pushkin's blocked energies? Clearly, it marked a departure from the lyrical habits criticized by Kiukhel'beker in 1824.[37] Pushkin's contemporaries would have classified it as a "historical elegy," in itself a Romantically hybrid genre, on the basis of its mixed meter (two chunks of four- and six-foot iambs) and its subject: a "historical scene" dominated by a dramatic monologue. Historical elegy could be seen as a compromise between the "mediocre" elegy and the high ode because it moved beyond the lyric poet's habitually narrow personal horizon into history.

The most popular genre of historical elegy took as its theme, however, the last words of the poet on the scaffold, and projected onto an imagined "objective" situation the poet's lyrical solipsism and sense of persecution / grandeur. Such were the many poems on the dying Tasso, the dying Byron, the dying Chatterton, and so on, including Pushkin's own "André Chénier."[38] In each of these the poet-hero bravely confronts his tormentor and tyrant as he never could have in history, and his glory, by the logic of the allegory, extends to the author of the poem within his own analogous historical situation. By the end of "Kleopatra" the contemporary reader might have recognized the trope of the poet on the scaffold, but in fully transmuted form. In the story of the Egyptian feast elegy is completely subordinated to history, the personal emphatically masked and made foreign. The silent poet-victim seems to be split up into three abstract attributes: manliness, intellect, and youth, while it is Kleopatra who does all the talking.

What would this poem have conveyed to a reader in 1824? I believe it would have been read as an emblem of tyranny, historically accurate yet symbolic. In much the same way that Byron's *Sardanapalus* could be read as an exploration of the temptations of an "effeminate," eastern, pleasure-loving and mind-destroying Regency rule, I suspect that in Russia on the eve of the Decembrist rebellion "Kleopatra" would have been read as a warning: Asian despotism suffocating in its mindless (female) luxury, devouring its best men, its best minds, its own European credentials. A similar possibility lurks in Pushkin's "Imaginary conversation with Alexander I": the mask and the language of enlightened monarchy may at any moment crack to reveal the abyss of Oriental tyranny, the two-faced mask of Kleopatra, bestowing the duplicitous blessing of sensual fulfillment and spiritual death on her slavish court. There is no need for the poet to speak on the scaffold. Read from this point of view, the victims' muteness is an eloquent and devastating portrayal of the fate of manliness and mind in an Oriental society. Once the Decembrist rebellion had happened, the interpretation of "Kleopatra" would have been sealed. How could the fate of the five victims not have been assimilated to the voluntary self-sacrifice of "the brightest and the best" of Kleopatra's court, and their savage fate?

Such a political interpretation fits in with other unfinished poems of the same year, including "A guard dozed motionless on the Tsar's threshold," which opens with the same atmosphere of somnolence, dynamized by the northern tsar's solitary thought, and the enigmatic fragment apparently addressed to Napoleon, "Why were you sent, and who sent you?"[39] This poem maintains in unresolved tension an apparent admiration for the charismatic greatness of the leader and a simultaneous contempt for the masses liberated by him, who, instead of following Napoleon's model of human freedom, slavishly invite renewed tyranny. This note of civic indignation would be sounded again in the historical elegy written the following year, "André Chénier," in which the concerns and language of intimate lyric poetry are quite legibly divorced from, and sacrificed to, the poet's "odic" obligation to speak fearlessly of freedom and justice, to assume his place in history. The erotic and the political are polarized stylistically and existentially as opposite ends of the human spectrum.

In "Kleopatra" there is no such convenient separation. As Henry Kissinger is supposed to have said, "Power is the greatest aphrodisiac." Pushkin was himself attracted like a moth to a flame by the sight of a society beauty surrounded by her crowd of admirers and the luxury and power her husband's position afforded her. "Kleopatra" is written not from a vantage point of satirical superiority, but by one for whom jostling in a crowd of rivals, being heartlessly played with, and skirting self-destruction at the hands of authority were a compelling fantasy. If "Kleopatra" can be read as a study in charismatic power, the erotic interaction of "great men" and crowds, it draws equally on the experience of a psyche imprinted in its most intimate fantasies with society's structures of domination and submission, of "mediated desire." But in "Kleopatra" Pushkin finally hit on a way of making the running leap into the "inexhaustible subject" of himself while bypassing elegy, love, sincerity, and the pronoun "I."

Царица голосом и взором
Свой пышный оживляла пир,
Все, Клеопатру славя хором,
В ней признавая свой кумир,
Шумя, текли к ее престолу,
Но вдруг над чашей золотой

Она задумалась—и долу
Поникла дивною главой.
И пышный пир как будто дремлет,
И в ожиданье все молчит...
Но вновь она чело подъемлет
И с видом важным говорит:
‹‹Внемлите мне: могу равенство
Меж вас и мной восстановить.
В моей любви для вас блаженство,
Блаженство можно вам купить:
Кто к торгу страстному приступит?
Свои я ночи продаю.
Скажите, кто меж вами купит
Ценою жизни ночь мою?››

Она рекла. Толпа в молчанье,
И все в волнении сердца.
Но Клеопатра в ожиданье
С холодной дерзостью лица:
‹‹Я жду,—вещает,—что ж молчите?
Иль вы теперь бежите прочь?
Вас было много; приступите,
Торгуйте радостную ночь.››
И гордый взор она обводит
Кругом поклонников своих...
Вдруг—из рядов один выходит,
Вослед за ним и два других.
Смела их поступь, ясны очи.
Царица гордо восстает.
Свершилось: куплены три ночи...
И ложе смерти их зовет.

И снова гордый глас возвысила царица:
‹‹Забыты мною днесь венец и багряница!
Неслыханно тебе, Киприда, я служу,
И новый дар теве ночей моих награда,
О боги грозные, внемлите ж, боги ада,
Подземных ужасов печальные цари!
Примите мой обет: до сладостной зари
Властителей моих последние желанья,
Всей чашею любви послушно упою...
Но только сквозь завес во храмину мою

Блеснет Авроры луч—клянусь моей порфирой,—
Главы их упадут под утренней секирой!»

Благословенные священною рукой,
Из урны жребии выходят чередой,
И первый Аквила, Клеврет Помпея смелый,
Изрубленный в боях, в походах поседелый.
Презренья хладного не снес он от жены
И гордо выступил, суровый сын войны,
На вызов роковых последних наслаждений,
Критон за ним, Критон, изнеженный мудрец,
От самых первых дней поклонник и певец
И пламенных пиров и пламенной Киприды.
Последний имени векам не передал,
Никем не знаемый, ничем не знаменитый;
Чуть отроческий пух, темнея, покрывал
  Его стыдливые ланиты.
  Огонь любви в очах его пылал,
Во всех чертах любовь изображалась—
И молча долго им царица любовалсь.

(3.2, 685–87)

Queen Cleopatra with her gazes
And voice adorned her splendid feast.
Exalting with a choir of praises
The chosen idol of the East,
Thronged to her throne the pleasure-seekers,
When all at once she stooped, and so
Fell still among the golden beakers,
Her wondrous forehead drooping low.
The rich assembly, never shifting,
Stands silently as in a daze...
Until the Queen announces, lifting
Her brow again, with solemn gaze:
"Hear me! This day it is my pleasure
To make us equals in my sight.
To you my love were highest blessing;
But you may buy this bliss tonight.
Behold the marketplace of passion!
For sale I offer nights divine;
Who dares to barter in this fashion
His life against one night of mine?"

Thus her decree. All breath abating,
The strange and stirring challenge looms.
Soon Cleopatra, coldly waiting,
With cold audacity resumes:
"Why are you silent? I am ready;
Or shall I see you all take flight?
Not few are here whose dreams were heady...
Now purchase an enchanting night!"

Her haughty glances scan the verges
Of her admirers' silent throng...
There! of a sudden one emerges,
Two others follow soon along.
Their step is bold, their gaze unclouded.
The Queen arises in her pride.
Three nights are bought: the couch is shrouded
For deadly pleasures at her side.

Once more they heard the Queen's imperious voice resound:
"Let none remember now I was in purple crowned!
I shall ascend the couch but as a common whore,
To serve thee, Lady Love, as no one has before,
And vow my nights' reward a novel gift to thee.
O awesome deities of Hades, hearken me,
Ye melancholy kings of nether realms forlorn!
Receive ye this my pledge: unto the languid dawn
I promise to obey my rulers' utmost wishes
With wondrous tenderness, strange arts, the deep delicious
Cup ever newly filled with love's entrancing wine...
But when into my chamber through the curtains shine
Young Eos' early rays—I swear by your grim shade
Their heads shall fall that morn beneath the headsman's blade!"

By holy augury each sanctified in turn
The lots assigned the three now issue from the urn:
First Archilaios' lot, of Pompey's noble guard,
Gone gray in his campaigns, in combat hewn and scarred.
A woman's cold disdain resolved to bear no more,
He haughtily stepped forth, the somber son of war
To heed the fateful lure, the last sweet test of mettle,
As earlier he had the glory-notes of battle.
Crito was the second drawn, Crito the gentle sage

Who, reared beneath the sky of Argolis,
Had glowing tribute paid, since barely come of age,
To Bacchus' fiery feasts, the Cyprid's fiery kiss.
The third one's name remains by annals unrecorded;
Unknown to all, unmarked, he would embrace his doom,
A downy youth as yet whose beard but faintly bordered
His tender cheek with bashful bloom.
With love's consuming fire his eyes now gleamed,
For Cleopatra meant his very life, it seemed;
And long and silently the Queen rejoiced in him.[40]

Our first response may be one of recognition. As in the opening scenes of "The Fountain of Bakhchisarai" and "The Bride of Abydos," the gaze and voice of an Oriental potentate spell life and death for the entire court. The difference, of course, is that the potentate is a woman; the dangerous power usually contained by the harem sits at the head of the table and "brings back to life" the homogeneous feasting throng; when she "bows her head in thought," the court falls into a fairy-tale torpor; when she speaks, men's bodies quiver mutely in response. The prerogatives of head, sight, and language have been monstrously usurped, and this is, to the western sensibility, reflected in the inhuman monstrosity of the "bargain" she proposes.

What prompts her proposal, simply unfettered feminine lust or insane Oriental luxury and satiation, as the Romans made out? Pushkin offers a different picture, that of a proud and deliberate enactment of a religious ritual, an unheard-of sacrifice performed by not only a queen but a goddess.[41] The plot of the poem repeats the essential moments of "Proserpine." Taking on herself the Isis/Venus role of priestess (which Cleopatra in fact did, for the two were often conflated in Hellenistic culture), she offers herself for ritual violation. The second half of the religious rite must follow with inexorable logic from the first. Having tasted divine love, the initiants must experience the other face of the goddess's identity in mystical proximity: at the first ray of dawn their *heads* will fall. They are not, in the manner of the Dionysian rites, to be torn to pieces, but precisely decapitated, severed from their reasoning, male, Roman half. In a later version Pushkin rearranged the order of the stanzas so that Kleopatra's first fateful gesture, the meditative bowing of her head, would be echoed by the last line of the poem: "Glava schastlivtsev otpadet" (The head of the lucky ones will fall), crystallizing the meaning of the sacrifice in a single image.[42] As in "Proserpine," the sacrificial victims of the queen are described as "schastlivtsy"—the lucky ones.

As is always the case in Pushkin's cross-cultural encounters, the two sides do not speak the same language. In contrast to the homogeneous Oriental throng that surrounds Kleopatra, the three men who volunteer to submit their fate, fairy tale–style, to the drawing of lots are highly individualized, and each participates in the rite on his own individual terms. The first, a Roman soldier, uses the rite to express his manhood in the face of Kleopatra's brazen feminine usurpation; the second, a Hellenistic Epicurean, sees in the rite the ultimate opportunity to pursue pleasure and knowledge; but the third, a "nameless young boy," is inspired by an ardor so pure that it startles the ritually dispassionate and rhetorical goddess into a moment of mute feeling. This is where the poem breaks off.

Coming as we do from our immersion in the repetitive scenarios of Pushkin's elegiac mode, we cannot help but recognize the scene's lyrical core. There he is again, the passionate youth, dissolved anonymously in a crowd of admirers ("poklonnikov tolpa"), silently transfixed by his erotic goddess. He actually emerges from the background of the crowd only at the end of the poem, at the very moment that Kleopatra's life-sustaining gaze and death-dealing words come to rest on him. There are no individual human figures until late in the poem. The crowd is depicted in rhythmic motion and choral praise, suggesting nothing so much as a beehive pulsating with collective life. Pushkin avoids the traditional topos of offering up the queen as a feast for the spectator's eyes, which would put her on the same existential level as the rest of her court.[43] Her physical beauty is not described at all. But when the charismatic power of her voice and gaze is withdrawn, the entire court's animation is suspended. The effect of her presence is like that of the (psychoanalytic) mother on the *corps morcelé* of the infant:[44] when the crowd is deprived of the unifying image of her face, it lapses into torpor and inchoateness. It lives only in her gaze, only as a materialization of her power.

The distribution of silence and speech, always structurally crucial and deliberate in Pushkin's poetry, and even, as we have seen in his account of the quarrel with his father, in his dramatic perception of life, is worth noticing here. The crowd's torpor is broken by Kleopatra's powerful speech: "She spoke. The crowd hushed, / And all hearts surged."[45] The crowd still does not speak, but it is at least released from its torpor into silent emotion. Then, as if in phenomenological response to her challenging address, three individuals materialize from the crowd. The "stage of the mirror" is followed by the "stage of language": individuation depends on language's ability to separate and "tell" identity from sensation. In naming experience, one names oneself. Or conversely, it is only when the individual experiences himself as separated that he can conceptualize desire, and hence his own subjectivity.

The proposition the queen makes is a classic Oedipal fantasy: the already differentiated, conscious child is allowed to reexperience union with the mother-goddess, but only for a finite time. Experience will have a narrative shape, a beginning, middle, and end, like her speech. When Kleopatra's words summon the three sacrifices out of the undifferentiated and plotless agitation of the crowd into temporary "equality" with her, she summons them into the domain of time and narrative. Their bodies will suddenly become discrete, visible, their actions nameable: they, not the crowd, will enter history. To accept the challenge of her language, of her imaginative refashioning of the borders and possibilities of life and desire, means to accept the death of the old self.

In "Proserpine" the happy initiate returns to the surface, only to discover that life is now invaded by a "false swarm of dreams." In "Kleopatra" there is no illusion, no regret: love has been openly offered as the death of the self. The narrative has been made maximally compact, one might say maximally archaic. No male god appears to force the lover out of his blissful experience of timeless and wordless union back into the real world of time, consciousness, and language. In "Kleopatra" the goddess's own speech forces the three victims out of the protective coloration of the crowd and into sculpted individuality and plotted action. Mute life has been delivered over into the power of the goddess of desire and speech; it becomes her images, her names, the subjects of her plots. Kleopatra does all the talking in the poem. No one answers her, except to take up assigned positions in her drama. Giving up their mute lives, they enter the eloquence of her story and are both preserved and killed by it. The poem breaks off just as her gaze comes mutely to rest on the boy, still passionately alive, not yet named, not yet inducted into language. "No ia, liubia, byl glup i nem." "Umru liubia."[46]

I hope it is clear that I am not attempting to identify Vorontsova or any of Pushkin's mistresses as "the original" for Proserpine, Kleopatra, or any other lyrical heroine.[47] If anything, the reverse is true: Pushkin was repeatedly drawn to erotic situations because they conformed to his own internal dramatis personae. As I said earlier, the opposing forces within a single, "hermaphroditic" human nature are often allegorized as gender opposites: the conscious self as "child-hero" and the unconscious as the supraordinate, demonic, two-faced mother / maiden.[48] Such a mythological emplotment of contradictory psychological impulses is only a slightly different way of expressing what we have been taught to call the unconscious—that is, an internal "other" with its own sometimes life-shattering agenda. Pushkin's Kleopatra is no mere goddess of sensual intoxication, of the usurping body. Her distinctive features are the animating power of her sight and speech, her transformative vision and language. Her language has the power to make things happen: to make men appear where there were none, to arouse them to unheard-of courage, to destroy them, and to make them remembered. She is the cannibalistic poet's mind, which must be fed a constant diet of human sacrifice: the sacrifice of his own manhood, reason, and love of life.

Recycling "Kleopatra"

Pushkin's urge to return to earlier texts, to either rework them or embed them in a frame tale that put their historical contexts into contrasting perspective, was not just an idiosyncratic solution to a personal creative predicament. It was influenced by the fashionable literary currents that accompanied the July Revolution in Paris in 1830, of which Pushkin kept very much abreast.[49] A glance at the front page of *Le Globe* for "Thursday, July 29, at midnight" conveys an instant impression of radical change.[50] Up until then the front page had consisted of one unbroken, lengthy exposition of a single topic the editors deemed to be of general importance and interest, such as French archaeological excavations in Greece. After the July Revolution the first page of *Le Globe* began to resemble a modern front page, a collage of up-to-the-minute reports on events occurring simultaneously all over the globe, in recognition both of the diversity of interests (and shorter attention span) of the newspaper's mass audience and the impossibility of predicting which events would eventually be deemed "central" and historical.

The front page was a visual icon of historical reality as it was now conceived of: fast paced, decentralized, requiring "information" rather than knowledge. Its fractured, collage-type presentation created a need for a new kind of journalistic presence: the cultural commentator like Sainte-Beuve, Jules Janin, or Charles Nodier, who provided an individualistic reading (very much in the nervous, buttonholing, street-corner-philosopher style of Diderot) of contemporaneity to itself.[51] The daily editorial column addressed the reader about the bewildering array of information that assaulted him and formulated his response for him. One prevalent way of providing historical perspective was to juxtapose contrasting moments in history—for example, 1688, 1789, and 1830—in order to show that what seemed like overnight change from a contemporary perspective had been long in the making: the July Revolution was really the completion of the French and even the Glorious Revolutions.[52]

There was also an impulse on the part of pro-July writers to look back to the social and literary movements that had accompanied the French Revolution and seek some form of continuity with them. Sainte-Beuve and other journalists excavated Diderot from the obscurity into which he had fallen and elected him the model for the new French man of letters, the *feuilletoniste*.[53] Jules Janin's *Barnave* was one of the best-sellers in the post-July frame tale genre. A latter-day *Decameron*, it presented the various self-incriminatingly decadent anecdotes of a group of French aristocrats on the eve of the French Revolution. More or less ignoring authenticity of language or detail, it created a maquette of the ancien régime salon calculated to satisfy the preconceptions of the post-July popular reading public.

One of the decadently self-mirroring stories told in the aristocratic salon was, as it happens, about Cleopatra.

Journalism, in other words, set new criteria for what was interesting in literature. The historical novel, which in the 1810's and 1820's had been valued for its poetic, imaginative resurrection of lost time—for being essentially the prose equivalent of elegy—was suddenly banished to the costume closet. How much more challenging was the interpretation of the opaque and agitated surfaces of contemporary life, where nothing was what it seemed to be. Stendhal was one of the first to argue (in his influential article "Sir Walter Scott and the Princess of Cleves," 1830) that "The doublet and the leather collar of the medieval serf are easier to describe than the emotions of the human heart."[54] His own novel *The Red and the Black*, whose final scene takes place in 1830, just weeks before it was actually published, was making quasi-journalistic contemporaneity fashionable, just as his minute analysis of the genesis of the passions in *On Love* established a perverse new conception of psychology for his generation. Honoré de Balzac chimed in with *Scenes from Private Life* and *The Physiology of Marriage*, published in Russian in 1831, and went on to explain in the first edition of his collected works, *Studies of Nineteenth-Century Life* (1833–37), "Walter Scott exhausted the only type of novel possible in the past . . . when caste provided each person with an appearance which dominated the individual; today the individual derives his appearance from nothing but himself . . . differences have disappeared and there are only nuances left."[55]

In her article "The Society Tale and the Innovative Argument in Russian Prose Fiction of the 1830's," Elizabeth Shepard describes the decline of the Scott novel's prestige in France and England, the concomitant rise of the predominantly Gallic society tale, and the latter's rapid proliferation on the Russian literary scene. For the pageantry of historical and local color, the society tale and the novel substitute the nuances of contemporary social ritual (or the "exoticism" of the aristocratic salon); for castles and landscapes, city streets and interiors; for national *Volksgeist*, the behavior and hidden motivations of individuals, interlocked with the specific social context that shaped them; for the long, long novel, the short story.[56] The writer who scrutinized the visible mores and invisible secrets of his contemporaries was no longer a "wizard," as Pushkin liked to call Scott, but a "doctor of the human heart," who offered a looking glass and the bitter medicine of analysis to his sick age. Not by accident, it was precisely two Romantic poets, Alfred de Musset and Lermontov, who in their alternate hypostases as prose writers prefaced their contemporary novels in this vein. The abandonment of historical subjects for contemporary ones and the retreat of poetry before prose—even in the works of poets—are the twin banners under which the approaching Age of Prose established its monopoly in the 1830's. Underlying these trends was the issue of class Balzac touched on; a democratized reading public was eager to peer through a literary keyhole into what had become the exotic customs of the upper class. To Pushkin, following the revolutionary contagion from Paris to Brussels to Warsaw in the pages of the (banned) French newspapers, none of this was heartening.

Few Russian readers kept as fully abreast of current literary trends in France as Pushkin did, yet he remained true to his old loyalties: Walter Scott figures in his critical articles of the 1830's (and in his private reading) as the measure of historical authenticity and poetic imagination against which virtually all modern writers are found wanting. "The chief fascination of Walter Scott's novels lies in the fact that we grow acquainted with the past not encumbered with the *enflure* of French tragedies, or with the prudery of the novels of sentiment, or with the dignité of history, but in a contemporary, homely manner. . . . What charms us in the historical novel is that what is historical is absolutely what we see."[57] In particular, he derides the efforts of French Romantic poets like Hugo and Alfred-Victor de Vigny to invest historical events with anachronistic modern significance (in *Cromwell* and *Cinq-Mars*) and prose with inept advertisements for poetry: "Milton, occupied with affairs of state, would inevitably suddenly have lost himself in poetical reveries and would have scribbled a few lines of *Paradise Lost* on the margins of some report; Cromwell would have noticed this, would have scolded his secretary, called him a rhymester and dissembler, all of which would produce an *effect* such as poor W. Scott never envisaged."[58]

Did modern novelists fare better, then, with the task of portraying contemporary society? Pushkin devoured each novel the moment it came out, and in 1831 outlined an article, "On the latest novels," which was to treat the popular novels of Jules Janin, Eugène Sue, Vigny, Hugo, Balzac, and Musset.[59] From what we know of Pushkin's tastes at the time, primarily from his letters to his principal purveyor of literary contraband, Elizaveta Khitrovo,[60] we can speculate that the essay would have criticized the *romans frénétiques* of Janin and Sue for their unhealthy and low-class sensationalism, the historical melodramas of Vigny and Hugo for their inauthenticity and misplaced poetic effects, and the society tales of Balzac for their "myopic triviality" (by which phrase Pushkin seems to mean that the plebeian Balzac did not know what counted in high society discourse and hence reported everything indiscriminately).[61] Underlying Pushkin's scattered comments one senses his impatience with the journalistic rawness, "tin ear" for nuance, and lack of what Tolstoy praised in Pushkin as "the correct hierarchy of objects" of the new literature of contemporaneity.[62] If in historical fiction Pushkin valued the poet's ability to fabricate the dense domestic reality and conflicting human interests left out of written documents, from the society tale he expected the opposite: a historian's distillation of the society's significant features, a dramatist's ability to sculpt symbolic conflict from the formless flow of everyday discourse, and a poet's ability to omit the rest. In short, he demanded a contemporary's view of history but a historian's view of contemporaneity.

Pushkin's experiments in the society tale genre of the 1830's confirm his affinity with the eighteenth-century culture of wit and anecdote,[63] one of the sources, as we saw, of Schlegel's new concept of irony. Just as the anecdote accidentally left behind by history contains its whole epoch in miniature, so the worldly anecdote cuts through the superfluous details of everyday life to its revealing conflicts and incongruities. All of Pushkin's society tale fragments are characterized by a tension between their light, anecdotic plots, dimensions, and style and the seeds of a minor tragedy buried beneath the surface of their dialogues. From a hybrid of the salon anecdote and the "dramatic scene," then, Pushkin produced his own highly condensed version of the society tale—what Akhmatova called "things in a new genre."[64]

Tales of high-society passion constituted a prolific genre. Pushkin, however, appears to have been interested in writing a single anecdote that would capture the paradoxes of his own existence in society once and for all. His notebooks are full of the ghosts of characters and situations migrating from draft to draft in apparent search of a society tale or novel that never materialized. Each of the early fragments ("The guests were arriving at the dacha," "A fragment," "At the corner of a small square," "My fate has been decided; I'm getting married") projects an aspect of Pushkin's problematic social life in St. Petersburg after his return from exile—his perpetual philandering, the tightening constraints on his personal and financial freedom, the troubled circumstances of his engagement—onto the framework of a fashionable novel. But the later unfinished stories (what I have been calling the "Kleopatra" tales—"We were spending the evening at the dacha," "A Tale of Roman Life," and "Egyptian Nights") move further away from autobiographical detail and attempt to do for Pushkin what he had always done in his poetry: to convey the duality of a life lived simultaneously on two planes, one "temporary," the other "for eternity"; in other words, to turn the society tale into an ironic representation of the poet's life in society.

Here again, Pushkin was scarcely entering uncharted territory. The *Künstler* tale as practiced by E. T. A. Hoffmann was the genre in which the Romantic fascination with the "artist in the midst of his creation" found fullest expression.[65] In the hands of a master ironist like Hoffmann, the solipsistic imaginative world of the artist overlaps uneasily both with the possibility of madness and crime and with the possibility of a supernatural reality; the reader cannot finally decide how to classify the story's phenomena. The underlying aim of a tale like Hoffmann's "Don Juan," David Wellbery has shown, is to create, by means of a particularly dramatic story of artistic reception, a model for the reader's own reading. Romantic hermeneutics teaches that understanding a work of art entails "the re-cognition of the sponsoring spiritual source of a work, a re-cognition made possible by the presence of this same spiritual source in the interpreter"[66]—a reaffirmation of Diderot's belief that "in order to be in a state to feel art strongly, one must be almost in a state to create it." I will return to this idea shortly.

In the hands of well-meaning imitators like A. A. Pogorelsky, V. F. Odoevsky, and N. A. Polevoy, artist tales could easily degenerate into worshipful expositions of the artist's incomprehensibility and suffering at the hands of a philistine society.[67] As Polevoy explained in "The Painter," "My aim is to show that the mad dreams of poets are not fit for the material world,"[68] particularly the new bourgeois world of the 1830's. In fact, the less poetry was read by a decreasingly exclusive public, the more poets were cast in popular prose as misfit heroes. It was not only that prose authors and their readers projected onto this "poet" figure a fictive world of shared values, of which they were in fact ignorant; it was that the poet as protagonist became the silent object of the author's and audience's pity, an unworldly, ridiculous, and often suicidal misfit incapable of adaptation and historically doomed. Vigny's Chatterton, Sainte-Beuve's invented poet Joseph Delorme,[69] Hugo's Milton all share this childlike emasculated fecklessness, irritatingly promoted by their authors as spirituality. Through the poet figure could be glimpsed the fate of a disempowered elite transformed into an object of patronizing commiseration tantamount to ridicule, its artifacts unintelligible to the surrounding society. The poet in prose was one step away from the mad clerk, the next figure into which modern society would project its own sense of disorientation and self-pity. (Pushkin understood this so well that he had his second Eugene [in "The Bronze Horseman"] incorporate the entire spectrum.)[70] In short, the poet's role in the prose of the 1830's was to be superannuated, to represent the dying of an age.

The idea Pushkin fastened on with such persistence from 1833 to 1835, the idea of creating a frame tale for "Kleopatra,"[71] must be related to his irritation with the shoddiness of these modern fables, and to his simultaneous and real sense of endangerment. He wants to tap into the fashion for the frame tale and at the same time change its rules. His first attempt, "A Tale of Roman Life," follows the strategy of Janin's *Barnave* in its portrayal of a society on the eve of collapse—in this case the decadent society of Nero's and Petronius's Rome—through a *Decameron*- or *Satyricon*-like feast of poetry and tales. Pushkin sharpens the apocalyptic atmosphere of the storytelling session by making it Petronius's last night of feasting and poetry even as he commits suicide to escape the emperor's persecution. Much as in *Barnave*, the historical scene is re-created by implicit contrast or analogy to modernity.

The question the frame tale always raises is one of interpretation: what is the relation of the inner to the outer narrative, the inner to the outer style? According to P. A. Annenkov, "Pushkin began his narrative with the mores of the ancient world, with the intention of expressing its false, pagan conception of death," while the Christian slave would have served as "the living condemnation of the indifference or intoxication with which the pagan world met death."[72] Briusov, on the other hand, discerns in the contrast an implicit glorification of the ancients' passionate, single-minded, courageous acceptance of life and death.[73] A third possibility would be a double take of recognition: despite the hermetically sealed authenticity of Pushkin's ancient anecdote, certain readers might ask themselves whether relations between Christian potentates and poets had noticeably improved. The polysemanticity that Pushkin's method of historical counterpoint engenders is realized in critics' opposing interpretations. My own inclination is to view "A Tale of Roman Life" as Pushkin's polemical response to the framing of "the poet" in contemporary literature and, perhaps less consciously, to the real decline in his own prestige.

Whereas the spectacle of the salon's decadence is revolved by Janin before the modern reader's prurient eyes, but is meant ultimately to justify the ancien régime's downfall, Pushkin puts an entirely different slant on Petronius's drily impersonal sensuousness and aestheticism. The writer's conversation provides a still enclave of humanism increasingly threatened by the menacing and mindless activities of Nero. Beginning as though on a chronicler's note ("Caesar was traveling," 8.1, 387), the story ends with Petronius's escape from the hyperactive world of political events inward to his own imperturbable world of aesthetic values. The "Tale of Roman Life" in which Petronius figures is itself a *satura*, like his own *Satyricon*, a mixture of poetry and prose.[74] Indeed, the conversation between the youthful narrator and Petronius is virtually a dialogue of citations from Greek and Roman verse. Petronius expresses his last thoughts on aging and dying to his young friend in the form of classical epigrams; the genre of choice for a young man's embrace of life, it serves equally well for his last meditations on death. In other words, far from being an outmoded and impractical form of expression within the worldly prose context, poetry is used by the conversationalists for particularly subtle and important communication. There is no superannuation of old poetic forms here. The vivid epigrams shine like jewels in the surrounding prose.[75]

In case his point is not yet clear, Pushkin has Petronius leave his friend with instructions on how to read between the poetic lines: "The shrewd versifier [Horace] wanted to make Augustus and Maecenas laugh at his faintheartedness only because he did not want to remind them that he had been a comrade-in-arms of Cassius and Brutus."[76] Piercing the bland surface of Horace's cordial relations with Augustus and Maecenas, Pushkin hints at the poet's virtuosity. Horace had actively participated in Brutus's republican rebellion against Julius Caesar and had suffered the confiscation of his property by Octavius before the latter extended a general amnesty to his former opponents (including the gift of the Sabine farm, which permitted Horace to devote the rest of his life to poetry). Petronius explains how Horace contrives to tread the fine line between poetic truth and wily self-preservation: by framing his reminiscences about Brutus's campaign in a funny anecdote about his own cowardice, the artful poet manages to shift attention away from the poem's forbidden yet central theme, the "phantom of liberty." Thus Pushkin's Petronius absolves Horace of "selling out" for the sake of creative tranquillity, something Pushkin was occasionally accused of and, as financial pressures accumulated, was perhaps increasingly forced to contemplate. No helpless child, Pushkin's poet virtuosically maneuvers between the forbidden and the banal in his historical context and still manages to express his ironic, forceful self. The timid child-victim is only one of the poet's many masks. The *Satyricon*, by implication, could be another.

The ultimate intentions of Petronius continue to be a subject of scholarly debate to this day: was he a typical product of Nero's decadent age, the greatest "immoralist" of them all, or is the *Satyricon* an insider's mocking exposé of his time?[77] Pushkin turns the missing poet, about whom we know nothing beyond Tacitus's famous phrase "arbiter elegantiae," into a figure of Renaissance *virtù* who bends reality to his own meanings: " 'Not only do I not intend to disobey

[Nero],' answered Petronius with a smile, 'but I propose to anticipate his wishes'" (240). His lordly refusal to succumb to the spirit of the times consists in the choice of his manner of dying. He not only preempts Caesar's order for execution by taking his own life, but he makes his suicide a kind of symposium, a reaffirmation of the values of philosophy, friendship, and love of art. Indeed, the morbid idea of alternating interludes of bloodletting with excerpts of poetry defiantly equates his life with poetry: the power to give and take is his alone.

One of the works to be recited during the three-day feast of poetry was "Kleopatra," about which Pushkin noted telegraphically in the draft: "our opinions on this." This shorthand suggests to me that Pushkin was aware of someone else's opinion—perhaps the use of the Cleopatra anecdote in *Barnave* as a sure sign of its teller's decadence and readiness for historical oblivion. Pushkin's text is, by contrast, thoroughly masculine, unusually so for Pushkin's prose; neither women nor carnal passions figure in it at all. Within the similar frame of Roman decadence, Petronius instead re-creates the role so often explored by Pushkin of the indomitable poet on the scaffold. Pushkin's youthful poem "Kleopatra" was to be juxtaposed on the one hand to the classical epigrams on death recited in the tale, and on the other to the *Satyricon*, Petronius's last word in the face of death and persecution and his means of seizing from the jaws of inimical history his own poetic immortality. In this context "Kleopatra" itself changes. Its erotic side in abeyance, it has become a poem about life's final choice, the artistry with which one lives and dies. The tyrannical whim of the Egyptian queen parallels the fatal whims of Nero and all tyrants. At the same time, the accent is shifted to her three sacrificial victims, who freely accept the lot fate has dealt them. With the same imaginative daring that impels Kleopatra to leave her unmistakable mark on her stagnant surroundings and her victims to differentiate themselves from them, Petronius chooses to fashion his suicide into his last *satura*.

Why did Pushkin abandon his historical tale? Although Pushkin ostensibly enters the narrative only as translator, I suspect the relative transparency of the palimpsest Petronius/Nero and Pushkin/Nicholas must have been as obvious to Pushkin as it is to us. This kind of "aesthetic irony" was too close, after all, to what he ridiculed in other modern writers' exploitations of history. The heart of the story is pedagogical; just as Petronius shows his young disciple how to read between the lines of Horace's ode, Pushkin imagines a historical context in which the slippery irony of the author of the *Satyricon* becomes a last refuge of human independence and self-respect. It is a clear, perhaps too clear, polemical effort to dislodge the "pitiful poet" cliché that had become so firmly rooted in Romantic prose.

The next time Pushkin returned to "Kleopatra" it was with a different frame tale in mind: the society tale of contemporary mores. "We were spending the evening at the dacha" displays a symmetrically opposite array of features, but can be thought of as Pushkin's response to the *Barnave* genre, take two. Pushkin abandons his historical setting for contemporary high society and a society that is predominantly feminine. The covert analogy between ancient and modern civilization and psychology has now become an overt contrast. When the "Kleopatra" anecdote finds itself in the company of a series of titillating French titles by Balzac, Dumas, and George Sand, it turns its erotic facets to the reader. In "We were spending the evening" it is the response of the modern audience to the ancient anecdote smuggled into its midst by Alexei Ivanovich, the surrogate for the absent poet "P.," which reveals its spiritual moribundness. Through its reactions to the topic of Cleopatra, St. Petersburg society inadvertently reveals its hodgepodge of European cultural pretensions, its unique combination of verbal prudery, vicarious thrills, and casual everyday lack of both passion and ethics, and above all, the divorce of the society's language from its real concerns and actions:

"This subject should be brought to the attention of Marquise George Sand, who is as shameless as your Cleopatra. She would adapt your Egyptian anecdote to contemporary mores."

"That would be impossible. It would completely lack verisimilitude. This is an anecdote exclusively of the ancient world; a bargain of this kind would be as impractical today as the erection of pyramids." . . . The young Countess K., a homely, plump little woman, tried to lend an air of importance to her nose, which looked like an onion stuck into a turnip, and said, "There are women even today who value themselves highly."

Her husband, a Polish Count who had married her out of (they say mistaken) calculation, cast his eyes down and drank up his tea.

"What do you mean by that, Countess?" asked the young man, hardly able to restrain a smile.

"What I mean is," answered the Countess K., "that a woman who respects herself, who respects . . ." But she became entangled in her thought. Vershnev came to her rescue.

"You think that a woman who respects herself will not wish death on the sinner, right?" (247)

Just as the Egyptian anecdote forces St. Petersburg society to reveal itself in a satirical light, the poem "Kleopatra" draws into erotic confrontation (the only field of action available to this society) the two characters, Vol'skaia and Alexei Ivanovich, whose imaginations have not been utterly stifled by it. She hides her passions (and the willfulness [*vol'ia*] advertised by her name) under lowered eyes and verbal prudery; he, standing in for his absent poet friend P., or perhaps simply disguising his authorship, represents the exclusion of poetry from society's language. Language continues to buzz, like a beehive without a queen, in a semblance of communication; but in fact it merely replicates its own phrases while action, imagination, and desire are forced into a silent, sublinguistic realm. It is no accident that Pushkin's little society tale, with its caricatural cast of characters caught in petrified poses and vapid conversation is at the last moment ignited—acquires a plot, passions, a raison d'être—by its searing contact with true poetry. In a clever reversal, social life is made the domain of spiritual paralysis, a plotlessness akin to death, which only the eternal vitality of a poem about an ancient subject—indeed, about violent and desired death—can revive. The poem turns out to be the essential catalyst that activates the frame tale, allowing modern life's shapeless raw material to coalesce into a representative anecdote.

In "A Tale of Roman Life" the imaginary portrait of the poet, Petronius, is the frame that recontextualizes the poetry. In "We were spending the evening" the poet is conspicuously absent, is, indeed, represented by an infinite regress of author figures. Alexei Ivanovich partly paraphrases, partly quotes fragments of a poem his friend P. began but never finished. It is based on a brief anecdote related by Aurelius Victor, a Roman mediocrity along the lines of the guests at the dacha, who intended to destroy Cleopatra's reputation once and for all and instead was briefly made a poet by his contact with her. There is no single authorial source, only a piece of poetic imagination so compelling that, despite age-old efforts to suppress it, it continually forces itself back into language.

"I suggested to P. that he write a narrative poem about it; he did start one, but gave it up."

"Very wisely so."

"What did he think he could get out of this subject? What was his main idea, do you remember?"

"He begins with a description of a feast in the Egyptian Queen's garden." (245)

That phrase, "What did he think he could get out of this subject?" gives us pause. It prompts us to ask the question of the endless series of men who have told and retold versions of Cleopatra's story to the scandalized shock of their audiences. What does Pushkin get out of it? The odd partnership of the two characters, one wearing a modified version of Pushkin's first name, the other the Latin letter he often used as his last initial, re-creates the relationship between the young poet of 1824, who wrote the original poem "Kleopatra," and the man of letters of 1835, who kept trying to insinuate it into a prose setting.

Alexei Ivanovich contributes the description of the exotic feast in the Egyptian queen's garden. Not only was it not part of the original poem, as we happen to know, but it is written in a different, not austerely classical but ornately exotic, key—in fact, in a style that, amazingly, anticipates the ornateness of late French Romantics like Théophile Gautier, who, coincidentally, wrote his own version of *Les Nuits de Cléopâtre* shortly after Pushkin.[78] Alexei Ivanovich's style is another frame within the frame tale of "We were spending the evening," quite different either from the spare dialogue of Pushkin's story or the powerful monologue of the poem.

Bright and noisy are the halls of Ptolemy: Cleopatra is spreading a feast before her friends; the table is set with ivory spoons; three hundred youths are waiting on the guests; three hundred maidens are bearing amphorae full of Greek nectar around the table, under the silent watchful gaze of three hundred eunuchs.

The colonnade of porphyry, exposed to the south and to the north, awaits the breath of Eurus; but the air is still, the lanterns' flame-tongues are burning still; the smoke from the incense-burners is borne aloft in a straight, still column; the sea, like a mirror, lies still by the steps of the rose-colored semicircular portico. In it the gilded claws and granite tails of guardian sphinxes find themselves reflected. Only the strains of the cithara and the lute ruffle the flames, the air, and the sea. (245)

The heightened exoticism and static luxury of Kleopatra's surroundings and the elaborate, Plutarchian description of her days and nights (compare Enobarbus's speech in Shakespeare's *Antony and Cleopatra*)—all revisions introduced in 1835—seem intended to intensify the anecdote's foreignness, in fact to kindle the audience's interest. The poetic prose paraphrase actually makes the boundary of the poem porous: it creates around Kleopatra the same atmosphere of luxurious idleness and bored satiation that surrounds the guests in the salon. Alexei Ivanovich transposes into his visual description of Oriental luxury the same features of collective satiation and stifling restriction that we have observed in the conversational decorum of the St. Petersburg salon. Kleopatra's bargain is, as it were, addressed not only to her court, but also, simultaneously, to the stifled inhabitants of St. Petersburg high society, whom in the earlier sketch "The guests were arriving at the dacha" Pushkin had called "Egyptian mummies."[79]

Although we are told nothing about the secret passions of the conversationalists, we are not surprised when Vol'skaia rises to the occasion and accepts Alexei Ivanovich's challenge to play Kleopatra. The poetic archetype provides the eternally living form of passion, which life acts out. Or, to put it in René Girard's terms, desire arises in response to a recognized image of desire; "private" passions always bear the imprint of a "public" form.[80] But the very process of translation creates its own distinctive form. The form of the modern Kleopatra's night-for-a-life bargain is of course quite different from the original (itself a product of an overheated Roman imagination): at the end of the night in which she has given her most precious possession—not love, or even ultimate erotic pleasure, but *her reputation*—her lover is obliged on *his word of honor* to shoot himself. The distinctive difference is probably in the means of the bargain's enforcement: internalized social opinion in the nineteenth century plays the role that ostentatious courtly display of power played in

Kleopatra's time; will-power, the power to make oneself do something, even to the limit of self-destruction, has replaced power over others. Thus, ironically, the very form the modern protagonists devise to violate society's mores demonstrates its indelible imprint on their imaginations.

Was this not perhaps what Alexei Ivanovich meant to "get out of" his recitation all along? In answer to the question "What was his main idea, do you remember?" Alexei Ivanovich implies that the poem originated in a feeling of social entrapment, almost a death wish, which his audience might well comprehend:

> When you consider, is the condition itself so hard to accept? Is life such a treasure that one would begrudge sacrificing it for happiness? Just think of it: the first scamp happening by, whom I despise, says something about me that cannot hurt me in any way, yet I expose my forehead to his bullet. I have no right to deny this satisfaction to the first bully coming my way who takes it into his head to test my sangfroid. And yet you think I would act like a coward when my bliss is at stake? What is life worth if it is poisoned by dejection and unfulfilled desires? What remains in it if all its delights have been sapped? (247)

The voice of Pushkin, circa 1835, is quite audible in these words. Alexei Ivanovich reads into the abandoned poetic fragment of P. his own current preoccupations, indeed substitutes his reading of the poem for an account of its original conception. By framing the poem for this particular salon audience he is actually reshaping its meaning. Or, to put it another way, he is using the poem to provoke a shapeless social life into dramatic self-representation (including his own). The evening at the dacha is his *satura*, a medley of poems and prose, script and improvisation. At the very moment that contemporary life coalesces into its own Kleopatra tale, Alexei Ivanovich "disappears," his artistic representation complete.

Whereas Pushkin plays no overt role in the "realistic" narrative of "A Tale of Roman Life," we have seen that it can be glossed as a lesson on reading poetry, a lesson Pushkin was very interested in getting across. In "We were spending the evening at the dacha" Pushkin moves one ironic step beyond that: he presents a man of letters somewhat similar to himself using a poem fragment to create a new artistic path out of the limited materials available to him that evening in the salon. The last level of the story emerges from Pushkin's ironic awareness of his own framing impulse. It raises not only the questions that are spoken: "What did he think he could get out of this subject? What was his main idea?" but also some unspoken ones: What did Alexei Ivanovich want to get out of his recital? And what role does the audience play in the making of this new kind of work of art? These were exactly the questions that Pushkin would pose more audibly in his next frame tale, written two months later, "Egyptian Nights."

I would like to return briefly to Hoffmann's story "Don Juan," in which I detect a typological affinity with Pushkin's late stories.[81] "Don Juan" exemplifies the sophisticated ironic possibilities of the artist tale that was beginning to emerge from the *Barnave* and society tale forms Pushkin was experimenting with. A look at its framing structures will bring us a step closer to "Egyptian Nights." Hoffmann's frame tale "is divisible into two symmetrical halves, the first being the narrator's experience of the opera performance, the second his writing of an interpretation of that experience in a document addressed to a certain 'Theodor.' (The entire text of 'Don Juan,' except perhaps for the title and subtitle, pretends to be that document.) One element of the story, then, is the production of the text that relates the story."[82] The framing anecdote of one man writing a letter describing an evening at the opera is conspicuously lacking in plot interest, as is the desultory society chatter in "We were spending the evening." This has the effect, in David Wellbery's view, of displacing the drama "from a primarily physical plane of execution to a cognitive plane. . . . Hoffmann's text . . . dramatizes interpretive processes."[83] Just as in "We were spending the evening" Alexei Ivanovich finally gets the audience to focus its wandering interest on the missing poet's original conception for "Kleopatra," the narrator of "Don Juan" is intent on conveying his own interpretive journey toward the creative source of *Don Giovanni*, Mozart's mind.

There is a whole drama in the way he describes his responses to the music, the way he penetrates what he deems to be the false, distracting surface of the opera's erotic, violent language and plot in order to reach its musical core, and the wholly different spiritual relationships the music reveals among the characters. Obviously an internal spiritual world is being valorized at the expense of the external world of mere action, sensuality, and language, and the subject's progress toward spiritual communion with the creative mind of Mozart is its quest plot. As Wellbery puts it, the opera and its story are the visible links in a much longer hermeneutic chain: "Mozart (sender) - *Don Giovanni* (message) - narrator (receiver/sender) - 'Don Juan' (message) - Theodor (receiver). The story structure thus enacts the problem of how it is possible to understand and to communicate to another what the truly originary meaning of an artwork is, 'wie es der grosse Meister in seinem Gemüt empfing und dachte!' "[84]

The question about what the "great master" in his heart of hearts experienced and thought is very similar to the question the gossipy socialites eagerly pose to Alexei Ivanovich about the original intentions of his friend P.: "What did he have in mind?" In Pushkin's story, authorship cannot be pinned down: the poet P., it turns out, got the idea from Alexei Ivanovich, who had found it in Aurelius Victor, whose only intention was to serve up a Cleopatra that suited Roman tastes and prejudices. Is it possible to locate "the moment of conception"? Pushkin's frame tale appears deliberately to muddy the Romantic idea of the single creative surge the salon audience clearly expected to hear about. Instead of a solitary inspired author, they get a series of interactions between writer and audience that essentially mirror Cleopatra's with her court; the night-for-a-life proposition is the composite product of Cleopatra's power and audacity and the untapped desire for self-expression of her subjects. Aurelius Victor's unforgettable portrait was elicited by the fantasies of his Roman audience, by their need for a Cleopatra who personified everything un-Roman. Even the poem "Kleopatra" appears to have been composed by P. at Alexei Ivanovich's suggestion and in sympathetic response to his nihilistic mood.[85]

We have already encountered the practice of fragmenting authorship and attributing it to a cultural collective; E. T. A. Hoffmann's *Kater Murr* was one of the most memorable of these "found manuscripts," as much the product of the forces that had thwarted the author as it is the realization of his intentions. Surely in Mozart's case a clearer path can be retraced from the work back to Mozart's mind? *Don Giovanni* presents another problem: it is a composite of musical and verbal media, soaring spirituality and sensuous seduction, tragedy and locker-room humor, virility and delicacy. The narrator's solution is straightforward: he imposes on *Don Giovanni* the same hierarchy of values with which he makes sense of the world. The verbal plot is to him a debased surface that must be penetrated to reach the opera's musical core, its real locus of value. The narrator's main concern in retelling the opera appears to be to establish a difference between a common, literal understanding (represented in the story by the hotel dining room) and his own, inspired interpretation (which emanates, as Wellbery points out, from the "faintly satanic space" of his study). In support of his claim, he quotes Goethe: "Only the poet can understand another poet; only a Romantic feeling can enter into the Romantic."[86] He bases his claim for privileged understanding both on his access to the natural language of music and to his understanding of Italian, which, according to Romantic biases, stands in poetic opposition to prosaic German in the same way that music does to mere language.[87]

In fact, however, the plot of the opera is decidedly skewed by its passage through the prism of the narrator's consciousness. His ideology of "pure music" versus tainted medium leads him to project a symbolic addition to the plot: he believes that Don Giovanni actually raped Donna Anna, in addition to killing her father. Another odd extrapolation is that Donna Anna herself (or the actress who sang her role) has recognized the narrator's kindred spirit and "visited" him. Having dismissed the plot of the opera as an unreal surface, the narrator now provides his own hallucinatory libretto: Donna Anna chooses him. Confirming the Romantic clichés he has just uttered, she speaks to him in Italian of music; she speaks to him as a native speaker of the language of genius. "The passage allegorizes the disclosure through music of a common stratum of identity, a single self, uniting the otherwise isolate individuals Mozart, Donna Anna, and the narrator."[88] It simultaneously raises the possibility of narcissistic mirage.

Donna Anna is refashioned into a mediating figure between the narrator's own and Mozart's "genius." Moreover, the "visitation" from Donna Anna takes place while the actress lies unconscious in a nearby room; it is as if her body has been appropriated for the enactment of the narrator's own script. The instinctual world that the narrator had eliminated from his pure conception of *Don Giovanni* comes back to haunt him. Wellbery views this as a "violation" of his original Mozartian communion. What the narrator and Don Juan have in common is "the fact that both violate Donna Anna."[89] Don Juan fails to recognize in his love for Donna Anna the face of his own spirituality, the infinity of longing that can never be quenched by physical satisfaction and that distinguishes him, Don Juan, from all other lovers; in raping her, he has reduced infinite spiritual longing to the physical and violated his own essence as much as he does her. The narrator's erotic fetishization of the actress whom he identifies with pure musical communion is a similar kind of betrayal. The tragedy of the aesthete is that

> at the very moment the narrator believes himself in possession of the spiritual source of the opera and experiences "eine lang verheissene Erfüllung" he in fact has violated that spiritual source in a manner analogous to Don Juan's rape of Donna Anna. The impulse of Romantic hermeneutics toward a reappropriation of the creative intuition is thus exhibited as a tragic impulse insofar as it violates the very thing it sought to know in its purity.[90]

It is when the narrator speaks the words of renunciation that Don Juan refused to speak in the opera that Donna Anna dies, freeing him from her disturbing presence into the "pure" absence of art. Curiously, Wellbery seems here to agree with the narrator's own high aesthetic terms: the admixture of his own desire and "plot" is seen as an impurity, distancing him tragically from his true apprehension of Mozart's music.

This is where I think another look at the frame tale structure is in order. The narrator's very style of narration, his corny Romantic formulas about "the great master's feelings and thoughts," wear almost visible ironic quotation marks. On the other hand, our Romantic narrator has a pedantic passion for classification and segregation. Pure, abstract music is segregated from transient passion and too-concrete verbal representation, the privileged, hermeneutically attuned listener in his solitary study from the common crowd in the dining room. His evening at the opera and his telling of the incident are separated into two sections, each of which is divided into three perfectly parallel subsections. He is in perfect control of his narrative.

However, a frame tale not only segregates, it also invites correlation. Does the plot of *Don Giovanni*, which the narrator is so eager to suppress, actually enter into his own act of interpretation in ways of which he is unaware?

We must not forget that this entire story is not a meditation but a letter. It is being told *to* someone, namely the narrator's bosom friend "Theodor." It is shaped through and through by the narrator's desire—to communicate, to *act* on, enter into, leave his imprint on another's being. The telling of the passionate, violent story of Mozart's opera enables that intimate contact to take place. An interpretation is always a performance made to or for someone. It is an act of communication not only with the original source but equally with an audience, and it bears the impress of both. Even as the narrator expounds his ultra-Romantic theory about the supremacy of music and the insignificance of language and plot in opera, the libretto begins to infiltrate his fantasy life. The opera invades all levels of his being, destroying the partitions he had erected against its intoxicating mixture (it is, after all, that most multisensorial of art forms, an opera, not a string quartet!). The repressed aesthete has failed to remodel the opera in his own image: its exuberant impurity has instead brought the segregated sections of his own psyche back into contact. Pace Wellbery, I would say that the mixed-up fantasy the opera arouses in the narrator is a fuller, less violating tribute to Mozart's imaginative power than his prudish vocabulary of spiritual exaltation. Moreover, even as he renounces desire, in the form of Donna Anna, he addresses his performance to Theodor. Mozart, the actress, music, eroticism, aesthetic theory, and violence are all included in the dramatic self-representation the narrator has offered up to his friend, a richer and more disturbing testimony to the power of art than the aesthetic credo he thought he was writing.

How can one tell when a reading has actually reconstituted the "original meaning" and when it has worked out its own? An answer might lie in Hoffmann's game with names: he gives to the ultimate addressee of the hermeneutic chain his own name Theodor, thus making the chain come full circle. Perhaps differentiation between true hermeneutic communion and inauthentic "violation" of the original is not really the issue? Wellbery himself suggests that "the self writes in order to reach its own center," supporting his observation with a passage from Friedrich Schlegel “on the ‘you’ or addressee as a higher ‘I’.”[91] By naming the letter’s addressee Theodor, Hoffmann adds another ironic frame to the tale. Not only is the narrator’s interpretation a passionate performance aimed at an audience, that audience is, in the end, himself. In Chapter 1 we explored Schlegel’s ideas about the dialogic structure of every utterance: what is banished from an utterance is as important as what is stated, what is given the name of other dramatis personae is as much a part of the subjectivity as the discrete figure labeled “I.” One of the conclusions we could draw from Hoffmann’s story might be that interpretation is not pious reconstitution of an anterior “creative source,” but an act of self-representation and communication in its own right. “Don Juan,” the story of his own fall from purity, is perhaps the closest the narrator will ever come to experiencing what he likes to call the spirit of Mozart—his own creativity.

In “We were spending the evening,” as we have seen, Pushkin sets up a similar structure, where the “real-life” frame hypnotically reenacts the imaginary situation it had attempted to disown. Cleopatra’s original provocation of her audience has been, as it were, passed down through the ages, each reader / teller of the previous text provoking his own audience into self-revelation. The “original meaning” of the poetic text is made cathartically manifest in the action or reactions it inspires, the audience’s almost chemical precipitation into a passively prurient herd and the two figures who ritually act out before its scandalized gaze exactly what it wants to see.

There is a compulsive aspect to the way “We were spending the evening” reenacts Kleopatra’s sacrificial “night.” I suggest that Pushkin was trying to represent precisely that which was missing as he repeatedly sat down to write in 1835: the invasive compulsion of inspiration. Its absence is, of course, the real source of life’s “meaninglessness” for Alexei Ivanovich. In its absence he constructs a “happening” that dramatizes the mystery of art’s origins and its compulsive power over human life; what he can no longer experience is poetry’s invasion of himself. P., the inspired poet, is just an old friend, in whose absence “We were spending the evening at the dacha” is composed—a suicide note disguised as a society tale.

The “Kleopatra” tales are the best illustration I know of the idea that “the self writes to find its own center.” In “We were spending the evening," as in "Don Juan," the compulsive power of art is demonstrated erotically: the poem "Kleopatra" takes over the erotic impulses of the salon. But in the summer of 1835 such an erotic subject was really a sidetrack from the main issue. Pushkin's copious letters to his wife talk about missing her for lack of any other name for his condition, but the real missing person, the elegiac addressee, the "lost love" he was mourning, was his own compulsively scribbling self—the self he had gone to Mikhailovskoe to find.

Although the society in "Egyptian Nights" is the same feminine and fashion-saturated milieu as in "We were spending the evening," the only passionate relationship develops between two male poets. Women have been conspicuously displaced to the story's periphery; the majestic beauty who lifts a gloved hand to draw the lots in the final scene is a last symbolic vestige of the willful heroine of the society tales, perhaps an elegiac invocation of the still earlier omnipotent goddess of Pushkin's poetry. Women are demoted from the role of muses or addressees to the role of consumers, as the poets' little "locker-room" colloquy suggests: " 'Last night at the rout I managed to recruit half of Petersburg; go ahead and print tickets and announcements. I guarantee you if not a triumph, then at least the ladie... ' - 'And that's the main thing!' cried out the Italian." [92] The word *ladies* is truncated, in the same way that the description of the society beauty stops at her glove. Lip service may be paid to the erotic theme, but in this story "the main thing" takes place between the poet and the improvisor.

The story opens on a series of hostile notes. First we overhear the two anonymous voices of the epigraph: " 'Who is this man?' - 'Ha, he's a great talent, he makes of his voice anything he wants.' - 'He ought, Madame, to make himself a pair of pants.' " [93] The first comment is as offensive as the second. "A talent" is someone who "makes" part of himself into something else, a commodity. The bon mot of the society wit only pushes the verb "make" (*faire*) to its logical extreme. Talent automatically makes its possessor not one of us; it neutralizes any ordinary social characterization that would give him a protective group identity and leaves him the naked object of collective scrutiny. The epigraph eavesdrops, as it were, on a typical vignette from the St. Petersburg milieu and sets the corrosive tone for the narrator's entry.

Not surprisingly, the narrator's style is preemptively laconic, defensively epigrammatic. His protagonist Charsky, one of the pillars of St. Petersburg society, is characterized as a man without qualities—not yet thirty, not married, not in the service, prosperous. He would have been blissfully anonymous and respectable if only he had not had the misfortune to write poetry.

> Despite all the great advantages enjoyed by versifiers (it must be admitted that apart from the privileges of using the accusative instead of the genitive case and one or two other acts of so-called poetic license, we do not know of any particular advantages Russian versifiers could be said to enjoy)—however that may be, despite all their advantages these people are subject to a great deal of trouble and unpleasantness. The most bitter and intolerable bane of the poet is his title, his sobriquet, with which he is branded and of which he can never rid himself. The reading public look on him as though he were their property: in their opinion, he was born for their *benefit and pleasure*. (249)

What kind of man is speaking? The narrator's angry sarcasm is apparently born of long personal injury, yet he speaks about the poet exclusively in the third person and at ironic, worldly arm's length. The description of Charsky is striking for its abundance of negatives:

> He was not yet thirty; he was not married; he was not burdened by the service. . . . He avoided the society of his brother-writers and preferred the emptiest of society people to them. His conversation was the most ordinary and never touched on literature. . . . In his study, decorated like a lady's bedroom, nothing recalled the writer; the couch was not spattered with ink; there was none of that disorder, which marks the presence of the muse and the absence of the broom and brush. . . . He pretended to be now a passionate horse enthusiast, now a desperate gambler, now the most exquisite gourmet; although he never could tell a mountain horse from an arab, could never remember the trump and secretly preferred a baked potato to any of the inventions of French cuisine. He led the most frivolous life; hung around at all the balls, stuffed himself at all the diplomatic suppers, and at every party was as unavoidable as . . . ice cream. Nevertheless, he was a poet, and his passion was unconquerable. (249–50)

The more intimately he goes into the details of Charsky's life, distorted at every step by the necessity for impersonating an ordinary, faceless nobleman, the more we suspect that the narrator is describing his own experience in the third person, disowned as "Charsky" (from *chary*, magic or charm).[94] Thus the narrator's language is torn between two allegiances: to the poet, and to the tastes and values of high society that dictate the tone of his narrative. His expression of rage and frustration takes the form of a defensive sarcasm, a rigid and reactive pose that strips his voice of its individuality and is in effect completely dictated by the society he professes to disdain. We hear only the uniformly sarcastic tone of a person under siege, one who sacrifices all playful and individual variation of tone and the risks of nuanced ironic communication to the necessity for self-defense—and thereby loses himself. Tormented by society's crass understanding of what it is to be a poet, he reacts not by thumbing his nose at society but by denying his "hated sobriquet" of poet. His empirical self, shaped very much by notions of social "face" and fear of ridicule, is trapped in a relationship with "the poet" that is characterized by perpetual tension and denial. What society thinks of the poet is much less important and destructive than the voices he himself has internalized and that shape his own speech to himself.[95]

This introductory paragraph ("Despite all the great advantages") was originally an independent piece written by Pushkin in 1830 under the title "A Fragment," perhaps with some intention of journalistic publication.[96] When the "fragment" of 1830 was quoted in 1835, however, it ceased to be a piece of self-expression and became a piece of characterization. Pushkin uses, as it were, a sample of his own speech at a certain moment to create the voice of his narrator, frozen with a monotonous chip on his shoulder. His litany of complaints ends with unsympathetic petulance: "And the little boy regales the poet with his [the poet's] own mutilated verses. And these are the high points of the craft!"[97] One can't help remembering a similar scene (also written in 1830) in which, to Salieri's high-minded disgust, Mozart drags a fiddler in off the street in order to share his delight at the fellow's popular version of his own aria.[98] Pushkin's narrator is touchily offended by any hint of attention that threatens to differentiate the poet from the blandly correct world of *comme il faut*, from his equal anonymity with all the other *hommes du monde*.

When the poetic "fit" is on him, Charsky goes into confinement, locking away from sight the incongruous pleasures of his invasive second self and denying the acquaintance once it is over. One particularly creative day, as this nonself is scribbling away, something happens that readers of Dostoevsky's "The Double," Dickens' *Great Expectations*, Kafka's *Metamorphosis*, Hoffmann's "Don Juan," or Diderot's *Le Neveu de Rameau* would readily recognize: the return of the repressed self. The door of his sanctuary squeaks open in a nightmarish way, and an "unknown head" appears. Charsky is confronted with a figure that incarnates his worst fears: the poet as visible *other*, a foreign body, a ridiculous man in his own society. Where the description of Charsky was a series of negatives designed to elude identification, the stranger is described in excruciating positive detail, as though through a society dandy's mocking lorgnette. Every external detail is laced with the ridicule of the narrator's gossipy internal voices:

> He was tall and thin, and looked about thirty. The features of his swarthy face were distinctive: his pale high forehead, framed in black locks, his sparkling black eyes, his aquiline nose and his thick beard, which encircled his sunken, tawny cheeks, all revealed the foreigner in him. He wore a black frock coat, already graying along the seams, a pair of summer trousers (though the season was well into the autumn); a fake diamond glittered on the yellowing shirtfront under his worn black tie; his fraying hat appeared to have seen both rain and sunshine in its day. If you had met this man in the woods, you would have taken him for a robber; in society, for a political conspirator; and in an anteroom, for a charlatan peddling elixirs and arsenic. (251)

Charsky seizes on the differences that allow him to avoid recognition—Italian, itinerant fiddler, selling tickets to a concert—then resorts to the man of the world's snooty repudiation: "What [do] you take me for?" (251). The more unequivocally the Italian praises Charsky's reputation as a poet, the more ferociously Charsky repudiates himself. It is only when the Italian shifts his gaze to the strange multicultural decor of Charsky's study and costume, with its hodgepodge of classical sculptures, Gothic knickknacks, Chinese robes, and Turkish shawls, that he begins to realize that culture for this Russian aristocrat is not a means of self-expression, but a disguise. With perfect ironic symmetry, Pushkin momentarily reverses the point of view, and we see Charsky's gentlemanly "morning suit" for the exotic disguise it is. It is only when Charsky's mask of "non-poet" is back in place and the risk of self-recognition is deflected that he can even begin to behave normally.

By the end of the chapter the distance between the two men has widened to a maximum: the Italian is not just a poet but, Charsky is happy to hear, an improvisor, a paid performer, a salon entertainer, which makes Charsky a society lion showing off his patronage. "They'll attend, don't worry: some from curiosity, others, to kill the evening somehow, still others, to show that they understand Italian; I repeat, all that's necessary is for you to be in fashion; and you will be in fashion, here's my hand on it" (*ruchaius'*) (8.1, 267). The brief European fad for salon improvisors was another symptom of the declining interest in poetry itself;[99] no one wanted to read poetry, but everyone wanted to witness the state of possession. Hence the unimportance of the improvisor's Italian, the signification of his visual presence. Most improvisor stories worked to expose the latter's spurious public performance in favor of the difficult and introspective production of true poetry. This simple opposition is not at all what Pushkin was after, as we shall see, and is preempted by his donation of his own poems to the improvisor.

The next day, knocking at the door of room number 35 in the dark and dirty corridor of the Italian's lodging house, Charsky informs him of the success of their marketing strategy and "guarantees" (*ruchaius'*—again the hand) "if not a triumph, then at least the ladie . . ." Why the marked repetition of the "hand of honor" in this obviously ironic context?[100] The phrase echoes a long-ago similar moment in Pushkin's poetry. In "Conversation of a Bookseller and a Poet" (1824), as I pointed out at the beginning of the chapter, the crass bookseller concluded his contract for the poet's work with these words: "Here is my manuscript [*rukopis'*]. Let's come to terms" (2, 1, 330). Ironically, that same fall Pushkin was getting himself out of (and back into) a financial jam by selling "tickets" for an almanac of poetry. Now in "Egyptian Nights" the two situations merge: a profitable literary arrangement and a fateful bargain. The corridor has the same "faintly satanic" aura of a Hoffmannian space from which demonic doings emerge;[101] the handshake clinching the bartering of creative powers has a Mephistophelean tinge; even the room number for which Charsky is searching suggests a (magical?) displacement of the year 1835. He, "not yet thirty," not married, not in the service, insisting that he is also not a poet, represents a denial of Pushkin's real situation from 1830 on. Why does he come knocking at door number thirty-five? To find the humiliating self he has choked off, hidden? To find a way back to being a poet in 1835?

One of the interesting asymmetries about the relationship of the two poets is that we are shown the work of only one. Earlier we are told about Charsky's creative "fits" by a narrator who seems to be half reminiscing about a state well known to him and half including the reader in a common experience, "when visions palpably sketch themselves before you and you invent lively, unexpected words for the incarnation of your visions, when poetic lines lie down easily before your pen and resonant rhymes run to meet elegant thought."[102] The lines closely paraphrase a passage from "Autumn (A Fragment)" (1833) that describes the experience of solitary inspiration and poetic readiness in similarly eroticized and populous metaphors and then peters out on the line "But where should we sail?"[103] The textual product of this particular writing spree of Charsky's remains invisible to us; what materializes instead is the figure of the swarthy Romantic poet, effortlessly and publicly speaking the language of poetry.

What takes place in room thirty-five is, by Charsky's standards, a striptease: Charsky incites the Italian to do what he himself does only in the strictest seclusion. Moreover, he assigns him a subject that reflects his own proud philosophy of independence, which in an improvisor's mouth can only sound like a mockery: "The poet chooses the subjects of his songs himself; the crowd has no right to command his inspiration" (254).[104] Although the poem speaks about the arbitrariness of inspiration as a fact of nature, controllable neither by the crowd nor by the poet himself, the production of the poem makes visible something different: "that close connection between one's own inspiration and another's external will" that makes poetry gush from the improvisor without the "labor, frigidity, or anxiety" so familiar to Charsky.[105] For a third time they cement their exchange with a handclasp, after which Charsky is referred to for the first time as "the poet." What has he gained from the transaction?

Seated on a suitcase in that dirty little hotel room, removed from the world of status and social partitions that has pitted his own psyche against itself, he has for the first time taken part in a nonadversarial poetic communion. The poem itself openly discusses the conflicted relationship between poet and audience, leaving the actual poet and audience (the improvisor and Charsky) free to model a different pattern of reception. That model is quite different from Charsky's paranoid involution, reflected in the topic he has proposed. It instead reveals an interactive creative process, one in which the audience's narrative desire is incorporated yet transformed by the poet into a new mirror, in which, "amazed and moved," it recognizes itself. Thus Charsky's stiff and rebarbative definition of the poet is modified by the Italian into a nature not elevated or godlike, but preternaturally responsive to unexpected aspects of the world:[106] "Such is the poet" (254)—an image of himself with which Charsky can reunite for the first time. The moment of reconciliation does not last long. "It was unpleasant for Charsk[y] to fall so suddenly from the height of poetry into the bookkeeper's office" (255). His reaction to the improvisor's "greedy" interest in his profits exactly reproduces the reader's scolding of the poet in the improvisation: "You've scarcely reached the heights when you lower your gaze and hurry to descend."[107] It is up to the reader to notice Charsky's ironic resemblance to the audience he professes to despise, their common squeamishness in the face of life.

Charsky's split identity is very much in evidence on the evening of the performance. A St. Petersburg lady has liberally left her salon at the disposal of the improvisor. What this means in practice is that the space has been partitioned in a formal, almost military manner, as though to guard the various participants against dangerous "fraternization" (to use Schlegel's word):[108]

> A platform had been erected, and the chairs had been arranged in twelve rows. On the appointed day . . . an old lady with a long nose, wearing a gray hat with drooping feathers and a ring on every finger, sat by the door behind a little table, charged with the sale and collection of tickets. Gendarmes stood by the main entrance. . . . Soon all the rows of armchairs were occupied by brilliant ladies; the men, as though forming a tight frame around them, stood by the platform, along the walls, and behind the last row of chairs. The musicians with their stands took up the space on either side of the platform. A porcelain vase stood on a table in the center of the room. (255–56)

Not only the stage is arranged with stiff symmetry, but no less so the part of the room reserved for the audience. The rigorously partitioned room is itself a stage set directed outward at the audience of readers; it reflects Charsky's and Petersburg society's social decorum. Pushkin no longer needs to plant a Spaniard in the salon, as he did in "The guests were arriving at the dacha," to comment aloud on the mausoleum-like formality and constraint of Petersburg social life. The "freely" adopted forms of their social life illustrate the extent to which the Petersburgers have internalized the order imposed on them; they are most exotic precisely when they are trying to be most European and civilized.

Charsky appears to be unaware of any oddity in the arrangements (even the outlandish old lady), but his touchy sense of sartorial decorum is once again offended by the Italian's explicitly theatrical costume. Dressed in black from head to foot, the lace collar of his shirt open to expose the strange whiteness of his neck framed by a black beard, his pale forehead shadowed by black locks, he resembles no one so much as the Romantic portrait of Pushkin done by V. A. Tropinin in 1827. By now the reader is inclined to look less at the object of Charsky's displeased scrutiny and more at the curious phenomenon of Charsky's exaggerated sense of comme il faut; one pictures him wearing an expression like that of the long-nailed dandy Pushkin in O. A. Kiprensky's more formal portrait of the same year.[109] What to the Italian is a conscious and perfectly natural performance represents to Charsky an embarrassing exposure of the poet—his ridiculous secret self.

It would seem that the demarcation of the salon's space has defined a priori who will be the object of scrutiny and who will be the scrutinizers. But an improvisation depends on its audience's willingness to participate, and the Russian audience is reluctant. Charsky, who had intended to watch the little comedy from an ironic distance, is repeatedly forced to save the performance, which thus becomes more and more his co-creation. It is he who breaks the ice and writes the first suggestion, it is he who interprets the selected topic for the Italian when its author, a homely young girl, is too humiliated by catty glances to step forward. Although the Italian seems to be on the spot, it is really the Petersburg audience that is spotlighted in the scene of the lots: its sheepish herd instinct, its automatic mockery of anyone willing to stand out, the morbid, revealing character of the topics themselves, most of which have to do with violent death or imprisonment, the snickering reaction to the erotic topic of Cleopatra, the "execution" (by eyes alone) of the girl who proposed it, the collective cry for "zhrebii, zhrebii" (draw lots)—the operation of fate, rather than choice—and finally the personification of that fate in the single figure of the self-possessed beauty, dipping her aristocratically gloved hand into the vase—these are the inadvertent self-revelations the Petersburg salon presents to the improvisor. They are all woven into the portrait he paints of an Egyptian court.

The uncooperative silence of the salon before the drawing of the lots, and its repressed whispering after the selection, are reproduced in the poem in the public's demeanor before and after Kleopatra's challenge:

> The beautiful girl unrolled the paper and read the words out: "Cleopatra e suoi amanti."
>
> She read these words in a soft tone, but the silence reigning over the room was so complete that everybody could hear her. . . . The music stopped... (258)

> И пышный пир как будто дремлет,
> Безмолвны гости. Хор молчит . . .
> Рекла—и ужас всех объемлет,
> И страстью дрогнули сердца...
> Она смущенный ропот внемлет
> С холодной дерзостью лица.
>
> (8.1, 274)

> And the luxurious feast seems to doze, the guests are speechless. The choir is mute. . . . She has spoken—and horror engulfs everyone, and hearts quiver with passion... She hearkens to the embarrassed murmur with a face of cold daring.[110]

The avidity with which the Petersburgers greet the idea of "zhrebii," as well as the image of a majestic beauty disposing of this fateful power, are of course transferred in the poem to the image of the "fateful urn" (260) from which the lots determining the order of Cleopatra's nights emerge. Perhaps most striking is the way the improvisor has understood his audience's overt and covert narrative desires. The topics written down by a few members of the audience are the following: the family Cenci (the subject of Shelley's gruesomely incestuous and violent melodrama); the last day of Pompeii; Cleopatra and her lovers; spring seen from a prison; and the triumph of Tasso. They are all high-Romantic literary topics, hallowed by fashion, hence a testimony to the writer's culture; but they also betray the kind of morbid attraction to sadomasochistic subjects that Mario Praz first identified in *The Romantic Agony*.[111] The improvisor appears to have detected precisely the repressed individuality and sexuality, literally the psychological imprisonment, that underlies the Petersburgers' choice of topics and eccentric behavior and which would best be satisfied by an image of thrilling self-immolation. The Italian's "suffering" from the crowd's indifference, his meek acceptance of its will, the sacrificial vulnerability with which he awaits the approaching "god" of inspiration are counterpointed by Kleopatra's ritual sacrifice of her body and her passion, and the three victims' clear-eyed sacrifice of their remaining life spans for one night of intensive Life.

—Клянусь... —о матерь наслаждений,
Тебе неслыханно служу,
На ложе страстных искушений
Простой наемницей всхожу.

(8.1, 275)

I swear... —O mother of delights, in an unheard-of way I serve you, to the couch of passionate seductions I ascend a common hireling.[112]

But the improvisatore already sensed the divine presence. . . . His face grew alarmingly pale; he trembled as if in a fever; his eyes sparkled with wondrous fire; he . . . suddenly stepped forward, folding his arms across his chest... The music stopped... The improvisation began. (258)

There is one more member of the audience whose narrative desires both coincide with and diverge from those of the crowd: Charsky. It is, after all, he who honed the topic from its general formulation (Cleopatra and her lovers) to the specific Roman anecdote with which we are familiar. In what way does the improvisor address Charsky?

The foreigner's two improvisations are active proofs of an interactive theory of poetry; in each case the Italian's performance addresses Charsky's preconceptions and overturns them. The poet's milieu may be hostile, uncomprehending, repressive—whatever it is, it not only offers him its subjects but shapes his own unconscious values and thought processes. His society's face is imprinted on his psyche and in his poetry. Pushkin leaves it up to his reader to discover the points of contact between the awkward circumstances of the salon evening depicted in the prose frame of "Egyptian Nights" and the inspired poem that emerges from the poet's painful contact with his audience. The implied process of production of the improvisation is then allegorized in the poem itself: "Kleopatra" is an allegory of the poet and audience's intercourse.

Whether Pushkin intended it or not, the terminal bracket of his prose frame remains unclosed.[113] The salon audience and Charsky disappear, and "Kleopatra" hangs suspended before another audience, the readers of "Egyptian Nights." This audience might be inclined to draw a different parallel between the night-for-a-life bargain proposed and accepted by Kleopatra and her victims and the relationship of the poet to his own life.

> [Charsky] was a poet nevertheless, and his passion for poetry was indomitable: when he felt this *nonsense* approach (that was what he called inspiration), he locked himself in his study and wrote from morning till late night. He confessed to his genuine friends that he knew true happiness only at such times. . . . But the improvisatore already sensed the divine presence... (250, 258)

"Kleopatra" represents metaphorically the "strastnyi torg" (passionate bargain) that defines the poet's own life: creative nights of "true happiness" in exchange for the dislocation of his whole mortal existence, a state of eternal readiness to utter his last word before the axe falls. Many of Pushkin's lyrical works of 1835–36 represent just such a conscious "last word." If "Journey to Arzrum," "A Tale of Roman Life," "We were spending the evening at the dacha," and "Egyptian Nights" constitute a new category of lyrical prose, it is not because they contain poetic citations, but because by repeating past poems in contemporary prose frames Pushkin recuperated and reinterpreted his own creative life, as though to will it to posterity. In the frame of "Egyptian Nights," which circles so persistently around the question of the poet's or the crowd's "right to choose," "Kleopatra" can be seen as the representation of an imaginative compulsion so irresistible that no choice is possible. Its final audience is Pushkin, who, in the summer of 1835, made a poem written eleven years earlier, at the end of a similar period of creative doldrums, stand in for the invasion of poetry itself.

And suddenly the writer's block that had produced only "Egyptian Nights" by the fall of 1835 broke, and *The Captain's Daughter* flowed quickly to completion. What had happened? For one thing, that September had not been so barren of creative nourishment as Pushkin had complained.

> I found everything as of old in Mikhailovskoe except that my nurse is no longer alive and that near the familiar old pine trees a young family of pines has grown in my absence, which makes me sad in the same way as I sometimes feel sad looking at young cavalry officers at balls at which I no longer whirl. There is nothing to be done about it: everything around me tells me that I am growing old. . . . I comport myself modestly and decently. I go for walks and rides, read Walter Scott's novels, from which I am in raptures, and sigh for you.[114]

This was a perfect elegiac recreation of his first autumn in Mikhailovskoe in 1824: historical research, Scott, horses, nostalgia for an absent love and balls from which he had been excluded, his nanny. That interlude had culminated in the composition of "Kleopatra"; Pushkin has now just finished framing it in "Egyptian Nights." It was exactly the kind of temporal rhyme that stimulated poetry. The next day Pushkin wrote his remarkable blank verse elegy "Again I have visited..." and stopped. He returned to St. Petersburg and the trap of his "empirical" existence tightened.

Suddenly, life vertiginously repeated the old imaginary figure:

> Every ingredient for a gay ball was present, judging from all the faces except that of Alexander Pushkin, who remained sad, pensive and care-worn. . . . His straying eyes, which were wild and distracted, were fixed with anxious concentration on his wife and d'Anthès alone. D'Anthès continued to play out his old farce, constantly linked up with Ekaterina Goncharov and at the same time casting oeillades from a distance at Natalia, with whom he none the less managed to finish up in the mazurka. It was pitiful to see Pushkin standing there facing them, framed in a doorway silent, pale and menacing.[115]

Pushkin must have begun to write day and night. Two months later, at the very height of the scandal that would lead to his fatal duel with d'Anthès, Karamzin's daughter Sophia reported, "To change the subject, the fourth *Sovremennik* [*Contemporary*] has just come out and contains a novel by Pushkin, *The Captain's Daughter*, which they say is delightful."[116]

Marina Tsvetaeva is the reader who recognized in *The Captain's Daughter* Pushkin's last major work of poetic, as opposed to prosaic, imagination.[117] On the surface, it would seem to represent a liberation from lyricism and personal anxiety into the refreshing impersonal world of folktale and history. Yet with laser-like vision (and the analogous experience of having switched from poetry to lyrical prose behind her), she recognizes in the objective tale one more ironic allegory of Pushkin's inner drama, a translation, in essence, of the starker "Kleopatra." The dramatis personae of 1824 are clearly represented: the father and son locked in life-and-death rivalry and betrayal; the fascinating pretender tsar, master of "the empty word," a second self of magical authority; the feminine now reduced to a faceless pretext for self-proof; and a scaffold. For the last time, a historical tale in the genre of Walter Scott allowed Pushkin to represent his own repeating, ruthlessly self-fulfilling imaginative patterns. Who plays "Kleopatra"? Certainly not the captain's daughter, as Tsvetaeva points out. The passion in the novel is between Grinev and Pugachev, the young nobleman buffetted by life and the self-created, poetic pretender who has taken over his destiny.

Who knows what Pushkin meant to convey by the swarthy Romantic rebel's last wink from the scaffold to his pale chronicler before, in January 1837, he chose his own manner of dying.

Autoportraiture: An Afterword

So the tremendous variety of Pushkin's representations is to be reduced to a series of fictional self-portraits or "psychodramas"? Yet, come to think of it, is this such a strange hypothesis for a writer who covered the margins of his manuscripts with self-sketches, always in medallion-like profile but in a variety of expressive styles and often embedded in a dream-like profusion of portraits of friends and enemies, sketches of situations recent, elegiac, and fictional—literally the "imagos" that contemporary theory sees as the stepping-stone between mute and imageless subjectivity and the "realistic" representation from which all trace of the subject has been effaced?[1]

What is the difference between autoportraiture and autobiography? Autobiography is an explanatory theory of the self's coherent existence in time, while autoportraiture suppresses discourse in favor of isolate, immanent cross sections, vivid and not entirely explainable images or "positions d'âme" (positions of the soul).[2] Stendhal's manuscript for his fictional autobiography, *The Life of Henry Brulard*, is studded with one hundred seventy diagrams, mnemonic stage sets for "feeling his way back to particular moments," located on "a border between the verbal and non-verbal."[3] In the words of Leo Bersani, "Literature hallucinates the world in order to accommodate desire. . . . The literary imagination reinstates the world of desiring fantasies as a world of reinvented, richly fragmented and diversified body-memories."[4] Michael Sheringham elaborates,

Art and discourse involve different "positions," what Lyotard calls the *figural* implies a relationship, partly physical and corporeal, between the mind and something intrinsically exterior and unassimilable to itself, while discourse dissolves difference into meaning. . . . The continuity of the graphic process, across the divide between verbal and visual communication, reflects in Stendhal the continuity in the autobiographical process between the adult and the child whose experiences are progressively rediscovered. Equally, the pictures in Stendhal's manuscript are like holes in a tattered fabric, manifesting the inward gaze of the "subject of recollection" who suddenly stops, breaks the chain of discourse, and makes a clearing in which the past is attended to in a different way. . . . We should perhaps think of the Stendhalian diagram as an area of transference, in Peter Brooks's sense, "a special 'artificial' space for the re-working of the past in symbolic form."[5]

More important than the identification of an invariant cluster that travels over generic and content boundaries unchanged is the mobile principle of creative self-translation, writing not to express the unchanging content of the self but rather to recognize itself in yet another phenomenological hypostasis, tracking the mind's effort to interpret to itself and make palpable to others "the movement of time in the author's life"—what Rousseau called "la succession de mon être" (the successiveness of my being). According to Brooks,

In [narrative] transference, desire passes through what Lacan calls the "defile of the signifier": it enters the symbolic order, where it can be reordered, reread, rewritten . . . in which affect, repeated from the past, is acted out as if it were present, yet eventually in the knowledge that the persons and relations involved are surrogates and mummers. . . . Plot [is] not a matter of typology or fixed structure, but rather a structuring operation. . . . The question of identity . . . can be thought only in narrative terms, in the effort to tell a whole life, to plot its meaning by going back over it to record its perpetual flight forward, its slippage from the fixity of definition.[6]

In the pre-psychological age of Russian literature, and with a writer who confessed that he found it "impossible to write about himself" and recoiled from exposing the smallest detail of his inner life as from an abyss,[7] "reading for the plot" can indeed reveal much about the twists and turns of Pushkin's self-exploration. What emerges, however, is quite a different view of the Romantic artist than the tired stereotype of the rigid Romantic egotist polemically espoused and denounced in Russian (anti-western) criticism. For the ideal aim of "high Romanticism" was quite different: nothing less than the artist's disappearance into the "plastic" world of his creative representations.[8]

I have tried in this book to reimagine the cultural materials, particularly the imported literary fashions (the Greek fragment, the Roman erotic elegy, rococo classical mythology, the Oriental drama of the self, the Shakespearean impostor/improvisor, the invisible quotation marks and embedded autoportraits of Romantic irony)—or, to use more fashionable Lacanian terminology, the "defile of the signifier"—through which Pushkin fashioned or retranslated his own creative energy, preoccupations, for lack of a better word, individuality into the kaleidoscopic array of his "hallucinated worlds."

It is instructive to compare the trajectory of Pushkin's self-fashionings with the mobile narrative of self told by Rembrandt's self-portraits in H. Perry Chapman's *Rembrandt's Self-Portraits: A Study in Seventeenth-Century Identity.*[9] Each portrait's half-historical, half-invented costume, hairstyle, props, and facial expression represent a different dimension of Rembrandt's invisible, individual spirituality—a restless *melancholia imaginativa* precipitating out in a protean series of intensely imagined selves. Seventeenth-century Dutch culture, entering European history and especially material culture through its military victories and wealth, much as Russia's would at the beginning of the nineteenth century, began to manifest what Stephen Greenblatt has identified as the flexibility of the Renaissance or western self, the fashioning of human identity as a manipulable, artful process.[10] Interestingly, the stages of Rembrandt's protean self-transformations are almost identical to Pushkin's as I have explored them in this book: (1) the solitary (elegiac) melancholic; (2) Romanticized, exotic costume dramas; (3) the Renaissance virtuoso, both appropriating the *sprezzatura* of the improvisational ideal and exploring its ambivalence (*Boris Godunov, Eugene Onegin*, "The Stone Guest"); (4) the proud native craftsman revealing the artist as maker (the prologues of "The Little House in Kolomna" and "The Bronze Horseman," "Egyptian Nights," and "To the Artist" ["Khudozhniku"]); (5) the landscape as an alternate form of self-examination, a phenomenological representation of the *vita contemplativa* ("Autumn" ["Osen' "]); (6) unfinished works and rough, improvisational technique as a deliberate part of the portrayal of the creative process; (7) historical self-portraiture with more than a little dose of irony, both vis-à-vis himself and his own increasingly alienated audience (Petronius, Pugachev); (8) self-portraits as madman and beggar, the negative side of creative melancholia ("Don't let me God go mad" ["Ne dai mne bog soiti s uma," 1833]); (9) and finally, in the last self-portraits, a tendency to circle back to the Romantic images of the artist's early career, so that *Self-Portrait at Age 63* refers to no other model than the self-portrait of Rembrandt's peak, *Self-Portrait at Age 34*, much in the way that Pushkin creates prose frame after prose frame for the unfinished, most exotic, and most self-effaced poetic image of his career, "Kleopatra": "Now, as if summing up his career, he emulates himself."[11]

The irrepressible flight from mode to representational mode traces the trajectory of the artist's inspired mental activity, yet eventually also reflects the difficulty of integrating and consolidating his identities, especially before an increasingly uncomprehending audience, hence the emphatic rhetoric of such programmatically Romantic "final statements" as "The Monument" ("Pamiatnik"). Yet even that solemn epitaph rings a little differently if we counterpoint it with the delightfully self-mocking self-portrait of the same year, "il gran' Padre AP" (which parodies traditional medallions of Dante).[12]

Pushkin's "distinctive feature" as a writer is refusal of closure, both closure of the discrete narrative and closure of meaning. Throughout his notebooks, the proliferation of representations, pictorial and verbal, feels like a race against the clock: the tiny sketches of dueling pistols that punctuate the flow of text seem to mark time.[13] In "A Tale of Roman Life" the equation is made explicit: Petronius lets a little more of his life's blood flow, then a little more poetry, in allegorical counterpoint. Narrative both moves toward "the quiescence and resolution of death" and "the definitive closure of meaning" and, in the plot's "dilatory loops and complications," works to postpone them.[14] If narrative is the expression of the self's wish to be "heard, recognized, understood," the kaleidoscopic dispersion of the self in an "infinite" series of representations prevents the closure of that understanding: Pushkin's self wants to be understood *ne do kontsa* (not to the end).

Deathliness inheres in the compulsive identification with the scene, which seals off the experience from the ordinary train of events, making outer and inner a function of each other, putting the spectator "on the spot" and immobilizing him in a death-like rigidity. . . . Central here is a connection between death and the phenomenon of representation itself—être détachés de notre propre histoire et la voir se jouer devant nous [to be detached from our own history and see it being played before us]. . . . The subject of representation is located midway between existence and a deathly world where everything has already occurred, where time has stopped and only repetition is possible.[15]

Recognition scenes, in which external reality suddenly "seems to mirror or allegorize inner mental space," are always accompanied in Pushkin's texts by death or a death-like torpor: the young Pushkin's "freezing" in the presence of the classical statues at Tsarskoe selo; the narrator Pushkin's slow-motion enactment of Lensky's killing; Don Juan's recognition that his infinite narrative of love is ending incarnated in the iron handshake of the statue; Eugene's recognition of the death grip of history in "The Bronze Horseman"; thirty-six-year-old Pushkin's mesmerized recognition that the fatal triangle of his imagination was being enacted before him in the Karamzins' salon. As I suggested at the end of the last chapter, it was perhaps that horrified moment of frozen "specular" recognition that unleashed Pushkin's longest and most self-effaced ("realistic") narrative, *The Captain's Daughter*, culminating in the long exchange of looks between the dark rebel-genius and the young scribe who survives to record his images.

Practitioners of the "autoportrait," from Montaigne [to] Barthes, lack confidence in a unified self, and therefore construct textual self-representations—non-narrative "miroirs d'encre" [mirrors of ink]—out of avowedly heterogeneous materials . . . "le sujet ne se dit qu'a tràvers ce qui le dépasse, le traverse, et le nie" [the subject doesn't speak itself except through what exceeds, traverses, and negates him]. . . . The autoportraitist's desire for textual incarnation leads to the cession of personal memory, and the wholesale acceptance of the self as a tapestry of disparate images and materials; by this acceptance of death and disunity the subject accedes to a phantom life of dispersion. Forsaking any relation to "pastness," the writer seeks to invest a succession of textual spaces with the capacity to act as surrogates of self, consigning himself to "l'infinie metempsychose que son écriture exige de lui" [the infinite metempsychosis that his writing exacts of him].[16]

If it is the movement from representation to representation that guarantees "the succession of self in time," the ironic escape from narrative closure and death, it works only when it generates an answering mobility and ironic liveliness of mind in the reader—a "new paradigm of subjectivity," the exercise of new "dimension[s] of selfhood."[17] It is this, I submit, that has kept succeeding generations of readers in Russia's intensely anti-individualistic culture both passively riveted and actively emboldened by Pushkin's endlessly counterpointed explorations of his own individuality.

When we reinterpret a writer through the lens of our own time's critical discourses, are we not also engaging in an act of autoportraiture? In taking aim at the long-accepted notion of Pushkin's evolution toward the values and image of the "mature" artist as defined by his culture—variegated objective representation instead of repetitive lyrical self-exposure, an interest in crystallizing the realistic, social, historical world around him rather than exploring the labyrinths of his own subjectivity—haven't I merely replaced the implicit values of past generations of critics with a focus molded willy-nilly by the intellectual climate and critical assumptions that nourished my generation, from Freudian compulsions to deconstruction to the "decentered" subject impaled on the vectors of its culture's discourses? Yes, inevitably—and why not? Certain writers are literally retranslated by each generation, and if American critics are joining their voices to, or raising their voices against, the always ongoing indigenous debate about Pushkin, it means that Pushkin has finally reached the world audience that has always been claimed for him.

REFERENCE MATTER

Notes

Introduction

1. B. Tomashevsky discusses the phenomenon of Pushkin's epigenesis in "Poeticheskoe nasledie Pushkina," *Pushkin*, bk. 2 (Moscow: Akademia nauk, 1961), pp. 345–443.

2. Letter to P. A. Viazemsky, Feb. 6, 1823. In Tatiana Wolff, ed. and trans., *Pushkin on Literature* (Stanford, Calif.: Stanford University Press, 1986), p. 63.

3. Iury Tynianov, "Pushkin," in his *Arkhaisty i novatory* (Leningrad: Priboi, 1929), p. 228.

4. Vissarion Belinsky, "Stati o Pushkine," *Polnoe sobranie sochinenii* (Moscow: Akademia nauk, 1955), vol. 7, p. 352; quoted in L. Ia. Ginzburg, "Liricheskii geroi russkogo romantizma," *Pushkin issledovania i materialy* (Leningrad: Nauka, 1962), p. 140.

5. Ginzburg, "Liricheskii geroi russkogo romantizma."

6. See Irina Reyfman, *Vasilii Trediakovsky: The Fool of the "New" Russian Literature* (Stanford, Calif.: Stanford University Press, 1990), pp. 1–21. She takes the concept of "culture hero" from Joseph Campbell's *The Hero of a Thousand Faces* (Princeton, N.J.: Princeton University Press, 1968).

7. P. V. Annenkov, *Materialy dlia biografii Pushkina*, photo-offset of original (St. Petersburg, 1873) edition (Moscow: Kniga, 1985).

8. See Boris Eikhenbaum, "Pushkin i Tolstoy," in his *O proze* (Leningrad: Khudozhestvennaia literatura, 1969).

9. Quoted phrases are from Tolstoy's letter to E. G. Golokhvastov (1873), cited in *ibid.*, p. 181.

10. F. M. Dostoevsky, "Otvet 'Russkomu vestniku' " (1861) and "Primechaniia," in *Polnoe sobranie sochinenii*, vol. 19 (Leningrad: Nauka, 1979), pp. 119–39 and 300–308. On Dostoevsky's polemic with Katkov, see B. Ia.

Kirpotin, "Dostoevsky i 'Egipetskie nochi' Pushkina," *Voprosy literatury*, 1962, no. 11: 112–21; and V. Komarovich, "Dostoevsky i 'Egipetskie nochi' Pushkina," *Pushkin i ego sovremenniki*, nos. 29–30 (Petrograd, 1918).

11. Marcus C. Levitt, "Pushkin in 1899," in Boris Gasparov, Robert P. Hughes, and Irina Paperno, eds., *Cultural Mythologies of Russian Modernism: From the Golden Age to the Silver Age* (Berkeley: University of California Press, 1992), pp. 183–203.

12. Osip Mandel'shtam, *Sobranie sochinenii*, ed. G. P. Struve and B. A. Filippov (Washington, D.C.: Mezhdunarodnoe literaturnoe sodruzhestvo, 1967), vol. 1, no. 118.

13. Omry Ronen, "The Dry River and the Black Ice: Anamnesis and Amnesia in Mandel'stam's Poem 'Ia slovo pozabyl, cto ia xotel skazat,'" *Slavica Hierosolymitana* 1 (1977). See also John Foster's article close to this subject: "Nabokov Before Proust: The Paradox of Anticipatory Memory," *Slavic and East European Journal* 33, no. 1 (Spring 1989): 78–94.

14. Vladimir Khodasevich, *Poeticheskoe khoziaistvo Pushkina*, bk. 1 (Leningrad: Mysl', 1924); Valerii Briusov, *Moi Pushkin*, ed. N. K. Piksanov (Moscow: Gosudarstvennoe izdatel'stvo, 1929); Marina Tsvetaeva, "Moi Pushkin," *Izbrannaia proza v dvukh tomakh. 1917–1937*, vol. 2 (New York: Russica Publishers, 1979), pp. 249–79; Osip Mandel'shtam, "Pushkin and Scriabin: Fragments," in *The Complete Critical Prose and Letters*, ed. and trans. Jane Gary Harris (Ann Arbor, Mich.: Ardis, 1979), pp. 90–95.

15. In "Kak my pishem," Iury Tynianov describes his favorite writers as "shershavykh, nedodelannykh neudachnikov, bormotatelei, za kotorykh nuzhno dogovarivat'." In V. Kaverin, ed., *Iury Tynianov. Pisatel' i uchenyi* (Moscow: Molodaia gvardiia, 1966), p. 199.

16. F. M. Dostoevsky, "Otvet russkomu vestniku," pp. 135–37; V. Briusov, "Kleopatra," in his *Izbrannye stikhotvoreniia, liricheskie poemy* (Moscow: Moskovskii rabochii, 1979); and B. M. Zhirmunsky, "*Egipetskie nochi* Valeriia Briusova," in his *Valerii Briusov i nasledie Pushkina. Opyt sravnitel'no-stilisticheskogo issledovaniia* (Petrograd: El'zevir, 1922), pp. 52–86; M. Gofman, *Egipetskie nochi* (Leningrad: S. Lifar', 1935); D. M. Thomas, *Ararat* (New York: Viking Press, 1983).

17. Aleksandr Pushkin, *Eugene Onegin: A Novel in Verse*, trans. and comm. Vladimir Nabokov, (Princeton, N.J.: Princeton University Press, 1981), vol. 2.

18. Iu. M. Lotman, *The Structure of the Artistic Text*, trans. Ronald and Gail Vroon (Ann Arbor: University of Michigan Press, 1977), pp. 283–84.

19. Osip Mandel'shtam, "On the Addressee," in *Complete Critical Prose*, pp. 71–73.

20. Viktor Shklovsky, "'Evgenii Onegin' (Pushkin i Stern)," *Ocherki po*

poetike Pushkina (Berlin: Epokha, 1923), and *Zametki o proze Pushkina* (Moscow: Sovetskii pisatel', 1937).

21. Iurii Tynianov, "Mnimyi Pushkin," in *Poetika, Istoria literatury, Kino* (Moscow: Nauka, 1977), pp. 78–92.

22. In "Simvolicheskoe opisanie," *Feniks* (Moscow, 1922), Pavel Florensky wrote, "It is appropriate to the artistic image that it possess the ultimate degree of incarnation, concreteness, and living truth, but the wise artist probably spends his greatest effort to keep his images, which have become symbols, from slipping from their pedestals of esthetic isolation and mixing with life." Quoted in Boris Uspensky, *A Poetics of Composition* (Berkeley: University of California Press, 1973), p. 139.

23. Tynianov, "Promezhutok," in *Poetika*, pp. 168–95.

24. I argue this point of view in "Tynianov, Pushkin and the Fragment: Through the Lens of Montage," in *Cultural Mythologies of Russian Modernism: From the Golden Age to the Silver Age* (Berkeley: University of California Press, 1992), pp. 264–92. See this excellent volume of essays for a many-faceted discussion of the relationship between the cultures of the Silver Age and Golden Age.

25. Here is a bibliography of interesting work on the fragment: Lucien Dallenbach and Christiaan L. Hart Nibbrig, eds., *Fragment und Totalität*, Neue Folge Band 107 (Frankfurt am Main: Suhrkamp Verlag, 1984); Umberto Eco, *The Role of the Reader* (Bloomington: Indiana University Press, 1979), pp. 47–66, 67–89; Monika Frenkel, " 'V malen'koi ramke': Fragmentary Structures in Pushkin's Poetry and Prose," (Ph.D. diss., Yale University, 1984); Michael Fried, *Absorption and Theatricality: Painting and Beholder in the Age of Diderot* (Berkeley: University of California Press, 1980); Laurence Goldstein, *Ruins and Empire* (Pittsburgh, Pa.: University of Pittsburgh Press, 1977); Anne F. Janowitz, "Parts and Wholes: Romantic and Modernist Fragment Poems" (Ph.D. diss., Stanford University, 1982); Lawrence D. Kritzman, ed., *Fragments: Incompletion and Discontinuity* (New York: New York Literary Forum, 1981); Philippe Lacoue-Labarthe and Jean-Luc Nancy, *L'Absolu littéraire: Theorie de la littérature du romantisme allemand* (Paris: Editions du Seuil, 1978), trans. Philip Barnard and Cheryl Lester as *The Literary Absolute* (Albany: State University of New York Press, 1988); Marjorie Levinson, *The Romantic Fragment Poem* (Chapel Hill: University of North Carolina Press, 1986); Thomas McFarland, *Romanticism and the Forms of Ruin: Wordsworth, Coleridge, and Modalities of Fragmentation* (Princeton, N.J.: Princeton University Press, 1981); Balachandra Rajan, *The Form of the Unfinished* (Princeton, N.J.: Princeton University Press, 1985); D. F. Rauber, "The Fragment as Romantic Form," *Modern Language Quarterly*, 1969, vol. 30, 212–31; Edward Stankiewicz, "Cen-

tripetal and Centrifugal Structures in Poetry," *Semiotica* 38, no. 3 / 4 (1982); Jack Undank and Herbert Josephs, eds., *Diderot: Digression and Dispersion* (Lexington, Ky.: French Forum, 1984); and Eddie Wolfram, *History of Collage* (New York: Macmillan, 1975).

26. See, for example, Efim Etkind, " 'Liricheskaia epigramma' kak zhanrovaia forma," in *Forma kak soderzhanie* (Würzburg: Jal-Verlag, 1977), and P. D. Timenchik, "Tekst v tekste u akmeistov," *Tekst v tekste, Uchenye zapiski Tartuskogo gos. universiteta*, no. 567. *Trudy po znakovym sistemam*, vol. 14 (Tartu: Izdatel'stvo Tartuskogo gosudarstvennogo universiteta, 1981), pp. 65–75.

27. B. M. Zhirmunsky, *Bairon i Pushkin* (Leningrad: Nauka, 1978), and Tynianov, *The Problem of Verse Language*, trans. Michael Sosa and Brent Harvey (Ann Arbor, Mich.: Ardis, 1981), p. 44.

28. See Paul Debreczeny, "The Reception of Pushkin's Poetic Works in the 1820's: A Study of the Critic's Role," *Slavic Review* 28, no. 3 (Sept. 1969): 394–415. Also Zhirmunsky, *Bairon i Pushkin*, pp. 57–61, 413. I realized to what extent Russian critics were repeating European reviews of Byron when I read John O. Hayden, *Romantic Bards and British Reviewers* (Lincoln: University of Nebraska Press, 1971); Theodore Redpath, *The Young Romantics and Critical Opinion, 1807–1824* (London: Harrap, 1973); Keith Walker, *Byron's Readers: A Study of Attitudes Towards Byron, 1812–1832* (Salzburg: Institut für Anglistik und Amerikanistik, 1979).

29. V. B. Sandomirskaia, " 'Otryvok' v poezii Pushkina dvadtsatykh godov," *Pushkin issledovania i materialy*, vol. 9 (Leningrad: Nauka, 1979), pp. 69–82.

30. Tynianov, "Tiutchev i Geine," in *Poetika*, pp. 29–37.

31. Tynianov, "Promezhutok," in *Poetika*, pp. 168–95.

32. See Herbert Eagle, *Formalist Film Theory* (Ann Arbor: Michigan Slavic Publications, 1985).

33. Cited in Iu. M. Lotman, *Struktura khudozhestvennogo teksta* (Moscow: Isdatel'stvo Iskusstvo, 1970), p. 358. See Sergei Eisenstein's *Izbrannye stat'i* (Moscow: Iskusstvo, 1975) or *Film Form: Essays in Film Theory and the Film Sense*, ed. and trans. Jay Leyda (N.Y.: Meridian, 1960), as well as Jacques Aumont, *Montage Eisenstein*, trans. Lee Hildreth, Constance Penley, and Andrew Ross (Bloomington: Indiana University Press, 1987).

34. Eagle, *Formalist Film Theory*, p. 97.

35. Letter to P. A. Viazemsky, Feb. 6, 1823. In Wolff, *Pushkin on Literature*, p. 63.

36. Eagle, *Formalist Film Theory*, p. 33.

37. *Ibid.*

38. Iury Tynianov, "Pushkin," in his *Arkhaisty i novatory*, p. 290.

39. Lacoue-Labarthe and Nancy, *L'Absolu littéraire*, pp. 57–80.

40. *Ibid.*

41. Quoted by Todd in *Fiction and Society*, p. 1.

42. Iu. M. Lotman, "Stsena i zhivopis' kak kodiruiushchie ustroistva kul'turnogo povedenia cheloveka XIX stoletia" and "Teatr i teatral'nost' v stroe kul'tury nachala XIX veka," *Stat'i po tipologii kul'tury* (Tartu: Izdatel'stvo Tartuskogo gosudarstvennogo universiteta, 1973), pp. 74–89 and 42–73.

43. The phrase comes from the title of Stephen Greenblatt's chapter on *Othello*, "The Improvisation of Power," in his influential study *Renaissance Self-Fashioning: From More to Shakespeare* (Chicago: University of Chicago Press, 1980). See also his *Shakespearean Negotiations: The Circulation of Social Energy in Renaissance England* (Berkeley: University of California Press, 1988).

44. I have borrowed the phrase and, I hope, the spirit of his innovative approach from Gregory Freidin's *A Coat of Many Colors: Osip Mandelstam and His Mythologies of Self-Presentation* (Berkeley: University of California Press, 1987).

Chapter 1

1. See Walter Vickery, "Parallelizm v literaturnom razvitii Bairona i Pushkina," in *American Contributions to the Fifth International Congress of Slavists*, vol. 2 (The Hague: Mouton, 1963), pp. 371–401; and my article "Pushkin's Byronic Apprenticeship: A Problem in Cultural Syncretism," *Russian Review*, July 1994.

2. John O. Hayden, *The Romantic Reviewers* (Chicago: University of Chicago Press, 1968); Paul Debreczeny, "The Reception of Pushkin's Poetic Works in the 1820's: A Study of the Critic's Role," *Slavic Review* 28, no. 3 (Sept. 1969): 394–415.

3. Philippe Lacoue-Labarthe and Jean-Luc Nancy, *The Literary Absolute*, trans. Philip Barnard and Cheryl Lester (Albany: State University of New York Press, 1988), p. 8. *L'absolu littéraire. Théorie de la littérature du romantisme allemand* (Paris: Editions du Seuil, 1978) includes the *Athenaeum Fragments*, Friedrich Schlegel's "Entretien sur la poésie," and other primary texts of the group translated into French; only Lacoue-Labarthe and Nancy's theoretical analysis of the Athenaeum is included in the English translation. See also Kathleen Wheeler, ed., *German Aesthetic and Literary Criticism: The Romantic Ironists and Goethe* (Cambridge, Eng.: Cambridge University Press, 1984), pp. 1–73.

4. Jack Undank, preface to Jack Undank and Herbert Josephs, eds., *Diderot: Digression and Dispersion* (Lexington, Ky.: French Forum Publishers, 1984), p. 12. About the influence of the *roman d'analyse*, see L. N.

Vol'pert, *Pushkin i psikhologicheskaia traditsiia vo frantsuzskoi literature* (Tallinn: Izdatel'stvo Eesti raamat, 1980); and Peter Brooks, *The Novel of Worldliness* (Princeton, N.J.: Princeton University Press, 1969). About Pushkin and Sterne, see Viktor Shklovsky, " 'Evgenii Onegin' (Pushkin i Stern)," in *Ocherki po poetike Pushkina* (Berlin: Epokha, 1923), and L. N. Stil'man, "Problemy literaturnykh zhanrov i traditsii v 'Evgenii Onegine' Pushkina. K voprosu perekhoda ot romantizma k realizmu," *American Contributions to the Fourth International Congress of Slavists* (The Hague: Mouton, 1958), pp. 321–65. When in Chapter 5 I turn to the oft-discussed subject of *Eugene Onegin*'s fragmentary structure, I will link it to the eighteenth-century skeptical tradition and Romantic irony, whereas Russian critics find foretastes of nineteenth-century Realism.

5. The chemical-molecular metaphors are Schlegel's and were part of the intellectual jargon of the time. See J. Bernard Cohen's account of the infiltration of political and philosophical thought by the "new nomenclature" of elements, compounds, mixtures, and combustion introduced by Lavoisier's "chemical revolution," *Revolution in Science* (Cambridge, Mass.: Harvard University Press, 1985). See especially chap. 4, "Changing Concepts of Revolution in the Eighteenth Century," and chap. 14, "Lavoisier and the Chemical Revolution."

6. Lacoue-Labarthe and Nancy discuss common features of the Athenaeum's selected genres in *L'Absolu littéraire*, pp. 16–27.

7. Fontenelle, *Entretiens sur la pluralité des mondes*, cited by Undank in the preface to Undank and Josephs, *Diderot*, p. 7.

8. Moi ("the great man") and Lui (the nephew) are the protagonists of Diderot's dialogical masterpiece *Le Neveu de Rameau*. The articles collected in the Undank and Josephs volume provide a convincing case for regarding Diderot as the first theoretician and practitioner of a deliberately fragmentary, antitotalizing, and reader-oriented language. See also Herbert Dieckmann, *Cinq leçons sur Diderot* (Geneva: Librairie E. Droz, 1959); Herbert Josephs, *Diderot's Dialogue of Language and Gesture* (Columbus: Ohio State University Press, 1969); J. J. Mayoux, "Diderot and the Technique of Modern Literature," *Modern Language Review* 31 (Oct. 1936): 518–31; and Franco Venturi, *Jeunesse de Diderot* (Paris: Albert Skira, 1939).

9. Sainte-Beuve's tribute to Diderot in *Le Globe* (Sept. 20, 1830) clearly meant to discover in the wreckage of the neoclassical legacy an unexpected Romantic forefather for French Romanticism—moreover, one whose fragments had to be reassembled by a creative reader: "He, the most synthetic genius of his century, left no monument. Or rather this monument exists, but in fragments; and as a unique and substantial mind is imprinted on all these scattered fragments, the attentive reader, who reads Diderot as he should be read, with sympathy, love, and admiration, easily recomposes what is

dashed off in apparent disorder, reconstructs what is unfinished, and ends by embracing in a single glance . . . the most German of all our heads, in which there are elements of Goethe, Kant, and Schiller all together." Sainte-Beuve, *Oeuvres*, vol. 1 (Paris: Editions le Roi, 1956), pp. 355–69.

10. Undank and Josephs, *Diderot*, p. 8.

11. See Carolyn C. Lougee, *Le Paradis des Femmes: Women, Salons, and Social Stratification in Seventeenth-Century France* (Princeton, N.J.: Princeton University Press, 1976).

12. Undank and Josephs, *Diderot*, p. 12. William Mills Todd III gives the best discussion of the institutionalization of the tastes and practices of the salon in nineteenth-century Russian literary life. See chaps. 1 and 2 of *Fiction and Society in the Age of Pushkin* (Cambridge, Mass.: Harvard University Press, 1986).

13. Denis Diderot, "Lettre sur les sourds et muets," cited in James Doolittle, "Hieroglyph and Emblem in Diderot's 'Lettre sur les sourds et muets,'" *Diderot Studies II*, ed. Otis Fellows and Norman Torrey (Syracuse, N.Y.: Syracuse University Press, 1952), p. 158.

14. See Goethe's brilliant use of the *tableau vivant* convention in *Elective Affinities*, trans. Elizabeth Mayer and Louisea Bogan (South Bend, Ind.: Gateway Editions, 1963), pp. 197–201. See also Jean Rousset, *Forme et signification* (Paris: J. Corti, 1962); Meyer Schapiro, "On Some Problems in the Semiotics of Visual Art: Field and Vehicle in Image-Signs," in A. J. Greimas et al., eds., *Sign, Language, Culture* (The Hague: Mouton, 1970), pp. 487–502; and Laurent Versini, *Le roman épistolaire* (Paris: Presses universitaires de France, 1979).

15. See Mario Praz's evocative account, "The Antiquities of Herculaneum," in his *On Neoclassicism*, trans. Angus Davidson (Evanston, Ill.: Northwestern University Press, 1969), pp. 70–90.

16. "I would say that, each having his own eyes, each sees and recounts differently. . . . I would say that between his ideas there is a choice." "Le Rêve de d'Alembert," in Denis Diderot, *Entretien entre D'Alembert et Diderot. Le Rêve de D'Alembert. Suite de l'entretien* (Paris: Garnier-Flammarion, 1965), p. 163.

17. Tsvetan Todorov, "Choderlos de Laclos et la théorie du récit," in Greimas et al., *Sign, Language, Culture*, pp. 601–12.

18. Harris, *Hermes* (1751), cited in Edward Stankiewicz, "The Dithyramb to the Verb in Eighteenth and Nineteenth Century Linguistics," in Dell Hymes, ed., *Studies in the History of Linguistics* (Bloomington: Indiana University Press, 1974), p. 167.

19. Denis Diderot, "Lettre sur les aveugles," *Oeuvres complètes*, vol. 1, J. Assézat, ed. (Paris: Garnier-frères, 1875), pp. 277–342; "Lettre sur les sourds et muets," *Diderot Studies VII*, ed. Otis Fellows (Syracuse, N.Y.:

Syracuse University Press, 1952). See also Ernst Cassirer, *The Philosophy of Symbolic Forms*, vol. 1 *Language*, trans. Ralph Manheim (New Haven, Conn.: Yale University Press, 1953); Pierre Juliard, *Philosophies of Language in Eighteenth-Century France* (The Hague: Mouton, 1970); Sterling A. Leonard, "The Philosophical Basis of Eighteenth-Century Language Theories," in Donald Hayden ed., *Classics in Linguistics* (London: Owen, 1968); Marlou Switten, "Diderot's Theory of Language as a Medium of Literature," *Romanic Review* 44 (Oct. 1953): 185–96.

20. Diderot, "Lettre sur les sourds et muets," p. 64.

21. Jean-Jacques Rousseau, *Essai sur l'origine des langues*, ed. Angèle Kremier-Marietti (Paris: Aubier Montaigne, 1974), p. 88.

22. Diderot, "Lettre sur les sourds et muets," p. 70.

23. S.v. *devise* in Denis Diderot and Jean le Rond D'Alembert, *L'Encyclopédie ou dictionnaire raisonné des sciences, des arts, et des métiers* (Paris: Briasson, David, Le Breton, et Durand, 1751), photo-offset compact edition (Elmsford, N.Y.: Pergamon Press, 1969), vol. 1, originally pp. 914–15, here p. 943: "It is not necessary that the word have a finished meaning, and the reason is that, before forming a composite with the figure, it must necessarily be divided, and consequently cannot signify everything, nor have the entire meaning that the word and the body have when joined together." See also Doolittle, "Hieroglyph and Emblem," pp. 152–58.

24. Diderot, *Salon de 1767*, in *Oeuvres complètes*, ed. J. Assézat, vol. 11 (Paris: Garnier-Frères, 1875), pp. 254–55; cited in Dieckmann, *Cinq leçons*, pp. 106–7. Cf. Johann Gottfried Herder: "Homer's rhapsodies and Ossian's songs were as it were impromptus, for at that time oratory was known only in impromptu delivery. . . . That is why so many of our recent poems lack that certainty, that exactness, that full contour which comes only from the first spontaneous draft, not from any elaborate later revisions. Our ridiculous versifying would have appeared to Homer and Ossian as the weak scribbles of an apprentice would have appeared to Raphael, or to Apelles, whose barest sketch revealed his mastery." "Extract from a Correspondence on Ossian and the Songs of Ancient Peoples" (1773), trans. Joyce P. Crick, in H. B. Nisbet, ed., *German Aesthetic and Literary Criticism: Winckelmann, Lessing, Hamann, Herder, Schiller, Goethe* (Cambridge, Eng.: Cambridge University Press, 1985), p. 159.

25. See Marc E. Blanchard, "Writing the Museum: Diderot's Bodies in the *Salons*," and Carol Sherman, "Changing Spaces," in Undank and Josephs, *Diderot*, pp. 21–36 and 219–30; and Jack Undank, "Between the Eye and the Word: Eighteenth-Century Readers and Viewers," *Boundary* 2, no. 10 (Spring 1982): 319–41.

26. See the bicentenary volume *Diderot et l'art de Boucher à David. Les Salons: 1759–1781* (Paris: Éditions de la Réunion des Musées nationaux, 1984), which reproduces Diderot's commentaries together with the paint-

ings, as well as articles on them. See in particular Jean Starobinski, "Diderot dans l'espace des peintres," pp. 21–40, and Jacques Chouillet, "Du langage pictural au langage littéraire," pp. 41–54.

27. Letter to P. A. Viazemsky, Feb. 6, 1823. In Tatiana Wolff, ed. and trans., *Pushkin on Literature* (Stanford, Calif.: Stanford University Press, 1986), p. 63.

28. Johann Gottfried Herder, *Briefe zur Beförderung der Humanität*, in his *Sämtliche Werke*, vol. 17 (Berlin: Bernhard Suphan, 1877–1913), p. 151. See also Heidi Owren, *Herders Bildungsprogramm und seine Auswirkungen im 18. und 19. Jahrhundert* (Heidelberg: Carl Winter, 1985), pp. 132–42.

29. Johann Gottfried Herder, "Shakespeare," trans. Joyce P. Crick, in Nisbet, *German Aesthetic*, pp. 161–67.

30. To quote Lacoue-Labarthe and Nancy in full, "The Schlegels' early work . . . gropes vaguely toward a new vision of Antiquity . . . a previously imperceptible hiatus in Greek 'classicism,' the traces of a savage prehistory and terrifying religion, the hidden, nocturnal, mysterious, and mystical face of Greek 'serenity,' an equivocal art barely detached from madness and 'orgiastic' (one of the Schlegels' pet words) fury. In sum, tragic Greece" (*The Literary Absolute*, p. 10). They are referring in particular to Friedrich Schlegel, *Über das Studium der griechischen Poesie* (1795, pub. 1797) (in Wolfdietrich Rasch, ed., *Kritische Schriften* [Munich: Hanser, 1970], pp. 113–230). For a thorough study of the intertwining of classical scholarship and German myths of identity, see Hugh Lloyd-Jones, *Blood for the Ghosts: Classical Influences in the Nineteenth and Twentieth Centuries* (Baltimore, Md.: Johns Hopkins University Press, 1982), which, however, oddly ignores Schlegel.

31. F. Schlegel, "On Incomprehensibility" (originally published in *Athenaeum* in 1800), trans. P. Firchow, in *Lucinde and the Fragments* (Minneapolis: University of Minnesota Press, 1971), pp. 257–71.

32. F. Schlegel, Fragment 24 from "Athenaeum Fragments," trans. P. Firchow, in *ibid.*, p. 164.

33. Jean Baptiste Colbert was Louis XIV's minister of finance and the interior. Quoted in Francis Haskell and Nicholas Penny, *Taste and the Antique: The Lure of Classical Sculpture, 1500–1900* (New Haven, Conn.: Yale University Press, 1981), p. 37.

34. *Ibid.*, pp. 88, 90.

35. *Ibid.*, pp. 37–52, 79–98.

36. For a more detailed account of the activities of the Dilettanti Society, see Richard Jenkyns, *The Victorians and Ancient Greece* (Cambridge, Mass.: Harvard University Press, 1980), pp. 3–5.

37. *Ibid.*, pp. 138–40, and Haskell and Penny, *Taste and the Antique*, pp. 62–73.

38. Jenkyns, *Victorians*, pp. 39–59.

39. Johann Joachim Winckelmann, *History of Ancient Art*, vols. 1–4, trans. G. Henry Lodge (N.Y.: Frederick Ungar Publishing Company, 1968), with Johann Gottfried Herder's essay, "Winckelmann," trans. Alexander Gode, pp. vii–xvii. See also Haskell and Penny, *Taste and the Antique*, pp. 100–105; Johann Wolfgang von Goethe, "Winckelmann," trans. H. B. Nisbet, in Nisbet, *German Aesthetic*, pp. 236–58.

40. Friedrich Schiller, "On Naive and Sentimental Poetry," trans. Julius A. Elias, in Nisbet, *German Aesthetic*, pp. 180–232.

41. Winckelmann, "Thoughts on the Imitation of the Painting and Sculpture of the Greeks" (1755), trans. H. B. Nisbet, in *ibid.*, p. 37.

42. Mario Praz brilliantly demonstrates the connection between Winckelmann's homoeroticism and the rhapsodic style of his sculptural commentary, where "the fixed, static character of Winckelmann's aesthetic ideal lies, essentially, in the transposition into terms of art of an erotic substratum such as his, where an immense sum of energy was employed in a hallucinatory idolization of the beloved object" (p. 41). Even more provocatively, Praz suggests that the ideal coldness and serenity that Winckelmann perceived even in a dramatic group like the Laocoön, which would dictate the way most people regarded classical sculpture in the nineteenth century, was actually a projection of his own repression. See his "Winckelmann," in *Neoclassicism*, pp. 40–69.

43. *Ibid.*

44. *Ibid.*, pp. 52–53.

45. Jenkyns, *Victorians*, pp. 47–54, 220–26.

46. Jean Starobinski, "Revery and Transmutation," in *Jean-Jacques Rousseau: Transparency and Obstruction*, trans. Arthur Goldhammer (Chicago: University of Chicago Press, 1988), pp. 352–64.

47. Haskell and Penny, *Taste and the Antique*, p. 84.

48. The classic example of the meditative ruin poem is Percy Bysshe Shelley's "Ozymandias," excellently analyzed by Anne F. Janowitz in "Parts and Wholes: Romantic and Modernist Fragment Poems" (Ph.D. diss., Stanford University, 1983), pp. 67–97. See her extensive bibliography on this subject.

49. Michel Foucault, *The Order of Things: An Archaeology of the Human Sciences* (New York: Vintage Books, 1970), pp. 226–32.

50. On the sham ruin, see Jenkyns, *Victorians*, pp. 39–59, and Janowitz, "Parts and Wholes," pp. 23–24.

51. The Greek Anthology is the name given to a collection of 4,500 short Greek epigrams by poets of ancient Greece, the Roman Empire, and Byzantium compiled from three sources in the tenth century by Constantinus Cephalus. It was rediscovered in the eighteenth century and translated into modern European languages, causing a stir in German scholarship and

poetry particularly. I have used the English translation of W. R. Paton (Cambridge, Mass.: Harvard University Press, 1980), vols. 1–4. For an analysis of the epigrammatic genre, see Barbara Herrnstein Smith, *Poetic Closure: A Study of How Poems End* (Chicago: University of Chicago Press, 1968), p. 26.

52. Janowitz, *Parts and Wholes*, pp. 24–25. For a discussion of the audience's awareness of the literary hoax's ironic status, see Marjorie Levinson, *The Romantic Fragment Poem* (Chapel Hill: University of North Carolina Press, 1986), pp. 34–54. In light of the proliferation of sham literary ruins, William Wordsworth's "On Epitaphs" probably constituted an attempt to restore to the epitaph its lost "authenticity." See *Wordsworth's Literary Criticism*, ed. W. J. B. Owen (London: Routledge and Kegan Paul, 1974). (The essay has been restored to prominence by Paul de Man's article, "Autobiography as De-facement," in *The Rhetoric of Romanticism* [New York: Columbia University Press, 1984], pp. 67–82.)

53. The popularity and influence of Ossian on nineteenth-century Russian literature is documented by Iu. D. Levin in *Ossian v russkoi literature konets XVIII-pervaia tret' XIX veka* (Leningrad: Nauka, 1980).

54. For a more detailed discussion of European-Russian cultural hybrids, see Iu. M. Lotman, "Stsena i zhivopis' kak kodiruiushchie ustroistva kul'turnogo povedeniia cheloveka XIX stoletiia" and "Teatr i teatral'nost' v stroe kul'tury nachala XIX veka," in *Stat'i po tipologii kul'tury* (Tartu: Tartuskii gosudarstvennyi universitet, 1973), pp. 74–89 and 42–73.

55. See, for example, K. N. Batiushkov's prose piece "Progulka v Akademiiu khudozhestv," in *Opyty v stikhakh i proze*, ed. I. M. Semenko (Moscow: Nauka, 1977), pp. 71–94.

56. This is my recontextualization of Tynianov's seminal study "Arkhaisty i Pushkin," in *Arkhaisty i novatory* (Petrograd: Priboi, 1929), photo-offset reprint (Ann Arbor, Mich.: Ardis, 1985), pp. 87–227.

57. Todd cogently differentiates the opposing cultures of court and *svet* (high society) in chap. 2 of *Fiction and Society*, pp. 45–105. See also Sam Driver, "The Dandy in Pushkin," *Slavic and East European Journal* 29, no. 3 (Fall 1985): 243–57.

58. On the relationship of spirituality and power, see Max Weber, *The Protestant Ethic and the Spirit of Capitalism*, trans. Talcott Parsons (New York: Scribner's, 1958); and Stephen Greenblatt, "The Word of God in the Age of Mechanical Reproduction," in *Renaissance Self-Fashioning: From More to Shakespeare* (Chicago: University of Chicago Press, 1980), pp. 74–114, 115–56.

59. See Stephen Greenblatt, "Power, Sexuality, and Inwardness in Wyatt's Poetry," in *Renaissance Self-Fashioning*, pp. 115–56. The comparison is not as farfetched as it may seem: the richness and dangers of cultural life at

the courts of the Romanovs and the Tudors and the highly personal, charismatic, and arbitrarily authoritarian relationships cultivated by Alexander I and Elizabeth I with poets and other leading figures left similar mythopoetic traces.

60. This is an *idée reçue* of Pushkinism. See even D. P. Iakubovich's thoughtful "Antichnost' v tvorchestve Pushkina," *Vremennik Pushkinskoi kommissii VI* (Moscow: Nauka, 1941), pp. 72–159.

61. "Essays upon Epitaphs," in *The Prose Works of William Wordsworth*, ed. Alexander B. Grosart (London: E. Moxon, 1876), vol. 2, pp. 45–119.

62. Lacoue-Labarthe and Nancy, *The Literary Absolute*, p. 30. The following pages are indebted to Lacoue-Labarthe and Nancy; to Wheeler, *German Aesthetic*; and above all, to Gary J. Handwerk, *Irony and Ethics in Narrative: From Schlegel to Lacan* (New Haven, Conn.: Yale University Press, 1985).

63. Handwerk, *Irony and Ethics*, pp. viii, 18–43. Page numbers in text correspond to this edition.

64. Wayne Booth, *A Rhetoric of Irony* (Chicago: University of Chicago Press, 1971), pp. 13, 28. See Handwerk on "normative irony," pp. 6–10.

65. The phrases are from Cleanth Brooks, "Irony as a Principle of Structure," in *Critical Theory Since Plato*, ed. Hazard Adams (New York: Harcourt Brace Jovanovich, 1971), pp. 1041–48; quoted and discussed by Handwerk in *Irony and Ethics*, p. 1.

66. For the rules governing privacy for the "familiar correspondence" of the early nineteenth century in Russia, see William Mills Todd III, *The Familiar Letter as a Literary Genre in the Age of Pushkin* (Princeton, N.J.: Princeton University Press, 1976).

67. Letter to L. S. Pushkin, Nov. 1824, from Mikhailovskoe. Trans. J. Thomas Shaw, *The Letters of Alexander Pushkin* (Madison: University of Wisconsin Press, 1967), pp. 189–90.

68. See Todd, *Fiction and Society*, chap. 2.

69. Originally, *parabasis* referred to the practice in Greek tragedy of the chorus's "breaking the illusion" by addressing the audience about the action just performed, but Handwerk greatly deepens its implications (*Irony and Ethics*, pp. 37–38, 52).

70. See Handwerk's illuminating discussion of Lacan's *Ecrits* and *Séminaires* and surrounding scholarship: "The Irony of Double Vision: Lacan's Liquidation of the Subject," in *Irony and Ethics*, pp. 125–71.

71. I will refer a number of times to V. K. Kiukhel'beker's important article "O napravlenii nashei poezii, osobenno liricheskoi, v poslednee desiatiletie" (1824), reprinted in *Puteshestvie. Dnevnik. Stat'i*, ed. N. V. Koroleva and V. D. Rak (Leningrad: Nauka, 1979), pp. 453–58.

72. Paul de Man, "The Rhetoric of Temporality," in his *Blindness and*

Insight: Essays in the Rhetoric of Contemporary Criticism (Minneapolis: University of Minnesota Press, 1983), pp. 211–13.

73. Particularly the last two stanzas of "Ia Muzu iunuiu, byvalo," quoted from V. A. Zhukovsky, *Izbrannye sochinenia* (Moscow: Khudozhestvennaia literatura, 1982), p. 131:

Все, что от милых, темных, ясных
Минувших дней я сохранил—
Цветы мечты уединенной
И жизни лучшие цветы,—
Кладу на твой алтарь священный,
О гений чистой красоты!

Не знаю, светлых вдохновений
Когда воротится чреда,—
Но ты знаком мне, чистый Гений!
И светит мне твоя звезда!
Пока еще ее сиянье
Душа умеет различать:
Не умерло очарованье!
Былое сбудется опять. (1822–24)

Everything that from sweet, dark, clear, bygone days I have preserved—flowers of solitary dream and the best flowers of life,—I place on your sacred alter, O Genius of pure beauty! I do not know when the succession of bright inspirations will return,—but you are known to me, pure Genius! And your star shines to me! As long as the soul knows how to distinguish its radiance: enchantment has not died! The past will come to pass again.

The theme of the unpredictable visitations of "genius" reappeared often in Zhukovsky's poetry. See for example "K mimoproletevshemu znakomomu geniiu" (pp. 116–17) and "Tainstvennyi posetitel' " (pp. 131–32).

74. Lidia Ginzburg, *O lirike* (Leningrad: Sovetskii pisatel', 1974), p. 23.

75. See again Greenblatt, "Power, Sexuality, and Inwardness in Wyatt's poetry," in *Renaissance Self-Fashioning*, pp. 115–56.

76. Handwerk, *Irony and Ethics*, p. 137.

77. De Man, "The Rhetoric of Temporality," in *Blindness and Insight*, p. 225.

78. See Todd's discussion of the disintegration of Russian salon discourse in chap. 5 of *Fiction and Society*, where he uses it to illuminate the denouement of Gogol's *Dead Souls*.

79. Pushkin wrote a spate of erotic elegies in Boldino on the eve of his marriage that beg to be regarded as his farewell to the genre. It is hard not to read "Chto v imeni tebe moem," perhaps the last in this series, as his meditation precisely on the bond of language. Found in the autograph album of

Karolina Sobańska, it begins as though in response to a specific "occasion," her request for his autograph, and ends on a wonderfully ironic, reversible piece of prosopopoeia: who is speaking and who is the "I" resurrected by the speech act depends entirely on whether we read the last two lines with quotation marks or without.

80. Writing against periphrastic diction in 1822, Pushkin called precision and brevity "the two virtues of prose. It [prose] demands matter and more matter—without [that] brilliant expressions serve no purpose." This has been turned into the cornerstone of the literal-minded Realistic doctrine of Pushkin, as opposed to the semiotic direction I propose. See Pushkin's "On Prose" in Wolff, *Pushkin on Literature*, p. 43.

Chapter 2

1. Ivan Kireevsky, "Nechto o kharaktere poezii Pushkina," *Moskovskii vestnik*, 1828, pt. 8, no. 6: 183; cited in B. M. Zhirmunsky, *Bairon i Pushkin* (Leningrad: Nauka, 1978), p. 71.

2. Out of the many reasons for this trend in national Pushkin criticism I will mention four: an ideological prejudice against the "egotistical" individualism of Romanticism; a tendency to identify Romanticism with its German and philosophical branches, to which Pushkin's indifference was well known; an inability to read western Romantic texts with nuanced understanding, in other words, as literature, not just as sources and subtexts; and an ignorance of the large body of sophisticated theoretical and comparative criticism that has been devoted to Romanticism in the last two or three decades. An important step in the direction of incorporating Pushkin into the study of comparative literature is made by John Bayley in *Pushkin: A Comparative Commentary* (Cambridge, Eng.: Cambridge University Press, 1971). See also B. Gasparov and I. Paperno, "K opisaniu motivnoj struktury liriki Puskina" (pp. 9–44), L. S. Flejsman, "K opisaniu semantiki 'Cygan'" (pp. 94–109), and other articles in Nils Ake Nilsson, ed., *Russian Romanticism: Studies in the Poetic Codes* (Stockholm: Almqvist and Wiksell, 1979).

3. Stephen Greenblatt, *Renaissance Self-Fashioning: From More to Shakespeare* (Chicago: University of Chicago Press, 1980).

4. D. P. Iakubovich, "Antichnost' v tvorchestve Pushkina," *Vremennik Pushkinskoi kommissii*, vol. 6 (Moscow: Akademia nauk, 1941), pp. 92–93.

5. See for example A. I. Malein, "Pushkin, Avrelii Viktor, i Tatsit," *Pushkin v mirovoi literature* (Leningrad: Gosudarstvennoe izdatel'stvo, 1926), pp. 11–12. Iakubovich hints that this classicizing trend in Pushkinism is "symptomatic" of the most recent period (1937–40), the period of both the Pushkin jubilee and the Stalinist crackdown on everything but literary conservatism.

He cites many more of these "symptomatic" works in his footnote on p. 92 of "Antichnost'."

6. See Francis Haskell and Nicholas Penny, *Taste and the Antique: The Lure of Classical Sculpture, 1500–1900* (New Haven, Conn.: Yale University Press, 1981), pp. 88–90, 212–21, 267–77.

7. Iakubovich, "Antichnost'," pp. 116–20.

8. Iu. M. Lotman, *Aleksandr Sergeevich Pushkin. Biografia pisatel'ia* (Leningrad: Prosveshchenie, 1982), pp. 13–30.

9. Letters to A. A. Bestuzhev and A. A. Del'vig, beginning of June 1825, from Mikhailovskoe. In Tatiana Wolff, ed. and trans., *Pushkin on Literature* (Stanford, Calif.: Stanford University Press, 1986), pp. 147, 149.

10. Letter to P. A. Viazemsky, early Apr. 1824, from Odessa. Trans. J. Thomas Shaw, *The Letters of Alexander Pushkin* (Madison: University of Wisconsin Press, 1967), p. 155.

11. Iakubovich, "Antichnost'"; M. P. Alekseev, "K istochnikam 'Podrazhanii drevnim' Pushkina," in *Pushkin. Sravnitel'no-literaturnye issledovaniiia* (Leningrad: Nauka, 1972), pp. 393–400; Iu. P. Suzdal'skii, "K voprosu ob istochnikakh perevodov A. S. Pushkina iz Anakreonta," *Gertsenovskie chteniia*, vol. 20 (Leningrad: LGPU im. Gertsena, 1967).

12. Iakubovich, "Antichnost'," p. 94.

13. K. N. Batiushkov, "Rech' o vlianii legkoi poezii na iazyk" (1816), in *Opyty v stikhakh i proze*, ed. I. M. Semenko (Moscow: Nauka, 1977), pp. 8–19. My translation.

14. G. A. Gukovskii, *Pushkin i russkie romantiki* (Moscow: Khudozhestvennia literatura, 1965), pp. 213–15.

15. Letter to L. S. Pushkin, Oct. 1822, from Kishinev. Trans. Shaw, *Letters of Alexander Pushkin*, p. 104. Shaw marks "hiatuses" in the manuscript with brackets.

16. N. M. Iazykov, "Pesnia," in *Poety Pushkinskoi pory*, ed. Vladimir Orlov (Moscow: Detskaia literatura, 1972), p. 267.

17. Erica Brendel, "The Poetry of Konstantin Batiushkov" (Ph.D. diss., University of California / Berkeley, 1969), p. 140.

18. "As a literary instrument Slavonic is unquestionably superior to all other European languages: its fate has been exceptionally fortunate. In the eleventh century the lexicon of classical Greek, a veritable treasure-house of harmony, was laid open to it. Greek endowed it with its carefully thought-out laws of syntax, its splendid nuances, its majestic flow of speech, in brief—adopted it, freeing it in this way from time's slow, perfecting processes." "Of M. Lemontey's introduction to the translation of I. A. Krylov's fables," published in *Moskovskii telegraf*, pt. V, no. 17 (1825). Trans. Wolff, *Pushkin on Literature*, p. 122.

19. S. S. Uvarov, "O Grecheskoi antologii," in *Sochineniia K. N. Batiush-*

kova, ed. L. N. Maikov and V. I. Santov (St. Petersburg: V. S. Balashev, 1885), vol. 1.2, pp. 423–33.

20. *Ibid.*, p. 424.

21. That Greek antiquity was a preoccupation of certain nineteenth-century homosexual circles, indeed almost a code word, is suggested by Richard Jenkyns in "The Consequences of Sculpture," *The Victorians and Ancient Greece* (Cambridge, Mass.: Harvard University Press, 1980), pp. 132–54. This certainly seems to apply to Uvarov, whose homosexual *kruzhok* was well known. See Simon Karlinsky, *The Sexuality of Nikolai S. Gogol* (Chicago: University of Chicago, 1976), pp. 56–58.

22. Uvarov, "O Grecheskoi antologii," p. 423.

23. Johann Gottfried Herder, *Briefe zur Beförderung der Humanität*, in his *Sämtliche Werke*, vol. 17 (Berlin: Bernhard Suphan, 1877–1913), p. 151.

24. Anthony Wilden, trans. and comm., "Lacan and the Discourse of the Other," in Jacques Lacan, *Speech and Language in Psychoanalysis* (Baltimore, Md.: Johns Hopkins University Press, 1968), p. 174.

25. *Ibid.*, p. 117.

26. M. H. Abrams, *Natural Supernaturalism* (New York: W. W. Norton, 1971), p. 375. Further citations from this source are made by page number in the text.

27. Samuel Coleridge, *Biographia literaria*, ed. J. Shawcross (Oxford: Oxford University Press, 1907), vol. 1, pp. 59–60. Quoted in Abrams, *Natural Supernaturalism*, pp. 379–80.

28. Friedrich Schiller, "On Naive and Sentimental Poetry," trans. Julias A. Elias, in H. B. Nisbet, ed., *German Aesthetic and Literary Criticism: Winckelmann, Lessing, Hamann, Herder, Schiller, Goethe* (Cambridge, Eng.: Cambridge University Press, 1985), pp. 189–90.

29. See also Efim Etkind, "'Liricheskaia epigramma' kak zhanrovaia forma," in *Forma kak soderzhanie* (Würzburg: Jal-Verlag, 1977), pp. 53–54.

30. Monika Greenleaf, "Lost in Translation: The Subject of Batiushkov's Poetry," in Monika Greenleaf and Stephen Moeller-Sally, eds., *Cultural Vectors and the Subject's Space: Russia's Golden Age Revisualized* (forthcoming).

31. Savely Senderovich, *Aleteiia. Elegiia Pushkina "Vospominanie" i problemy ego poetiki*, Wiener Slawistischer Almanach Sonderband 8 (Vienna: A. Hansen-Löve, 1982), pp. 132–37.

32. V. K. Kiukhel'beker, "O napravlenii nashei poezii, osobenno liricheskoi, v poslednee desiatiletie," in *Puteshestvie. Dnevnik. Stat'i* (Leningrad: Nauka, 1979), p. 457.

33. See Roberta Reeder, "The Greek Anthology and Its Influence on Pushkin's Poetic Style," *Canadian-American Slavic Studies* 10, no. 2 (Summer): 205–27. I use her translation (p. 208) of Pushkin's "O poeticheskom sloge" (11, 73).

34. Letter to P. A. Viazemsky, Dec. 1–8, 1823, from Odessa. In Wolff, *Pushkin on Literature*, p. 75.

35. V. B. Sandomirskaia, "'Otryvok' v poezii Pushkina dvadtsatykh godov," *Pushkin issledovaniia i materialy*, vol. 9 (Leningrad: Nauka, 1979), pp. 69–82; and "Iz istorii Pushkinskogo tsikla 'Podrazhaniia drevnim' (Pushkin i Batiushkov)," *Vremennik Pushkinskoi kommissii* (Leningrad: Nauka, 1975), pp. 15–30.

36. The earliest pieces, written still in St. Petersburg in 1819, "Dorida" and "Doride," were published in *Nevskii zritel'* in 1820, while "Muza" was actually published the year it was written, 1821, in *Syn otechestva*. Although Pushkin conducted a lively correspondence with Bestuzhev about getting his "anthological fragments" past the censorship, most of the poems found their way into print only in 1824 or 1825. "Nereida" and "Redeet oblakov letuchaia griada," written in 1820, were published in *Poliarnia zvezda* for 1824, the former with a large censorial excision; "Krasavitsa pered zerkalom" (1821) in *Sorevnovatel' prosveshchenia* in 1825; "Zemlia i more" and "Dioneia" (both 1821) in *Novosti literatury* in 1825; while "Primety" (1821) was published for the first time only in 1826. Commentary to A. S. Pushkin, *Polnoe sobranie sochinenii v desiati tomakh*, 4th ed. (Leningrad: Nauka, 1977), vol. 2.

37. Sandomirskaia, "Iz istorii Pushkinskogo tsikla," p. 17.

38. André Chénier, *Oeuvres complètes*, ed. Henri de Latouche (Paris: Bibliothèque-Charpentier, 1907).

39. Neil Fraistat, *The Poem and the Book: Interpreting Collections of Romantic Poetry* (Chapel Hill: University of North Carolina Press, 1985).

40. Chénier, *Oeuvres*, pp. 224–331.

41. Sandomirskaia, in "'Otryvok' v poezii Pushkina," p. 70, writes, "This stage of preliminary publication in fragments, under the heading 'A fragment from,' was traversed by all of Pushkin's narrative poems (except 'Angelo') and all the chapters of his novel *Eugene Onegin*."

42. A comparable example of modern self-fashioning through the traditional topoi of erotic elegy and epigram is Johann Wolfgang von Goethe's *Roman Elegies and Venetian Epigrams*, trans. and ed. L. R. Lind (Lawrence: University Press of Kansas, 1974).

43. See, for example, L. Ia. Ginzburg's discussion of Pushkin's generic system of styles and personae, in "Pushkin i liricheskii geroi russkogo romantizma," *Pushkin issledovania i materialy*, vol. 4 (Leningrad: Nauka, 1962), pp. 140–45.

44. Chénier, "La Jeune Captive," in *Oeuvres*, p. 267. See Sandomirskaia, "Iz istorii Pushkinskogo tsikla," p. 21.

45. Reeder points out somewhat comparable examples in both the Greek Anthology and André Chénier.

46. Chénier, *Oeuvres*, pp. 224–31.

47. Compare Sappho's poem on the same theme in Guy Davenport, trans., *Archilochos, Sappho, Alkman: Three Lyric Poets of the Seventh Century B.C.* (Berkeley: University of California Press, 1980), p. 81: "And you O Kika weave with your slender hands / A crown of flowers and dill into those lovely curls, / For she comes first before the serendipitous Graces / Who comes in flowers. The uncrowned they turn away."

48. See Lidia Ginzburg, *O lirike* (Leningrad: Sovetskii pisatel', 1974), p. 29, on the "poetics of recognition" in the lyric poetry of the 1820's.

49. K. N. Batiushkov, "Iz Grecheskoi antologii," no. 8, in *Opyty v stikhakh i proze*, ed. I. M. Semenko (Moscow: Nauka, 1977), p. 346.

50. W. R. Paton, trans., *The Greek Anthology* (Cambridge, Mass.: Harvard University Press, 1980), vol. 1, bk. 5, no. 250.

51. *Ibid.*, bk. 5, no. 232.

52. Paul de Man, "The Intentional Structure of the Romantic Image," in his *Rhetoric of Romanticism* (New York: Columbia University Press, 1984), p. 13.

53. David Wellbery states that Romantic texts tend to mythologize "the sponsoring source of the work" and to try to kindle a corresponding "sense of the presence of this same spiritual source" in the reader. See his "E. T. A. Hoffmann and Romantic Hermeneutics: An Interpretation of Hoffmann's 'Don Juan,'" *Studies in Romanticism* 19 (Winter 1980): 455.

54. Kiukhel'beker, "O napravlenii nashei poezii," pp. 456–57.

55. *Ibid.*, p. 458.

56. *Ibid.*

57. B. Tomashevsky, "Pushkin i Batiushkov," in *Batiushkov, K. N. Stikhotvorenia* (Moscow: Sovetskii pisatel', 1936), pp. 5–49.

58. Senderovich, *Aleteiia*, p. 138.

59. See John W. Draper, *The Funeral Elegy and the Rise of English Romanticism* (New York: New York University Press, 1929); and Abbie Findlay Potts, *The Elegiac Mode: Poetic Form in Wordsworth and Other Elegists* (Ithaca, N.Y.: Cornell University Press, 1967).

60. See Senderovich, *Aleteiia*, pp. 110–19, for a compilation of eighteenth-century definitions of the elegy.

61. *Ibid.*, pp. 62–63.

62. Peter M. Sacks, *The English Elegy* (Baltimore, Md.: Johns Hopkins Press, 1985), pp. 19–20. Further citations are noted by page number in the text.

63. St. 58, line 14 (in Pushkin, *Polnoe sobranie sochinenii*, vol. 6).

64. On the episode of the "fort/da" game, Sacks (*The English Elegy*, p. 333) cites the accounts of Sigmund Freud, *Beyond the Pleasure Principle*, trans. James Strachey (London: Hogarth Press, 1950); and Jacques Lacan,

"The Function and Field of Speech and Language in Psychoanalysis," in *Ecrits: A Selection*, trans. Alan Sheridan (N.Y.: Norton, 1977), pp. 30–113.

65. The rough draft of a letter to A. N. Raevsky, written between Oct. 15 and 22, 1823, in Odessa, refers to a convoluted epistolary intrigue involving Raevsky and Madame Sobańska, but announces, "My passion has cooled considerably and . . . in the meantime I have fallen in love with somebody else." Pushkin would renew his affair with Sobańska in 1828 in St. Petersburg and eventually address two of his most famous love poems to her, "Ia vas liubil" and "Chto v imeni tebe moem?" See Roman Jakobson, "The Police Accomplice Sung by Puskin and Mickiewicz," in *Puskin and His Sculptural Myth* (The Hague: Mouton, 1975), pp. 76–86; and Anna Akhmatova, "Dve novye povesti Pushkina," in her "Neizdannye zametki Anny Akhmatovoi o Pushkine," *Voprosy literatury*, 1970, no. 1: 176–87.

66. V. Veresaev, *Pushkin v zhizni*, 1st ed. (Moscow: Sovetskii pisatel', 1936), vol. 1, p. 239.

67. See Lilja Saava, *The Roman Elegists' Attitude to Women* (Helsinki: Suomalairen Tiede akatemia, 1965).

68. P. V. Annenkov, *Pushkin v Aleksandrovskuiu epokhu*, quoted in Veresaev, *Pushkin v zhizni*, p. 222.

69. P. P. Viazemsky, quoted in Veresaev, *Pushkin v zhizni*, p. 230.

70. Evariste Parny, *Les désguisements de Vénus. Tableaux imités du grec*, in *Oeuvres de Parny, Elegiés et poésies diverses* (Paris: Garnier-frères, 1862), pp. 296–98.

71. See Pushkin's letter to Alexander N. Raevsky, Oct. 15–22, 1823, from Odessa (rough draft, in French). Trans. Shaw, *Letters of Alexander Pushkin*, pp. 138–39.

72. Kiukhel'beker, "O napravlenii nashei poezii," p. 456.

73. In "Kamennyi gost'," the commander whose statue is so imposing is described by Don Juan as having been in reality too small to reach his own (statue's) nose.

74. Parny, *Oeuvres*, p. 55.

75. I am drawing, with her permission, on Jenny Hixon's unpublished paper "'Iz glubiny sobstvennoi dushi': Pushkin's Translation of Parny in 'Prozerpina'" (1989).

76. Parny, *Oeuvres*, pp. 296–98.

77. Mary M. Innes, trans., *The Metamorphosis of Ovid* (London: Penguin, 1955), bk. 5, p. 127, lines 421–25.

78. *Ibid.*, bk. 11, pp. 262–63, lines 599, 609–11, 626.

79. S. S. Uvarov's *Essai sur les mystères d'Eleusis* (Paris: Imprimerie royale, 1816) must have been read and discussed in the Grecophile circles frequented by the young Pushkin in St. Petersburg. Uvarov was obviously conversant with the fabulous flowering of interpretive writing on the language

of myth, particularly in late-eighteenth-century German scholarship, a good sampling of which is given in Burton Feldman and Robert D. Richardson, eds., *The Rise of Modern Mythology, 1680–1860* (Bloomington: Indiana University Press, 1972), for example Antoine Pernety, *Egyptian and Greek Fable Unveiled*; Christian Gottlob Heyne, *An Interpretation of the Language of Myths*; Friedrich Schlegel, "Talk on Mythology;" F. W. J. Schelling, *Introduction to the Philosophy of Mythology*; and the famous work by Richard Payne Knight, *A Discourse on the Worship of Priapus*, originally published in 1786 and republished in a watered-down version, *The Symbolical Language of Ancient Art and Mythology*, in 1818. It is difficult to imagine such books not being discussed by the more learned members of the Uvarov and A. N. Olenin *kruzhki*. See also Harold Segel, "Classicist and Classical Antiquity in Eighteenth- and Early-Nineteenth-Century Russian Literature," in J. Garrard, ed., *Eighteenth-Century Russia* (Oxford: Clarendon, 1973); and Marilyn Butler, *Romantics, Rebels and Reactionaries: English Literature and its Background, 1760–1830* (Oxford: Oxford University Press, 1981), pp. 130–32.

80. Innes, *Metamorphoses of Ovid*, bk. 5, p. 129, lines 505–9.

81. C. Kerenyi, "Kore," in C. G. Jung and C. Kerenyi, eds., *Essays on a Science of Mythology*, trans. R. F. C. Hull (New York: Pantheon Books, 1964), pp. 109, 125–29.

82. Joseph Campbell, *The Masks of God: Occidental Mythology* (New York: Viking Press, 1964), pp. 177, 234.

83. C. G. Jung, "Introduction" and "Psychological Aspects of the Kore," in Jung and Kerenyi, *Essays*, pp. 83 and 157–59.

84. Sacks, *English Elegy*, pp. 20, 26–31.

85. James Hillman, *The Dream and the Underworld* (N.Y.: Harper and Row, 1979), pp. 48–57.

86. Hixon, "Pushkin's Translation of Parny," p. 11.

87. Sacks, *English Elegy*, pp. 16–17.

88. Erich Neumann, *The Great Mother: An Analysis of the Archetype*, trans. Ralph Manheim (New York: Pantheon Books, 1955), p. 303.

89. Quoted in Kerenyi, "Kore," in Jung and Kerenyi, *Essays*, p. 114.

90. The journey of initiation is discussed by Hillman, *Dream and Underworld*, pp. 48–57; Neumann, *Great Mother*, pp. 294–98; and Mircea Eliade, *Mephistopheles and the Androgyne*, trans. M. J. Cohen (New York: Sheed and Ward, 1965), pp. 97–102.

91. Jung, "Psychological Aspects of the Kore," in Jung and Kerenyi, *Essays*, p. 173.

92. Pushkin's prophet in "Prorok" also submits to cleaving and emasculation in exchange for shamanistic empowerment.

93. Sacks, *English Elegy*, p. 2.

94. Hixon, "Pushkin's Translation of Parny," pp. 13–14.

95. Letter to Viazemsky, second half of Nov. 1825, trans. Shaw, *Letters of Pushkin*, pp. 263–64.

96. See B. Tomashevsky, "Kleopatra," in *Pushkin*, bk. 2 (Moscow: Izdatel'stvo Akademii nauk, 1961), pp. 55–64.

Chapter 3

1. "Imaginary conversation with Alexander I" (draft), in Tatiana Wolff, ed. and trans., *Pushkin on Literature* (Stanford, Calif.: Stanford University Press, 1986), p. 111.

2. My discussion of Orientalist discourse is much indebted to Edward Said's study *Orientalism* (New York: Pantheon Books, 1979). Said seems to be largely unaware of the subject's Russian ramifications (see p. 1).

3. See Denis Davydov's fascinating and long-suppressed memoir, *Zapiski Denisa Vasil'evicha Davydova, v Rossii tsensuroiu ne propushchennye* (begun in 1828 and first published in Brussels in 1863), especially "Anekdoty o raznykh litsakh, preimushchestvenno ob Aleksee Petroviche Ermolove," in *Sochineniia* (Moscow: Gosudarstvennoe izdatel'stvo khudozhestvennoi literatury, 1962), pp. 471–516. See also Iurii Tynianov's novel on the subject, *Smert' Vazir-Mukhtara* (Kishinev: Literatura artistike, 1984).

4. See Leonid Grossman, "Lermontov i kul'tury vostoka," *Literaturnoe nasledvstvo*, vols. 43–44 (Moscow: Nauka, 1941), pp. 673–744 (reprinted in his *Ispoved' odnogo evreia* [Jerusalem: Ia. Vaiskopf, 1987], pp. 184–262); N. N. Kholmukhamedova, "Vostok v russkoi poezii 30-kh godov XIX v.: V. K. Kiukhel'beker i M. Iu. Lermontov," *Izvestiia Akademii nauk*, Seriia literatury i iazyka, vol. 44, no. 1 (1985): 57–79.

5. See Albert Resis, "Russophobia and the 'Testament' of Peter the Great, 1812–1980," *Slavic Review* 44, no. 4 (Winter 1985): 681–85.

6. Katya Hokanson defines the terms of this problem in her excellent study "Russian Orientalism" (Master's thesis, Stanford University, 1988), pp. 1–32, 79–89.

7. Quoted by Said, *Orientalism*, p. 100.

8. *Ibid.*, p. 51.

9. See Victor Hugo, "Preface" to *Les Orientales*, in *Odes et ballades. Les Orientales* (Paris: Garnier-Flammarion, 1968), pp. 319–23.

10. Michel Foucault, *The Order of Things: An Archaeology of the Human Sciences* (New York: Vintage Books, 1970), quoted in Anne F. Janowitz, "Parts and Wholes: Romantic and Modernist Fragment Poems" (Ph.D. diss., Stanford University, 1983), p. 43.

11. Said, *Orientalism*, pp. 103, 32–78.

12. *Ibid.*, pp. 62, 81–86.

13. *Ibid.*, pp. 123, 125, 129, 132.

14. See Hokanson, "Russian Orientalism," pp. 33–49, and Louis Pedrotti, *Józef-Julian Sękowski: The Genesis of a Literary Alien* (Berkeley: University of California Press, 1965).

15. Said, *Orientalism*, pp. 1–2.

16. *Ibid.*, p. 96.

17. *Ibid.*

18. See Steven Marcus, *The Other Victorians: A Study of Sexuality and Pornography in Mid-Nineteenth-Century England* (New York: Basic Books, 1967), pp. 197–216, and Bram Dijkstra, *Idols of Perversity: Fantasies of Feminine Evil in Fin-de-Siecle Culture* (Oxford: Oxford University Press, 1986).

19. Said, *Orientalism*, p. 106.

20. Samuel Taylor Coleridge, "Kubla Khan," in *Christabel, Kubla Khan, A Vision: The Pains of Sleep* (London: John Murray, 1816).

21. See Janowitz, "Parts and Wholes," pp. 98–141; Elisabeth Schneider, *Coleridge, Opium and "Kubla Khan"* (Chicago: University of Chicago Press, 1953); John Livingston Lowes, *The Road to Xanadu: A Study in the Ways of the Imagination* (Boston: Houghton Mifflin, 1930); Marjorie Levinson, *The Romantic Fragment Poem* (Chapel Hill: University of North Carolina Press, 1986).

22. Cited in Brian Wilkie, *Romantic Poets and Epic Tradition* (Madison: University of Wisconsin Press, 1965), pp. 23, 191.

23. See Philip W. Martin, *Byron: A Poet Before His Public* (Cambridge, Eng.: Cambridge University Press, 1982), pp. 21–29.

24. Edmund Burke's treatise *A Philosophical Enquiry into the Origin of Our Ideas of the Sublime and Beautiful* (ed. James T. Boulton [London: Routledge and Kegan Paul, 1958]) established "sublime" as a literary term much discussed throughout the late eighteenth century and Romantic period. See Thomas Weiskel, *The Romantic Sublime: Studies in the Structure and Psychology of Transcendence* (Baltimore, Md.: Johns Hopkins University Press, 1986), pp. 3–33.

25. Letter to P. A. Viazemsky, Jan. 2, 1822, from Kishinev. Trans. J. Thomas Shaw, *The Letters of Alexander Pushkin* (Madison: University of Wisconsin Press, 1967), p. 89.

26. Like most Soviet commentators, Lotman explains Byron's framing practice in a "monological" way, to contrast it with Pushkin's dialogism. See "K strukture dialogicheskogo teksta v poemakh Pushkina (problema avtorskikh primechanii k tekstu)," *Pushkin i ego sovremenniki, Uchenye zapiski*, vol. 434 (Pskov: Pskovskii gosudarstvennyi universitet, 1970), pp. 103–10.

27. See Hokanson, "Russian Orientalism," pp. 79–89.

28. Marcus, *The Other Victorians.*

29. See Leonid Grossman, "U istokov 'Bakhchisaraiskogo fontana,'"

Pushkin issledovaniia i materialy, vol. 3 (Leningrad: Nauka, 1960), pp. 49–100.

30. Rose Bradwardine and Flora McIvor in *Waverley* and Rebecca and Rowena in *Ivanhoe* are two such famous pairs. See Judith Wilt, *Secret Leaves: The Novels of Walter Scott* (Chicago: University of Chicago Press, 1985), pp. 26–36.

31. Two studies pursue a more purely feminist approach: Stephanie Sandler, "The Two Women of Bakhchisarai," *Canadian Slavonic Papers* 29, nos. 2 & 3 (June–Sept. 1987): 241–54; Joe Andrew, "'Not Daring to Desire': Male / Female and Desire in Narrative in Pushkin's 'Bakhchisaraiskii fontan,'" *Russian Literature* 24 (1988): 259–74.

32. See Sandler, "Two Women of Bakhchisarai," pp. 247–48, on the goldfish bowl image. It is frequently encountered in Matisse's oriental paintings.

33. *Ibid.*, pp. 248–50.

34. See Pushkin's letters of Jan. 12, Feb. 8, and June 29, 1824 (Wolff, *Pushkin on Literature*, pp. 80–81, 84, 93), in which he so pointedly castigated A. A. Bestuzhev for printing "the very verses which I asked you not to publish" and possibly betraying the identity of the young woman who had inspired the writing of "Bakhchisaraiskii fontan" that one wonders whether he wasn't intentionally attracting attention to the autobiography behind the suspension dots, à la Byron. See my article "Pushkin's Byronic Apprenticeship: A Problem in Cultural Syncretism," *Russian Review*, July 1994, and Grossman, "U istokov 'Bakhchisaraiskogo fontana.'"

35. Letters to P. A. Viazemsky of Oct. 14, 1823, from Odessa, and late Mar. / early Apr. 1825, from Mikhailovskoe. Trans. in Wolff, *Pushkin on Literature*, pp. 70–71, 141.

36. Letter to Viazemsky of Nov. 4, 1823, from Odessa. Trans. in *ibid.*, pp. 70–71.

37. Lotman, "K strukture dialogicheskogo teksta," pp. 103–10.

38. Pushkin, "On Prose" (1822 draft), in Wolff, *Pushkin on Literature*, p. 43.

39. Letter to P. A. Viazemsky, Oct. 14, 1823, from Odessa. Trans. in Shaw, *Letters of Alexander Pushkin*, p. 137.

40. More typically, he fantasized to Viazemsky from his exile in 1826, "Where is my poet? . . . He has escaped to Paris and will never return to accursed Russia" (14, 56). In January 1830 he even requested Benckendorff's permission to go to China.

41. "Puteshestvie V.L.P.," 1836, unpublished note on I. I. Dmitriev's poem of the same title. Trans. in Wolff, *Pushkin on Literature*, p. 403. Original in vol. 12, p. 93 of the collected works.

42. "Cherez nedeliu budu v Parizhe nepremenno . . ." under "Dramatic Fragments" (7, 251–53).

43. For more on the relation between the two works, see Ia. L. Levkovich,

"Kavkazskii dnevnik Pushkina," *Pushkin issledovania i materialy*, vol. 11 (Leningrad: Nauka, 1983): pp. 19–26.

44. "In Stavropol I saw at the sky's edge the clouds that so struck my eyes exactly nine years ago. They were still the same, in the same place. These are the snowy peaks of the Caucasian chain" (8, 1, 447).

45. Although the itineraries of his two sets of travels were quite different, Pushkin relates their landscapes, sometimes quite directly: "Asian structures and bazaars reminded me of Kishinev" (8, 1, 456).

46. See Michael Seidel, *Exile and the Narrative Imagination* (New Haven, Conn.: Yale University Press, 1986); Victor Brombert, *The Romantic Prison: The French Tradition* (Princeton, N.J.: Princeton University Press, 1978); and Paul M. Austin, "The Exotic Prisoner in Russian Romanticism," *Russian Literature* 16 (1984): 217–74.

47. The suppression of *Boris Godunov*, a multiplied censorship, retrospective investigations of "André Chénier" and "Gavriliada," the financial as well as critical failure of "Poltava," journalistic harassment by literary critics in the pay of the Third Section, and police surveillance of his movements and social contacts all revealed the disadvantages lurking in Pushkin's "special relationship" with the tsar and Nicholaevan society. His personal life in 1828, his "wildest year," exhibited a similar alternation between freedom and restriction, featuring a series of simultaneous romances, courtships, and abrupt disentanglements enacted on the stage of high society. See Iu. M. Lotman, *Aleksandr Sergeevich Pushkin. Biografia pisatel'ia* (Leningrad: Prosveshchenie, 1982); V. E. Vatsuro and M. I. Gillel'son, *Skvoz' umstvennye plotiny* (Moscow: Kniga, 1972); and A. A. Akhmatova, "Neizdannye zametki o Pushkine," *Voprosy literatury*, 1970, no. 1: 196.

48. The passport restrictions listed in *Polnoe sobranie zakonov rossiiskoi imperii* for the 1820's and 1830's, for example, apply almost exclusively to merchants, Jews, and foreign residents. For a structural analysis of the nobleman's options, see Iu. M. Lotman, "The Poetics of Everyday Behavior in Eighteenth-Century Culture," in Alexander D. Nakhimovsky and Alice Stone Nakhimovsky, eds., *The Semiotics of Russian Cultural History* (Ithaca, N.Y.: Cornell University Press, 1985), pp. 67–94; and Seymour Becker, *Nobility and Privilege in Late Imperial Russia* (Dekalb: Northern Illinois University Press, 1985), pp. 28–31.

49. Laurence Sterne, *A Sentimental Journey Through France and Italy*, ed. Graham Petrie (Baltimore, Md.: Johns Hopkins University Press, 1974). See Seidel on Sterne as "expatriated adventurer" in *Exile and Narrative Imagination*, pp. 107–30.

50. Victor W. Turner, *The Ritual Process: Structure and Anti-Structure* (Chicago: Aldine, 1969), p. 95; see also pp. 94, 96–130.

51. See excerpts from contemporaries' memoirs about Pushkin's dress,

violations of social and military decorum, and laughter en route to Arzrum, particularly those of N. B. Potoksky and Prince E. O. Palavandov in V. Veresaev, *Pushkin v zhizni* (Moscow, 1936), pp. 10–12.

52. See Hokanson, "Russian Orientalism," pp. 56–76.

53. *Ibid.*, p. 65.

54. See V. L. Komarovich's "K voprosu o zhanre 'Puteshestvia v Arzrum,'" *Vremennik Pushkinskoi komissii*, vol. 3 (Leningrad: Nauka, 1937), pp. 326–38. He identifies as the generic model for Pushkin's work Chateaubriand's "journey of a poet," the *Itinéraire de Paris à Jérusalem et de Jérusalem à Paris*, where he avowed his aim to research the background of his poetic work in progress, *Les Martyres* (p. 53 of Chateaubriand, *Itinéraire de Paris à Jérusalem* [Paris: Garnier-Flammarion, 1968]).

55. Chateaubriand finds a Greek translation of his own *Atala* on the roadside in an equally improbable manner. Other parodistic moments such as the citation of Horace's Ode 14 in book 2 ("Eheu fugaces, Postume"), the apostrophe about Catholic missionaries, the rush to overtake the army, the "civilized European's" resorting to a stick to reinforce his wishes, and then being mistaken for a doctor are cited by Komarovich in "K voprosu," pp. 334–37.

56. "Monastyr' na Kazbeke" (1829) was one of the poems about his journey that Pushkin published in 1832. See N. V. Izmailov, "Liricheskie tsykly v poezii Pushkina kontsa 20-30-kh godov," in *Ocherki tvorchestva Pushkina* (Leningrad: Nauka, 1975), pp. 213–69; and Komarovich, "K voprosu."

57. Iu. M. Tynianov, "O 'Puteshestvii v Arzrum,'" *Vremennik Pushkinskoi Kommissii*, vol. 2 (Moscow: Nauka, 1936), pp. 56–73; Piotr Bitsilli, "Puteshestvie v Arzrum," in E. V. Anichkov, ed., *Belgradskii pushkinskii sbornik* (Belgrade: Slovo, 1937), pp. 247–64; V. L. Komarovich, "K voprosu," pp. 326–38; and Krystyna Pomorska, "Structural Peculiarities in 'Puteshestvie v Arzrum,'" in *Alexander Pushkin Symposium*, ed. Andrej Kodjak and Kiril Taranovsky (New York: New York University Press, 1976), pp. 119–29. For an approach more oriented to traditional Realism, see Anthony Olcott, "Parody as Realism: The *Journey to Arzrum*," *Russian Literary Triquarterly* 10 (Fall 1974): 245–59; G. P. Makogonenko, *Tvorchestvo A. S. Pushkina v 1830-ye gody (1833–1836)* (Leningrad: Khudozhestvennia literatura, 1982), pp. 256–346. A prose genre analysis is provided by T. Roboli, "Literatura puteshestvii," *Russkaia proza*, ed. Boris Eikhenbaum and Iurii Tynianov (The Hague: Mouton, 1963 reprint), translated by Ray Parrott in *Russian Prose* (Ann Arbor, Mich.: Ardis, 1985), pp. 45–66, and more recently by Andrew Wachtel in "Voyages of Escape, Voyages of Discovery: Transformations of the Travelogue," in Boris Gasparov, Robert P. Hughes, and Irina Paperno, eds., *Cultural Mythologies of Russian Modernism: From the Golden Age to the Silver Age* (Berkeley: University of California Press, 1992), pp. 128–49.

58. I have borrowed the notion of the "notes of a gentleman" from Tynianov, who first pointed out the parodistic thrust of the preface in "O 'Puteshestvii v Arzrum.'" Not only had satirical intent been attributed to Pushkin by the French, but Russian critics, F. V. Bulgarin and N. I. Nadezhdin among them, had bewailed the non-epic results of Pushkin's trip to the front (in *Severnaia pchela*, 1830, no. 35 and *Vestnik Evropy*, 1830, no. 2, respectively). Hence Pushkin's reaction in the preface: "To arrive at the front with the idea of singing its future exploits [*vospevat' budushchie podvigi*] would be for me, on the one hand, too arrogant, and on the other—too undignified." His rejection of the Chateaubriand conception of a "poet's journey" is also slightly indirect: "*To search for inspiration* always seemed to me a silly and awkward eccentricity: inspiration cannot be sought; it must itself find the poet." In the end he claims to have found what he, as a "man in no need of patronage," desired: simply a "cordial and hospitable" reception (8.1, 443–44).

59. After several attempts, Pushkin was granted permission to publish a journal in 1836. A literary quarterly severely limited in scope and spirit by a veto on political topics and current events, it was also surrounded by the shades of Pushkin's many uncensored, unpublished projects. "Call it Arion or Orion—I love names that make no sense," Pushkin instructed P. A. Pletnev (in his letter of Oct. 11, 1835, from Mikhailovskoe; trans. in Shaw, *Letters of Alexander Pushkin*, p. 728). He opted in the end for *The Contemporary*, an ironic choice for a journal permitted to touch on anything but what was going on in Russia. About Pushkin's problems with the censorship, see Vatsuro and Gillel'son, *Skvoz' umstvennye plotiny*, pp. 216–72. About "Journey to Arzrum" as a kind of graveyard for dead projects, see my "Illegibility in Pushkin's 'Puteshestvie v Arzrum,'" in Andrej Kodjak and Stephen Rudy, eds., *Pushkin Symposium III* (N.Y.: New York University Press, forthcoming).

60. *Biblioteka dlia chteniia*, vol. 10, p. 63. Cited on p. 210 of Leonid Grossman's discussion of Orientalist publications in "Lermontov i kul'tury vostoka" (in *Ispoved'*, pp. 209–14). See also Pedrotti, *Józef-Julian Sękowski*, pp. 49–68.

61. Said, *Orientalism*, pp. 80–86. See also Paul Carter's argument against Anglo-Australian historicism and geography in *The Road to Botany Bay: An Exploration of Landscape and History* (New York: Alfred A. Knopf, 1988), pp. 34–68.

62. P. I. Chaadaev, *Lettres philosophiques adressées à une dame* (Paris: Librairie de Cinq Continents, 1970). The first letter was written and privately circulated in 1829.

63. Pushkin's review "O vtorom tome 'Istorii russkogo naroda' Polevogo" (11, 127).

64. Said gives many examples of Europe's fragmentary practices of display in *Orientalism*, pp. 123–66.

65. *Ibid.*, pp. 170–78.

66. Byron did not need to travel to Russia to "suppose [Juan] then at Petersburgh" and satirize "Moscow's climes" and Catherine's court. See *Don Juan*, can. 11, st. 42 to can. 12, st. 49.

67. See Tynianov's admirable analysis of "Journey to Arzrum" as a covert satire on Paskevich's exploits in "O 'Puteshestvii v Arzrum,'" pp. 63–72. See also his historical novel *Smert' Vazir-Mukhtara* for a suggestive depiction of the cult of Ermolov among Pushkin's contemporaries.

68. "A graceful solitary minaret bears witness to the existence of a vanished settlement . . . from which the voice of the mullah no longer resounds. There I found several unfamiliar names scratched on the bricks by travelers hungry for fame" (8, 1, 448). "We met more grave mounds, more ruins. Two or three funeral monuments stood at the roadside. . . . A Tartar inscription, the representation of a sabre . . . were carved into the stone by predatory grandsons in memory of a predatory ancestor" (8, 1, 449). Even in the capital city of Arzrum, "The monuments consist usually of columns, decorated with a stone turban . . . they have no refinement: no taste, no thought. . . . One traveler writes that out of all the Asian cities, only in Arzrum did he find a clock tower, and that one was broken" (8, 1, 479). "I asked for water first in Russian, then in Tartar. He didn't understand me. Amazing obliviousness! Thirty versts from Tiflis and on the road to Persia and Turkey, he knew not a word of Russian or Tartar" (8, 1, 460).

69. This hissingly alliterative phrase accompanies Paskevich so frequently that it contributes to the aura of derision Tynianov first detected in Pushkin's treatment.

70. I borrow this phrase from Paul Zweig's stimulating chapter "The Flight from Women" in his *The Adventurer* (New York: Basic Books, 1974), p. 61.

71. The phrase is Pushkin's ("Demon neterpenia opiat' mnoiu ovladel," 8.1, 462); Pomorska, in "Structural Peculiarities," sees it as the surreal leitmotiv of the "Journey."

72. Dante, *Purgatorio*, trans. Charles S. Singleton (Princeton, N.J.: Princeton University Press, 1980), can. 9, st. 19–78 (pp. 89–91). See my article "Illegibility in 'Journey to Arzrum'" on the Dantean structure of Pushkin's "Journey."

73. Turner, *The Ritual Process*, p. 96.

74. The dervish, a Muslim religious ascetic who expressed divine "possession" by his whirling dance, was adopted, for example by Coleridge in "Kubla Khan" (1816), as a prototype of the Romantic poet ("His flashing

eyes! His floating hair!"). Pushkin probably had in mind the dialogue between the pasha and the captive "Dervise," who throws off his disguise to reveal himself as the hero Conrad himself, in Byron's "The Corsair" (can. 2, st. 64–195).

75. The circumstances of Griboedov's patronage by Ermolov, then Paskevich, the cause for his transfer to the Persian capital, the behind-the-scenes maneuvers of English diplomats in Persia, and the circumstances of Griboedov's death were long suppressed and speculated on. See Denis Davydov's *Zapiski.*

76. Zweig, *The Adventurer*, pp. 89–114.

77. Cited in Bitsilli, "Puteshestvie v Arzrum," p. 255.

78. Chaadaev introduced the equation of St. Petersburg and Egypt by signing his *Philosophical Letter* of Dec. 1, 1829, "Necropolis." See Leslie O'Bell, *Pushkin's "Egyptian Nights": The Biography of a Work* (Ann Arbor, Mich.: Ardis, 1983), p. 63.

79. Pushkin's last unfinished story, "Egyptian Nights" (1835), takes this logic to its conclusion.

Chapter 4

1. Letter to V. F. Viazemskaia, from Mikhailovskoe, late Oct., 1824. Trans. J. Thomas Shaw, *The Letters of Alexander Pushkin* (Madison: University of Wisconsin Press, 1967), pp. 183–84.

2. Pushkin's frequent requests for books in his correspondence give us an unusually complete sense of his reading during this period: Thomas Medwin's *Conversations of Lord Byron*, Walter Scott's novels, Nikolai Karamzin's *History of the Russian State*, Russian chronicles, the Bible, and August Wilhelm Schlegel's *Course Lectures on Dramatic Art and Literature* figured among his most urgent requests. For an excellent analysis of the circumstances in which *Boris Godunov* was composed, see Stephanie Sandler, " 'Boris Godunov': The Expectations of an Audience," in her *Distant Pleasures: Alexander Pushkin and the Writing of Exile* (Stanford, Calif.: Stanford University Press, 1989), pp. 77–139.

3. "A tragedy without love appealed to my imagination," Pushkin recalled in a letter drafted to N. N. Raevsky on Jan. or June 30, 1829 (trans. Shaw, *Letters of Alexander Pushkin*, p. 365). Pushkin seems to have had in mind the difference between lyric poetry and mimetic representation when he wrote exultantly to N. N. Raevsky in July 1825, "I feel that my soul has become fully developed; I can create" (trans. Shaw, *Letters of Alexander Pushkin*, p. 237).

4. St. 35, lines 5–8 (in Pushkin, *Polnoe sobranie sochinenii*, vol. 6).

5. The various "audiences" a history of *Boris Godunov*'s early reception

would have to include are Pushkin himself, who concluded his own solitary reading of the play with the famous cry, "Ai da Pushkin, ai da sukin syn!" (10, 148), as he reported to P. A. Viazemsky Nov. 7, 1825, from Mikhailovskoe (see Shaw, *Letters of Alexander Pushkin*, p. 261); the various "neighbors" to whom he read parts of the manuscript in Mikhailovskoe; those present at several salon readings that took place in St. Petersburg in 1828; and the government censors, including Nicholas I himself and Faddei Bulgarin, who recommended that the play be rewritten as a historical novel in the style of Walter Scott.

6. The critical reviews quoted are N. I. Nadezhdin's, published in *Teleskop* 1831, pt. 1, no. 4, and N. A. Polevoy's, published in *Moskovkii telegraf* 1833, pt. 49, no. 11. They are quoted in M. G. Zel'dovich and L. Ia. Livshits, eds., *Russkaia literatura XIX veka (Khrestomatiia kriticheskikh materialov)* (Moscow: Vysshaia shkola, 1975), pp. 167–69.

7. In a rare attempt at self-justification, Pushkin wrote to N. N. Raevsky that his tragedy should be read only after perusing "the last volume of Karamzin. My play is full of good jokes and delicate allusions to the history of the time. . . . It is a *sine qua non* that they be understood." Draft of letter to Raevsky, Jan. or June 30, 1829, from St. Petersburg; trans. Shaw, *Letters of Alexander Pushkin*, p. 365. Iu. D. Levin discusses the problem of the disappearance of an "initiated" readership in his assessment of the dramaturgical failure of Pushkin's supposedly Shakespearean techniques in *Boris Godunov*. See his "Nekotorye voprosy Shekspirizma Pushkina," *Pushkin issledovaniia i materialy*, vol. 7 (Leningrad: Nauka, 1974), pp. 58–86.

8. Similar conclusions are drawn on the basis of a more linguistic, and less culturally contextualized, analysis by Kevin Moss in "The Last Word in Fiction: On Significant Lies in *Boris Godunov*," *Slavic and East European Journal* 32, no. 2 (1988): 187–97.

9. Letter to Vasily Andreevich Zhukovsky (Oct. 31, 1824, from Mikhailovskoe). Trans. in Shaw, *Letters of Alexander Pushkin*, pp. 185–86. A more complete discussion follows in the Chap. 6 of this book.

10. My emphasis. Letter to L. S. Pushkin, late Jan. / early Feb. 1825, from Mikhailovskoe to St. Petersburg. Trans. Shaw, *Letters of Alexander Pushkin*, p. 202.

11. The concept was established by Alexander Welsh in *The Hero of the Waverley Novels* (New Haven, Conn.: Yale University Press, 1963); see also Avrom Fleishman, *The English Historical Novel: From Walter Scott to Virginia Woolf* (Baltimore, Md.: Johns Hopkins University Press, 1970); and Judith Wilt, *Secret Leaves: The Novels of Walter Scott* (Chicago: University of Chicago Press, 1985).

12. N. I. Nadezhdin, review in *Teleskop*, quoted in Zel'dovich and Livshits, *Russkaia literatura XIX veka*, pp. 167–69.

13. That *Boris Godunov* remained incomprehensible to readers who shared Pushkin's fascination with Shakespearean dramaturgy is a paradox Caryl Emerson discusses with great thoroughness in "The Shakespeare Connection," in her landmark study *Boris Godunov: Transpositions of a Russian Theme* (Bloomington: Indiana University Press, 1986), pp. 110–21. Her notes cite most of the Pushkin-Shakespeare studies I found useful as background research, including M. P. Alekseev, "Pushkin i Shekspir," in his *Pushkin: Sravnitel'no-istoricheskie issledovaniia* (Leningrad: Nauka, 1974), pp. 240–80; S. M. Bondi, "Dramaturgiia Pushkina," in his *O Pushkine: Stat'i i materialy* (Moscow: Khudozhestvennaia literatura, 1941), pp. 192–208; Iu. D. Levin, "Pushkin," in his *Shekspir i russkaia literatura XIX veka* (Leningrad: Nauka, 1988); Tatiana Wolff, ed. and trans., *Pushkin on Literature* (Stanford, Calif.: Stanford University Press, 1986), pp. 99–109.

14. Herbert Lindenberger, *Historical Drama: The Relation of Literature and Reality* (Chicago: University of Chicago Press, 1975), pp. 4–5, 42–43, 134–136. On the "emplotment of history," see Hayden White, *Metahistory: The Historical Imagination in Nineteenth-Century Europe* (Baltimore, Md.: Johns Hopkins University Press, 1973), pp. 1–80.

15. Lindenberger, *Historical Drama*, pp. 95–130.

16. See Roger Bauer, Michael de Graat, and Jürgen Wertheimer, eds., *Das Shakespeare-Bild in Europa zwischen Aufklärung und Romantik* (Bern: Peter Lang, 1988).

17. I have chosen to follow up on what Emerson calls an "intriguing thesis: that Pushkin's 'Shakespearism' might have been incomprehensible to his early nineteenth-century audiences because Pushkin, consciously or no, was reflecting in his play a *Renaissance* understanding of Shakespeare, one that contradicted the accepted received image of the Bard in the 1820's" (*Boris Godunov: Transpositions*, p. 111). I am convinced that Pushkin owes this richer apprehension of Shakespeare at least in part to August Schlegel's excellent analysis both of the Renaissance cultural context and innovative dramaturgy of Shakespeare's history plays in *A Course of Lectures on Dramatic Art and Literature*, trans. John Black (Philadelphia: Hogan and Thompson, 1833). Pushkin ordered the French edition, *Cours de littérature dramatique* (Paris, 1814) in the spring of 1825. See his letter to L. S. Pushkin of Mar. 14, 1825, from Trigorskoe to St. Petersburg, in Shaw, *Letters of Alexander Pushkin*, p. 206. Schlegel also drew my attention to the particular plays through which I believe Pushkin filtered his historical materials to produce the specific scenes and metapoetic language of *Boris Godunov*.

18. Lindenberger, *Historical Drama*, p. 133.

19. Pushkin's review "Istoriia russkogo naroda, sochinenie Nikolaia Polevogo" (11, 120).

20. See Nancy Anderson's (as yet unpublished) paper "Shakespeare's History Plays and Karamzin's Boris Godunov."

21. Emerson, *Boris Godunov: Transpositions*, pp. 32–35.

22. Ivan Kireevsky, "Obozrenie russkoi literatury za 1831 god," in *Evropeets* 1832, pt. 1, no. 1, quoted in Zel'dovich and Livshits, *Russkaia literatura*, pp. 171–72.

23. N. A. Polevoy's review of *Boris Godunov* in *Moskovskii telegraf* 1833, pt. 49, no. 11, quoted in Zel'dovich and Livshits, *Russkaia literatura*, pp. 169–70.

24. Letter to L. S. Pushkin, late Jan./early Feb. 1825, in Shaw, *Letters of Alexander Pushkin*, p. 202.

25. Iu. M. Lotman, "Problema khudozhestvennogo prostranstva v proze Gogolia," *Trudy po russkoi i slavianskoi filologii*, vol. 11 (Tartu, 1968), p. 9. (This article was translated by Susan Toumanoff as part of her Master's thesis for Stanford University in 1977.)

26. My thinking on *Boris Godunov* has been shaped above all by Stephen Greenblatt's *Renaissance Self-Fashioning: From More to Shakespeare* (Chicago: University of Chicago Press, 1980), and his "Invisible Bullets," in *Shakespearean Negotiations: The Circulation of Social Energy in Renaissance England* (Berkeley: University of California Press, 1988), pp. 21–65.

27. N. A. Polevoy's review, in Zel'dovich and Livshits, *Russkaia literatura*, p. 170.

28. Emerson, *Boris Godunov: Transpositions*, p. 102.

29. See Edmund S. Morgan, *Inventing the People: The Rise of Popular Sovereignty in England and America* (New York: W. W. Norton, 1988), pp. 11–121. The best discussion of Karamzin's political philosophy is Richard Pipes's "Karamzin's Conception of Monarchy," in N. M. Karamzin, *Memoir on Ancient and Modern Russia*, trans. and ed. Richard Pipes (Cambridge, Mass.: Harvard University Press, 1959), pp. 105–26.

30. Karamzin's argument here bears a striking resemblance to Wordsworth's in "On Epitaphs," *Wordsworth's Literary Criticisms*, ed. W. J. B. Owen (London: Routledge and Kegan Paul, 1974).

31. Emerson gives a history and refutation of this interpretation (*Boris Godunov: Transpositions*, pp. 132–41). See also M. P. Alekseev, "Remarka Pushkina 'Narod bezmolvstvuet,'" in *Pushkin. Sravnitel'no-istoricheskie issledovania* (Leningrad: Nauka, 1984), pp. 221–52. Rachel Wilson gives a refreshing approach to the vocal and subvocal roles of the *narod* in "The Politics of Noise in Pushkin's 'Boris Godunov'" (unpublished).

32. See Efim Etkind, "'Sei ratnik, vol'nost'iu venchannyi': Grishka Otrep'ev, imperator Napoleon, marshal Nei, i drugie," *Revue des études slaves* 59 (1987): 55–62.

33. Lindenberger, *Historical Drama*, pp. 33–34.

34. Kevin Moss, "The Last Word in Fiction: On Significant Lies in *Boris Godunov*," *Soviet and East European Journal* 32, no. 2 (1988): 187–97.

35. Emerson (*Boris Godunov: Transpositions*, pp. 125–26) discusses Ilia Serman's thesis about the medieval miraculous mentality that he feels permeates *Boris Godunov*'s "chronotope" and plausibly accounts for behavior that to a modern mentality seems unmotivated. See I. Z. Serman, "Pushkin i russkaia istoricheskaia drama 1830-kh godov," in *Pushkin: Issledovania i materialy*, vol. 6 (Leningrad: Nauka, 1969), pp. 118–49. The most interesting quotations are, however, from Serman's unpublished essay "Paradoxes of the Folk Mind in Pushkin's *Boris Godunov*." As will be seen, a great deal of what Serman attributes to the folk mind (Pimen's hagiographical "miracles," what he calls Grigory / Dmitry's "immediate, sensuous perception of life," the ability of the *narod* to hold two contradictory beliefs at once) I find consistent instead with Renaissance modes of behavior.

36. Greenblatt, *Renaissance Self-Fashioning*, p. 230.

37. Nicholas V. Riasanovsky's analysis of Ivan IV's reign (*A History of Russia* [Oxford: Oxford University Press, 1984], pp. 143–56) corroborates this view.

38. I have borrowed the phrase from a chapter of the same title in Sebastian de Grazia, *Machiavelli in Hell* (Princeton, N.J.: Princeton University Press, 1989), pp. 295–97.

39. Indeed, Shakespeare's chronicle plays can be regarded as a revision of "the older and still vigorous historiography" based on divine predestination in light of the new Italian doctrine. Ernest A. Strathmann writes in his introduction to *William Shakespeare: The Complete Works*, ed. Alfred Harbage (Baltimore, Md.: Penguin, 1969), p. 6, "Although there was no English translation of *The Prince* in print until 1640, translations circulated in manuscript and the work was available in Latin and French as well as Italian. Informed Elizabethans understood the principles advanced by the Italian writers, but the unsophisticated got their knowledge of *The Prince* at second hand, in part from an attack upon 'Machiavellianism' popularly known as the *Contre-Machiavel*. . . . When the Duke of Gloucester catalogues the talents which may enable him to eliminate all obstacles on his path to the throne, one of them is that he can 'set the murderous Machiavel to school' (*3 Henry VI*, III, ii, 193)." See also Greenblatt, *Renaissance Self-Fashioning*, especially "The Improvisation of Power," pp. 222–54, and *Shakespearean Negotiations*, especially "Invisible Bullets," pp. 21–65. Pushkin had two volumes of Machiavelli in his library: *Oeuvres complètes de Machiavel*, trans. J. V. Peries (Paris, 1823–26); and *Machiavel, ou morçeaux choisis et pensées de cet écrivain sur la politique, la législation, la morale, l'histoire et l'art*

militaire, "preceded by an essay on Machiavelli and accompanied by a new and complete translation of *The Prince*" (Paris, 1823). See Tatiana Wolff's appendix to *Pushkin on Literature* (p. 508), a list of titles of foreign books in Pushkin's library as catalogued by B. L. Modzalevsky, published in *Pushkin i ego sovremenniki*, nos. 9–10 (St. Petersburg, 1910).

40. Letter to L. S. Pushkin, trans. Shaw, *Letters of Alexander Pushkin*, p. 202.

41. Niccolo Machiavelli, *The Prince*, trans. Peter Bondanella and Mark Musa (Oxford: Oxford University Press, 1984), p. 9. Further quotations from this work will be cited by page number in the text.

42. "Draft articles on *Boris Godunov*" (1828), trans. Wolff, *Pushkin on Literature*, p. 222. In a letter to Chaadaev in 1836, Pushkin reiterated that "the Russian clergy, up to Feofan, was worthy of respect; it was never besmirched by the infamies of papism, and most certainly it would never have provoked the Reformation at the moment when humanity had the most need of unity" (Shaw, *Letters of Alexander Pushkin*, p. 780). In the rough draft of that letter he contrasted the modern Orthodox clergy, isolated from "good society" and from real historical action: "Like eunuchs, it has no passion but for power. Consequently it is dreaded. And, I know, a certain one [Nicholas I], in spite of all his energy, yielded to it on one grave occasion. I was enraged by this at the time" (*ibid.*, p. 798).

43. In the canceled scene, "At the Monastery Wall," based in its narrative details on Karamzin, the *zloi chernets* baldly suggests to Grigory that he "play a trick on our stupid and superstitious people," upon which they shake hands. Emerson writes, "This disappointing scene so clearly resembles a pact with the devil that some critics have linked Grigory with Faust. . . . But ultimately that scene, along with other similarly melodramatic passages in other scenes, was eliminated. Motivation for Grigory's act was to come not from the demonic but from the godly monk, not from the devil but from Pimen" (*Boris Godunov: Transpositions*, pp. 122–23). If, on the other hand, Pushkin had a visceral ambivalence about clerics and father figures with a childlike loyalty to the tsar, he had good reason for it. See pt. 4, "Exile under Surveillance—Mikhaylovskoe," in Shaw, *Letters of Alexander Pushkin*, pp. 181–298.

44. As an illustration of the usage of *taf'ia*, Dal' quotes Karamzin: "Tsar' dal oprichnikam taf'i," which suggests that Pushkin preserved the details he found in Karamzin. Vladimir Dal', *Tolkovyi slovar' zhivago velikorusskogo iazyka*, 2nd ed., vol. 4 (St. Petersburg: Izdanie knigoprodavtsa-tipografa M. O. Wol'fa, 1882), p. 393.

45. Greenblatt, *Renaissance Self-Fashioning*, pp. 224–25.

46. *Ibid.*, p. 228.

47. Emerson, *Boris Godunov: Transpositions*, p. 128. The "miracle" can of course be explained by the well-known physiological reflexes that follow beheading.

48. The most thorough and illuminating analysis of Boris's soliloquy is Stephanie Sandler's second chapter on *Boris Godunov* in her *Distant Pleasures*, pp. 108–39.

49. Judith Wilt discusses Scott's predilection for Prince Hal in *Secret Leaves*, p. 28.

50. The line is from *I Henry IV*, act 2, sc. 4, lines 17–18; quoted in Greenblatt, *Shakespearean Negotiations*, p. 45.

51. One of Henri Bergson's famous definitions of the comic is "something mechanical in something living." See *Laughter: An Essay on the Meaning of the Comic* (N.Y.: Macmillan, 1913), p. 77.

52. Greenblatt, *Shakespearean Negotiations*, pp. 56–57.

53. In his letter to N. N. Raevsky the Younger (Jan. 30 or June 30, 1829, from St. Petersburg to the Caucasus or in Erzerum [rough draft]), Pushkin compared Dmitry to Henry IV: "There is a great deal of Henri IV in Dmitry. He is like him, bold, generous and a Gascon, like him indifferent to religion—both of them abjuring their faith for a political cause, both loving pleasure and war, both throwing themselves into chimerical projects—both the butt of conspiracies." Both Wolff (*Pushkin on Literature*, p. 250) and Shaw (*Letters of Alexander Pushkin*, p. 396) conclude that Pushkin is referring to the Protestant French king Henri de Navarre (who with famous irreligion said, "Paris is well worth a mass"). The text does not warrant Caryl Emerson's conclusion (in *Boris Godunov: Transpositions*, p. 234) that Pushkin is referring to "Shakespeare's Henry IV," who was not the amiable adventurer Hal, but his ambitious father. Unfortunately, there is no hard proof for the intuition I share with her that Hal is the model Pretender.

54. Greenblatt, *Shakespearean Negotiations*, p. 46.

55. *Ibid.*, p. 53.

56. See historical details in M. A. Schaaber, "Introduction" to *I Henry IV*, in *Shakespeare: The Complete Works*, p. 669.

57. It is probably no accident that this barb was aimed at an ancestor of Karolina Sobańska, the Polish-born consort of Count de Witt; both were employed by Alexander I's and then Nicholas I's secret police, and both spied on Pushkin. There is a good possibility that Sobańska was also a Polish counteragent. See Roman Jakobson, "The Police Accomplice Sung by Pushkin and Mickiewicz," in his *Puskin and His Sculptural Myth* (The Hague: Mouton, 1975), pp. 76–86, and Izabela Kalinowska's as yet unpublished paper on Sobańska and Marina Mniszek, "The False Dmitri and Pushkin's Polish Passion: An Analysis of the Scene by the Fountain from *Boris Godunov*." I appreciate her drawing my attention to two additional articles by Maria Czap-

ska, "Podejrzane towarzystwo" and "Karolina i szef żandarmów," reprinted in her *Szkice Mickiewiczowskie* (London: B. Świderski, 1963).

58. Letter of Feb. 6, 1823, responding to Prince P. A. Viazemsky's criticisms of "Kavkazskii plennik" (Wolff, *Pushkin on Literature*, p. 63).

59. J. Thomas Shaw, "*Romeo and Juliet*, Local Color, and 'Mniszek's Sonnet' in *Boris Godunov*," *Soviet and East European Journal* 35, no. 1 (1991): 1–35.

60. Shaw, *Letters of Alexander Pushkin*, pp. 365–66.

61. Evgeny Baratynsky, *Stikhotvoreniia i poemy* (Petrozavodsk: Izdatel'stvo Kareliia, 1979), p. 53.

62. Moss, "Last Word," p. 195.

63. Sandler, *Distant Pleasures*, pp. 77–78.

64. This is a point which Caryl Emerson makes exceedingly well: "Events matter less than rumors about events and everyone with a story to tell is aware of the power of storytelling. . . . Pushkin's plot, like the Boris tale at its base, is itself a *samozvanets*, a pretender that invites and engenders response without identifying any source of authority within itself" (*Boris Godunov: Transpositions*, pp. 140, 103). I have arrived, as does Kevin Moss in his excellent piece, with a certain inevitability but by a different route, at the same conclusions.

Chapter 5

1. Aleksandr Pushkin, *Eugene Onegin: A Novel in Verse*, trans. and comm. Vladimir Nabokov (Princeton, N.J.: Princeton University Press, 1981, vol. 2, pp. 311–12.

2. *Ibid.*, p. 312.

3. Jan M. Meijer, "The Digressions in 'Evgenii Onegin,'" *Dutch Contributions to the Sixth International Congress of Slavists*, ed. A. G. F. Van Holk (The Hague: Mouton, 1968), pp. 122–52. See also Boris Filippov, "Zavershennaia nezakonchennost' u Pushkina," *Transactions / Zapiski of the Association of Russian-American Scholars in the U.S.A.*, vol. 20 (Richmond Hill, N.Y.: Association of Russian-American Scholars in the U.S.A., 1988), pp. 33–40; Iu. M. Lotman, *Roman A. S. Pushkina* (Leningrad: Prosveshchenie, 1980), and "Khudozhestvennaia struktura 'Evgeniia Onegina,'" *Trudy po russkoi i slavianskoi filologii* 9, literaturovedenie (Tartu: Tartuskii gosudarstvennyi universitet, 1966); L. N. Stil'man, "Problema literaturnykh zhanrov i traditsii v 'Evgenii Onegine' Pushkina. K voprosu perekhoda ot romantizma k realizmu," *American Contributions to the Fourth International Congress of Slavists: Moscow, September, 1958* (The Hague: Mouton, 1958), pp. 321–65; Iurii Tynianov, "O kompozytsii 'Evgeniia Onegina,'" *Poetika, istoria literatury, kino* (Moscow: Nauka, 1977), pp. 52–77.

4. William Mills Todd III, *Fiction and Society in the Age of Pushkin* (Cambridge: Harvard University Press, 1986), pp. 121–36.

5. The generic term is Marjorie Levinson's. See *The Romantic Fragment Poem* (Chapel Hill: University of North Carolina Press, 1988), pp. 7–17.

6. Studies of Romantic irony I have found useful include Wayne Booth, *The Rhetoric of Irony* (Chicago: University of Chicago Press, 1956); Paul de Man, "The Rhetoric of Temporality," in *Blindness and Insight: Essays in the Rhetoric of Contemporary Criticism* (Minneapolis: University of Minnesota Press, 1983), pp. 187–228; Gary Handwerk, *Irony and Ethics in Narrative: From Schlegel to Lacan* (New Haven, Conn.: Yale University Press, 1985); Søren Kierkegaard, *The Concept of Irony, with Continual Reference to Socrates*, ed. and trans. Howard V. Hong and Edna H. Hong (Princeton, N.J.: Princeton University Press, 1989); Anne Mellor, *English Romantic Irony* (Cambridge, Mass.: Harvard University Press, 1980); D. C. Muecke, *The Compass of Irony* (London: Methuen, 1969); Dan Sperber and Deirdre Wilson, "Irony and the Use-Mention Distinction," in *Radical Pragmatics*, ed. Peter Cole (New York: Academic Press, 1981).

7. See Pushkin's letters to N. N. Pushkina written in September from Mikhailovskoe, which culminate in this announcement to Pletnev on Oct. 11, 1835: "I've never had such a fruitless autumn in my life. I'm writing, but bungling the job. For inspiration, one must have spiritual tranquility, and I'm not tranquil at all." Trans. Shaw, *Letters of Alexander Pushkin*, p. 728.

8. Vladimir Nabokov, "Commentary" to Pushkin, *Eugene Onegin: A Novel in Verse*, vol. 2, p. 296. See Pushkin, *Polnoe sobranie sochinenii* (3.2, 992–95) for other variations of Pushkin's response to Pletnev's request for a sequel to *Eugene Onegin*.

9. See excerpts from Bulgarin and Nadezhdin's critiques of Pushkin's recent work in Iurii M. Tynianov, "O 'Puteshestvii v Arzrum,'" *Vremennik Pushkinskoi kommissii II* (Moscow: Nauka, 1936), p. 71; and Sonia Hoisington, *Russian Views of Pushkin's Eugene Onegin* (Bloomington: Indiana University Press, 1988).

10. A. S. Pushkin, *Polnoe sobranie sochinenii v desiati tomakh* (Leningrad: Akademia nauk, 1977), vol. 3, pp. 323, 430–31.

11. B. Tomashevsky, "Desiataia glava 'Evgeniia Onegina.' Istoriia razgadki," in *Pushkin*, vol. 2 (Moscow: Nauka, 1961), pp. 200–243; I. L. Feinberg, *Nezavershennye raboty Pushkina* (Moscow: Sovetskii pisatel', 1964); Nabokov, "Commentary" to Pushkin, *Eugene Onegin*, vol. 2, pp. 311–75; Viktor Kozhevnikov, "Shifrovannye strofy 'Evgeniia Onegina,'" *Novyi mir* 6 (June 1988): 259–68.

12. Quoted in Tynianov, "O 'Puteshestvii v Arzrum,'" p. 71.

13. See Nabokov's background discussion of chap. 10 in his "Commentary" to Pushkin, *Eugene Onegin*, vol. 2, p. 364.

14. *Ibid.*, p. 319.

15. See "Zapis' A. N. Wul'fa ot 16 sentiabria 1827 goda," in "Vyderzhki iz dnevnika," *Russkaia starina*, Mar. 1899: 512; and Feinberg, *Nezavershennye raboty Pushkina*, p. 397. Prince Andrei Mikhailovich Kurbsky was exiled by Ivan IV to Poland, from whence he conducted an impassioned and critical correspondence with the tsar.

16. Sam Driver, *Pushkin: Literature and Social Ideas* (New York: Columbia University Press, 1989).

17. On the theatricality of Petersburg culture under Alexander I, see Iu. M. Lotman, "Teatr i teatral'nost' v stroe russkoi kul'tury nachala XIX v," in his *Stat'i po tipologii kul'tury*, no. 2 (Tartu: Tartusskii gosudarstvennyi universitet, 1973), pp. 42–73. Translated in Henryk Baran, ed., *Semiotics and Structuralism: Readings from the Soviet Union* (White Plains, N.Y.: International Arts and Sciences Press, 1976). See also Boris Gasparov, "Introduction" to Alexander D. Nakhimovsky and Alice Stone Nakhimovsky, eds., *The Semiotics of Russian Cultural History* (Ithaca, N.Y.: Cornell University Press, 1985), pp. 13–29.

18. "Projected preface to the last chapters of *Evgenii Onegin*," in Tatiana Wolff, ed. and trans., *Pushkin on Literature* (Stanford, Calif.: Stanford University Press, 1986), p. 274.

19. All quotations from *Eugene Onegin* in this chapter are cited in the text by chapter, stanza, and line. I have used the version of *Onegin* found in Pushkin, *Polnoe sobranie sochinenii*, vol. 6.

20. Levinson, *Romantic Fragment Poem*, pp. 55–56.

21. See Pushkin's letter to A. A. Bestuzhev of Mar. 24, 1825 (from Mikhailovskoe) in Shaw, *Letters of Alexander Pushkin*, pp. 209–10.

22. See Nabokov, "Commentary" to Pushkin, *Eugene Onegin*, vol. 2, p. 257. On the relationship between Byron and Childe Harold, see Philip W. Martin, *Byron: A Poet Before His Public* (Cambridge, Eng.: Cambridge University Press, 1982), pp. 21–29.

23. Levinson, *Romantic Fragment Poem*, p. 47.

24. Nabokov, "Commentary" to Pushkin, *Eugene Onegin*, vol. 2, pp. 257, 293, 302.

25. Gary Handwerk, "The Irony of Double Vision: Lacan's Liquidation of the Subject," in *Irony and Ethics*, pp. 125–71.

26. Levinson, *Romantic Fragment Poem*, pp. 199, 24–25.

27. *Ibid.*, pp. 30–33.

28. *Ibid.*, p. 199.

29. Letter to Kiukhel'beker (Apr. / May 1824, from Odessa); trans. Shaw, *Letters of Alexander Pushkin*, p. 156.

30. Levinson, *Romantic Fragment Poem*, p. 214.

31. Denis Diderot, "Lettre sur les sourds et muets," cited in James Doo-

little, "Hieroglyph and Emblem in Diderot's 'Lettre sur les sourds et muets,'" *Diderot Studies II*, ed. Otis Fellows and Norman Torrey (Syracuse, N.Y.: Syracuse University Press, 1952), p. 158.

32. All translations of *Eugene Onegin* in this chapter are based on Vladimir Nabokov's in Pushkin, *Eugene Onegin*, vol. 1. I have, however, modified syntax and selected more commonly used synonyms for the sake of clarity and stylistic accuracy (for example, I translate *pole* as "field" rather than "champaign" and *mladost'* as "youth" rather than "juventude").

33. Diderot, *Salon de 1767*, in *Oeuvres complètes*, J. Assézat, ed., vol. 11 (Paris: Garnier-frères, 1875), pp. 254–55. Cited in Herbert Dieckmann, *Cinq leçons sur Diderot* (Geneva: Librairie E. Droz, 1959), pp. 106–7.

34. Handwerk, *Irony and Ethics*, p. 52.

35. Lotman, *Roman A. S. Pushkina*, p. 121.

36. See Sperber and Wilson, "Irony and the Use-Mention Distinction," pp. 295–318. I am indebted to David Kropf for calling my attention to this and other discussions of irony.

37. Booth, *Rhetoric of Irony*, p. 13.

38. *Ibid.*

39. Handwerk discusses Booth's view of irony in *Irony and Ethics*, p. 6.

40. *Ibid.*, p. 5.

41. *Ibid.*, p. 8.

42. *Ibid.*, pp. viii, 2, 18–43, 125–71.

43. *Ibid.*, pp. 9, 47.

44. De Man, *Blindness and Insight*, pp. 212–13.

45. Nabokov's "Commentary" to *Onegin* is saturated with this narcissistic conception of Pushkin's self-reflective irony, a projection of Nabokov's own aesthetic attitude. The equation of Romantic and aesthetic irony is common also in Soviet criticism. See Iu. M. Lotman, "Khudozhestvennaia struktura 'Evgeniia Onegina,'" *Trudy po russkoi i slavianskoi filologii* 10 (Tartu: Tartuskii gosudarstvennyi universitet, 1966).

46. "If the reader has understood the mechanism of this pursuit he has grasped the basic structure of Chapter One." See Nabokov in Pushkin, *Eugene Onegin*, vol. 2, p. 108.

47. De Man, *Blindness and Insight*, p. 225.

48. Sergei Eisenstein analyzed Pushkin's narrative technique as an early instance of montage. See "Pushkin i kino," in *Iskusstvo kino* 4 (1955), translated as "Lessons from Literature" in *Film Essays with a Lecture*, trans. and ed. Jay Leyda (Princeton, N.J.: Princeton University Press, 1981), pp. 77–83.

49. See Norman Bryson, *Looking at the Overlooked: Four Essays on Still Life Painting* (Cambridge, Mass.: Harvard University Press, 1990).

50. See Leonid Grossman, "Pushkin i dendizm," and other essays in

Pushkin v teatral'nykh kreslakh. Kartiny russkoi stseny 1817–1820 godov (Orange, Conn.: Antiquary, 1987).

51. Handwerk, *Irony and Ethics*, p. 46.

52. For vivid pictorial examples of the convention of the dandy-collector and his exotic study in European painting, see Clive Wainwright, *The Romantic Interior: The British Collector at Home, 1750–1850* (New Haven, Conn.: Yale University Press, 1989).

53. Barry P. Scherr calls this device "homonym or echo rhyme." See his *Russian Poetry: Meter, Rhythm, and Rhyme* (Berkeley: University of California Press, 1986), p. 206.

54. For some recent thoughts on an old subject, see Richard Tempest, "The Young Pushkin and Chaadaev," in J. Douglas Clayton, ed., *Issues in Russian Literature Before 1917* (Columbus, Ohio: Slavica, 1989), pp. 49–61.

55. Marina Woronzoff drew my attention to this thread of imagery in her unpublished paper "The Tale of Echo and Narcissus Retold: Pushkin's Tatiana and Eugene."

56. See B. Tomashevsky, "Malen'kaia nozhka," in "Melochi o Pushkine," *Pushkin i ego sovremenniki*, nos. 38–39, (Leningrad, 1930), pp. 76–81; Nabokov's ruminations on the "candidates" in his "Commentary" 1975, 120–135; and more recently, Helena Goscilo, "Feet Puskin Scanned, or Seeming Idée Fixe as Implied Aesthetic Credo," *Slavic and East European Journal* 32, no. 4 (Winter 1988): 562–73.

57. De Man, *Blindness and Insight*, p. 207.

58. Handwerk on Lacan's *Ecrits*, *Irony and Ethics*, p. 156.

59. Jacques Lacan, *Ecrits* (Paris: Editions du Seuil, 1966), p. 447. Quoted by Handwerk in *Irony and Ethics*, p. 146.

60. See Grossman, "Pushkin i dendizm," in *Etiudy o Pushkine* (Moscow: L. D. Frenkel', 1923), pp. 5–36; Sam Driver, "The Dandy in Pushkin," *Slavic and East European Journal* 29, no. 3 (1985): 243–57; and particularly Domna Stanton, *The Aristocrat as Art: A Study of the Honnête Homme and the Dandy in Seventeenth- and Nineteenth-Century French Literature* (New York: Columbia University Press, 1980), pp. 54–61, 110, 127–30, 155–59.

61. Pushkin wrote to his brother from Mikhailovskoe, Nov. 1–10, 1824: "Here is a little picture for *Onegin*—find a skilled and speedy artist. If you have a different picture let the *positioning* of everything be exactly the same. The same scene, do you understand? That I must have, without fail." Trans. in Wolff, *Pushkin on Literature*, p. 113. Wolff adds, "Pushkin annotated his sketch as follows: the left-hand figure (clearly representing himself, seen from the back) had to be 'handsome'; the right-hand figure (representing Evgeny) had to be '*leaning on the granite*'; and 'the fortress of Peter-and-Paul' had to appear in the background. An illustration based on this sketch was first published in 1829, not in the first edition of Chapter I of *Evgeny Onegin*."

62. De Man, *Blindness and Insight*, pp. 209–10.

63. See Handwerk's synthesis of Lacan's argument on the splitting of the subject in *Ecrits* and *Séminaires*, bks. 1 and 2 (Paris: Editions du Seuil, 1975, 1978), in *Irony and Ethics*, pp. 125–71.

64. Traditionally it is identified with a place, Lake Onega. Another possibility might be Pushkin's favorite elegiac word *nega*, to match Lensky's *len'*. (In the latter case the connection would be, however, associative, not etymological, since *len* and *len'* are different roots.) The type of semantic name so typical of Gogol is considered to be uncharacteristic of Pushkin.

65. Todd analyzes Russian social life through concepts taken from Erving Goffman, *The Presentation of Self in Everyday Life* (Garden City, N.Y.: Doubleday, 1959). See Todd, *Fiction and Society*, pp. 121–36.

66. Tynianov favored Kiukhel'beker, others proposed N. M. Iazykov. See Lotman, *Roman A. S. Pushkina*, pp. 180–92.

67. Indeed, the whole "quacking critic" and "audience of ducks" complex is Pushkin's extended joke on Kiukhel'beker's criticism of the contemporary elegiac poet: "Dushe legche—govoriu,—esli on vdobavok ne snabdit nas podrobnym opisaniem svoei kladovoi i biblioteki i shvabskikh gusei i russkikh utok svoego priiatelia" (It's a relief to the soul,—I say—if he doesn't in addition furnish us with a detailed description of his pantry and library and his friend's Schwabian geese and Russian ducks). V. K. Kiukhel'beker, "O napravlenii nashei poezii, osobenno liricheskoi, v poslednee desiatiletie" (1824), reprinted in *Puteshestvie. Dnevnik. Stat'i*, ed. N. V. Koroleva and V. D. Rak (Leningrad: Nauka, 1979), p. 455.

68. In other words, "triangular desire"; see René Girard, *Deceit, Desire, and the Novel: Self and Other in Literary Structure*, trans. Yvonne Freccero (Baltimore, Md.: Johns Hopkins University Press, 1976).

69. J. Douglas Clayton discusses *Romeo and Juliet* as a subtext for Tatiana's love story in *Ice and Flame: Aleksandr Puskin's Eugene Onegin* (Toronto: University of Toronto Press, 1985).

70. For example, in Jean-Baptiste Greuze's *Le Tendre Ressouvenir* (Salon of 1763), the girl's dishabille is ostensibly motivated by her preoccupation with her sorrow. See Michael Fried, *Absorption and Theatricality: Painting and Beholder in the Age of Diderot* (Berkeley: University of California Press, 1980), pp. 57–61.

71. Todd, chap. 3 in *Fiction and Society*. See also I. A. Paperno, "O dvuiazychnoi perepiske pushkinskoi pory," *Uchenye zapiski Tartuskogo gosudarstvennogo universiteta* 358 (1975), *Trudy po russkoi i slavianskoi filologii* 24, pp. 148–56.

72. Pushkin liked to consider Baratynsky a specialist in the feminine psychology of both the "native girl" and the worldly type, as demonstrated in Baratynsky's narrative poems "Eda" and "Bal," respectively.

73. David Wellbery writes, "The opposition between naive and civilized languages . . . is homological with several other oppositional pairs: south and north, passion and reason, poetry and prose, all of which are commonplace in literature after Rousseau. . . . This is a variant of the Romantic myth (cliché) of a naive or natural language, a language unspoiled by civilization, poetic and creative. Whenever one of the speakers of this language is heard, either the message itself is only faintly understood or much of its affective grace and charm is lost in translation." See his article "E. T. A. Hoffmann and Romantic Hermeneutics: An Interpretation of Hoffmann's 'Don Juan,'" *Studies in Romanticism* 19 (Winter 1980): 463.

74. See Peter Brooks, "The Text of Muteness," in *The Melodramatic Imagination* (New Haven, Conn.: Yale University Press, 1976), pp. 56–80.

75. Wellbery, "E. T. A. Hoffman," p. 463.

76. Nabokov, "Commentary" to Pushkin, *Eugene Onegin*, vol. 2, p. 384.

77. See M. H. Abrams, *The Mirror and the Lamp: Romantic Theory and the Critical Tradition* (Oxford: Oxford University Press, 1953), pp. 161–76, 282–83.

78. Percy Bysshe Shelley, "A Defense of Poetry," in *Complete Works of Percy Bysshe Shelley*, vol. 7, ed. Roger Ingpen and Walter E. Peck (New York: Gordian Press, 1965), p. 135.

79. The ritual emasculation of the shaman or initiant is described by Erich Neumann in *The Great Mother: An Analysis of the Archetype*, trans. Ralph Manheim (New York: Pantheon Books, 1955), pp. 294–98; and Mircea Eliade, *Mephistopheles and the Androgyne*, trans. M. J. Cohen (New York: Sheed and Ward, 1965), pp. 97–102.

80. V. A. Zhukovsky, *Izbrannye sochinenia* (Moscow: Khudozhestvennaia literatura, 1982), p. 116; and K. N. Batiushkov, *Opyty v stikhakh i proze*, ed. I. M. Semenko (Moscow: Nauka, 1977), p. 220.

81. V. K. Kiukhel'beker, "O napravlenii nashei poezii," p. 456.

82. P. A. Viazemsky, "O Kavkazkom plennike, povesti soch. A. Pushkina" (1822), in *Polnoe sobranie sochinenii*, vol. 1 (St. Petersburg: Izdanie grafa S. D. Sheremeteva, 1878), pp. 73–78.

83. See Tony Tanner, *Adultery in the Novel: Contract and Transgression* (Baltimore, Md.: Johns Hopkins University Press, 1979).

84. See, for example, one of the first nature lyrics Pushkin wrote upon arrival in Mikhailovskoe, "Nenastnyi den' potukh" (2.1, 348).

85. See Lotman, *Roman A. S. Pushkina*, pp. 268–77, for a folkloric interpretation of the dream imagery, and Daniel Rancour-Laferriere's "Puskin's Still Unravished Bride: A Psychoanalytic Study of Tat'jana's Dream," *Russian Literature* 25 (1989): 215–58, for a quite different interpretation.

86. Rancour-Laferriere focuses on the *zherdochki* (two thin poles, coated with ice) as a symbol of masturbation. J. Douglas Clayton further develops

this idea in his "A Feminist Reading of *Evgenii Onegin*," *Canadian Slavonic Papers* 29, nos. 2 and 3 (June–Sep. 1987): 263–65.

87. The phrase is from Roman Jakobson, "The Statue in Puskin's Poetic Mythology," in *Puskin and His Sculptural Myth* (The Hague: Mouton, 1975), p. 3.

88. For details of the Vorontsov-Raevsky affair, see Nabokov in Pushkin, *Eugene Onegin*, vol. 2, pp. 129–30.

89. Emphasis mine. *Vzbesit'* (to enrage) contains the root *bes* (demon), while *chertit'* (to sketch, from *cherta*, line) contains an associative link with *cherti* (devils).

90. L. Ia. Ginzburg discusses Pushkin's acute sensitivity to this kind of mixing of concrete and abstract planes in her chapter on poetic formulas, "Shkola garmonicheskoi tochnosti," in *O lirike* (Leningrad: Sovetskii pisatel', 1974), pp. 32–43.

91. See the entries *kupa* (clump, pile; in Polish, feces), *kuplet*, *kupor*, *zakuporit'* (to plug up) in M. Fasmer, *Etimologicheskii slovar' russkogo iazyka*, trans. from the German by O. N. Trubachev (Moscow: Izdatel'stvo Progress, 1967), vol. 4, pp. 418–20.

92. See Leighton Brett Cooke, "Pushkin and the Pleasure of the Text: Anal and Erotic Images of Creativity," in Daniel Rancour-Laferriere, ed., *Russian Literature and Psychoanalysis* (Amsterdam: John Benjamins, 1990).

93. For a narratologically similar approach to the duel, see Thomas Barran, "Who Killed Lensky?: The Narrator as Assassin in *Eugene Onegin*," *Selected Proceedings of the Kentucky Foreign Language Conference: Slavic Section, 1987–1988* 5, no. 1: 7–15.

94. An outgrowth of "graveyard poetry," it was practiced especially frequently by Zhukovsky in such poems as "Pevets."

95. I am referring to Peter M. Sacks's theoretical description of elegy's origins in Greek rites of mourning and poetic competition, discussed at greater length in chap. 1 of his book *The English Elegy* (Baltimore, Md.: Johns Hopkins University Press, 1985), pp. 1–37.

96. This stanza's influence on the Russian elegiac tradition can be clearly seen in Vasily Zhukovsky's elegy on Pushkin's death, "A. S. Pushkin," in *Izbrannye sochineniia* (Moscow: Khudozhestvennia literatura, 1982), p. 140; and in Mikhail Lermontov's "Son," in *Sobranie sochinenii*, vol. 1 (Moscow: Izdatel'stvo Akademii nauk, 1961), p. 530.

97. Translations: "Scarcely out of swaddling clothes / He wilted!" (6, 36, 5–6); "Maybe it was for the good of the world / or at least for fame that he was born" (6, 37, 1–2); "And maybe even this" (6, 39, 1).

98. See Sacks's discussion of the conventions of Thomas Gray's "Elegy Written in a Country Churchyard," in *The English Elegy*, pp. 133–37; and Paul de Man's essay on Wordsworth's "On Epitaphs," "Autobiography As De-

Facement," in his *The Rhetoric of Romanticism* (N.Y.: Columbia University Press, 1984), pp. 67–82.

99. Soviet critics usually treat the "bast sandal" scene as an example of Pushkin at his most realistically anti-Romantic. For a deconstructive approach to this type of landscape, see Paul de Man's analysis of Rousseau's "allegorical" use of landscape in "The Rhetoric of Temporality," *Blindness and Insight*, pp. 204–6, as well as his essays on Wordsworth and landscape in *The Rhetoric of Romanticism*. Another interesting collection of essays on the relationship of nature tropes to acts of consciousness can be found in Harold Bloom, ed., *Romanticism and Consciousness: Essays in Criticism* (N.Y.: W. W. Norton, 1970).

100. William Wordsworth, "On Epitaphs," in *Wordsworth's Literary Criticism*, ed. W. J. B. Owen (London: Routledge and Kegan Paul, 1974), p. 132.

101. Meijer, "The Digressions in 'Evgenii Onegin,'" pp. 122–52; and Todd, *Fiction and Society*, pp. 121–36.

Chapter 6

1. Letter to P. A. Pletnev (Oct. 11, 1835, from Mikhailovskoe). Trans. J. Thomas Shaw, *The Letters of Alexander Pushkin* (Madison: University of Wisconsin Press, 1967), p. 728.

2. In answer to his own similar questions about Pushkin's creative motivations in 1835, G. P. Makogonenko stresses the renewed issue of the Decembrists and amnesty. See chap. 3 and 4 in *Tvorchestvo A. S. Pushkina v 1830-e gody (1833–1836)* (Leningrad: Khudozhestvennaia literatura, 1982). For an excellent account of the turn against Scott and the historical novel, see Elizabeth C. Shepard, "The Society Tale and the Innovative Argument in Russian Prose Fiction of the 1830's," *Russian Literature* 10, no. 2 (Aug. 15, 1981): 111–62; also B. Tomashevsky, *Pushkin i Frantsiia* (Leningrad: Sovetskii pisatel', 1960), pp. 62–174, and "Pushkin i romany frantsuzskikh romantikov (k risunkam Pushkina)," *Literaturnoe nasledstvo* (Moscow: Akademia nauk, 1934), pp. 947–58; P. B. Iezuitova, "Put' k razvitiiu romanticheskoi povesti" and "Svetskaia povest'," in *Russkaia povest' XIX veka* (Leningrad: Nauka, 1973), pp. 77–107, 169–99.

3. Paul de Man, "The Rhetoric of Temporality," in *Blindness and Insight: Essays in the Rhetoric of Contemporary Criticism* (Minneapolis: University of Minnesota Press, 1983), p. 225. See earlier discussion of this concept in Chaps. 1 and 5.

4. When referring to Pushkin's poetic heroine, as opposed to the Cleopatra of western historical and literary tradition, I will retain the Russian spelling (Kleopatra).

5. For a cogent discussion of the development of the Pugachev texts, see Paul Debreczeny, *The Other Pushkin: A Study of Alexander Pushkin's Prose Fiction* (Stanford, Calif.: Stanford University Press, 1983), pp. 239–73.

6. Letters to Natalia Nikolaevna Pushkina and Vladimir Fedorovich Odoevsky, from Boldino to St. Petersburg, trans. J. Thomas Shaw, *Letters of Alexander Pushkin*, pp. 613–14, 618.

7. P. A. Viazemsky, "Vzgliad na literaturu nashu posle smerti Pushkina," quoted in L. S. Sidiakov, "Nabliudenia nad slovoupotrebleniem Pushkina ('proza' i 'poeziia')," *Pushkin i ego sovremenniki, Uchenye zapiski LPGI imeni Gertsena*, vol. 434 (Pskov, 1970), p. 8.

8. Paul Debreczeny gives a useful account of the sequence of rough drafts in chaps. 4 and 6 of *The Other Pushkin*, pp. 148–65, 239–56. See also Ia. L. Levkovich, "Printsipy dokumental'nogo povestvovania v istoricheskoi proze Pushkinskoi pory," *Pushkin issledovania i materialy VI* (Leningrad: Nauka, 1969), pp. 171–96; N. N. Petrunina, "K tvorcheskoi istorii 'Kaptanskoi dochki,'" *Russkaia literatura*, 1970, no. 2: 79–92; P. Kaletskii, "Ot *Dubrovskogo* k *Kapitanskoi dochke*," *Literaturnyi sovremennik*, 1937, no. 1: 148–68.

9. The compositional history of the various drafts of "Kleopatra" and the sequence of its prose frames have been most clearly set forth by N. N. Petrunina, "'Egipetskie nochi' i russkaia povest' 1830-kh godov," *Pushkin issledovania i materialy*, vol. 8 (Leningrad: Nauka, 1978), pp. 22–50; but see A. A. Akhmatova's differing opinion about the stories' order of precedence, in "Dve novye povesti Pushkina," in "Neizdannye zametki Anny Akhmatovoi o Pushkine," ed. E. G. Gershtein, *Voprosy literatury* 1970: 175–87. See also P. V. Annenkov, *Materialy dlia biografii Pushkina* (St. Petersburg: A. S. Suvorin, 1873), pp. 387–93, and his "Literaturnye proekty Pushkina," in *P. V. Annenkov i ego druz'ia* (St. Petersburg: A. S. Suvorin, 1892), p. 457; Ia. Bagdasar'ianets, "K istorii teksta 'Egipetskikh nochei,'" in M. P. Alekseev, *Pushkin stat'i i materialy*, no. 2 (Odessa: Odesskii dom uchenykh, 1926), pp. 88–91; S. M. Bondi, "K istorii sozdaniia 'Egipetskikh nochei,'" in his *Novye stranitsy Pushkina* (Moscow: Mir, 1931), pp. 148–205; M. Gorlin, "'Noce egipskie' (kompozycja i geneza)," *Puszkin 1837–1937* (Kraków: Polskie Towarzystwo dla badań Europy, nos. 16/17, 1939); E. Kazanovich, "K istochnikam 'Egipetskikh nochei,'" *Zven'ia*, vols. 3–4 (Moscow: Akademia, 1934), pp. 191–204; Wacław Lednicki, "Pochemu Pushkin ne okonchil 'Egipetskie nochi,'" *Novyi zhurnal* 90 (1968): 244–55, and "Z istorii poetyckiej przyjaźni," in his *Aleksander Puszkin* (Kraków: Krakowska Spółka Wydawnicza, 1926), pp. 162–225; and more recently, Leslie O'Bell, *Pushkin's "Egyptian Nights": The Biography of a Work* (Ann Arbor, Mich.: Ardis, 1983).

10. B. Tomashevsky, *Pushkin*, bk. 2 (Moscow: Akademia nauk, 1961), pp. 55–64.

11. Letter to Viazemsky from Mikhailovskoe to Moscow, trans. Shaw, *Letters of Alexander Pushkin*, p. 191.

12. Letter to Zhukovsky from Mikhailovskoe and Trigorskoe to St. Petersburg, in *ibid.*, p. 185.

13. See Caryl Emerson, "Grinev's Dream: *The Captain's Daughter* and a Father's Blessing," *Slavic Review* 40, no. 1 (1981): 60–76. The subtextual connections between Pushkin and Scott have been extensively studied, most thoroughly by D. P. Iakubovich, "*Kapitanskaia dochka* i romany Val'ter Skotta," *Pushkin: Vremennik Pushkinskoi kommissii*, vols. 4–5 (1939): 165–97; George Lukács, *The Historical Novel*, trans. Hannah and Stanley Mitchell (London: Merlin Press, 1962); Donald Davie, "*The Captain's Daughter*: Pushkin's Prose and Russian Realism," in his *Heyday of Sir Walter Scott* (New York: Barnes and Noble, 1961), pp. 7–20. Recent studies of Scott have focused on the way he molded historical material to the patterns of quest and romance, and indeed, to the patterns of psychological "family romance." The best of these, in my opinion, is Judith Wilt's *Secret Leaves: The Novels of Walter Scott* (Chicago: University of Chicago Press, 1985). See also Alexander Welsh, *The Hero of the Waverley Novels* (New Haven, Conn.: Yale University Press, 1963); and Avrom Fleishman, *The English Historical Novel: Walter Scott to Virginia Woolf* (Baltimore, Md.: Johns Hopkins University Press, 1971). In a related vein, see Gerald E. Mikkelson, "The Mythopoetic Element in Pushkin's Historical Novel *The Captain's Daughter*," *Canadian-American Slavic Studies* 7 (1973): 296–313.

14. Translated by Tatiana Wolff, "Imaginary conversation with Alexander I," in Tatiana Wolff, ed. and trans., *Pushkin on Literature* (Stanford, Calif.: Stanford University Press, 1986), pp. 110–11.

15. *Ibid.*

16. *Ibid.*

17. *Ibid.*, pp. 99–100.

18. Letter to Viazemsky, Oct. 8 or 10, 1824. Trans. Wolff, *Pushkin and Literature*, p. 111.

19. Letter to V. F. Viazemskaia, late Oct. 1824, in *ibid.*, p. 112.

20. Letter to Lev Pushkin, first half of Nov. 1824, in *ibid.*, pp. 113–14.

21. Letter to Viazemsky, Jan. 25, 1825, in *ibid.*, p. 131.

22. Pushkin read Thomas Medwin's best-selling *Conversations of Lord Byron* in the French edition of 1824.

23. Letter from second half of Nov. 1825, in Shaw, *Letters of Alexander Pushkin*, pp. 263–64.

24. The most complete discussion of Pushkin's vestigial autobiography

is in I. L. Feinberg, *Nezavershennye raboty Pushkina* (Moscow: Sovetskii pisatel', 1962), pp. 272–428.

25. Pushkin describes his activities in a letter to his brother Lev, Apr. 22–23, 1825, from Mikhailovskoe to St. Petersburg. Trans. Shaw, *Letters of Alexander Pushkin*, p. 215.

26. See Margaret Lamb, *Antony and Cleopatra on the English Stage* (Rutherford, N.J.: Farleigh Dickinson University Press, 1980); Marilyn L. Williamson, *Infinite Variety: Antony and Cleopatra in Renaissance Drama and Earlier Tradition* (Mystic, Conn.: Lawrence Verry, 1974); Hans Volkmann, *Kleopatra: Politik und Propaganda* (Munich: R. Oldenburg, 1953). The richest discussion of historical, dramatic, and pictorial reinterpretations of Cleopatra as cultural icon is Lucy Hughes-Hallett's *Cleopatra: Histories, Dreams and Distortions* (New York: Harper and Row, 1990). See also Bertrand d'Astorg, "Cléopâtre et la vieille Europe," in his *Les noces orientales* (Paris: Editions du Seuil, 1980), pp. 52–66; and Rana Kabbani, *Europe's Myths of Orient* (Bloomington: Indiana University Press, 1986).

27. Jean-François La Harpe, *Lycée, ou cours de la littérature ancienne et moderne* (Paris: Baudouin, 1827–29).

28. *Larousse grand dictionnaire universel du XIXe siècle*, 1982, s.v. "Alexandre Soumet."

29. Stendhal gives the most cogent formulation of the terms of the debate in *Racine et Shakespeare* (Paris: Le Divan, 1928).

30. For an illuminating discussion of political allusion and historical drama, see Herbert Lindenberger, *Historical Drama: The Relation of Literature and Reality* (Chicago: University of Chicago Press, 1975), pp. 38–45.

31. G. A. Gukovsky discusses the unexpectedly radical political symbolism of Oriental images of luxury and sensuality in Russian writing of the early 1820's, in *Pushkin i russkie romantiki* (Moscow: Khudozhestvennaia literatura, 1965), pp. 257–58.

32. Hughes-Hallett, who covers an enormous number of reworkings of the Cleopatra theme in all the major European languages, regards Pushkin as the first modern resuscitator of Aurelius Victor's night-for-a-life bargain, which a few years later would form the nucleus of Théophile Gautier's "Une Nuit de Cléopâtre" (p. 233). Her chapter on nineteenth-century "Killer-Cleopatras" (pp. 225–51) proves in much greater detail than does Mario Praz in *The Romantic Agony* (Oxford: Oxford University Press, 1933, pp. 213–16), how fecund this sadomasochistic image would be after 1837. It does not indicate how Pushkin's text, published posthumously in Russian in *Sovremennik*, managed to penetrate to Paris by 1838.

33. Hughes-Hallett, *Cleopatra*, pp. 9–69.

34. I am inclined to suspect a common anterior source for Pushkin's and Gautier's sudden interest in a Roman historian much too obscure (classicists

assure me) for either of them to have run across in the ordinary course of his schooling or literary pursuits: perhaps a salon anecdote like the one recounted by Alexei Ivanovich in "We were spending the evening at the dacha." The fact that Pushkin conceived of his "Kleopatra" in 1824, the year of Soumet's succès de scandale, suggests that such anecdotes were making the rounds.

35. Leonid Grossman, "Iskusstvo anekdota u Pushkina," in his *Etiudy o Pushkine* (Moscow: L. D. Frenkel', 1923), pp. 46–48.

36. "We were spending the evening at the dacha," trans. Paul Debreczeny, *Alexander Pushkin: Complete Prose Fiction* (Stanford, Calif.: Stanford University Press, 1983), p. 244.

37. I am referring to V. K. Kiukhel'beker's influential article "O napravlenii nashei poezii, osobenno liricheskoi, v poslednee desiatiletie," reprinted in *Puteshestvie. Dnevnik. Stat'i*, ed. N. V. Koroleva and V. D. Rak (Leningrad: Nauka, 1979), pp. 453–58 (see the discussion in Chap. 3).

38. Examples include Batiushkov's most famous poem, "Dying Tasso" (1817); P. Gabbe's "Byron in a Dungeon" (1822); Byron's own "The Lament of Tasso"; B. V. Raevsky's "Singer in a Dungeon" (1822); Pushkin's own "André Chénier in a Dungeon," the original title of "André Chenier" (1825); Lamartine's "Napoleon" and "Le Poète mourant"; and the innumerable other poems portraying Napoleon's last words, Byron's death, or an intertwining of the two, as in Pushkin's "To the Sea" (1824). Even against this background the quotation of poetic "last words" a moment before execution recurs in Pushkin with striking regularity: Lensky's elegy on the eve of the duel in *Eugene Onegin*; Kochubei's last night in prison before execution in "Poltava"; the entirety of "Feast in the Time of the Plague"; Mozart's performance of his requiem before the poisoning in "Mozart and Salieri"; "Scenes from chivalrous times," a dramatic fragment in which the troubadour's improvisation helps commute his execution to imprisonment for life; Maria Schoning's last words on the scaffold; and above all, Petronius's feast.

39. O. S. Murav'eva, "Pushkin i Napoleon (Pushkinskii variant 'napoleonovskoi legendy')," *Pushkin issledovaniia i materialy*, vol. 14 (Leningrad: Nauka, 1991), pp. 5–32.

40. Trans. Walter Arndt, *Alexander Pushkin: Collected Narrative and Lyrical Poetry* (Ann Arbor, Mich.: Ardis, 1984).

41. Cleopatra's performance of rituals connected with the cult of Isis is well documented. See Hughes-Hallett, *Cleopatra*, pp. 70–110.

42. See rough draft versions of "Kleopatra" in *Polnoe sobranie sochinenii* (3.2, 677–92).

43. See Hughes-Hallett's commentary to illustrations of the pictorial tradition in *Cleopatra*.

44. I am referring to Jacques Lacan's famous formulation of the "mirror stage" of infant development. See "The Mirror Stage as Formative of the

Function of the I as Revealed in Psychoanalytic Experience," in *Ecrits: A Selection*, trans. Alan Sheridan (New York: W. W. Norton, 1977).

45. My translation of lines 21–22 of "Kleopatra" (1824) (3.2, 685).

46. *Eugene Onegin* (st. 58, line 14); "The Gypsies" (4, 200).

47. See T. G. Zenger (Tsiavlovskaia), "Tri pis'ma Pushkina k neizvestnoi," *Zven'ia*, vol. 2 (Moscow: Akademia, 1933), pp. 200–221, and M. A. Tsiavlovsky's commentary "Dva chernovykh pis'ma K. A. Sobanskoi," in M. A. Tsiavlovsky, L. V. Modzalevsky, and T. G. Zenger, eds., *Rukoiu Pushkina* (Moscow: Academia, 1935), pp. 179–208. See also Akhmatova's "Neizdannye zametki," pp. 158–206, for interesting arguments supporting the candidacy of the Polish agent Karolina Sobańska—with whom Pushkin was in love in 1823 and apparently again in 1830—for the role of the demonic Kleopatra.

48. "The illusions that swarm in the male Eros are naively identified with certain women," according to C. G. Jung, "Psychological Aspects of the Kore," in C. G. Jung and C. Kerenyi, eds., *Essays on a Science of Mythology*, trans. R. F. C. Hull (New York: Pantheon Books, 1964), p. 173.

49. For a list of the French periodicals that were, despite a government ban, made available to Pushkin through the diplomatic connections of Elizaveta Khitrovo, see B. Tomashevsky's "Pushkin i Iiul'skaia revoliutsiia 1830–1831 gg. (Frantsuzskie dela 1830–1831 gg v pis'makh Pushkina k E. M. Khitrovo)," in his *Pushkin*, bk. 2 (Moscow: Akademia nauk, 1961), pp. 291–344.

50. The first issues of the newspaper, although they covered news from Argentina, Turkey, Greece, England, Prussia, and Russia on the front page, were preoccupied with the unifying theme of social unrest. Thus the feuilleton on Russia brings up past history—"Quelques détails sur la mort de l'empereur Alexandre Ier"—that has relevance to French current events.

51. About the post-July *feuilletonistes*, see Lise Queffelec, *Le roman-feuilleton français au XIXe siècle* (Paris: Presses universitaires de France, 1989).

52. "L'Angleterre en 1688 et la France en 1830," *Le Globe*, Aug. 25, 1830.

53. In the Sept. 20, 1830 issue, *Le Globe* published a long, laudatory review of *Mémoires, correspondance et ouvrages inédits de Diderot* with the clear intention of remodeling Diderot into the first French Romantic (rather than rationalist), hence an appropriate role model for the post-July ferment. See Sainte-Beuve, "Diderot," in *Premiers lundis*, vol. 1 of *Oeuvres* (Paris: Editions le Roi, 1956), pp. 355–69.

54. Quoted in Shepard, "Society Tale," p. 117.

55. Quoted in *ibid.*, pp. 126–27.

56. *Ibid.*

57. "Of Walter Scott's novels," trans. Wolff, *Pushkin on Literature*, p. 275. My translation of last sentence's French.

58. "On Milton and on Chateaubriand's translation of *Paradise Lost.*" *Ibid.*, p. 460.

59. "O noveishi kh romanakh," in *Polnoe sobranie sochinenii* (12, 204).

60. See B. Tomashevsky's discussion of Pushkin's view of modern novels in "Frantsuzskaia literatura v pis'makh Pushkina k E. M. Khitrovo," *Pushkin i Frantsiia*, pp. 360–404.

61. In his review "Tri povesti N. Pavlova," Pushkin criticizes Pavlov's descriptions for sharing the "myopic triviality of the current French novelists" (12, 9).

62. The quoted phrase is from Leo Tolstoy's letter to E. G. Golokhvastov (1871), cited in Boris Eikhenbaum, "Pushkin i Tolstoy," in his *O proze* (Leningrad: Khudozhestvennaia literatura, 1969), p. 181.

63. For more on the eighteenth-century culture of wit and anecdote, see Grossman, *Etiudy o Pushkine*, pp. 45–93; and Peter Brooks, *The Novel of Worldliness* (Princeton, N.J.: Princeton University Press, 1969).

64. Akhmatova, "Neizdannye zametki," pp. 179–80.

65. See, for example, the discussion of Hoffman as "Teller of Tales" in P. M. Pasinetti, *Life for Art's Sake: Studies in the Literary Myth of the Romantic Artist* (New York: Garland Publishing, 1985), pp. 108–25; Leo Weinstein, "Hoffman's Romantic Interpretation of Don Juan," in his *Metamorphoses of Don Juan* (New York: AMS Press, 1967); and especially David Kropf, *Authorship as Alchemy: Subversive Writing in Pushkin, Scott, Hoffman* (Stanford, Calif.: Stanford University Press, 1994).

66. David E. Wellbery, "E. T. A. Hoffmann and Romantic Hermeneutics: An Interpretation of Hoffmann's 'Don Juan,'" *Studies in Romanticism* 19 (Winter 1980): 455.

67. Russian examples of the *Künstler* tale include: V. F. Odoevsky's "La Sylphide," Pogorelsky [pseud. of A. A. Perovsky]'s "Lafertovskaia makovnitsa" and "Dvoinik," N. A. Polevoi's "Zhivopisets," and N. V. Gogol's "Nevskii prospekt." See John Mersereau, *Russian Romantic Fiction* (Ann Arbor, Mich.: Ardis, 1983).

68. Polevoy, "Zhivopisets," published in *Mechty i zhizn'*, pt. 2 (Moscow: n.p., 1834), pp. 8–70. See N. N. Petrunina, "'Egipetskie nochi' i russkaia povest'," p. 31.

69. Sainte-Beuve published a little book of elegiac poetry under the pseudonymous title *Vie, poésies et pensées de Joseph Delorme* (Paris: Delande Frères, 1829). The introductory frame tale, Pushkin wrote in his 1831 review, "read like a novel," and the poetic talent was "extraordinary," "diseased," and "charming." See Wolff, *Pushkin on Literature*, pp. 290–97.

70. I am referring to the evolving conception of the protagonist of "The Bronze Horseman," which began with the impoverished nobleman of "Moia rodoslovnia" and culminated in the petty clerk Eugene, whose "poet-like" dreams of family happiness collide with the impersonal fatality of the city.

71. Although most of the rich critical literature refers to "Egyptian Nights" in the title, it has become customary to treat the three frame tales as related conceptions. I don't believe that any critic comments on the obsessiveness of Pushkin's circling back, or entertains the possibility that Pushkin abandoned each story in turn because it failed to capture what he was looking for. Here is a bibliography of the works I have found helpful in addition to those cited earlier in this chapter: S. J. Bocharov, *Poetika Pushkina Ocherki* (Moscow: Nauka, 1974), pp. 105–27; Paul Debreczeny, *The Other Pushkin*, pp. 274–99; F. M. Dostoevsky, "Otvet 'Russkomu vestniku' " (1861) and "Primechaniia," in *Polnoe sobranie sochinenii*, vol. 19 (Leningrad: Nauka, 1979), pp. 119–39, 300–308; M. Gofman, "Introduction" to *Egipetskie nochi* (Paris: S. Lifar, 1935), and "Les nuits égyptiennes de Pouchkine et leur héroine," *Le monde slave* 4 (1933): 346–59; D. P. Iakubovich, "Antichnost' v tvorchestve Pushkina," *Vremennik Pushkinskoi kommissii VI* (Moscow: Nauka, 1941), pp. 151–59; V. Khodasevich, "Knigi i liudi. 'Egipetskie nochi,' " *Vozrozhdenie* 13, no. 12 (1934); Nadezhda Mandel'shtam, *Mozart and Salieri*, trans. Robert McLean (Ann Arbor, Mich.: Ardis, 1973); V. Ia. Kirpotin, "Dostoevsky i 'Egipetskie nochi' Pushkina," *Voprosy literatury*, 1962, no. 11: 112–21; V. Komarovich, "Dostoevsky i 'Egipetskie nochi' Pushkina," *Pushkin i ego sovremenniki* 7, nos. 29–30 (Leningrad: Izd. Akademii nauk, 1927), pp. 36–48; Ralph E. Matlaw, "Poetry and the Poet in Romantic Society as Reflected in Pushkin's 'Egipetskie nochi,' " *Slavic and East European Review* 33, no. 80: 102–19; B. Meilakh, *Pushkin i russkii romantizm* (Moscow: Akademia nauk, 1937), pp. 174–97, and *Khudozhestvennoe myshlenie kak tvorcheskii protsess* (Moscow: Akademia nauk, 1962), pp. 83–84; N. N. Mikhailova, "Tipologiia povestvovaniia v khudozhestvennoi proze A. S. Pushkina" (diss. for *kandidat* of philology, Moskovskii gosudarstvennyi universitet, 1976), pp. 17–56; V. Nepomniashchii, "K tvorcheskoi evoliutsii Pushkina v tridtsatye gody," *Voprosy literatury*, 1973, no. 11: 124–68, and "Sobiraites' inogda chitat' moi svitok vernyi," *Novyi mir*, 1974, no. 6: 248–66; P. I. Novitskii, ed., "Introduction" to *Egipetskie nochi* (Leningrad: Akademia, 1927); I. M. Nusinov, " 'Antonii i Kleopatra' i 'Egipetskie nochi' Pushkina," in his *Istoriia literaturnogo geroia* (Moscow: Gosizdat. Khudozhesvennoi literatury, 1958), pp. 231–95; L. S. Sidiakov, "K izucheniiu 'Egipetskikh nochei,' " *Pushkin issledovaniia i materialy*, no. 4 (Moscow: Nauka, 1962), pp. 173–82, and *Khudozhestvennaia proza A. S. Pushkina* (Riga: Uchebnoe posobie, 1973); I. M. Toibin, " 'Egipetskie nochi' i nekotorye voprosy tvorchestva Pushkina 1830–kh godov," *Uchenye zapiski Orlovskogo*

pedagogicheskogo instituta, vol. 30 (1966): 122–24; B. Val'be, " 'Egipetskie nochi,' " *Zvezda*, 1937, no. 3: 143–57.

72. Annenkov, *Materialy dlia biografii Pushkina*, p. 396.

73. V. Briusov, " 'Egipetskie nochi," in *Moi Pushkin* (Moscow: Gosudarstvennoe izdatel'stvo, 1929), pp. 107–18; B. M. Zhirmunsky, "*Egipetskie nochi* Valeriia Briusova," in his *Valerii Briusov i nasledie Pushkina. Opyt sravnitel' no-stilisticheskogo issledovaniia* (Petrograd: El'zevir, 1922), pp. 52–86.

74. The original Latin meaning was "medley," although it gradually acquired connotations of mockery and protest, according to J. A. Cuddon, *A Dictionary of Literary Terms and Literary Theory* (Oxford: Basil Blackwell, 1991), pp. 827–28. See Mikhail Bakhtin's discussion of *menippea*, *satura*, and Petronius in his *Problems of Dostoevsky's Poetics*, trans. Caryl Emerson (Minneapolis: University of Minnesota Press, 1984), pp. 106–80.

75. Pushkin inserts here his own translations of Anacreon's Odes 56 and 61, as well as of Horace's Ode 7, Book 2. Not one of Pushkin's habitual pastimes, translations account for a significant proportion of his lyrics during the years 1832–35. See Jean Kim, "Making Another Voice Mine: Pushkin and the Poetics of Translation" (Ph.D. diss., Yale University, 1992).

76. Trans. in Debreczeny, *Pushkin: Complete Prose Fiction*, p. 242. Subsequent quotations from Debreczeny's translation of "Egyptian Nights" are cited by page number in the text.

77. "Introduction" to Petronius, *Satyricon*, ed. and trans. William Arrowsmith (Ann Arbor: University of Michigan Press, 1959).

78. Théophile Gautier, "Une Nuit de Cléopâtre," in *Nouvelles* (Paris: Charpentier, 1907).

79. " 'You are so open and kind,' said the Spaniard, 'that I feel encouraged to ask you to solve a riddle for me. I have wandered all around the world, have been introduced at all the European Courts and frequented high society everywhere, but nowhere have I felt as constrained and awkward as I do in your accursed aristocratic circles. Every time I enter Princess V.'s drawing room and see these speechless and motionless mummies, which bring to mind Egyptian burial grounds, I feel frozen to the bones. I am not aware of anyone with spiritual authority among them, nor has fame impressed anyone's name on my memory—why then do I feel so timid?' " "The guests were arriving at the dacha," trans. Debreczeny, *Pushkin: Complete Prose Fiction*, p. 45. Leslie O'Bell, in *Pushkin's "Egyptian Nights,"* presents an informative discussion of the St. Petersburg–as–Egypt metaphor (pp. 57–68).

80. René Girard, *Deceit, Desire, and the Novel: Self and Other in Literary Structure*, trans. Yvonne Freccero (Baltimore, Md.: Johns Hopkins University Press, 1976).

81. Most Pushkin / Hoffman studies tend to be thematic, although

Charles Passage describes the German revival of the medieval frame tale by Goethe, Wieland, Tieck, and especially Hoffmann, which created a "second wave" of Romantic storytelling after the Byronic fashion had abated. See Passage's *The Russian Hoffmannists* (The Hague: Mouton, 1963), pp. 47–49. See also Sergei Ignatov, "Gofman i Pogorel'sky," *Russkii filosofskii vestnik* 72 (1914): 249–78; and N. V. Izmailov, "Fantasticheskaia povest'," *Russkaia povest' XIX veka* (Leningrad: Nauka, 1973), pp. 134–68.

82. Wellbery, "E. T. A. Hoffmann," p. 459.

83. *Ibid.*, p. 458.

84. *Ibid.*, pp. 460–61.

85. Pushkin expressed a similar idea in the form of a lyrical epigram in "Ekho" (1831).

86. Wellbery, "E. T. A. Hoffmann," p. 461.

87. *Ibid.*

88. *Ibid.*, p. 465.

89. *Ibid.*, p. 467.

90. *Ibid.*, pp. 468–69.

91. *Ibid.*, p. 472.

92. My translation of Pushkin, "Egipetskie nochi" (8.1, 268).

93. My translation of the French epigraph in "Egipetskie nochi" (8.1, 263).

94. Lev Pushkin was the first to draw this conclusion (in 1837).

95. This kind of analysis of "internally dialogized speech" and heteroglossia was developed by Mikhail Bakhtin, particularly in his analyses of Dostoevsky's characters (see *Problems of Dostoevsky's Poetics*). See also Bakhtin's "Avtor i geroi v esteticheskoi deiatel'nosti," in *Estetike slovesnogo tvorchestva* (Moscow: Iskusstvo, 1979), pp. 7–180. I believe that it was this pronounced characteristic of the language of "Egyptian Nights" that attracted Dostoevsky so powerfully to the story.

96. See Debreczeny, *The Other Pushkin*, p. 335.

97. My translation of "Otryvok" (8.1, 409–10).

98. Boris Gasparov gives a sympathetic reading of this moment in " 'Ty, Motsart, nedostoin sam sebia,' " *Vremennik Pushkinskoi kommissii*, 1974 (Leningrad: Nauka, 1977), pp. 115–22.

99. See Petrunina, " 'Egipetskie nochi' i russkaia povest'," pp. 39–42, for an overview of the Improvisatore fashion in both salons and literature.

100. As Roman Jakobson says, "The conversion of a sign into a thematic component is a favorite formal device of Pushkin's." See his discussion of this in "The Statue in Pushkin's Mythology," in *Pushkin and His Sculptural Myth* (The Hague: Mouton, 1975), pp. 28–38. In Russian the metonymic play with the *hand* as symbolic guarantee of a man's *word* (which relies on accepting the substitution of another sign for something of substance) is

more pronounced. The fact that Charsky's promise—"*Ruchaius'* esli ne za uspekh, to po krainei mere za barysh . . ."—is incomplete suggests that Pushkin is deliberately calling attention to the incommensurability of signifier and signified, uttered / claimed and understood, in social discourse.

101. Wellbery, "E. T. A. Hoffmann," p. 459.

102. My translation of "Egipetskie nochi" (8.1, 264).

103. I tut ko mne idet nezrimyi roi gostei,
Znakomtsy davnie, plody mechty moei.

I mysli v golove volnuiutsia v otvage,
I rifmy legkie navstrechu im begut
I pal'tsy prosiatsia k peru, pero k bumage,
Minuta—i stikhi svobodno potekut.

(3.1, 321)

And now an invisible throng of guests comes to me, old acquaintances, fruits of my dream. And thoughts surge courageously in my head, and light rhymes rush to meet them, and fingers beg for the pen, the pen for paper, a minute—and verses will flow freely.

104. Roman Jakobson first noted the logical paradox implicit in the topic; see "The Statue in Pushkin's Poetic Mythology," *Pushkin and Sculptural Myth*, p. 31.

105. My translation (8.1, 270).

106. This is close to Pushkin's lyrical definition of the poet's nature in such poems as "Zemlia i more," the first half of "The Demon," and "Ekho."

107. My translation (8.1, 269).

108. See Philippe Lacoue-Labarthe and Jean-Luc Nancy, *The Literary Absolute*, trans. Philip Barnard and Cheryl Lester (Albany: State University of New York Press, 1988), p. 9, on the Athenaeum salon's "fraternization of [different spheres of] knowledge" and social classes, from which a modern literature liberated from genre, caste, and propriety would be generated.

109. These portraits are frontispieces to vols. 2 and 4 of A. S. Pushkin, *Polnoe sobranie sochinenii v desiati tomakh*, 4th ed. (Leningrad: Nauka, 1977), but can be found in many other editions.

110. My translation.

111. See Praz, *Romantic Agony*, pp. 116–19 for Sadean elements in Shelley's *The Cenci* and other works, pp. 213–29 and 250–52 on Cleopatra as fatal woman, and of course the entire book for evidence of "the shadow of the divine marquis" on the nineteenth-century literary imagination. See also O'Bell (*Pushkin's "Egyptian Nights"*), who calls "society a stage where dramas are performed" (p. 49) and "the poet an instrument, a medium of society's desires to itself" (p. 101). *L'Ultimo giorno di Pompei* was the title

of a Giovanni Pacini opera performed to mark the opening of the Théâtre Italien in Paris soon after the July Revolution (see feuilleton in *Le Globe*, Aug. 26, 1830), as well as the subject of a K. P. Briullov canvas displayed in St. Petersburg in 1834. Silvio Pellico's *Le Mei Prigioni*, the story of his ten-year political incarceration for Carbonarism, was published in 1832, followed by *Dei Doveri degli Uomini* in 1834; the former was reviewed warmly by Pushkin in *Sovremennik* 3 (1836). The topic of the Triumph of Tasso was well worn after Byron's "The Lament of Tasso" and Batiushkov's "Umiraiushchii Tass" and must have seemed old hat in this fashionable salon.

112. My translation.

113. The question of whether Pushkin deliberately broke off the story or never got back to it is addressed by virtually every study of "Egyptian Nights" I have cited, but there is no textological evidence with which to answer it conclusively. Dostoevsky insists that "to develop and complete this fragment in an artistic respect is impossible." He realizes that its effect on the imagination relies precisely on the selective illumination of "a corner" of life in "Kleopatra," and on the fact that the audience's arousal beyond the borders of the text is part of the story's subject. "In 'Egyptian Nights' Pushkin himself artistically expressed a question dear to his heart about *certain relations between art and society*. The question stands to this very day. Even now the Improvisor of the 'Nights' might be able to hear the renewed laughter of the northern barbarians" ("Otvet 'Russkomu vestniku,' " pp. 137–38). In Dostoevsky's view, the poem with which the story concludes is left deliberately facing us, its new readers, creating yet another frame tale of response. See "Otvet 'Russkomu vestniku," pp. 119–39, and "Primechaniia," pp. 300–308.

114. Letter to Natalia Pushkina, Sept. 25, 1835, from Trigorskoe. Trans. Wolff, *Pushkin on Literature*, p. 369.

115. Sophia Karamzina, Sept. 19, 1836, in *ibid.*, p. 378.

116. *Ibid.*, pp. 379–80.

117. Marina Tsvetaeva, "Pushkin i Pugachev," in *Izbrannaia proza v dvukh tomakh. 1917–1937*, vol. 2 (New York: Russica Publishers, 1979), pp. 280–304.

Afterword

1. See Michael Sheringham's superb overview of recent autobiographical theory in *French Autobiography: Devices and Desires* (Oxford: Clarendon Press, 1993), pp. 1–30. The recent critical literature is, of course, immense: I refer the reader to Sheringham's bibliography.

2. The phrase is Stendhal's, quoted by Sheringham in *French Autobiography*, p. 93. According to Michel Beaujour, "The anamnesis of the autoportrait

is opposed to autobiographical reminiscence, always founded to a certain degree on the belief in the permanance of an individual me whose interiority is anteriority" (*Miroirs d'encre. Rhétorique de l'autoportrait* [Paris: Editions du Seuil, 1980], p. 167; my translation). Sheringham comments that this narrative order automatically commits the autobiographer to a particular unifying view of memory that erases the "work" of remembrance, that "recounts the contents of memory, not the process of its invention or rememoration" (p. 293).

3. *Ibid.*, p. 73.

4. Leo Bersani, *A Future for Astynax: Character and Desire in Literature* (New York: Marion Boyars, 1978), p. 314. Quoted in Sheringham, *French Autobiography*, p. 88.

5. Sheringham, *French Autobiography*, pp. 94–96.

6. Peter Brooks, *Reading for the Plot: Design and Intention in Narrative* (Oxford: Oxford University Press, 1984), pp. 234–35, 10, 33. Quoted in Sheringham, *French Autobiography*, pp. 27–29.

7. Aleksandr Pushkin, letter to P. A. Viazemsky, second half of Nov. 1825. Trans. J. Thomas Shaw, *The Letters of Alexander Pushkin* (Madison: University of Wisconsin Press, 1967), p. 264.

8. See Harold Bloom, ed., *Romanticism and Consciousness: Essays in Criticism* (New York: W. W. Norton, 1970), esp. his "The Internalization of Quest-Romance" (pp. 3–23) and Geoffrey H. Hartman's "Romanticism and 'Anti-Self-Consciousness'" (pp. 46–56).

9. H. Perry Chapman, *Rembrandt's Self-Portraits: A Study in Seventeenth-Century Identity* (Princeton, N.J.: Princeton University Press, 1990).

10. See Stephen Greenblatt, *Renaissance Self-Fashioning: From More to Shakespeare* (Chicago: University of Chicago Press, 1980), esp. "The Improvisation of Power" (pp. 222–54); and "Invisible Bullets," in his *Shakespearean Negotiations: The Circulation of Social Energy in Renaissance England* (Berkeley: University of California Press, 1988), pp. 21–65.

11. Chapman, *Rembrandt's Self-Portraits*, p. 131.

12. See T. G. Tsiavlovskaia's discussion of Pushkin's self-portraits in *Risunki Pushkina* (Moscow: Iskusstvo, 1980), pp. 340–80.

13. Tsiavlovskaia proves that the pistol sketch was Pushkin's code for his own planned or completed duels (*Risunki Pushkina*, pp. 390–405).

14. Sheringham, *French Autobiography*, p. 28.

15. *Ibid.*, p. 261.

16. *Ibid.*, pp. 307–9. Sheringham is again quoting Beaujour, *Miroirs d'encre*, pp. 105 and 68.

17. Sheringham, *French Autobiography*, pp. 200, 308. See Thomas C. Heller and David E. Wellbery's more pessimistic analysis in Thomas C. Heller, Morton Sosna, and David E. Wellbery, eds., *Reconstructing Individualism:*

Autonomy, Individuality, and the Self in Western Thought (Stanford, Calif.: Stanford University Press, 1986), p. 12: "What begins to take shape is an unstable individuality, always circling among the alternative descriptions it deploys to reflect on its own condition. . . . The individual is actor when observer and artifact when observed. It is a self in motion that makes use of the discourse of autonomous individuality in conjunction with an ongoing series of displacements of its position in order to reinterpret the history of its own behavior from continuously shifting vantage points. In an extreme form, this transitory self, which experiences a coherent sense of individuality and uniqueness as one of several competing but mutually vivid accounts of existence, may undergo a kind of intellectual vertigo." See also other essays in that book and in Richard Rorty, *Contingency, Irony, and Solidarity* (Cambridge, Eng.: Cambridge University Press, 1989).

Index

In this index an "f" after a number indicates a separate reference on the next page, and an "ff" indicates separate references on the next two pages. A continuous discussion over two or more pages is indicated by a span of page numbers, e.g., "57–59." *Passim* is used for a cluster of references in close but not consecutive sequence.

Library of Congress Cataloging-in-Publication Data

Greenleaf, Monika.
Pushkin and romantic fashion : fragment, elegy, Orient, irony / Monika Greenleaf.
p. cm.
Includes index.
ISBN 0-8047-2287-0 (cl.) : ISBN 0-8047-2799-6 (pbk.)
1. Pushkin, Aleksandr Sergeevich, 1799–1837—Criticism and interpretation. 2. Romanticism. I. Title.
PG2258.R6G74 1994
891.71'3—dc20
[B]
94-15593
CIP

∞ This book is printed on acid-free paper.